A COMMENTARY ON HESIOD

Works and Days, vv. 1-382

BY

W. J. VERDENIUS

Emeritus Professor of Greek Language and
Literature in the University of Utrecht

LEIDEN E. J. BRILL 1985

ISBN 90 04 07465 1

A COMMENTARY ON HESIOD
Works and Days, vv. 1-382

MNEMOSYNE

BIBLIOTHECA CLASSICA BATAVA

COLLEGERUNT

A. D. LEEMAN · H. W. PLEKET · C. J. RUIJGH

BIBLIOTHECAE FASCICULOS EDENDOS CURAVIT

C. J. RUIJGH, KLASSIEK SEMINARIUM, OUDE TURFMARKT 129, AMSTERDAM

SUPPLEMENTUM OCTOGESIMUM SEXTUM

W. J. VERDENIUS

A COMMENTARY ON HESIOD
Works and Days, vv. 1-382

LUGDUNI BATAVORUM   E. J. BRILL   MCMLXXXV

CONTENTS

PREFACE

A commentary should be concise and exhaustive at the same time. Whether I have attained this ideal will be doubted by many readers. On the one hand, I have included many questions of grammar and idiom which might seem too elementary. On the other hand, I have omitted to discuss many subtleties of composition discovered by others. Criticism of these extremes will not weigh heavy upon my conscience. My attention has always been focused on the difficulties hampering our understanding of the text, and I have tried to show that these are much more numerous and serious than is commonly assumed. This view, too, may be disputed, and it may be argued that we should not expect complete clarity of thought and expression from a primitive mind such as Hesiod's. It is my sincere conviction, however, that the work of a man who proclaims 'to tell the truth' should be approached with careful observation and intellectual respect.

I have confined myself to the first part of the poem because this seemed to me to need more detailed explanation than the rest. A short analysis of the sequel has been given in Entret.s.l'ant.class. 7 (1962), 148 ff., and some notes on 383-404 and 504-35 have been published in Mnem. IV 38 (1980), 379 ff.

Zeist, February 1984   W. J. V.

LIST OF ABBREVIATIONS

Aufbau — W. J. Verdenius, *Aufbau und Absicht der Erga*, in: K. von Fritz et al., *Hésiode et son influence* (Entret. s. l'ant. class. 7, Vandœuvres-Genève 1962), 110-70.

Becker — O. Becker, *Das Bild des Weges und verwandte Vorstellungen im frühgriechischen Denken* (Hermes Einzelschr. 4, Berlin 1937).

Bolkestein — H. Bolkestein, *Wohltätigkeit und Armenpflege im vorchristlichen Altertum* (Utrecht 1939).

Bruhn — E. Bruhn, *Sophokles. Anhang* (Berlin 1899).

Chantr. — P. Chantraine, *Grammaire homérique*, I (⁵Paris 1973), II (Paris 1953).

Chantr., *Dict. étym.* — P. Chantraine, *Dictionnaire étymologique de la langue grecque* (Paris 1968-80).

Col. — A. Colonna, *Esiodo. Le opere e i giorni* (Milan 1967).

Denn. — J. D. Denniston, *The Greek Particles* (²Oxford 1954).

Dover — K. J. Dover, *Greek Popular Morality in the Time of Plato and Aristotle* (Oxford 1974).

Edwards — G. P. Edwards, *The Language of Hesiod in its Traditional Context* (Oxford 1971).

Ev. — H. G. Evelyn-White, *Hesiod, the Homeric Hymns and Homerica* (Loeb Libr., ²London-New York 1936).

Fehling — D. Fehling, *Die Wiederholungsfiguren und ihr Gebrauch bei den Griechen vor Gorgias* (Berlin 1969).

Fink — G. Fink, *Pandora und Epimetheus* (Erlangen 1958).

Fränkel — H. Fränkel, *Dichtung und Philosophie des frühen Griechentums* (²Munich 1962).

Fränkel, *W.u.F.* — H. Fränkel, *Wege und Formen frühgriechischen Denkens* (²Munich 1960).

Fuss — W. Fuss, *Versuch einer Analyse von Hesiods Ἔργα καὶ Ἡμέραι* (Leipzig-Borna 1910).

van Groningen — B. A. van Groningen, *La composition littéraire archaïque grecque* (Amsterdam 1958).

Hays — H. M. Hays, *Notes on the Works and Days* (Chicago 1918).

Heitsch — E. Heitsch (ed.), *Hesiod* (Darmstadt 1966).

Hoffmann — M. Hoffmann, *Die ethische Terminologie bei Homer, Hesiod und den alten Elegikern und Jambographen* (Tübingen 1914).

Humbert — J. Humbert, *Syntaxe grecque* (³Paris 1960).

Kaufmann-Bühler — D. Kaufmann-Bühler, *Hesiod und die Tisis in der Odyssee*, Hermes 84 (1956), 267-95.

Kerschensteiner — J. Kerschensteiner, *Zu Aufbau und Gedankenführung von Hesiods Erga*, Hermes 79 (1944), 149-91.

K.B. — R. Kühner - F. Blass, *Grammatik der griechischen Sprache*, I: *Elementar- und Formenlehre* (Hannover 1890-2).

K.G. — R. Kühner - B. Gerth, *Grammatik der griechischen Sprache*, II: *Satzlehre* (Hannover 1898-1904).

KP — K. Ziegler - W. Sontheimer (edd.), *Der kleine Pauly* (Stuttgart 1964-75).

Krafft — F. Krafft, *Vergleichende Untersuchungen zu Homer und Hesiod* (Göttingen 1963).

Kühn — J. Kühn, *Eris und Dike. Untersuchungen zu Hesiods Ἔργα καὶ Ἡμέραι*, Würzb.Jbb. 2 (1947), 259-94.

Latt. — R. Lattimore, *Hesiod* (Ann Arbor 1959).

Leaf — W. Leaf, *The Iliad* (²London 1900-2).

Lendle — O. Lendle, *Die Pandorasage bei Hesiod* (Würzburg 1957).

Lenz   — A. Lenz, *Das Proöm des frühen griechischen Epos* (Bonn 1980).
Less. pol.   — L. Bertelli - I. Lana (edd.), *Lessico politico dell'epica greca arcaica*, fasc. 1-
                      2 (Turin 1977-8).
Lex.   — B. Snell *et al.*, *Lexikon des frühgriechischen Epos*, fasc. 1-9 (Göttingen
                      1955-78).
Lex. II   — *Id.*, fasc. 10 (Göttingen 1982).
Livrea   — E. Livrea, *Il proemio degli Erga considerato attraverso i vv. 9-10*, Helikon 6
                      (1966), 442-75.
LSJ   — H. G. Liddell - R. Scott - H. Stuart Jones - R. McKenzie, *Greek-English
                      Lexicon* (Oxford 1925-40).
Luther   — W. Luther, *Wahrheit und Lüge im ältesten Griechentum* (Borna-Leipzig
                      1935).
Marg   — W. Marg, *Hesiod* (Zürich 1970).
Maz. (I)   — P. Mazon, *Hésiode. Les Travaux et les Jours* (Paris 1914).
Maz. (II)   — P. Mazon, *Hésiode* (Coll. Budé, Paris 1928).
Meyer   — H. Meyer, *Hymnische Stilelemente in der frühgriechischen Dichtung*
                      (Würzburg 1933).
Neitzel   — H. Neitzel, *Homer-Rezeption bei Hesiod* (Bonn 1975).
Neitzel, *Pandora* — H. Neitzel, *Pandora und das Fass*, Hermes 104 (1976), 387-419.
Nicolai   — W. Nicolai, *Hesiods Erga. Beobachtungen zum Aufbau* (Heidelberg 1964).
Nilsson   — M. P. Nilsson, *Geschichte der griechischen Religion*, I (²Munich 1955).
Onians   — R. B. Onians, *The Origins of European Thought* (Cambridge 1951).
Pal.   — F. A. Paley, *The Epics of Hesiod* (London 1883).
Péron   — J. Péron, *L'analyse des notions abstraites dans les Travaux et les Jours
                      d'Hésiode*, REG 89 (1976), 267-91.
Quaglia   — L. Bona Quaglia, *Gli 'Erga' di Esiodo* (Turin 1973).
RE   — A. Pauly - G. Wissowa (edd.), *Real-Encyclopädie der classischen Alter-
                      tumswissenschaft* (Stuttgart 1893-1978).
Renehan   — R. Renehan, *Progress in Hesiod* [review of West's edition], CP 75 (1980),
                      339-58.
Rohde   — E. Rohde, *Psyche* (⁹⁻¹⁰Tübingen 1925).
Rudhardt   — J. Rudhardt, *Le mythe hésiodique des races et celui de Prométhée*, Rev.
                      europ. d. sciences soc. 19 (1981), no. 58, 245-81.
Ruijgh   — C. J. Ruijgh, *Autour de 'TE épique'* (Amsterdam 1971).
Rz.   — A. Rzach, *Hesiodi carmina* (³Leipzig 1913).
Schm.   — W. Schmid, *Geschichte der griechischen Literatur*, I (Munich 1929).
Schw.   — E. Schwyzer, *Griechische Grammatik* (Munich 1939-50).
Sellschopp   — I. Sellschopp, *Stilistische Untersuchungen zu Hesiod* (Hamburg 1934).
Si.   — T. A. Sinclair, *Hesiod, Works and Days* (London 1932).
Sittl   — C. Sittl, *Ἡσιόδου τὰ ἅπαντα* (Athens 1889).
Snell   — B. Snell, *Die Entdeckung des Geistes* (⁴Göttingen 1975).
So.   — F. Solmsen, *Hesiodi Theogonia, Opera et Dies, Scutum* (²Oxford 1983).
Solmsen, *Hes.*   — F. Solmsen, *Hesiod and Aeschylus* (Ithaca, N.Y. 1949).
Troxler   — H. Troxler, *Sprache und Wortschatz Hesiods* (Zürich 1964).
Wackernagel   — J. Wackernagel, *Vorlesungen über Syntax* (²Basel 1926-8).
Walcot, *Near East* — P. Walcot, *Hesiod and the Near East* (Cardiff 1966).
Walcot, *Peasants* — P. Walcot, *Greek Peasants, Ancient and Modern* (Manchester 1970).
Waltz (I)   — P. Waltz, *Hésiode et son poème moral* (Paris 1906).
Waltz (II)   — P. Waltz, *Hésiode. Les Travaux et les Jours* (Brussels 1909).
We.   — M. L. West, *Hesiod, Works and Days* (Oxford 1978).
We., *Th.*   — M. L. West, *Hesiod, Theogony* (Oxford 1966).
Wil.   — U. von Wilamowitz, *Hesiodos, Erga* (Berlin 1928).
Wil., *Gl.*   — U. von Wilamowitz, *Der Glaube der Hellenen* (Berlin 1931-2).

COMMENTARY

1: Πιερίηθεν. Not to be connected with κλείουσαι (for in that case they would not have to come δεῦτε) or with δεῦτε (for in that case we should have expected a future instead of κλείουσαι), but with Μοῦσαι (cf. Hom. Ν 363 Ὀθρυονῆα Καβησόθεν). We. rightly observes that the genitive is not simply a gen. of origin, but that "the poet has the Muses' coming in mind". A more precise explanation is that one idea, viz. that the Muses belong in Pieria, where they were born (*Th.* 53), is dominated by another idea, viz. that they have to come from their 'official' dwelling-place to that of the poet. Cf. the anticipatory use of ἐκεῖθεν, ἔνδοθεν, οἴκοθεν *et sim.*: K.G. I, 546-7, Schw. II, 434.

1: ἀοιδῆσι κλείουσαι. Called by We. "an echo of *Th.* 44 κλείουσιν ἀοιδῇ": this is misleading because there the verb has an explicit object, whereas in the present passage no specific object, such as τά τε θεῖα καὶ τὰ ἀνθρώπινα (Pal.), should be supplied. For this absolute use of the verb cf. 5 βριάει, 9 ἰδὼν ἀίων τε, 44 ἔχειν, Hom. Α 132 κλέπτε, Ι 501 ὑπερβήῃ, Pind. *O.* 1, 29 ἐξαπατῶντι, Antiph. Ι 2 ἠνάγκασαν, Hdt. III 54, 2 ἔκτεινον, S. *Ai.* 157 ἔχοντα, Ε. *H.F.* 697 ὑπερβάλλων, Pl. *Meno* 76 b 7 ἐπιτάττεις, *Rep.* 339 b 4 προστίθης. See further K. W. Krüger, *Griechische Sprachlehre* (⁵Leipzig 1875), § 52, 1, 2, J. Bechert, Münch. Stud. z. Sprachwiss. 19 (1966), 87-102.

For the association of 'song' and 'celebration' cf. Hom. α 338 ἔργ' ἀνδρῶν τε θεῶν τε, τά τε κλείουσιν ἀοιδοί, and my remarks in Mnem. IV 36 (1983), 47 and n. 148 [1].

2: δεῦτε. P. von der Mühll, *Ausgewählte kleine Schriften* (Basel 1975), 265, argues that the word does not mean 'come hither' but is equivalent to ἄγετε δή. But (1) in such passages as Hom. Ν 481 and θ 307 δεῦτε obviously implies an appeal to local approach (as is admitted by von der Mühll) [2], and (2) such an appeal is a *topos* in cletic hymns: cf. Ar. *Nub.* 564, *Ran.* 326 [3]. The present use of this motif has a special purpose: the beginning of the *Th.* shows that Hes. worshipped the Muses of Helicon [4]; on the other hand, he could not

---

[1] For ἀοιδή, ἀοιδός, ἀείδειν cf. A. Pagliaro, *Saggi di critica semantica* (²Messina-Florence 1961), 5 ff.

[2] On the other hand, the local sense has weakened in such cases as Η 350: cf. W. Beck, *Lex.* II, 257.43 ff., 69 ff.

[3] Cf. Renehan, 345. See further E. Fraenkel, *Kleine Beiträge zur klassischen Philologie*, I (Rome 1964), 357 ff.

[4] On the cult of the Muses there cf. Paus. IX 29, 1, and J. G. Frazer, *Pausanias' Description of Greece*, V (²London 1913), 141, 147-8, M. Mayer, RE XVI, 697, B. A. van Groningen, AC 17 (1948), 287-96, A. R. Burn, ABSA 44 (1949), 323, J. R. T. Pollard, CR N.S. 2 (1952), 61, G. Roux, BCH 78 (1954), 22-48, P. von der Mühll, *Ausgewählte kleine Schriften* (Basel 1975), 249-52. See also my remarks in Mnem. IV 25 (1972), 225-6.

ignore the epic tradition of the Olympian Muses. In the *Th.* (11 ff., 68) he tried to reconcile the two conceptions by making the Muses go from Helicon to Olympus; he now establishes a similar compromise by asking them to come from Pieria to Boeotia, so that they can assist him in his task [5]. For the nature of this assistance see below, on 2 ὑμνείουσαι.

2: Δι' ἐννέπετε. The contrast with the beginning of the *Odyssey* seems to be intentional: not a man, but Zeus is the centre of Hes.'s thoughts [6]. There are more of such adversative allusions to Homer (see below, on 3 φατοί, 10 ἐτήτυμα, 15 οὔ ... φιλεῖ, 317 αἰδὼς δ' οὐκ ἀγαθή) [7], but this does not imply that the whole of Hes.'s poetry sprang from rivalry with Homer [8].

2: σφέτερον. Equivalent to ὑμέτερον, just as at Alcm. 4 D. = 85 a P. It can also refer to the first person (e.g. Xen. *Cyr.* VI 1, 10). We. speaks of "the extension of reflexive σφεῖς, σφέτερος, and ἑαυτ- to the second and first persons", but it is more correct to say that these reflexives (just as ἑός and ὅς) originally had the general meaning of 'one's own': cf. Leaf, App. A, K.G. I, 572-3, Wackernagel, II, 94-5, Chantr., I, 266-7, Schw. II, 201-2, 204-5, G. M. Bolling, Lang. 23 (1947), 30-3. See also below, on 58 ἑόν and 381 ᾗσιν.

2: πατέρα. The genealogical definition is a stock element in hymns, but in the present case it also suggests that Zeus is the most congenial theme of their songs (Lenz, 213-4).

2: ὑμνείουσαι. We. rightly observes that σφέτερον πατέρα stands in apposition to Δία, so that no comma should be put after ἐννέπετε. But in that case it is difficult to maintain that ὑμνείουσαι "means no more than 'sing'" (We.): 'speak of' is specified by 'singing', and this has the pregnant sense of 'celebrating' (cf. *Th.* 11, 101, etc.), for their song is virtually identical with the hymn to Zeus of vv. 3-8. This leads us to the question why this hymn is not directly uttered by Hes. himself. At 662 he says that the Muses have taught him ἀθέσφατον ὕμνον ἀείδειν: so why should he leave the task to them? There is a similar paradox in the *Th.*: the Muses ordered him ὑμνεῖν μακάρων γένος αἰὲν ἐόντων (33), but nevertheless he bids them: κλείετε δ' ἀθανάτων ἱερὸν γένος αἰὲν ἐόντων (105). This difficulty cannot be solved by regarding the invocation of the Muses as a metonymy for the poet's own desire to sing, as is suggested by Wil. (40). The proem of the *Th.* shows that Hes. really

---

[5] Cf. also U. von Wilamowitz, *Die Ilias und Homer* (Berlin 1916), 472, Mazon (II), 7-8, P. Walcot, SO 33 (1957), 39.

[6] For Zeus in Hes. cf. H. Schwabl, RE Suppl. XV (1978), 1266 ff. See also Solmsen, *Hes.*, 132-3, J. S. Rexine, CB 42 (1966), 37-9, 41-3.

[7] Similarly, 707 seems to oppose θ 546-7. Cf. also my note on Th. 27 ψεύδεα, Mnem. IV 25 (1972), 234, and my remarks in Mnem. IV 36 (1983), 28 and n. 70.

[8] As is maintained by H. Munding, *Hesiods Erga in ihrem Verhältnis zur Ilias* (Frankfurt 1959). Cf. the review by J. Kerschensteiner, Gnom. 34 (1962), 1-7, Krafft, 155 ff., G. Broccia, *Tradizione ed esegesi* (Brescia 1969), 24 ff.

believed in the Muses [9], and this also appears from *Op.* 658-9. This belief did
not imply, however, that the poet felt himself a mere instrument in their
hands. He called the singer a 'servant of the Muses' (*Th.* 100), but this did
not exclude his own initiative. The archaic Greeks did not yet reflect on
the border-line between human and divine activities, but contented themselves with assuming a complementary relation often imagined as a kind of
cooperation [10]. Accordingly, divine inspiration is always presupposed in
Hes.'s poetry, and conversely the words of the Muses are always spoken by
the poet himself at the same time [11]. It depends on the special situation
whether the divine or the human aspect of this cooperation gets the stronger
accent. Here, at the beginning of his poem, the Muses dominate the picture
because the poet intuitively felt that his ascription of absolute powers to Zeus
required a divine sanction. This sanction is given in the belief that through the
poet's mouth the Muses themselves will glorify Zeus. Thanks to the help of
the same Muses Hes. is able 'to proclaim the will of Zeus' (661-2). This task is
not confined to the immediate context of these lines (as is assumed by
Fränkel, 105, 141, and We.), but it is rather assumed that anything said by the
poet should be understood as a manifestation of the will of Zeus. This
ambitious claim is also implied in the proem: the fact that the Muses are
called on to celebrate Zeus means that the whole of the poem will be a song of
praise to Zeus [12].

The rhyme (κλείουσαι-ὑμνείουσαι) is a characteristic of hymnic poetry: cf.
5-8, and see further E. Norden, *Agnostos Theos* (Leipzig 1923), 258-60,
Meyer, 39. It is no mere embellishment, but it serves to enforce the Muses'
present action by closely connecting it with their permanent function (Lenz,
210). Elsewhere (e.g. at 243-4 and 471-2) the emphatic character of rhyme has
a didactic purpose (cf. Troxler, 4-6). It should be added that the lengthened
form ὑμνείουσαι also has a metrical reason: cf. Edwards, 119.

3: ὅν τε. Col. and We. rightly put a comma (not a semicolon) at the end

---

[9] As is now generally assumed: cf. the literature mentioned in Mnem. IV 11 (1958), 21 n. 3,
Aufbau, 115 n. 3, Mnem. IV 25 (1972), 233 n. 1. See also my remarks in Mnem. IV 36 (1983), 40
n. 124.

[10] I have elaborated this point in Mnem. IV 36 (1983), 40.

[11] Cf. my note on *Th.* 32 κλείοιμι, Mnem. IV 25 (1972), 238, and H. Schwabl, Proc. Afr.
Class. Ass. 2 (1959), 26, who, after comparing *Th.* 31-3 with 37-9, concludes that "the
correspondences bring out the identity of the singing of the Muses and the poet's song".
Accordingly, it is misleading to say that "die an den Zeusnamen sich anschliessenden Prädikationen nicht von den Musen, sondern von dem Dichter selbst in Eigeninitiative geäussert werden"
(Lenz, 215; similarly 223: "Die Selbständigkeit, mit der der Dichter neben die Musen tritt ...",
and 228: "In der Polarisation des dichterischen Vorgangs tritt der Dichter neben die Musen als
Garant der Wahrheit seiner Darstellung, insofern er selbst unmittelbar an der Situation beteiligt
ist, auf die sich die Dichtung bezieht"; cf. also 238 and 249). Wil. (146) seems to me wrong in
thinking that the poet felt more dependent on the Muses in the *Th.* than in the *W.a.D.*

[12] Similarly Quaglia, 32, whose argument, however, seems to me too specific (see below,
n. 43).

of 2: the relative connection belongs to the hymnic style (cf. We. on *Th.* 2). For 'epic' τε in Hesiod cf. Ruijgh, 885 ff. His explanation ('digressive-permanent') seems to me to do less justice to the specifying force of the relative sentence than that proposed by J. Gonda, Mnem. IV 7 (1954), 206-7 ('complementary'). For τε introducing a specification cf. Denn., 502 (e), and my notes on *Th.* 66, Mnem. IV 25 (1972), 248, Men. *Epitr.* 338, Mnem. IV 27 (1974), 31-2, A. *Prom.* 152, *Miscellanea* ... J. C. *Kamerbeek* (Amsterdam 1976), 455, E. *Ba.* 54, Mnem. IV 33 (1980), 13-4, Pind. *N.* 11, 45, ICS 7, 1 (1982), 35.

3: διά. 'By aid of': cf. Hom. θ 520 νικῆσαι διὰ μεγάθυμον Ἀθήνην, LSJ B III 1, K.G. I, 484. Hes. alludes to the name Δία: similarly Hom. θ 82 Διὸς μεγάλου διὰ βουλάς, A. *Ag.* 1485-6 διαὶ Διός/παναιτίου πανεργέτα[13]. We. is too cautious when he writes that " 'etymologizing' word-play is certainly not foreign to Hesiod", for Hes. is really fond of it, as appears e.g. from 256 Δίκη, Διὸς ἐκγεγαυῖα, *Th.* 207-10 Τιτῆνας ... τιταίνοντας ... τίσιν, 281-2 Πήγασος ... Ὠκεανοῦ περὶ πηγάς[14]. It should be added that the application of such 'etymologies' is more than a witticism: it creates an atmosphere of solemnity, as has been observed by W. B. Stanford, G & R 28 (1981), 132.

3: ἄνδρες. The copula is often omitted in generalizing sentences: cf. 13, 24, etc., K.G. I, 40, Schw. II, 623[15].

3: ἄφατοι. Elsewhere 'unutterable', here 'not named', 'unknown' (schol. ἀνονόμαστοι ... ἄδοξοι): cf. Pind. *P.* 3, 112 Νέστορα καὶ Λύκιον Σαρπηδόν', ἀνθρώπων φάτις[16]. Wil. writes: "Um die Menschheit, die von Zeus abhängt, in ihrer Ganzheit auszudrücken, wählt H. die sogenannte polare Zerteilung, 'die, von denen man sprechen kann, und auch die, wo man es nicht kann' " (apparently taking 'they are' in the sense of 'they exist'), but the sequel shows that the adjectives are predicates, not attributes.

---

[13] See further Norden, *Agnostos Theos*, 259 n. 1, Sellschopp, 113 n. 174, L. Ph. Rank, *Etymologiseering en verwante verschijnselen bij Homerus* (Assen 1951), 43-4, K. Deichgräber, Zt. f. vergl. Sprachforsch. 70 (1952), 19-28, B. Snell in Entret. s. l'ant. class. 1 (1954), 11-2, K. von Fritz, Glotta 34 (1955), 300, Lendle, 119-20, O. Weinreich, *Religionsgeschichtliche Studien* (Darmstadt 1968), 409-12, Quaglia, 19 n. 12, Renehan, 345.

[14] See further Rzach, RE VIII, 1199-1200, Sellschopp, 112-3, E. Risch, in *Eumusia: Festschrift E. Howald* (Erlenbach-Zürich 1947), 72-91, P. Walcot, SO 34 (1958), 11, the discussion in Entret. s. l'ant. class. 7 (1962), 53-5, Troxler, 8-13, T. P. Feldman, SO 46 (1971), 7 ff.

[15] See further Ch. Guiraud, *La phrase nominale en grec d'Homère à Euripide* (Paris 1962), 33 ff.

[16] Although φημί may be etymologically connected with φαίνω (cf. Chantr., *Dict. étym.*, 1196), I doubt whether Hes. still felt this connection, as is suggested by H. Ioannidi, Φιλοσοφία 12 (1982), 226 n. 48. Von der Mühll, *Ausgew. Schr.* (above, n. 4), 184, even thinks that φατός is derived from φαίνω, so that ἄφατοι-φατοί is synonymous with ἀφανεῖς-ἐπιφανεῖς. He compares Pind. *O.* 1, 116 πρόφατον (for πρόφαντον), but ἄφαντος usually means 'disappeared' (e.g. Hom. Υ 303 ἄφαντος ὄληται), not 'obscure'. Sittl compares ἐν οὐδενὶ λόγῳ, but λέγειν in this connection does not mean 'to speak' but 'to count' (cf. 'to be of no account', Dutch 'niet in tel zijn'). A. von Blumenthal, Hermes 74 (1939), 96, translates 'Lebende und Tote' (referring to Hsch. φατοί· τεθνεῶτες), but this is out of tune with 5-7. See also M. Schmidt, *Lex.*, 1699.

3: φατοί. Polar expressions are often used to denote divine omnipotence: cf. 669, *Th.* 442-3, 447, Hom. O 490-2, Υ 242, π 211-2, Archil. 58 D. = 130 W., Thgn. 172. See further Fehling, 277, H. S. Versnel, Mnem. IV 27 (1974), 380 and n. 66. In addition to the hymnic style we should also take into account Hes.'s general predilection for antithetical diction (cf. Troxler, 6-8).

Hes. expresses the omnipotence of Zeus in a very drastic way: in contradistinction to the common, and especially Homeric, view, according to which it depends on men whether somebody is spoken of (cf. e.g. I 461 δήμου φάτις, φ 323 φάτις ἀνδρῶν), Hes. solemnly declares that in reality this depends on Zeus. It should be added that there is no absolute contrast between the Homeric and the Hesiodic views, for in Homer κλέος is sometimes given by the gods (e.g. γ 380), and Hes. speaks of a βροτῶν φήμη (*Op.* 760)[17]. We. suggests that "Hesiod may think of his ἄφατοι and φατοί in terms of social class", but the poet is more likely to refer to general prominence or success, for in his view these find their expression and consummation in fame (313).

4: ῥητοί. In Homer 'fixed by agreement'[18], here 'spoken of', 'famous'. This meaning reappears in Aratus *Phaen.* 2 and 180. V. 4 is synonymous with 3, but it should not be regarded as an interpolation (Schm., 278 n. 5), for repetitions are characteristic of the hymnic style (cf. Norden, *Agnostos Theos*, 258 ff., Meyer, 39), and Plutarch in a solemn passage (*Is. Os.* 383 a) uses the tautology μὴ φατὸν μηδὲ ῥητόν.

4: Διός. Maz. and Nicolai (14) rightly point out the chiastic composition of 3-4 (see below, on 10 μυθησαίμην), but fail to observe that it serves to emphasize the power of Zeus. For emphatic repetition see below, on 188 γηράντεσσι.

5: ῥέα. For the synizesis cf. Troxler, 51-2, We., *Th.*, 100, Chantr. I, 84-5, K.B. I, 227-8, Schw. I, 244-5. Ease is characteristic of divine action: cf. 325, 379, *Th.* 90, 254, 442-3, Hom. Γ 381, Π 690, π 198, Thgn. 14, Alc. 34, 7, A. *Suppl.* 100 (and Friis Johansen-Whittle *ad loc.*), Meyer, 43 f.

5: βριάει. 'Makes strong', used absolutely (see above, on 1 κλείουσαι).

5: βριάοντα. The intransitive use reappears in Oppian *Hal.* 5, 96. Conversely, βρίθω usually means 'to be heavy', but in Pindar *N.* 8, 18 it means 'to make heavy'. A transitive and an intransitive use also coexist in Hom. M 433-4 ἀλλ' ἔχον ὥς τε τάλαντα γυνὴ χερνῆτις ἀληθής, / ἥ τε σταθμὸν ἔχουσα καὶ εἴριον ἀμφὶς ἀνέλκει and ι 21-3 ναιετάω δ' Ἰθάκην ... ἀμφὶ δὲ νῆσοι /

---

[17] Cf. also 311 and 313, referred to by Quaglia, 23 n. 17. She is wrong, however, in maintaining: "Omero sa che quel κλέος che l'eroe gode, a s'aspetta di godere, fra gli uomini gli viene però concesso da Zeus": the case of Achilles, who does not care about public opinion but only about the honour bestowed on him by Zeus, cannot be generalized.

[18] The formula ῥητὰ καὶ ἄρρητα (e.g. S. *O.C.* 1001) usually has the meaning of *dicenda tacenda* (Hor. *Ep.* I 7, 72).

πολλαὶ ναιετάουσι. These examples show that for the linguistic feeling of the Greeks the transitive and the intransitive were not so widely apart as they are for us. Accordingly, in such expressions as διδόναι 'indulge in', ἔχειν 'come to a stop', ἐσβάλλειν 'invade', ῥίπτειν 'throw oneself', ἰέναι 'flow', ἐλαύνειν 'sail', 'drive', ἄγειν 'advance', προσέχειν 'land' we should not assume the ellipse of an object (as is done by K.G. I, 96, Schw. II, 219 [19]) but an actually intransitive meaning [20].

After βριάοντα we should not mentally supply τινα, for the participle is used as a substantive: cf. *Th.* 437 νικήσας, Hom. Κ 47 αὐδήσαντος, ε 400 βοήσας, K.G. I, 36, Schw. II, 408-9 [21]. Similarly below, 12 νοήσας, 309 ἐργαζόμενος.

5: χαλέπτει. 'Presses hard': cf. Hom. δ 423 θεῶν ὅς τίς σε χαλέπτει. For the idea that the ups and downs in human life are caused by the gods cf. Hom. Υ 242 Ζεὺς δ᾽ ἀρετὴν ('excellence') ἄνδρεσσιν ὀφέλλει τε μινύθει τε, π 211-2 ῥηίδιον δὲ θεοῖσι ... / ἠμὲν κυδῆναι θνητὸν βροτὸν ἠδὲ κακῶσαι, J. Krause, Ἄλλοτε ἄλλος. *Untersuchungen zum Motiv des Schicksalswechsels in der griechischen Dichtung bis Euripides* (Munich 1976), espec. 68; and We., 139-40, who rightly points out that vv. 5-6 merely emphasize the power of Zeus [22], but that v. 7 adds a moral motivation.

6: ῥεῖα. The form is explained by We. The anaphora (similarly Hom. Ρ 461-2 ῥέα ... / ῥεῖα ...) has emphatic force (cf. Fehling, 197-8) and belongs to the hymnic style: cf. Norden, *Agnostos Theos*, 149 ff., H. S. Versnel, Mnem. IV 27 (1974), 368 ff.

6: ἀρίζηλον. For -ζηλος = -δηλος cf. E. M. Voigt, *Lex.*, 1273, and We. In Homer the word is used in a literal sense ('conspicuous'), here in a figurative sense ('illustrious'), just as Hom. Ε 2-3 ἵν᾽ ἔκδηλος μετὰ πᾶσιν / Ἀργείοισι γένοιτο. The transition from the literal to the figurative sense can be explained from the pregnant use found at Σ 519, where the opposite is ὑπολίζονες. The figurative sense reappears in Hellenistic literature, e.g. Theocr. 17, 57, Callim. *Epigr.* 51 [23].

---

[19] Similarly, Ameis-Hentze on η 130 and λ 239 ἵησιν: "sc. ὕδωρ" (they refer to Φ 158 ὕδωρ ἐπὶ γαῖαν ἵησιν, but this does not prove anything). Stanford rightly takes the meaning to be intransitive.

[20] Cf. Humbert, § 161: "Aucun verbe n'est, par lui-même, transitif ou intransitif ... le verbe le plus constamment transitif peut toujours être employé sans objet direct". See also Bruhn, § 99 ('Transitive verba intransitiv gebraucht'), my note on Callin. 1, 3 μεθιέντες, Mnem. IV 25 (1972), 3, and the literature mentioned in *Lex.* II, 95.29 ff.

[21] Cf. also my notes on Callin. 1, 15 φυγών, Mnem. IV 25 (1972), 7, Pind. *I.* 2, 38 νομίζων, Mnem. IV 35 (1982), 28, Arist. *Top.* 142 b 33 ἀποδούς, in G. E. L. Owen (ed.), *Aristotle on Dialectic* (Oxford 1968), 36-7, Verdenius-Waszink on Arist. *GC* 336 b 15, and A. C. Moorhouse, *A Syntax of Sophocles* (Leiden 1982), 258-9.

[22] Lenz (212, 214, 217, 227, 230) wrongly thinks that they imply the idea of restoring a balance: see below, n. 26.

[23] See further my remarks in Mnem. IV 30 (1977), 80 and 34 (1981), 410-1.

6: μινύθει. Cf. Hom. Y 242 quoted above, on 5 χαλέπτει. For the use with personal object cf. Hom. O 492.

6: ἄδηλον. Elsewhere 'unknown' in a strict sense (e.g. S. *O.R.* 475, Pl. *Leg.* 874 a 4), here 'obscure'.

6: ἀέξει. 'Increases in power and/or prestige': cf. Sol. 8 D. = 11 W., 3, Thgn. 823, Pind. *O.* 8, 88, and LSJ αὐξάνω I 2. For the transition from a purely quantitative to a more qualitative sense cf. S. R. Slings, Mnem. IV 29 (1976), 47-8. See also *Less. pol.,* 251-5.

7: ἰθύνει σκολιόν. Interpreted by Sittl and Quaglia (20-1 n. 13) as 'he lifts up the bent one' (cf. Thgn. 525-6 οὔ ποτε δουλείη κεφαλὴ ἰθεῖα πέφυκεν, / ἀλλ' αἰεὶ σκολιή, καὐχένα λοξὸν ἔχει), but Hes. always uses the contrast ἰθύς–σκολιός in a moral sense (36, 194, 219-24, 230, 250, 263-4)[24]. Quaglia objects that the conception of Zeus as a rectifying god, i.e. as a god of salvation, is foreign to Hes.'s mind. But (1) the idea of divine rectification is implied in 9 ἴθυνε θέμιστας (where Quaglia's translation [24] 'guida', explained by "ponendo a guida e modello della giustizia umana la vera giustizia che è sua propria" [similarly 30 n. 34], is too weak), and (2) rectification is not identical with salvation in so far as the former presupposes a higher degree of human cooperation (see below, on 16 ἀθανάτων βουλῇσιν).

The image underlying the figurative use of σκολιός may originally belong to a way (cf. 226 παρεκβαίνουσι δικαίου, 262 παρκλίνωσι δίκας σκολιῶς ἐνέποντες, Pind. *P.* 2, 85 πατέων ὁδοῖς σκολιαῖς, and see Becker, 85 ff.), but ἰθύνει rather points to a jointing-rule or a carpenter's line: cf. Hom. ε 245 ἐπὶ στάθμην ἴθυνεν, ξ 131 ἔπος παρατεκτήναιο, Thgn. 543-4 χρή με παρὰ στάθμην καὶ γνώμονα τήνδε δικάσσαι, / Κύρνε, δίκην[25].

It is from such phrases as the present one that the meaning 'to punish' (Hdt. II 177, 2 etc.) seems to have developed. The use of εὐθύνω, which originally was synonymous with ἰθύνω (cf. Sol. 3 D. = 4 W., 36 εὐθύνει δὲ δίκας σκολιάς), in the sense of 'call to account' is to be explained in the same way.

7: ἀγήνορα. E. Risch, *Lex.,* 65, classes this passage with Hom. I 699, but the context shows that the meaning is much more unfavourable than 'stolz, hochmütig': similarly Hom. B 276 (Thersites), α 106 (the suitors), *Th.* 641 (the Titans). See further *Less. pol.,* 59-63.

7: κάρφει. 'Withers'. Used of the body at 575 and Hom. v 398, 430. It is misleading to call the present use 'metaphorical' (LSJ) or to speak of "Übertragung vom Körper auf den Geist" (Troxler, 167), for both corporeal

---

[24] Accordingly, Quaglia's reference to the literal use of ἰθύς at 443 does not carry any weight. Her argument that the anaphora suggests that 5-7 express the same idea is not very impressive either.

[25] See further Luther, 144-8, K. Latte, A & A 2 (1946), 65 = *Kleine Schriften* (Munich 1968), 235-6.

and mental strength were conceived as a kind of liquid: cf. Hom. κ 460-3 ἐσθίετε βρώμην καὶ πίνετε οἶνον, / εἰς ὅ κεν αὖτις θυμὸν ἐνὶ στήθεσσι λάβητε / ... νῦν δ' ἀσκελέες καὶ ἄθυμοι. See further Onians, 192 ff., 254 ff. Cf. the similar use of αὐαίνω at Sol. 3 D. = 4 W., 35, S. *El.* 819, *Phil.* 954. See also below, on 66 γυιοκόρους.

We. writes: "In so far as the phrase [ἰθύνει σκολιόν] implied restoring to the wronged man what he had lost, it would provide an antithesis to ἀγήνορα κάρφει and so make the line more parallel with 5 and 6". But the wronged man is not always a modest man. It is more natural to recognize that Hes. abandons his scheme of contrasts because his mind was obsessed by the evil done to himself and by the conviction that the wrong-doer will be punished. At the same time this puts the preceding lines in a new, viz. moral, perspective: whenever Zeus intervenes in human life, strengthening the weak or weakening the strong, this always implies a correction, either of direction (ἰθύνει) or of magnitude (κάρφει)[26].

8: Ζεύς. Pal. writes: "This verse reads very tamely as the subject to the verbs which have preceded. Perhaps it was interpolated". But a similar epanalepsis occurs at 518 (see my note in Mnem. IV 33, 1980, 385) and at Hom. Z 154. See further K.G. I, 282, Schw. II, 615, Fehling, 184-5. We. speaks of "a ring", but this is misleading, for Hes. wanted emphasis, not a formal composition.

8. Krafft (86 n. 2) writes: "Als Abschluss des kurzen Zeushymnos wird ein Vers aus Formelstücken [Hom. A 354 etc. Ζεὺς ὑψιβρεμέτης, α 51 etc. δώματα ναίει] zusammengestellt, um zu dokumentieren, dass diese Eigenschaften dem allbekannten Zeus, nicht dem eines Lokalmythos zukommen". This is correct but insufficient: Hes. uses the traditional formulae to emphasize the superior position of Zeus[27], but this superiority now has a more

---

[26] Wil. (42) wrongly maintains: "An Zeus wird die Allmacht gepriesen, nicht die Gerechtigkeit". In *Gl.* I, 346, he admits that "wenn auch seine Allmacht ganz besonders gepriesen wird, so glaubt doch Hesiod auch an seine Gerechtigkeit", but this is too vague: in Hes.'s view the omnipotence of Zeus is identical with his justice. This identity need not be derived from some more universal concept, as is done by H. Diller (in Heitsch, 248), who argues that the justice of Zeus is "unter einem umfassenderen Aspekt gesehen, der auch für das ganze Gedicht gilt, unter dem Aspekt der ausgleichenden göttlichen Macht". This conclusion is based on a wrong interpretation of the connection between 3-4 and 5-6: the former couplet shows that the latter does not illustrate Zeus' intention to restore a balance, but only his power. Cf. also Livrea, 458 n. 58. He speaks of "l'evoluzione (o rivoluzione?) del concetto della divinità che è ormai come una sublimazione del sentimento di giustizia del poeta" (469). It is true that the moral aspect of Zeus is more prominent in the *W.a.D.* than in the *Th.*, but this is a question of emphasis (connected with the subject of the poem), not of evolution. For the general problem of the relation between divine power and divine justice cf. J. Dalfen, *Wandlungen einer antiken Deutung menschlicher Existenz* (Salzburg-Munich 1974), and the critical remarks made by H. Hommel, Gymn. 84 (1977), 546-51.

[27] Lenz (213) rightly observes: "vom Traditionellen wird nur das übernommen, was die ausserhalb des Traditionellen stehende Wesensbeschreibung sinnfällig zu machen vermag".

systematic function: in the epic stories it manifests itself in incidental interventions, but in Hes.'s view it determines the permanent order of the world (Lenz, 230).

8: ὑπέρτατα. This does not mean that his house is higher than those of the other gods, but only that he himself is the highest (18 ὑψίζυγος, *Th.* 529 ὑψιμέδοντος): similarly Ὀλύμπια δώματ' ἔχοντες (Hom. Β 13 etc.) is equivalent to Ὀλύμπιοι.

8: δώματα. The plural is explained by K.G. I, 18 as referring to a collection of parts, but it more probably has augmentative or amplifying force: cf. 96 δόμοισιν, A. *Ag.* 3 στέγαις, K.G. I, 18-9, Schw. II, 43-4.

9: κλῦθι. The epic introduction of a prayer (Α 37 etc.). We. thinks that it "takes the place of the typical χαῖρε"[28], but χαῖρε in the Homeric Hymns has a different function. The abrupt transition from the third to the second person is characteristic of the hymnic style: cf. Norden, *Agnostos Theos*, 163. It confirms our impression that in Hes.'s thought there was no sharp distinction between the song of the Muses and his own words. The latter fact also explains the main difference between this hymn and the Homeric Hymns: "auf die Prädikationen folgt eine Hinwendung zu der Gottheit, die die Musen besingen sollen, nicht an sie selbst" (Lenz, 216): Hes.'s cooperation with his Muses is so intimate that the simple imperative ἐννέπετε (2) suffices to guarantee their continuous assistance.

9: ἰδών. Si. concludes that κλύω is not restricted to the sphere of hearing. But κλῦθι always means 'give ear to'. Accordingly, 'seeing and hearing' is a complementary expression one of the components of which does not have factual relevance, but serves to round off the phrase: cf. Hom. Γ 277 (similarly λ 109, μ 323) Ἥλιός θ', ὃς πάντ' ἐφορᾷς καὶ πάντ' ἐπακούεις, *Th.* 32 ἐσσόμενα, 34 ὕστατον (see my notes in Mnem. IV 25, 1972, 239-40). See further K.G. II, 587-8, Bruhn, § 221, 228, Wilamowitz on E. *H.F.* 1106, E. Kemmer, *Die polare Ausdrucksweise in der griechischen Literatur* (Würzburg 1903), 43, 101, G. E. R. Lloyd, *Polarity and Analogy* (Cambridge 1966), 90 ff., Fehling, 274 ff., S. Fogelmark, HSCP 83 (1979), 121-2[29]. See also below, on 175 ἔπειτα. In the present case ἰδών may have a certain relevance in so far as it expresses a subordinate idea: in order to give ear to the poet's call for justice Zeus will first have to notice the evil practices of men[30].

9: ἀϊών. To be taken as an aorist (cf. *Lex.*, 331)[31]. The original meaning is

---

[28] Similarly R. Janko, Hermes 109 (1981), 16.

[29] See also my notes on Semon. 7, 9 ἀμεινόνων, Mnem. IV 21 (1968), 135-6, Hes. *Op.* 385, Mnem. IV 33 (1980), 380, and Pind. *I.* 2, 42, Mnem. IV 35 (1982), 31, and the literature mentioned there.

[30] We. rightly refers to 267-9, but his quotation of A. *Suppl.* 77 κλύετ' εὖ τὸ δίκαιον ἰδόντες is misleading because there ἰδόντες means 'observing' in the sense of 'attending to'.

[31] Renehan (345) refers to fr. 199, 3 ἰδών ... ἀκούων, but there the participles do not stand in immediate sequence.

'to hear something that implies an appeal to action': here it refers to the poet's call for justice (cf. the use in a prayer at Hom. Ο 378, Ψ 199). This object, however, has not been expressed, so that from a grammatical point of view both participles are used absolutely (see above, on 1 κλείουσαι).

9: δίκῃ. The dative is not adverbial or modal (e.g. Latt. 'in righteousness') but instrumental: 'by means of righteousness'. In Homer this meaning of δίκη occurs as a human quality honoured by the gods (ξ 84), in Hes. it is at the same time a divine power (220-4, 256-60, *Th.* 902-3). As such it is expected to be used here by Zeus. The original meaning of the word is 'judicial sentence' (see below, on 36 δίκης). The transition to 'justice' has been well explained by V. Ehrenberg, *Die Rechtsidee im frühen Griechentum* (Leipzig 1921), 63: "Schon als die richterliche Entscheidung im Streit ist sie ein Höheres über den Anschauungen der Parteien"[32]. It should be added that this general justice is not to be understood as an abstract principle in the sense of 'Recht' (as is done by M. Schmidt, *Lex.* II, 304.49), but as a human or divine quality in the sense of 'righteousness'. In this respect it is misleading to call Hes. a precursor of Greek philosophy[33].

9: δέ. Introduces the specification of κλῦθι: cf. my notes on Men. *Epitr.* 352, Mnem. IV 27 (1974), 32-3, and E. *Ba.* 13, Mnem. IV 33 (1980), 3. See also below, on 70, 102, 117, 186.

9: ἴθυνε. *Scil.* if they are σκολιαί (194, 219, 221): see above, on 7 ἰθύνει. The ἰθεῖαι δίκαι are ἐκ Διός (36). For ἰθύς used of jurisdiction cf. Hom. Σ 508 ὅς μετὰ τοῖσι δίκην ἰθύντατα εἴποι, Π 387, Ψ 580. Sellschopp (107 n. 165) rightly remarks that Hes. "sich an das Wort klammert, so dass das Wort Einheit und Fortgang der Rede bestimmt". Thus ἰθύνει used in a moral sense suggests ἴθυνε used in a juridical sense[34]. This is the first instance of the association of ideas which, as we shall see, plays an important part in the composition of the poem[35].

---

[32] On the other hand, his translation of δίκη by 'im Urteil' seems to me wrong. At p. 98 the translation is explained by "durch ein nach richtiger Beweisführung erfolgendes Urteil", but there are no parallels for such a pregnant sense: when a righteous judgement is meant Hes. uses ἰθεῖη δίκη (36, *Th.* 86). See further Hoffmann, 39-40, 42-3, Luther, 129-33, D. Loenen, *Dike*, Meded. Kon. Ned. Akad. v. Wet., afd. Lett. N.R. 11:6 (1948), H. Hommel, A & A 15 (1969), 168-74, M. W. Dickie, CP 73 (1978), 91-101, espec. 96-7, where he disproves the view put forward by Gagarin (below, n. 158), 86, that at Hom. ξ 84 δίκη means 'legal process', Livrea, 469, and the literature mentioned in *Lex.* II, 302-3. Krafft's discussion of δίκη (76 ff.) is full of confusion: see my review in Mnem. IV 21 (1968), 82-3. See also below, on 35 νεῖκος, 36 δίκης, 39 δίκην, 269 δίκην. The considerations put forward by D. B. Claus, TAPA 107 (1977), 73 ff., are based on an uncritical acceptance of Gagarin's view (see further below, n. 560).

[33] As is done by H. Diller (in Heitsch, 702), who speaks of "das abstrakte Prinzip der Gerechtigkeit".

[34] This seems to me a more obvious connection than the one assumed by Quaglia (25), who thinks that if men are guided by the justice of Zeus they will become more famous.

[35] For vv. 383 ff. see *Aufbau*, 148 ff., and my notes in Mnem. IV 33 (1980), 379 ff. For the principle of association in Homer and Theognis cf. my remarks in REG 73 (1960), 345 ff. Nicolai

The exhortation implied in ἴθυνε does not refer to an impending process [36] (see below, on 35 νεῖκος), but "the state expressed in the command has to become, as it were, a mental possession, a feature of the hearer, so that, whenever the appropriate occasion occurs, he can react in the right way" [37].

9: θέμιστας. 'Judgements', 'sentences': cf. H. Vos, Θέμις (Assen 1956), 9-11, and the literature mentioned by Livrea, 457 n. 56 and 473 n. 98. The word does not refer to the judgements of Zeus (Maz., Ev., Latt.), for these need not be made straight (van Groningen, 298), but to those of the human judges: cf. 221, *Th.* 85, Hom. Π 387.

10: τύνη. An emphatic τύ: cf. Schw. I, 606, Chantr. I, 264, We. on *Th.* 36, Livrea, 450 n. 40. The word no doubt refers to Zeus: cf. Livrea, 455 ff.

10: ἐγώ. The frequent use of this pronoun (106, 286, etc.) is characteristic of Hes.'s self-confidence: cf. Luther, 122-3, Livrea, 451.

10: Πέρση. It is not until 633 that we hear that Perses is Hes.' brother. The poet obviously assumes his audience to be familiar with the situation [38]. The dative is better than the vocative Πέρση: Zeus will especially concern himself with the judges (implied in θέμιστες), Hes. with his brother [39]. This does not mean, however, that Perses need not be 'made straight'; conversely, the sequel shows that the truths proclaimed by Hes. are also addressed to the judges, and even to a wider public, for the personal and the general aspects of his themes are constantly interwoven [40]. See also next note.

The addition of the disjunction τύνη-ἐγώ has been called "ineptissima" (Goettling-Flach), but it may be explained as an adaptation of the farewell formula which is found at the end of most of the Homeric Hymns [41]. The adaptation is determined by the principle of association mentioned above.

(78 ff.) argues that association is only an external and formal principle of order, but B. A. van Groningen in his review, Gnom. 37 (1965), 330, rightly remarks that form and content are but two aspects of one and the same thing.

[36] As is held by Wil., E. Meyer (in Heitsch, 477-8), Nicolai, 14, 16, Lenz, 218. He observes that in the Homeric Hymns the prayer implies "dass das Wesen der Gottheit in einem bestimmten, den Bittsteller unmittelbar betreffenden Einzelfall sich auswirken soll". But Hes. did not follow his hymnic models slavishly.

[37] W. F. Bakker, *The Greek Imperative* (Amsterdam 1966), 33. Cf. also van Groningen, 298-9, Quaglia, 28.

[38] However, it should not be concluded that the poem was intended to be performed at a session of the court in the agora, as is assumed by M. Skafte Jensen, Class. Med. 27 (1966), 6 (at p. 8 she even calls the poem "the speech for the defence"): see below, on 35 νεῖκος.

[39] Cf. E. Meyer, in Heitsch, 475 n. 9. The objections against Πέρση raised by R. Harder, *Kleine Schriften* (Munich 1960), 167 (similarly Diller, in Heitsch, 249 n. 17), are insignificant. See further Livrea, 458 ff.

[40] Cf. Fränkel, 124, Solmsen, *Hes.*, 96, Livrea, 459 ff. On the other hand, it is certainly wrong to regard the personal utterances in Hes.'s poems "as myth, not as history", as is done by M. Lefkowitz, CQ N.S. 28 (1978), 460-1.

[41] As has been suggested by Nicolai (15-6), who compares *H. Ap.* 545-6 καὶ σὺ μὲν οὕτω χαῖρε Διὸς καὶ Λητοῦς υἱέ· / αὐτὰρ ἐγὼ καὶ σεῖο καὶ ἄλλης μνήσομ' ἀοιδῆς. Cf. also W. W. Minton, TAPA 93 (1962), 198.

The word θέμιστας reminds the poet of the fact that there are not only men administering justice but also men seeking 'justice' by violating justice, and that the latter, too, may have some influence on the administration of justice (cf. 38-9, 190-4, 282-3). What is needed, therefore, is a general education to justice. This is a joint task of Zeus and the poet[42], the first concentrating on the direction of the factual course of events (ἰθύνειν), the latter on the enlightenment of his fellow-men (μυθεῖσθαι). It is this connection between practice and theory which holds the two lines together[43]. The fact that v. 9 refers to the judges only and v. 10 to Perses only is again to be explained by the principle of association. Hes. uses ἰθύς and σκολιός mostly in connection with the administration of justice. Accordingly, the words ἰθύνει σκολιόν especially refer to the judges, an implication made explicit in 9 ἴθυνε θέμιστας. But in thinking of the judges Hes. realized that their malversations personally affected him through his brother. Consequently, he begins by addressing the latter[44].

10: ἐτήτυμα. Not 'some home truths' (E. Meyer, in Heitsch, 475 n. 9: 'ich selbst aber will dem Perses ins Gewissen reden') but 'objectively true things' (cf. Luther, 42, Quaglia, 26 n. 26). We. writes that "Hesiod uses a vague, catch-all expression for the content of the coming poem", but the choice of the term ἐτήτυμα has a very special reason: Perses is a σκολιός, a man twisting the truth, and Hes. will answer his intriguing by basing himself on true facts. The meaning of ἔτυμος and ἐτήτυμος is 'factual', and they may even be used for 'real' (e.g. Hom. γ 241 κείνῳ δ' οὐκέτι νόστος ἐτήτυμος): cf. Luther, 51 ff., T. Krischer, Phil. 109 (1965), 166-7, 172-4, J. P. Levet, *Le vrai et le faux dans la pensée grecque archaïque*, I (Paris 1976), 161 ff., and for the subjective-objective ambivalence of the Greek terms for 'true', Luther, 30 ff. and *id.*, *Wahrheit, Licht und Erkenntnis in der griechischen Philosophie bis Demokrit*, Arch. f. Begriffsgesch. 10 (1966), 42.

---

[42] As is rightly observed by Quaglia (18 n. 8), whose interpretation is vitiated, however, by making man's education to justice the central theme of the poem. It is misleading, for instance, to call wealth "il giusto fine della vita umana" (38), and the good Eris "un aspetto, per quanto particolarissimo, della giustizia" (*ibid.* n. 10; similarly 43 n. 14, 46).

[43] Quaglia (31) seems to me to go too far in maintaining that Hes. "misura e fonda sulla giustizia di Zeus la veridicità del suo canto". She refers to 270-3, but 273 does not imply that the truth of the poet's expectation is guaranteed by Zeus. Quaglia argues that it is guaranteed by the Muses, who are the daughters of Zeus (see below, on 10 ἐτήτυμα). But neither the fact that they reveal the intentions of Zeus (661-2) nor the fact that they inspire just judges (*Th.* 80-93) implies that truth is based on justice.

[44] This connection has often been misunderstood, e.g. by Maz. (II), 71: "Hésiode en appelle de la justice des hommes à la justice des dieux. *En attendant*, il va donner à son frère *quelques* bons avis"; 83: "Je *ne* veux *que* faire entendre à Persès *quelques* vérités" (my italics). Similarly van Groningen, 299: "L'antithèse est purement formelle; elle ne sert qu'à effectuer la transition". Livrea (472) argues that v. 10 serves "per allontanare la vera δίκη da una sfera astrattamente concettuale e calarla nella piena realtà umana". But δίκη δ' ἴθυνε θέμιστας already implies the application of divine justice to human practice.

It has been observed that "we never get the feeling that the poem is a pleading on Hesiod's part"[45], but this does not imply that "Richter und Perses sind Adressaten, die nur als herausgegriffene Muster von Lesern, wie Hesiod sie sich wünscht, Bedeutung haben" and that they are merely introduced "um ein Lehrgedicht lebendiger zu machen"[46]. The words σοὶ δ' οὐκέτι δεύτερον ἔσται κτλ. (34 ff.) and the high tone taken by Hes. with his brother throughout the poem show that he tried to deter him from taking further legal action (see below, on 35 νεῖκος). On the other hand, the truths proclaimed by the poet have a much wider scope than that of a personal quarrel: they refer to the good kind of life as contrasted with the wrong kind of life. The revelation of these truths was a task imposed on Hes. by the Muses, as appears from *Th.* 27-8[47].

10: μυθησαίμην. Not 'ich denke, es wird wahr sein, was ich sagen werde' (Wil.; similarly 136: "er hofft, dass es Wahrheit ist"), for the modesty conveyed by the potential refers to the verb, not to its object. Besides, the modesty does not imply hesitation, but is an urbane expression of determination: cf. Hom. E 32-3 οὐκ ἂν δὴ Τρῶας μὲν ἐάσαιμεν καὶ Ἀχαιοὺς / μάρνασθαι, K.G. I, 233, Schw. II, 329, Fraenkel on A. *Ag.* 838.

The authenticity of the proem was doubted by Aristarchus, Crates, and other ancient critics. Praxiphanes, a pupil of Theophrastus, is said to have come across copies of the text which did not contain the proem, and Pausanias relates that the Boeotians in the neighbourhood of Helicon did not acknowledge the proem (cf. Rz., *ed. mai.*, 127). This is to be explained by the rivalry between the inhabitants of Ascra and Orchomenus and those of Thespiae. The first tried to claim Hes. for themselves by clinging to an old cult of three Muses on mount Helicon and repudiating the nine Muses of Pieria (Maz. (I), 37-9). The absence of the proem from a number of ancient editions may be connected with the practice of the rhapsodes to begin their recitations with an invocation of the god at whose festival they appeared. They could seldom use Hes.'s own proem, because there were but few festivals of Zeus (Wil., 39; cf. *Gl.* II, 172). See also We., 136-7[48].

---

[45] S. Østerud, Hermes 104 (1976), 17. Cf. Lenz, 229 and n. 1. B. A. van Groningen, *Hésiode et Persès*, Meded. Kon. Ned. Akad. v. Wet., afd. Lett. N.R. 20:6 (1957), 3, is certainly wrong in suggesting that when Hes. proposes to settle the quarrel in private "son plaidoyer à lui sera le poème".

[46] F. Dornseiff, in Heitsch, 133, quoted with approval by Østerud, n. 13.

[47] For the interpretation of these lines cf. my note in Mnem. IV 25 (1972), 234-5, and my remarks in Mnem. IV 36 (1983), 28 and n. 70. That Hes. felt himself a prophet of truth is acknowledged e.g. by Schm., 250, Luther, 125-6, O. Gigon, *Der Ursprung der griechischen Philosophie* (Basel 1945), 15-8, H. Diller, in Heitsch, 691, K. Latte, A & A 2 (1946), 161-2 = *Kl. Schriften* (above, n. 25), 73-4, K. von Fritz, in *Festschrift B. Snell* (Munich 1956), 35-6. For the differences in outlook between Hes. and the Hebrew prophets cf. Wil., 158, Sellschopp, 103, Gigon, *op. cit.*, 20.

[48] And cf. L. Massa Positano, in *Studi V. di Falco* (Napels 1971), 27-30.

In modern times the authenticity has been called in question both on linguistic and on stylistic grounds. It has been argued that the proem contains a comparatively large number of words and meanings which are not to be found elsewhere in Hes. or in early Greek literature[49]. This usage, however, is not quite unparalleled: it is true, for instance, that φατός and ῥητός in the sense of 'famous' are singular, but Homer has φάτις in the sense of 'common talk', 'report', and ῥῆσις in the sense of 'speech'.

The figures of speech found in the proem, such as anaphora, antithesis, chiasmus, alliteration, rhyme, have been said to belong to the second half of the 5th century[50], but they already occur in Homer[51]. There are also parallels in the W.a.D., e.g. 101, 150-1, 182-4, 317-9, 578-80 (anaphora), 275, 341 (antithesis)[52], 227, 300, 346 (chiasmus), 471-2 (rhyme), 497, 701 (alliteration). Cf. also Troxler, 4-8, We., Th., 75-7. It should be borne in mind that there are different kinds of rhetoric: the figures of speech in archaic literature do not have an ornamental function, but in most cases serve to lend emphasis to the expression of thought or emotion[53].

11: οὐκ ἄρα. We. thinks that "Hesiod had the idea of saying 'There is such a goddess as Emulation' ... but he realized that this was a different Eris from the one he had spoken of in the Theogony (225 f.)". But instead of using such a contamination Hes. obviously takes the view expressed in the Th., viz. that Eris is an evil power, for granted, and he immediately proceeds to a supplementary correction[54]. This correction is connected with the preceding line by means of an association arising from the word ἐτήτυμα: Hes. claims to tell

---

[49] See espec. S. Martin, Das Proömium zu den Erga des Hesiodos (Würzburg 1898). His arguments are summarized by Hays (23-5), who concludes that "the first eight lines may well have been a rather general proem of some rhapsodist, while the last two lines were added to attach it more fittingly to the Works and Days".

[50] Cf. K. Ziegler, ARW 14 (1911), 392 ff.

[51] Cf. O. Navarre, Essai sur la rhétorique grecque avant Aristote (Paris 1900), 92 ff., Norden, Agnostos Theos, 259 n. 3, E. Drerup, Homerische Poetik, I (Würzburg 1921), 127 n. 2, V. Bérard, Introduction à l'Odyssée, I (Paris 1924), 383 ff., Fehling, passim, G. Avezzù, Boll. Ist. Fil. Padova 11 (1974), 61 ff., A. J. Karp, Areth. 10 (1977), 237 ff.

[52] See further K. Reich, Der Einfluss der griechischen Poesie auf Gorgias, II (Würzburg 1909), 5-12, 23-6.

[53] Cf. F. Dornseiff, Pindars Stil (Berlin 1921), 14-5, E. Norden, Logos und Rhythmus (Berlin 1928), 8-20, Sellschopp, 112 n. 171.

[54] In Homer both a bad ἔρις and a good ἔρις occur, but the latter does not appear as a divine power. H. Munding, Gymn. 67 (1960), 409 ff., argues that Hes. opposes the good Eris to the sporting ἔρις in Homer, but the Homeric examples of good ἔρις (ζ 92, θ 210, σ 366) show that it was not limited to the sports field. D. Bremer, Licht und Dunkel in der frühgriechischen Dichtung (Bonn 1976), 188, maintains that Eris in the Th. comprises both a good and a bad aspect, but this is disproved by the context (224 ὀλοή, 225 οὐλόμενον, 226 στυγερή, etc.). See further J. Gruber, Über einige abstrakte Begriffe des frühen Griechischen (Meisenheim/Glan 1963), 40-55, Walcot, Peasants, 87-8. Cf. also L. M. Oostenbroek, Eris-Discordia. Zur Entwicklungsgeschichte der ennianischen Zwietracht (Pijnacker 1977), 16 ff., espec. 23, where the author wrongly calls the good Eris "eine bedauerliche Gegebenheit": cf. 12 κεν ἐπαινήσειε, 24 ἀγαθή (see below, ad loc.).

the truth, but in the *Th.* he had told a half-truth[55]. Accordingly, the asyndeton has specifying force: cf. We. on *Th.* 533 καί περ, K.G. II, 344-5, and my notes on Men. *Epitr.* fr. 2, Mnem. IV 27 (1974), 17-8, and Pind. *I.* 2, 37 αἰδοῖος, Mnem. IV 35 (1982), 27[56]. For the corrective force of οὐκ ἄρα ('it now appears that not') cf. K.G. I, 145-6, Schw. II, 279-80, Denn., 36-7, Renehan, 345[57].

Lenz (221) rightly remarks: "Die Berichtigung der Aussage über die Eris gehört unmittelbar zur Darstellung der bestehenden Zeusordnung, unterliegt somit der Intention der Erga, wie das Proöm sie zum Ausdruck bringt". This is correct (cf. 18-9), but it should be added that the intention of praising Zeus is carried out in an indirect way and does not determine the argument as a kind of program[58].

This is not the only passage which suggests that the *Th.* was composed before the *W.a.D.*: 48 ἐξαπάτησε refers to *Th.* 538-41, and 659 may be assumed to refer to the proem of the *Th.*, for Hes. is unlikely to have alluded to his consecration by the Muses in one single line and to have postponed a full description to the proem of a second poem[59]. Cf. also We., *Th.*, 44-5. On the other hand, it is improbable that the poet should have started the composition of the *W.a.D.* many years after the completion of the *Th.* (as is assumed by Wil., *Gl.* I, 343). We do not know when the quarrel about the inheritance, which seems to have given the impulse to the composition of the *W.a.D.*, occurred. But there is no difficulty in assuming that by that time the *Th.* had not yet received its final form[60].

11: μοῦνον. Equivalent to ἕν μόνον: cf. *Th.* 143 and We. *ad loc.* To the parallels mentioned there may be added S. *O.R.* 1280.

---

[55] Wil. is certainly wrong in calling the proem "ein Vorspruch ohne jede Verbindung mit dem Folgenden". On the other hand, Livrea (465) goes too far in maintaining: "La verità generale, anzi universale che Esiodo bandisce è la duplicità di Eris": the double nature of Eris is *a* truth, not *the* truth under which anything and everything might be subsumed.

[56] It should be emphasized that this specification does not narrow the import of the general claim ἐτήτυμα μυθησαίμην, as is wrongly concluded by Quaglia (34 n. 2, 37 n. 9) from *Aufbau*, 119.

[57] Si. argues that "it is unnecessary to see any allusion to *Theog.* 225. The imperfect with ἄρα expresses what was true all along and still is" (cf. Latt. 'It was never true that ...'). He refers to Dem. 55, 1 οὐκ ἦν ἄρ', ὦ ἄνδρες Ἀθηναῖοι, χαλεπώτερον οὐδὲν ἢ γείτονος πονηροῦ καὶ πλεονέκτου τυχεῖν, but this does not mean 'you will have observed, gentlemen ...' but 'you will now have come to realize that ..., a truth not fully understood before'. Fuss (28) thinks that Hes. disputes a common view, and Livrea (465-6) argues that he explains ἐτήτυμα while implicitly opposing a view held by Perses. But the use of the term γένος obviously alludes to a view expressed in the *Th.* Cf. also Broccia, *Tradizione* (above, n. 8), 56, Quaglia, 33-4 n. 1.

[58] Lenz himself observes (226) "dass das Anliegen der Dichtung nicht mehr darin besteht, das Thema in seiner Vollständigkeit darzustellen, sondern nur, soweit es sich auf diese Situation bezieht".

[59] The arguments put forward by C.M. Bowra, *Tradition and Design in the Iliad* (Oxford 1930), 262, and J. Latimer, TAPA 61 (1930), 78, to defend the priority of the *W.a.D.* can be easily disproved: cf. my remarks in Mnem. IV 11 (1958), 20-1.

[60] Cf. E. Meyer, in Heitsch, 472-3, 478.

11: ἔην. The imperfect logically refers to the speaker's former belief, but this is transferred to the object of that belief: cf. L. Reinhard, *Die Anakoluthe bei Platon* (Berlin 1920), 6 ff.

11: Ἐρίδων γένος. Strictly speaking this is illogical, for in the *Th.* Hes. did not yet think of a 'race' of Ἔριδες. He wants to say: "It has now appeared that there are two Ἔριδες, so that the race of Ἔρις does not consist of one person only, as my former view implied" (cf. γένος 'descendant': Hom. Z 180, T 124, π 401). We should not translate 'one kind of strife', for (1) this meaning of γένος does not occur before Plato, and (2) Hes. did not conceive of Ἔρις as a mere abstraction but as a power which may manifest itself as a divine person. The same holds good with regard to his other so-called personifications: they are no literary fictions[61] but real divinities[62]. Hes. (763-4) first defines φήμη as a human utterance (ἥντινα πολλοὶ λαοὶ φημίξουσι) and then adds: θεός νύ τίς ἐστι[63]: it is not true that "to him the very word 'god' (θεός) had taken on an abstract meaning"[64], for θεός denotes the superhuman element in nature as well as in human actions[65]. These divine powers have an abstract and a personal aspect, and it depends

---

[61] As is held, e.g., by J. Burnet, *Early Greek Philosophy* ([4]London 1930), 14. Waltz (II), 25, speaks of "allégorie" and "une divinité symbolique".

[62] Cf. Wil., 155-6 (but wrongly 157: "gerade bei der Dike merkt man, dass alles Persönliche Mythologie ist"), Meyer, 58, K. Latte, A & A 2 (1946), 161 = *Kl. Schriften*, 72, G. Vlastos, Philos. Quart. 2 (1952), 99-100, Snell, 45 ff., espec. 49, We., *Th.*, 33-4. Péron (290) speaks of "des puissances intermédiaires entre les dieux et les hommes, issues de la volonté des uns pour l'imposer aux autres". But the abstract notions have their own divinity because they are conceived as superhuman powers. A perversion of this point of view is to be found in E. Bethe, *Die griechische Dichtung* (Wildpark-Potzdam 1924), 61: "da er [Hes.] Begriffe noch nicht fassen kann, werden sie ihm Göttergestalten". See also below, on 73 Πειθώ and 224 ἔνειμαν.

[63] Walcot's assumption (*Near East*, 83-4) of a ring-composition ("Thus the beginning and end of the Works are linked tightly together as the only places in the poem where Hesiod adds to the gods and goddesses of the Theogony") makes the worst pages in a sensible book.

[64] As is maintained by H. J. Rose, *A Handbook of Greek Literature* ([4]London 1950), 63.

[65] Cf. Wil., *Gl.* I, 18: "Er redet so, weil er in ἔρις und φήμη eine wirkende Kraft anerkennt, stärker als der Mensch". Similarly *Platon*, I, 348, *Pindaros*, 202, and his note on E. *H.F.* 557, where he adds the important remark that the religious value of such concepts is independent of the question whether there existed a corresponding cult. Accordingly, it is wrong to call the use of θεός as a predicate of social events such as 'recognizing friends' (E. *Hel.* 560) a "Verwässerung des Wortes θεός" (Nilsson, 813), or "metaphorical" (LSJ) or "whimsical" (Dale). Similarly, Pearson on S. fr. 605 wrongly calls the personifications in Sophocles "literary rather than religious". See further Meyer, 58, E. Ehnmark, *The Idea of God in Homer* (Uppsala 1935), 50 ff., H. Kleinknecht in *ThWNT* III (1938), 68, E. Peterich, *Die Theologie der Hellenen* (Leipzig 1938), 152 ff., Ch. Picard, REG 55 (1942), 25-49, W. Pötscher, WS 72 (1959), 5-25, Fränkel, 64-70, Dodds on E. *Ba.* 370, K. J. Stelkens, *Untersuchungen zu griechischen Personifikationen abstrakter Begriffe* (Bonn 1963), F. W. Hamdorf, *Griechische Kultpersonifikationen der vorhellenistischen Zeit* (Mainz 1964) and the review by U. Hausmann, Gnom. 38 (1966), 705-9, who rightly observes (707) that cultic worship is not a decisive criterium of religious significance, Dover, 141-4, A. J. Podlecki, AC 49 (1980), 45-86. Cf. also my note on Pind. *N.* 11, 8 Θέμις, ICS 7, 1 (1982), 19-20. Personifications in archaic art should also be taken seriously: thus Eris was represented on the chest of Cypselus (Paus. V 19, 2), and she appears on a 6th cent. vase: cf. D. M. Robinson, AJA 34 (1930), 353-9.

on the circumstances which of these two aspects becomes predominant[66]. This also explains the fact that we find 'reification' as well as personification: personal names such as Ares, Aphrodite, and Hephaestus are also used for 'war' and 'warlike spirit' (LSJ II), 'love' and 'love-making' (LSJ II 1), and 'fire' (LSJ II)[67].

11: ἐπὶ γαῖαν. We. writes: "This unemphatic phrase would have gone better at the end of a clause". But it probably is emphatic: in that case it does not mean that Hes., in contradistinction to *Th.* 782, now banishes Eris from Olympus (Sittl)[68], but rather that besides strife there is also salutary emulation in human life (the latter hardly plays a part among the gods, because each of them has his well-marked task and prerogative). See also below, on 19 ῥίζῃσι. For ἐπί with acc. denoting omnipresence ('extending over', 'everywhere on') cf. 487, 505, *Th.* 95, 187, 531, Hom. P 447, ψ 371. Similarly Sa. 16, 2 ἐπὶ γᾶν, E. *Med.* 1269 ἐπὶ γαῖαν.

12: εἰσί. Scil. Ἔριδες, not γένη[69].

12: δύω. The two aspects of ἔρις already occur in Homer (see above, n. 54), but Hes. was the first to distinguish them consciously and explicitly. He also distinguishes between a good and a bad αἰδώς (318), a good and a bad φιλότης (*Th.* 206, 224), etc.[70]. More generally, he has a keen sense of contrasts, e.g. 311 ἔργον–ἀεργίη, 319 ὄλβος–ἀνολβίη, 471-2 εὐθημοσύνη–κακοθημοσύνη[71]. In this respect (and in other respects, too) he is a precursor of Greek philosophy[72], but he is no real philosopher, for his conceptions lack systematic unity: there is no universal frame comprising all divisions and polarities. It is true that his thought is dominated by the contrast 'good–bad', but this is not further defined.

---

[66] C. J. Rowe, JHS 103 (1983), 124 ff., points out that multiple but complementary approaches are characteristic of Hes.'s thought.

[67] For Ἄρης cf. W. Pötscher, Gymn. 70 (1963), 398, and my remarks in Mnem. IV 30 (1977), 80. See also below, on 32 Δημήτερος and 145 Ἄρηος.

[68] On the other hand, W. W. Briggs, *Narrative and Simile from the Georgics in the Aeneid* (Leiden 1980), 4, is certainly wrong in maintaining: "*Works* 11-16 mentions the wars of heaven, the same strife that is recounted at greater length in the *Theogony*, 225 ff.": N.B. 15 βροτός and its connection with 16 τιμῶσι.

[69] As is held by E. A. Havelock, Yale Cl. St. 20 (1966), 68, who translates 'two different strife-families'.

[70] Cf. K. J. McKay, AJP 80 (1959), 385-6 and AJP 84 (1963), 19-27, F. Martinazzoli, SIFC 21 (1946), 11-22, Broccia, *Tradizione* (above, n. 8), 41-64, E. Livrea, Helikon 7 (1967), 81-100, E. Heitsch, *Die Entdeckung der Homonymie*, Abh. Akad. Mainz 1972: 11, 11 ff., and the critical remarks made by Th. Szlezák, Gymn. 81 (1974), 454.

[71] See further Sellschopp, 92 ff., Krafft, 59 ff., Péron, *passim*.

[72] Cf. Sellschopp, 99-100, Gigon, *Ursprung* (above, n. 47), 13 ff., F. Solmsen, SIFC 24 (1950), 235-48 = *Kleine Schriften*, I (Hildesheim 1968), 68 ff., G. Vlastos, Gnom. 27 (1955), 74-5, Fränkel, 112-28, 289-90, H. Diller, in Heitsch, 688-707, M. C. Stokes, Phron. 7 (1962), 1-35 and 8 (1963), 1-34, E. Heitsch, RhM 109 (1966), 196-201, B. Gladigow, Philol. 111 (1967), 1-20, V. Krafft, Sudh. Arch. 55 (1971), 152-79, C. J. Rowe, JHS 103 (1983), 124-35. See also my remarks in *Archaïsch-Griekse wetenschap*, Meded. Kon. Vlaamse Acad. v. Wet., Lett. 30:5 (1968), 4-5 and nn. 7-9.

12: ἐπαινήσειε. Not *scil.* τις, for the participle νοήσας is used as a substantive: see above, on 5 βριάοντα.

12: νοήσας. 'When he came to understand her' (Ev.) rather than 'seeing her at work' (We.): for νοέω 'to notice that something is a definite thing', 'to realize the true nature of a thing' cf. Hom. α 322-3 νοήσας/θάμβησεν, K. von Fritz, CP 38 (1943), 85, 88-90 = H. G. Gadamer (ed.), *Um die Begriffswelt der Vorsokratiker* (Darmstadt 1968), 259-60, 266-9, W. Luther, Arch. f. Begriffsgesch. 10 (1966), 13-29[73]. Similarly 89 ἐνόησεν, 202 νοέουσι, 267 νοήσας, 293 νοήσῃ.

13: ἐπιμωμητή. Parallels are Hellenistic, but ἐπιμέμφομαι is Homeric. A. A. Parry, *Blameless Aegisthus* (Leiden 1973), 254, observes that "this is the earliest example of a usage common later, in which a word connected with μῶμος is a general antonym for a word meaning 'praise' ".

13: διά. Not to be connected with ἔχουσιν (Schw. I, 598 n. 4), for διέχω means 'to keep apart', but with ἄνδιχα: cf. Hom. A 189 etc. διάνδιχα μερμηρίζειν. For the tmesis We. compares Hom. ι 157 διὰ δὲ τρίχα. Hes. generalizes the Homeric phrase δίχα θυμὸν ἔχοντες (Υ 32), not only "zur Füllung des Verses" (Krafft, 87 n. 6) but also to emphasize the contrast. For the transition from 'separately' to 'different' cf. Hom. Σ 510 δίχα δέ σφισι ἥνδανε βουλή, Thgn. 91 ὃς δὲ μιῇ γλώσσῃ δίχ' ἔχει νόον, A. *Prom.* 927 τό τ' ἄρχειν καὶ τὸ δουλεύειν δίχα. For a similar use of χώρις cf. my note on Semon. 7, 1, Mnem. IV 21 (1968), 133.

13: δέ. Has explanatory (motivating) force: cf. Denn., 169-70.

13: θυμόν. Not 'nature' (Ev., Latt.) or 'character' (Maz. 'cœur'), but 'impulse', 'tendency' (Marg 'Trachten'). The word originally denotes (the organ of) inner motion: cf. J. Böhme, *Die Seele und das Ich im homerischen Epos* (Leipzig-Berlin 1929), 19-23, Onians, 44 ff., Snell, 19-22. See also my remarks in Lampas 5 (1972), 100-1.

14: ἥ. The last-mentioned.

14: πόλεμον. Cf. Hom. Ξ 389, Ρ 253 ἔρις πολέμοιο, *Th.* 228 (the children of Eris) Ὑσμίνας τε Μάχας τε Φόνους τ' Ἀνδροκτασίας τε. See also Quaglia, 34 n. 3.

14: κακόν. Not 'evil' (Ev., Latt.), for the word does not imply condemnation on the part of the poet, but means 'terrible', just as in the Homeric model Δ 15 and 82[74].

---

[73] G. Plamböck, *Erfassen–Gegenwärtigen–Innesein* (Ph. D. diss. Kiel 1959), 27, seems to me wrong in explaining νοέω 'erfassen' as "sich ganz zu eigen machen": see my review in Mnem. IV 17 (1964), 304-5.

[74] Cf. also Π 494 νῦν τοι ἐελδέσθω πόλεμος κακός and Leaf's remark *ad loc.* that this is not intended as an oxymoron. It is true that all the Homeric epithets of war are unfavourable (κυδιάνειρα being the only exception), but these are intended to heighten the pathos of the story: cf. J. Griffin, *Homer on Life and Death* (Oxford 1980), 103 ff. We. writes that "the prevailing Homeric and later Greek attitude is that war is an evil". He refers to Τ 221-4, but these lines

14: τε ... καί. 'And generally': cf. de Vries on Pl. *Phdr.* 230 b 8, and my note on Pind. *O.* 7, 55, Mnem. IV 29 (1976), 250.

14: ὀφέλλει. A reminiscence of Hom. Δ 445 (Eris) ὀφέλλουσα στόνον ἀνδρῶν. See further Péron, 285 n. 2.

15: σχετλίη. 'Horrible': cf. Hom. ι 295 etc. σχέτλια ἔργα. This meaning is a generalization of 'hard-hearted' (e.g. B 112), which in its turn is a specialization of the original meaning 'tenacious' (derived from ἔχω)[75].

15: οὐ. The asyndeton has consecutive force: cf. K.G. II, 342-3, and my notes on Semon. 7, 29, Mnem. IV 21 (1968), 140, and Men. *Epitr.* 378 and 579, Mnem. IV 27 (1974), 34 and 38.

15: οὖ ... φιλεῖ. Cf. *Th.* 226 Ἔρις στυγερή. The phrase perhaps implies a rejection (or rather, a suppression) of the heroic ideal denoted by the epithet φιλοπτόλεμος. This also appears from the fact that the destruction of the fourth race is not ascribed to their bellicose character, as in the case of the third race (cf. 146 ὕβριες), but to forces represented as a kind of fate (161).

15: ὑπ' ἀνάγκης. Not identical with ἀνάγκῃ but 'under the pressure of ἀ.'. Similarly ὑπὸ δέους, etc.: cf. LSJ A II 3, K.G. I, 523, Schw. II, 528.

16: ἀθανάτων βουλῆσιν. Causal dative: specifies ὑπ' ἀνάγκης. We. wrongly thinks that Hes. "would as readily have said Διὸς βουλῆσι if it had suited his verse". The ultimate responsibility for human wrongdoing is laid on the gods[76]. On the other hand, Zeus punishes ὕβρις τε κακὴ καὶ σχέτλια ἔργα (238 ff.), and Dike is a daughter of Zeus (256). Just men are never punished by Zeus (225-9). Hes. draws a distinction between 'the gods', who are almost identical with Fate (ἀνάγκη), and Zeus, who upholds the moral world-order (see also below, on 138 Ζεύς)[77]. In the *Iliad* (A 2-5; cf. η 81-2) Zeus causes war without any justification, but Hes. makes him send war only as a

---

serve to show the necessity of a good meal. We. further quotes Achilles' wish that ἔρις would disappear from the world, but this idea is prompted by his own situation and cannot be regarded as typical.

[75] J. R. Wilson, AJP 92 (1971), 293, is undoubtedly wrong in writing: "Connected with σχεθεῖν, it implies a withholding of one's natural reactions of pity and fear".

[76] This fact is undervalued by Quaglia (37), who wrongly concludes from ἀθανάτων βουλῆσιν: "è lasciato dunque agli uomini ... il dono della scelta delle proprie azioni".

[77] On the other hand, Wil. (*Gl.* I, 346) goes too far in maintaining: "die Olympier kommen nicht vor, Zeus ist der einzige". Solmsen (*Hes.*, 132-3) observes that "Hesiod's Justice is conceived as an obligation of and among men, and his Zeus will watch over the fulfilment of this obligation", but thinks that "Zeus himself is under no obligation to treat the entire human race justly and fairly". He refers to the story of Prometheus as told in the *Th.* and remarks: "It does not occur to him [Hes.] to wonder whether Zeus was not after all unwarrantly cruel, whether Prometheus did not have Justice on his side. The wrath of Zeus was aroused (554, 561, 568); this fact suffices for Hesiod, but not for Aeschylus, as explanation for the cruel punishment". But (1) Prometheus had tried to deceive Zeus (537, 565), and (2) Hes., just as Homer (A 410) and Aeschylus (*Sept.* 605-8), takes it for granted that often a whole community has to pay for a misdeed committed by one of its members (*Op.* 240). Accordingly, W. Kraus, Gnom. 49 (1977), 243, is wrong in arguing "dass Zeus Prometheus gegenüber durchaus nicht das Recht vertritt. Er könnte sonst für Prometheus' Taten nicht die Menschen büssen lassen".

punishment (225). It is true that 42 κρύψαντες θεοί is followed up by 47 Ζεὺς
ἔκρυψε. This has been called "a very interesting proof that to him the two
expressions meant much the same. He was on the road to a philosophical
monotheism"[78]. This is not correct, for 42 describes the fatalistic aspect of
the situation (N.B. ἔχουσι), whereas 47 states the moral motive: Zeus sends a
retribution for deceit (N.B. χολωσάμενος). Similarly the existence of a bad
Eris is accepted as a given fact, whereas good Eris is intentionally instituted
by Zeus, i.e. as a power serving to redress the moral balance in the world[79].
It should be added, however, that Hes. does not offer a satisfactory solution
of the problem of human responsibility. On the one hand, it is man himself
who has to make a choice between good and bad Eris, between justice and
injustice, between work and deceit (cf. Lenz, 233-4); on the other hand, bad
Eris is a divine power, and Hes.'s warning against it is moulded into the form
of a wish (28). Similarly, the fact that justice is rewarded by Zeus (225 ff.)
suggests that it is a human merit and as such is based on a free decision, but
the perspective of a brighter future for the present generation is immediately
followed by a picture of doom (179 ff.). In the Homeric epics the fatalistic
and the moral aspects of divine determination are not clearly coordinated
either[80]. This vagueness may be explained from "the dual rôle of the
Olympians, as nature gods and as gods of a social order"[81], combined with
the fact that in archaic thought no sharp distinction is made between nature
and culture[82]. Even the deeply religious and at the same time highly rational
mind of Solon did not arrive at a synthesis of divine justice and divine
power[83]. Aeschylus still wavers between three different solutions, viz. (1) God
lures man into a trap (e.g. *Pers.* 93, *Ag.* 273, fr. 301 N. = 601 M.), (2) man

---

[78] Rose, *Handbook* (above, n. 64), 58 n. 5. Similarly Wil. on 42.

[79] This difference has not been observed by Kerschensteiner, 157, who maintains that both
Erides have been instituted by Zeus, a view rightly criticized by Quaglia, 47 n. 23.

[80] Cf. W. C. Greene, *Moira* (Cambridge, Mass. 1944), 19-23. The importance of divine justice
in Homeric religion has often been underestimated, e.g. by Wil., *Gl.* I, 353, and Schm., 176-7 (cf.
IV, 522, 525). A healthy reaction against this tendency is to be found in H. Kelsen, *Society and
Nature* (London 1946), 188-96, although it is not true that "divine retribution is the chief motive
of both epic poems" (190). A similar extreme thesis has been proposed by H. Lloyd-Jones, *The
Justice of Zeus* (Berkeley-Los Angeles 1971): see the critical remarks made by C. J. Herington,
AJP 94 (1973), 395-7, H. R. Rawlings, CJ 70 (1975), 62, W. Kraus, Gnom. 49 (1977), 241-2, and
by me, Mnem. IV 30 (1977), 440-1. Cf. also Ehnmark, *Idea of God* (above, n. 65), 87-100,
P. Chantraine in Entret. s. l'ant. class. 1 (1954), 73-8, Kaufmann-Bühler, *passim*, P. Janni, SIFC
40 (1968), 148-68, J. E. Rexine, CB 54 (1977), 1-6.

[81] Greene, *op. cit.*, 11. Cf. Kelsen, *op. cit.*, 192.

[82] See my remarks in Lampas 3 (1970), 98-101.

[83] Cf. Wil., *Gl.* II, 116: "Also steht für Solon neben der unerbittlich und gerecht strafenden
Gottheit, die er Zeus nennt, die Willkür der Götter, die dem Streben der Menschen Erfolg und
Misserfolg geben ... Er empfindet darin keinen Widerspruch, weil der Weltlauf ihm beides gezeigt
hat".

takes the initiative, and God joins him in the execution (e.g. *Pers.* 742, *Ag.* 1508), (3) human and divine activities go side by side (e.g. *Cho.* 910)[84].

16: ἀθανάτων. Cf. *Less. pol.*, 266 ff.

16: βουλῆσιν. Not because the gods form a plurality, for cf. 79 Διὸς βουλῆσι and 71 Κρονίδεω διὰ βουλάς. K.G. I, 16, observe that in early Greek abstract notions are not sharply distinguished from their concrete manifestations. See further below, on 146 ὕβριες.

16: τιμῶσι. Not 'honour' but 'cultivate': cf. Sol. 1 D. = 13 W., 11 (πλοῦτον) τιμῶσιν, Thgn. 189 χρήματα τιμῶσι, Pind. *O.* 6, 72 τιμῶντες ἀρετάς, E. *Ba.* 885 τοὺς τὰν ἀγνωμοσύναν τιμῶντας (similarly *Ion* 1045-6, *Phoen.* 549-50, fr. 354).

16: βαρεῖαν. Not 'heavy to bear' but 'oppressive', 'overwhelming': cf. Hom. B 111 ἄτη ἐνέδησε βαρείῃ, Υ 55 ἔριδα ῥήγνυντο βαρεῖαν, η 197 Κλῶθες βαρεῖαι, and *Lex.* II, 39.46 ff., where the explanation 'quälend' seems to me misleading (because the Greek word does not imply subjective reactions).

17: προτέρην. This implies that good Eris ranks above bad Eris: cf. Hom. Β 707 etc. πρότερος καὶ ἀρείων, Ν 355, Ν 429-31, Ο 165-6. Similarly *Th.* 361 προφερεστάτη is explained by 777 πρεσβυτάτη[85].

17: μέν. Si.'s note, "emphatic, not adversative", is based on a misunderstanding: the sense of δέ at 18 is certainly not adversative, but μέν still has preparative force (cf. Denn., 369 ff.).

17: Νύξ. Supposed to be known from *Th.* 224-5. G. Calvo, Emer. 23 (1955), 217, proposes to punctuate as follows: τὴν δ' ἑτέρην – προτέρην (i.e. bad Eris) μὲν ἐγείνατο Νὺξ ἐρεβεννή –, but Hes. deliberately adapts his innovation as closely as possible to his original picture. To that end he tacitly omits Night's epithet ὀλοή.

18: θῆκε. See below, on 19 τε.

18: δέ. Has consecutive force ('and therefore'): cf. Denn., 170, Chantr. II, 358. Similarly 95, 193, 243, 326, 380.

18: Κρονίδης. Zeus not only assigns a specific function to the 'new' Eris (Quaglia, 36 n. 5, We.), but also gives her a moral sanction: see above, on 7 κάρφει and 16 ἀθανάτων.

18: ὑψίζυγος. As a helmsman seated on a higher ζυγόν than the rowers: cf. Fraenkel on A. *Ag.* 182 and 1618, and D. van Nes, *Die maritime Bildersprache des Aischylos* (Groningen 1963), 102-5.

---

[84] Cf. W. Kranz, *Stasimon* (Berlin 1933), 68-9, Fraenkel on A. *Ag.* 811, K. Deichgräber, *Der listensinnende Trug des Gottes* (Göttingen 1952), 108 ff., A. Lesky, *Die tragische Dichtung der Hellenen* (³Göttingen 1972), 162-8.

[85] Walcot (*Near East*, 85) probably goes too far in suggesting "that Hesiod as a living representation of the good spirit of competition, compared to Perses who equals the bad Eris, was also the first born". It is rather his superior tone which shows that he was the elder brother.

18: αἰθέρι. 'Bright sky': cf. Ch. H. Kahn, *Anaximander and the Origins of Greek Cosmology* (New York 1960), 140 ff., who rightly points out that "the primary contrast between ἀήρ and αἰθήρ is a question of visibility, not of relative location". See also H. Vos, Mnem. IV 16 (1963), 25-7. For the locative dative cf. K.G. I, 443-4, Schw. II, 154-5.

19: τε. Wrongly bracketed or omitted by many editors (some even printing a comma after ῥίζῃσι and supplying οὖσαν or connecting ἀμείνω with ἐγείνατο): θῆκε is used first in a local, and then in a modal, sense, just as at Pind. *P.* 1, 40 ταῦτα νόῳ τιθέμεν εὐανδρόν τε χώραν. This construction should not be called 'zeugma' (as is done e.g. by Col. and We.), for 'to place' and 'to make' are connected by the idea of 'establishing' and so are only different aspects of the general meaning of τίθημι. A real zeugma is, e.g., Hom. υ 312-3 οἴνοιό τε πινομένοιο/καὶ σίτου, and Hdt. IV 106 ἐσθῆτά τε φορέουσι τῇ Σκυθικῇ ὁμοίην, γλῶσσαν δὲ ἰδίην, but not Hom. P 476 ἵππων ἀθανάτων ἐχέμεν δμῆσίν τε μένος τε (called by Leaf "a slight zeugma", but 'to have' and 'to hold' are different aspects of one and the same notion), Pind. *O.* 1, 88 ἕλεν δ᾽ Οἰνομάου βίαν παρθένον τε σύνευνον (cf. the use of 'to get' for killing or injuring) [86].

19: ἐν. C. R. Beye, HSCP 76 (1972), 32-3, argues that this points forward to the idea of 'within' which binds together the next sections: 31 ἔνδον, 41 ἐν, 42 κρύψαντες, 50 κρύψε, 63 εἶδος (concealing her true nature), 97 ἔνδον. I mention this as a warning example of the wrong way of explaining Hes.'s train of thought: it is true that his transitions are often based on mental associations, but he does not use formal concepts as if they were themes.

19: ῥίζῃσι. This does not mean that she is as old as the world (Maz.) [87], but that she is a fundamental principle of human life. Yet the expression is not to be taken metaphorically (as is done e.g. by Col. and We.), for the roots of the earth are a cosmological reality (cf. *Th.* 728, 812). They belong to the conception of the earth as a tree, which is also found in Anaximander (A 10), Pherecydes (B 2), Xenophanes (A 47), Parmenides (B 15 a), Pindar (*P.* 9, 8), Aeschylus (*Prom.* 1046-7). Eris, after being put in the roots of the earth, will imbue the whole earth, including human life (which originated from it [88]).

---

[86] For more examples cf. K.G. II, 570-1, Bruhn, § 198 III, Fehling, 278-9, who quotes e.g. Hom. Π 505 τοῖο δ᾽ ἅμα ψυχήν τε καὶ ἔγχεος ἐξέρυσ᾽ αἰχμήν (Leaf: "The curious zeugma ... has almost a comic effect", but ψυχή as life-breath was a kind of substance: cf. my remarks in Lampas 3, 1970, 105-6), Ψ 182-3 Ἕκτορα δ᾽ οὔ τι / δώσω Πριαμίδην πυρὶ δαπτέμεν, ἀλλὰ κύνεσσιν (but fire was imagined as a living being: cf. Lampas 2, 1969, 97-8).

[87] It is true that the description of the Erides implies a contrast "zwischen einer vom Himmel zeitweise auferlegten Schickung und einer dauernd auf Erden beheimateten Kraft" (Fränkel, 128), but the phrase ἐν ῥίζῃσι does not contain the idea of duration.

[88] For the conception of Earth as the mother or origin of human life cf. W. Fauth, *Gaia*, KP II (1967), 657-8, We. on *Th.* 571, A. Motte, *Prairies et jardins de la Grèce antique* (Brussels 1973), 79 ff., P. H. Schrijvers, Mnem. IV 27 (1974), 247 ff.

19: ἀμείνω. In a utilitarian sense: see below, on 24 ἀγαθή. Similarly 294, 314, 320 [89].

20: ἤ τε. Cf. 3 ὅν τε.

20: ἀπάλαμον. Hom. E 597 (ἀπάλαμνος) 'helpless', 'desperate', here 'shiftless', 'unhandy' (as a permanent quality). The translation 'indolent' (Maz., Col., *Lex.* 989.21, Quaglia, 39 n. 11) is not correct, for the literal meaning is 'who is unable to use his hands', not 'who is unwilling to use his hands' [90].

20: ὅμως. We. rightly rejects the reading ὁμῶς because an ellipse of 'as the man of gumption' is improbable. The adversative ὅμως came to be used as a reinforcement of the concessive καί(περ): cf. A. *Sept.* 712 πείθου γυναικὶ καίπερ οὐ στέργων ὅμως, S. *O.C.* 958-9 πρὸς δὲ τὰς πράξεις ὅμως/καὶ τηλικόσδ᾽ ὢν ἀντιδρᾶν πειράσομαι (Jebb and Dain wrongly put a comma after ὅμως), Hdt. V 63, 2 ἐξελῶντα Πεισιστρατίδας ἐξ Ἀθηνέων ὅμως καὶ ξείνους σφι ἐόντας. See further Schw. II, 390, 582-3 and We. *ad loc.*, who compares the similar use of ἔμπης [91].

20: ἔργον. At 311 ἔργον is used as the contrary of ἀεργίη, but there is no need to assume this abstract meaning here, as is done by Krafft, 66 n. 1.

20: ἔγειρεν. The gnomic aorist alternates with the present (23 ζηλοῖ), just as at 217-8, 450-1, Hom. Δ 442-3, P 177. See further K.G. I, 159-60. The reading ἐγείρει, adopted by Pal., Wil., and So., is a *lectio facilior* [92].

21: εἰς. Expresses intensity of looking and suggests admiration: cf. my note on *Th.* 82 ἐσίδωσι, Mnem. IV 25 (1972), 252.

21: γάρ τίς τε. It is a debated question whether in such cases τε belongs to τις or to γάρ: cf. K.G. II, 240-1, Schw. II, 574, Chantr. II, 340-1, Ruijgh, 739-40, 898-9. J. Gonda, Mnem. IV 7 (1954), 283, argues that in the present sentence τε emphasizes the complementary relation between τις and ἕτερον. But it seems more natural to take τε as expressing the complementary character of this sentence and the preceding one (cf. Gonda, *ibid.*, 270-1).

---

[89] Hes. nowhere suggests that good ἔρις is an aspect of justice, as is assumed by Quaglia (25 n. 22).

[90] We. refers to D. Page, *Sappho and Alcaeus* (Oxford 1955), 315 (note on Alc. 360, 2), but (1) his translation of Pind. *O.* 1, 59 by 'helpless' is misleading, for there the meaning is πρὸς ὃν οὐκ ἔστι παλαμήσασθαι (schol.), and (2) his explanation of the meaning 'wicked' (Thgn. 281, Pind. *O.* 2, 57) is unsatisfactory: it is true that "a number of words in Greek draw no sharp distinction between 'folly' and 'wickedness'", but a transition from 'shiftless' to 'wicked' is difficult to understand. D. Müller, *Handwerk und Sprache* (Meisenheim/Glan 1974), 17 (followed by D. E. Gerber in his note on *O.* 1, 59), suggests that the ἀπάλαμος "kann auch durch seine Unbeholfenheit Schaden anrichten", but this does not lead to 'wicked'. The latter meaning is more easily derived from the passive use, 'unmanageable' becoming 'terrible', 'evil' (cf. a similar development in ἀμήχανος: LSJ II 2 b).

[91] Cf. also my note on Mimn. 1, 6, Mnem. IV 6 (1953), 197.

[92] Broccia, *Tradizione* (above, n. 8), 26-8, suggests that the choice of this verb has a polemic intention, in so far as Homer mostly uses it with regard to war (cf. espec. E 517-8 πόνος ... ὃν ... ἔγειρεν ... Ἔρις). But Homer does not have ἐγείρειν τινα ἐπί τι, and Hes. may just as well have given a figurative sense to the epic ἐπέγειρειν 'wake up'.

Denn. (528) observes that "the great majority of passages in which τε is coupled with another particle contain general propositions, or describe habitual action", but I doubt whether this warrants his conclusion that "τε generalizes".

21: τις. Not 'everyone' (Col.) but 'many a one': cf. Hom. H 201 etc. ὧδε δέ τις εἴπεσκεν, Schw. II, 214.

21: ἰδών. So. unnecessarily reads ἴδεν: for the anacolouthon see below, on 22 ὅς[93].

21: χατίζων. Some editors adopt the reading χατίζει, but (1) this is the *lectio facilior*, viz. an attempt to supply the sentence with a main verb; (2) ἔργοιο χατίζει cannot mean 'il prend le goût du travail' (Maz.; similarly Quaglia, 41 n. 11: 'si sente preso dalla voglia di lavorare'), for χατίζω and χατέω used in the sense of 'to desire' always refer to a desire the fulfilment of which does not depend on the subject itself[94]; (3) τις needs a qualification. The explanation proposed by A. Hoekstra, "quelqu'un qui a besoin de travail (c'est-à-dire pour gagner sa vie, donc un homme ordinaire)"[95], is not convincing, for in Hesiod's view everyone has to work. We must assume a transition from 'being in want of work' to 'being without work', 'not working': similarly Hom. Γ 294 θυμοῦ δευομένους for 'dead'. Si. observes that we expect 'letting work slide' (cf. Wil. 'der nicht arbeitet wie er sollte'), and Col. even translates 'riluttante al lavoro', but cf. 312-3 εἰ δέ κε ἐργάζῃ, τάχα σε ζηλώσει ἀεργὸς/πλουτεῦντα, where ἀεργός shows that the idea of unwillingness or neglect should not be sought in χατίζων but is implied in the context[96].

22: ὅς. Deleted by Wil. because σπεύδει "kann unmöglich von dem Reichen ausgesagt werden"[97]. This is to forget that rich farmers have to exert themselves if they wish to remain rich, and that they have to remain rich and, if possible, to become still richer in order to keep up their public reputation (see below, on 313 κῦδος)[98]. With regard to the metre Wil. writes: "Die Freiheit des Versbaues wird uns öfters begegnen", but a trochee instead of a

---

[93] G. Arrighetti, in *Studi A. Ardizzoni*, I (Rome 1978), 29-30, rightly objects that ἴδεν would have to carry the implication of emulation which is only explained at 23-4.

[94] Cf. e.g. 394, Hom. Σ 392, θ 156. The importance of this point is ignored by Quaglia (*loc. cit.*) and underestimated by N. J. Richardson, JHS 99 (1979), 170, when he states: "I am not convinced that the question of availability is relevant here".

[95] Mnem. IV 3 (1950), 108. Similarly M. Hofinger, Rech. de Philol. et de Ling. 2 (1967), 10: "*qui a besoin de travailler*, entendons: qui en a besoin pour vivre, parce qu'il est pauvre". Cf. the absolute use of χατίζων in the sense of 'needy' at 394 and Hom. χ 50 and 351.

[96] Cf. also B. M. Palumbo Stracca, Boll. d. Com. Ediz. Naz. 24 (1976), 37-9, who rightly criticizes the views of Wil. and Col., but wrongly defends χατίζει.

[97] Similarly O. A. Danielsson, Eran. 1 (1896), 5, who proposes πλησίον instead of πλούσιον, and Hofinger (above, n. 95), 9.

[98] Cf. also below, on 23 ζηλοῖ.

dactyl occurs only in those places where he has himself altered the text![99] Waltz and Si. take ὅς as equivalent to οὗτος (cf. 429, Hom. α 286, etc.). But (1) if σπεύδει referred to τις we should have expected ὅ γε[100]; (2) 24 εἰς ἄφενος σπεύδοντα echoes and specifies ὅς σπεύδει[101] (accordingly, γείτων is not a third person, as is assumed by Si.); (3) the construction ἕτερον .../πλούσιον, ὅς is paralleled by 31-2 βίος .../ὡραῖος, τόν, 38-9 βασιλῆας/ δωροφάγους, οἵ, etc.[102]. Consequently, we have to assume an anacolouthon: the sentence should proceed with ζηλοῖ αὐτόν, but the poet replaced this by a standing proverb ζηλοῖ δέ τε γείτονα γείτων[103]. Accordingly, not a semicolon but a comma should be put after θέσθαι (as is done by We.).

22.: μέν. Precedes apodotic δέ: cf. Hom. I 508-9 ὅς μέν τ᾽ αἰδέσεται κούρας Διὸς ἆσσον ἰούσας, / τὸν δὲ μέγ᾽ ὤνησαν, λ 385-7 αὐτὰρ ἐπεὶ ψυχὰς μὲν ἀπεσκέδασε ... / ἦλθε δ᾽ ἐπὶ ψυχὴ Ἀγαμέμνονος, Denn., 379.

22: ἀρώμεναι. So. prints ἀρόμεναι, but cf. Hom. Κ 125 καλήμεναι, Ξ 502 γοήμεναι, We., *Th.*, 84, Edwards, 108-9 (who compares Hom. ἀλώμεναι, γνώμεναι, and plausibly suggests that ἀρώμεναι "may be an analogical formation rather than an original Aeolism"). For the contrast 'plow-plant' cf. Hom. Μ 313 φυταλιῆς καὶ ἀρούρης[104].

23: οἶκον. The farmhouse including the supplies (LSJ II): cf. We. *ad loc.*

23: τε. Often introduces the last item of a series (Denn., 500), because it conveys the idea of completion (see above, on 3 ὅν τε).

23: εὖ θέσθαι. Not 'faire prospérer son bien' (Maz.) or 'crearsi una bella casa' (Col), but 'to put his house in good order' (Ev.): cf. Thgn. 846 εὖ δὲ θέμεν τὸ κακῶς κείμενον ἀργαλέον, LSJ A VII 1, Renehan, 345.

23: ζηλοῖ. The explanation given by LSJ (I 1 a), "in bad sense, *to be jealous of, envy*", is misleading: there are two kinds of jealousy, one inspired by emulation (ζῆλος), the other by grudging (φθόνος: see below, on 26 φθονέει): cf. P. Walcot, *Envy and the Greeks* (Warminster 1978), 2 ff., espec. 8-10. Whether jealously is good or bad in Hes.'s eyes depends on its results, not on the kind of feeling which is behind it (see below, on 24 ἀγηθή)[105].

---

[99] *Th.* 454 Ἱστίην is a proper name which cannot enter the hexameter. For *Th.* 466 cf. We. *ad loc.*, and for *Th.* 532 and 961 see We., *Th.*, 92.

[100] Cf. A. Hoekstra, Mnem. IV 3 (1950), 111-2.

[101] As is observed by Hoekstra, 108-9.

[102] See further Hoekstra, 110.

[103] Cf. Hoekstra, 113-4. For the anacolouthon cf. Arrighetti (above, n.93), 30-1, who compares Hom. Κ 224 σύν τε δύ᾽ ἐρχομένω, καί τε πρὸ ὃ τοῦ ἐνόησεν. For proverbs in Hes. see below, on 40 πλέον.

[104] More examples are given by We. They show that Hofinger (above, n. 95), 10-3, is wrong in arguing that "les verbes labourer et planter ne sont pas ceux qui se rapprochent naturellement". He proposes the translation 'to sow' (similarly AC 36, 1967, 5-21, and *Études sur le vocabulaire du grec archaïque*, Leiden 1981, 36-8), but this meaning is not found before the 5th cent. See further *Lex.*, 1341.

[105] It is true that these results are connected with specific intentions (cf. 13 διὰ δ᾽ ἄνδιχα

Thus φθόνος may be good, when it stimulates one to work (26), and ζῆλος may be bad, when it brings about mere destruction (195-6). On the other hand, good ζῆλος increases the farmer's property and hence his prestige: now he in his turn will be envied by others (312-3, 482)[106]. See further Walcot, *Peasants*, Ch. V: 'Envy and the Spirit of Competition', espec. 82, where he states: "Hesiod wants wealth not because it confers power over others, but because it makes a man needed and envied". Cf. also his essay *A Study of Rural Communities: The Greeks and the Welsh* (Cardiff 1974), 7: "the man of honour must always strive for yet more honour and will envy it being recognized in others"[107].

23: δέ τε. Proverbs are often introduced by δέ τε, e.g. 218 παθὼν δέ τε νήπιος ἔγνω, Hom. I 497 στρεπτοὶ δέ τε καὶ θεοὶ αὐτοί, δ 397 θεοὶ δέ τε πάντα ἴσασιν[108]. In such cases the force of δέ is explanatory, that of τε complementary: see above, on 21 γάρ τε, and J. Gonda, Mnem. IV 7 (1954), 266-7[109]. Here, however, the proverb takes the place of an apodosis: for δέ *in apodosi* cf. K.G. II, 277, Schw. II, 562, Denn., 177-81; it is most easily explained as a weak form of δή: see my notes on Semon. 7, 110, Mnem. IV 21 (1968), 154, and E. *Ba.* 23, Mnem. IV 33 (1980), 5-6. For apodotic δέ τε cf. 284, *Th.* 609, 784, and Ruijgh, 898. For proverbs in Hes. see below on 40 πλέον.

23: γείτονα γείτων. For the polyptoton cf. 182-3, We., *Th.*, 76, Fehling, 229. For the importance of neighbourship cf. 343-51, 395-400, etc.[110].

24: ἄφενος. For the variant ἄφενον (most MSS.) cf. We. *ad loc.* and on *Th.* 112-3; Hes. perhaps used it here for euphonic reasons. Pal. thinks that "by ἄφενος, as distinct from πλοῦτος, the wealth of the farmer is meant", but the original meaning seems to be 'abundant supply': cf. *Th.* 112 and my note *ad loc.*, Mnem. IV 25 (1972), 258. See further B. Mader, *Lex.*, 1702-3, and A. Heubeck, Gymn. 90 (1983), 296.

24: ἀγαθή. 'Profitable' rather than 'morally good', although Hes. does not

---

θυμὸν ἔχουσιν), but it is significant that Hes. does not define these intentions but concentrates on the results.

[106] Walcot (*Peasants*, 8) rightly points out that 482 παῦροι δέ σε θηήσονται implies "the envy felt by the needy". Ζῆλος at *Th.* 384 is not the envy felt by Zeus but refers to the admiration which he incites in others: cf. We. *ad loc.* and Walcot, *Peasants*, 90-1.

[107] Cf. also J. K. Campbell, *Honour, Family and Patronage* (Oxford 1964), 43, where he observes that among the Sarakatsani "property is itself an element in prestige", 317: "Reputation is impossible without strength", and 298-9 on the importance of wealth for family prestige.

[108] Cf. A. Hoekstra, Mnem. IV 3 (1950), 113 and n. 86.

[109] I do not believe that τε answers τε at 21, as is assumed by Arrighetti (above, n. 93), 32.

[110] See further L. Radermacher, *Beiträge zur Volkskunde aus dem Gebiet der Antike*, SB Akad. Wien, phil.-hist. Kl. 187:3 (1918), 3 ff., who remarks (5): "Wir dürfen annehmen, dass der Nachbar in einem antiken Gemeinwesen mit grösster Unbefangenheit und Selbstverständlichkeit sich an allem beteiligte, was der Anwohner zur Rechten und Linken trieb und verhandelte".

clearly distinguish the two aspects, as appears e.g. from 265 and 703-4[111]. See further *Lex.*, 27, *Less. pol.*, 9-14.

24: ἀγαθὴ ... βροτοῖσιν. Rightly printed as a parenthesis by Col.: καί at the beginning of 25 and 26 is not corresponsive but continuative[112]. Another parenthesis is 107 σὺ δ᾽ ἐνὶ φρεσὶ βάλλεο σῇσιν (cf. also 268 οὐδέ ἑ λήθει). See further K.G. II, 602, Schw. II, 706. Hes. adds the remark because there is also a bad ζῆλος (195-6), and he wants to preclude any ambiguity.

25-6. Nicolai (20) rightly observes that these lines look like an appendix, but that their real function is to show the universal character of the principle of emulation. They might be called a reversed priamel[113]. The authenticity of the lines is doubted by Quaglia (41-2 n. 12) on insufficient grounds (see below).

25: κεραμεῖ. For the contraction see below, n. 538.

25: κοτέει. Refers to malevolent envy: cf. *Scut.* 403 ἀλλήλοις κοτέοντες. We. thinks that "κότος and φθόνος are not in the spirit of the good Eris" (similarly Quaglia, *loc. cit.*, Péron, 266, who wrongly speaks of "incertitudes"), but ἀγαθή (see above, *ad loc.*) does not exclude malevolence. The Greek spirit of emulation was so fierce that it was often allied to envy and easily led to malevolence. This even appears in the sphere of sporting contests. Pindar (*P.* 8, 82) praises a young wrestler for having flung himself on his adversaries κακὰ φρονέων, and this is not "an unfortunate reminiscence of Π 783 Πάτροκλος δὲ Τρωσὶ κακὰ φρονέων ἐνόρουσεν" (Farnell) but a reality. The challenge of a boxer, Hom. Ψ 673 ἀντικρὺς χροά τε ῥήξω σύν τ᾽ ὀστέ᾽ ἀράξω, even if we abstract the element of bluff, is still remarkably harsh[114].

---

[111] Waltz (I), 86, however, goes too far when he writes: "Le principe de la morale hésiodique est purement utilitaire ... Le premier devoir d'un homme est d'entretenir et d'augmenter son patrimoine ... L'équité, la piété, une honnêteté scrupuleuse sont avant tout des conditions de succès dans l'existence" (similarly Luther, 132-3): a predominantly moral point of view appears e.g. at 185 ff. Cf. also Péron, 282.

[112] Rather than explanatory, as I suggested in *Aufbau*, 120 n. 2. The only undeniable example of corresponsive καί in Homer is N 260: cf. Denn., 323-4.

[113] B. A. van Groningen, Gnom. 37 (1965), 332, is certainly wrong in proposing to print these lines as a parenthesis and to put a comma at the end of 24.

[114] Cf. the quarrel between Idomeneus and Ajax the Lesser at Ψ 448-98, on which Ameis-Hentze remark: "die Szene befremdet durch die Art, wie Aias gezeichnet ist, die der feinen ritterlichen Sitte des Epos nicht entspricht". It is also typical that at θ 208 Odysseus motivates his refusal to wrestle or to sprint with a ξεῖνος by the words τίς ἂν φιλέοντι μάχοιτο; Nietzsche's essay *Homers Wettkampf* is still worth reading. Cf. also R. J. Littman, *The Greek Experiment: Imperialism and Social Conflict 800-400 B.C.* (London 1974), 18: "The Greeks were obsessively concerned with the admiration and approval of their peers. This fostered a character which was vain, boastful, ambitious, envious and vindictive. Above all the arousal of envy and the obtaining of revenge were esteemed most highly". See further Walcot, *Peasants*, 87 ff., who rightly disproves the view proposed by E. A. Havelock, YCS 20 (1966), 63-4, that 25-6 express "rather cynical sentiments" and that the intent of these lines "can be viewed as satirical".

The Greeks made a competition of everything. Cf. Hom. ζ 92 στεῖβον δ᾽ ἐν βόθροισι θοῶς ἔριδα προφέρουσαι, σ 366 Εὐρύμαχ᾽, εἰ γὰρ νῶϊν ἔρις ἔργοιο γένοιτο. A potters' contest and a doctors' competition are known from inscriptions[115]. The inscription on the base of the Nike of Paeonius (*Syll.*[3] 80) mentions a contest of sculptors. Xenophon (*Vect.* III 3) proposes to put up prizes for those ὅστις δικαιότατα καὶ τάχιστα διαιροίη τὰ ἀμφίλογα[116]. The best speaker in the βουλή was honoured with a wreath (*Syll.*[3] 227). After the battle of Salamis the Greeks went to the Isthmus, ἀριστήϊα δώσοντες τῷ ἀξιοτάτῳ γενομένῳ Ἑλλήνων ἀνὰ τὸν πόλεμον τοῦτον (Hdt. VIII 123, 1), and during the preparation of the Sicilian expedition the crews as well as the troops competed with one another (Thuc. VI 31, 3-4). In short, life was πολύζηλος (S. *O.R.* 381)[117].

We. thinks that 25 and 26 were existing proverbs because alliteration often occurs in proverbs, but if we omit the initial καί (see above, on 24 ἀγαθὴ … βροτοῖσιν) the metre does not suit a proverb. Hes. probably modelled the phrases on 23 ζηλοῖ δέ τε γείτονα γείτων.

26: πτωχός. Well-known from the quarrel between Odysseus and Irus, which has rightly been called "une véritable concurrence professionnelle"[118]. The fact that the beggar is mentioned in the same breath as the artisan shows "dass man keinen prinzipiellen, oder wenigstens wesentlichen, sittlich begründeten Unterschied im Urteil über die angeführten Mittel zum Erwerb des Lebensunterhalts kannte" (Bolkestein, 205). It is misleading to call a professional beggar "a man forfeiting all honour", as is done by Walcot, *Peasants*, 62. He refers (63) to the reproaches addressed by the maid Melantho to Odysseus (σ 321 ff. and τ 65 ff.), but these refer to the fact that he does not leave the palace, not to his way of making a living[119].

---

[115] A. Wilhelm, *Beiträge zur griechischen Inschriftenkunde* (Vienna 1909), 40-2, J. Keil, Österr. Jahresh. 8 (1905), 133-4. We. mentions the inscription on an amphora of Euthymides, ὡς οὐδέποτε Εὐφρόνιος.

[116] Hom. Σ 507-8 is to be interpreted in this light: the judges compete for justice and the best spokesman gets a prize. Cf. Leaf, App. I, §§ 28-30, R. Köstler, *Homerisches Recht* (Vienna 1950), 73-4, H. Hommel, *Symbola*, I (Hildesheim 1976), 87-9.

[117] For the agonistic spirit of the Greeks see further V. Ehrenberg, *Ost und West* (Brünn 1935), Ch. IV, Bolkestein, 152-3, M. Pohlenz, *Der hellenische Mensch* (Göttingen 1947), 425-32, J. Huizinga, *Homo ludens* ([3]Haarlem 1951), 72-7, H. Berve, *Gestaltende Kräfte der Antike* ([2]Munich 1966), 14-8, H. O. Weber, *Die Bedeutung und Bewertung der Pleonexie von Homer bis Isokrates* (Ph. D. diss. Bonn 1967), 23-4, W. J. Froleyks, *Der ἀγὼν λόγων in der antiken Literatur* (Bonn 1973), J. Weiler, *Der Agon im Mythos. Zur Einstellung der Griechen zum Wettkampf* (Darmstadt 1974), J. P. Hershbell, *The Idea of Strife in Early Greek Thought*, The Personalist 55 (1974), 205-15, W. Burkert, *Griechische Religion* (Stuttgart 1977), 173-4, Walcot, *Envy* (above, on 23 ζηλοῖ).

[118] P. Waltz, Rev. hist. 39 (1914), 27. Quaglia (41-2 n. 12) objects that Odysseus explicitly denies to be jealous and proposes to keep the place open to both (σ 15-9). But this does not testify to his humanity (Quaglia speaks of "l'umanissimo discorso di Odisseo") but to his sense of superiority.

[119] Cf. Bolkestein, 210: "Natürlich haben viele mit Verachtung auf sie [the beggars] herab-

26: φθονέει. 'Bears a grudge against' rather than 'is jealous': the meaning is that he does not want the other to have something (cf. 25 κοτέει), not that he wants to have what the other has[120]. It is true that the latter notion is implied in the good ἔρις, but this is the result of φθόνος rather than its equivalent.

26: ἀοιδός. Hes. himself mentions a singers' contest (654-7). Cf. also Hom. B 594-600, *H. Ap.* 146-50, *H. Ven.* VI 19-20, Thgn. 995[121]. It has been suggested that the joining of beggar and singer in one and the same line betrays the poet's self-irony[122]. Apart from the question whether the wandering singer was looked upon in the same manner as a beggar[123], it may be doubted whether self-irony is compatible with Hes.'s self-esteem as expressed, e.g., in *Th.* 26. It is equally doubtful whether the poet here "speaks slightingly of his colleagues"[124]. He simply describes the actual situation.

27: ὦ. "Tandis que, chez Platon, ὦ est devenu la formule de politesse banale, l'usage de la particule répond chez Homère à une intention: l'interjection exprime souvent un ton assez vif et brusque" (Chantr. II, 37). Cf. 213, 248, etc.[125].

27: δέ. The use of δέ after an apostrophe is commonly explained as a case of postponement (Denn., 174-5, 189; cf. We.: "It is impossible in Greek to say ὦ Πέρση δέ or ὦ δὲ Πέρση") or adversative (with implied opposition or turning from one person to another) (LSJ II 4), but it is much more natural to take δέ as a weak form of δή[126].

---

gesehen, aber diese Haltung wird eher aus der Geringschätzung entsprungen sein, mit der jeder Vermögenslose und umsomehr der vermögens- und rechtlose Fremde betrachtet und behandelt wurde, als aus sittlicher Entrüstung über die Faulheit, die doch manchen zum Betteln getrieben haben wird".

[120] Cf. B. Snell, *Aischylos und das Handeln im Drama* (Leipzig 1928), 72 n. 108, J. L. Myres, CR 51 (1937), 163. Neglect of the difference between 'grudge' and 'jealousy' has obscured most discussions of the φθόνος θεῶν.

[121] See further R. Hirzel, *Der Dialog*, I (Leipzig 1895), 17 ff., J. Frei, *De certaminibus thumelicis* (Basel 1900), E. E. Sikes, *The Greek View of Poetry* (London 1931), 7-10, who rightly concludes (10) that "the whole idea of the critic's function was powerfully affected by the theory and practice of poetic competitions" (κριτής originally means 'umpire'), E. Vogt, RhM 102 (1959), 196 n. 4, Pagliaro, *Saggi* (above, n. 1), 52 ff., Krafft, 21-4, H. Maehler, *Die Auffassung des Dichterberufs im frühen Griechentum bis zur Zeit Pindars* (Göttingen 1963), 16.

[122] Fränkel, 127, Nicolai, 19-20, P. Rose, Hist. 24 (1975), 135, W. Stroh, in H. Görgemanns - E. A. Schmidt (edd.), *Studien zum antiken Epos* (Meisenheim/Glan 1976), 102.

[123] As is assumed by Fränkel, 127 n. 3, and Renehan, 345-6. Fränkel's reconstruction of the wandering singer from the wandering Odysseus (11-2) is highly hypothetical.

[124] Maehler (above, n. 121), 42 n. 1.

[125] Schw. II, 61, defines ὦ in Homer as "ein Zeichen der Vertraulichkeit", but this aspect does not seem to predominate in Hes. We. on *Th.* 544 wrongly suggests that it is inexpressive. Cf. also my note on Tyrt. 6-7 D. = 10 W., 15, Mnem. IV 22 (1969), 345.

[126] Cf. M. Leumann, MH 6 (1949), 85-9 = *Kleine Schriften* (Zürich 1959), 229 ff. This explanation also accounts for δέ in questions (Denn., 173-7) and exclamations (Denn., 172), and δέ at the beginning of a speech (Denn., 172-3). I have discussed inceptive δέ in Mnem. III 13 (1947), 274-5, IV 8 (1955), 17, and IV 27 (1974), 173-4. Cf. also my notes on Men. *Epitr.* 512 and 728, Mnem. IV 27 (1974), 36 and 41.

27: ἐνικάτθεο. Properly 'lay up in store in yourself': cf. 627 ἐγκάτθεο οἴκῳ. Similarly Hom. ψ 223 ἄτην ἑῷ ἐγκατθέτο θυμῷ.

27: θυμῷ. Although the θυμός has its principal seat in the φρένες the two words are not synonymous, θυμός being the power of mental movement and often leading to action. Accordingly, it is used in situations (like the present one) where consideration is, or should be, followed by prompt action: cf. Hom. Ο 566 ἐν θυμῷ δ᾽ ἐβάλοντο ἔπος, φράξαντο δὲ νῆας, δ 729-30 οὐδ᾽ ὑμεῖς περ ἐνὶ φρεσὶ θέσθε ἑκάστη / ἐκ λεχέων μ᾽ ἀνεγεῖραι, ἐπιστάμεναι σάφα θυμῷ, ψ 223 τὴν δ᾽ ἄτην οὐ πρόσθεν ἑῷ ἐγκάτθετο θυμῷ (cf. 222 τὴν δ᾽ ἤ τοι ῥέξαι θεὸς ὤρορεν ἔργον ἀεικές). Cf. also such phrases as *Th*. 443 ἐθέλουσά γε θυμῷ, 536 πρόφρονι θυμῷ.

28: μηδέ. 'And therefore not': for consecutive οὐδέ cf. Hom. Α 342, Λ 330, β 44, κ 214, ν 269, and my note in Mnem. IV 9 (1956), 249 [127]. See also above, on 18 δέ.

28: σε. We. rightly argues that this is more probable than σοι: he compares Hom. Γ 438 μή με, γύναι, χαλεποῖσιν ὀνείδεσι θυμὸν ἔνιπτε. Cf. also *Op*. 714 σὲ δὲ μή τι νόος κατελεγχέτω εἶδος. The construction, a σχῆμα καθ᾽ ὅλον καὶ μέρος, is not to be explained as an apposition (K.G. I, 289), but as a 'parathesis', i.e., both objects directly depend on the verb [128].

28: Ἔρις. Hes. does not tell us what the quarrel was about. Maz. plausibly suggests that Perses had ceded some land to Hes. in exchange for metals (representing money). The brothers had probably made their agreement without witnesses (cf. 371), so that Perses now tried to claim more 'money' than was agreed upon.

28: κακόχαρτος. Not 'rejoicing in the ills of others' [129], but 'rejoicing in evil deeds', 'wont to do evil'. Cf. Hom. Ι 257 Ἔρις κακομήχανος, and χαίρειν used in the sense of 'to be wont to do' (LSJ I 3 b) [130].

28: ἀπ᾽ ἔργου. For the neglect of the digamma cf. We., *Th*., 91, 99-100, and Si. *ad loc*. [131]. The sequel shows that 'work' means 'tillage' (LSJ I 3 a). We. (36) thinks that "the bad Eris ought to be the cause of war and fighting

---

[127] Cf. also my notes on A. *Prom*. 212 in *Miscellanea ... J. C. Kamerbeek* (Amsterdam 1976), 457, and Pind. *I*. 2, 45, Mnem. IV 35 (1982), 34.

[128] Cf. B. A. van Groningen, *La parathèse grammaticale en grec*, Mnem. III 9 (1941), 258-80, espec. 274-5. See also Schw. II, 81, who speaks of "Zusammenziehung von zwei Sätzen".

[129] As is suggested by Broccia, *Tradizione* (above, n. 8), 26 n. 22, who compares Hom. Λ 73 Ἔρις δ᾽ ἄρ᾽ ἔχαιρε πολύστονος εἰσορόωσα.

[130] E. A. Havelock, YCS 20 (1966), 64, thinks that "the Greek more naturally reads as initiating a fresh argument, to the effect that strife of any kind can menace hours of labor ... On this showing, the poet at this point has abandoned the formal division with which he had begun". However, it will be hard to deny the antithetic connection between 20 ἐπὶ ἔργον ἔγειρεν and 28 ἀπ᾽ ἔργου θυμὸν ἐρύκοι. Havelock's suggestion is based on his misapprehension of the Greek sense of emulation (above, n. 117).

[131] See further A. Hoekstra, Mnem. IV 10 (1957), 205 ff., A. Athanassakis, CSCA 2 (1969), 33 ff., Edwards, 132 ff.

(14), not of idleness", and that the antithetic character of Hes.'s thought made him transform the bad Eris into a cause of idleness as the counterpart of good Eris as the cause of industry. The difficulty disappears if we ask why Perses was watching and listening to the legal disputes of others. Not out of curiosity or to fill his leisure, but obviously to get acquainted with the tricks of legal action with a view of using them against his brother[132]. Hence bad Eris is the cause of idleness in that this idleness consists in the preparation of a legal strife. Accordingly, it is misleading to say that at 286 ff. "Perses has changed back from a perjurer to an idler" (We., 39). It is true that Hes. emphasizes his dishonesty and his idleness according to the context of the argument, but this does not imply a "shift in Perses' circumstances" (We., 35). The two aspects of his nature are so closely related that one is never absent when the other is mentioned.

28. θυμόν. 'Inclination' is better than 'mind' (Pal.): see above, on 13. It is true that at 27 the intellectual aspect predominates, but in such cases (e.g. Hom. M 119 γνῶ δ᾽ Αἴας κατὰ θυμὸν ῥίγησέν τε, ι 299 βούλευσα κατὰ θυμόν) the emotional or volitional aspect is not absent.

29: ὀπιπεύοντα. 'Watching closely', a reduplicated *intensivum* of ὁράω[133]. It has been suggested that the word implies "des sentiments analogues à ceux que peut ressentir l'homme à la vue d'une femme désirable"[134], but cf. 806 εὖ μάλ᾽ ὀπιπεύοντα. Perses' interest in lawsuits was shared by most Greeks[135], but we have seen above (on 28 ἀπ᾽ ἔργου) that it also had a practical purpose.

29: ἀγορῆς. Not to be connected with ἐπακουόν (LSJ, Latt.), for νείκεα needs a qualification. Wil. translates ἀγορῆς by 'Gerede': "denn der Plural [30 ἀγορέων] schliesst es aus, ἀγορή lokal zu fassen". He refers to Hom. δ 818 νήπιος, οὔτε πόνων εὖ εἰδὼς οὔτ᾽ ἀγοράων, which he explains by "Er kann sich in der Gesellschaft nicht benehmen". But ἀγοραί here means 'deliberations in assemblies' (cf. B 275, 788), and πόνοι does not refer to the difficulties of travel (Wil.) but to the toils of war: cf. I 440-1 νήπιον, οὔ πω εἰδόθ᾽ ὁμοιίου πολέμοιο / οὐδ᾽ ἀγορέων, ἵνα τ᾽ ἄνδρες ἀριπρεπέες τελέθουσι. This

---

[132] I do not believe that Perses tried to win the favour of the judges by his presence and his plaudits, as is suggested by van Groningen, *Hés. et Persès* (above, n. 45), 5.

[133] Cf. Schw. I, 648. The reading ὀπιπτεύω, which is also found in MSS. of Homer, seems to be due to confusion with ἐποπτεύω.

[134] Van Groningen, *op. cit.*, 2. He refers to Hom. τ 67 and Λ 385, but forgets Δ 371 and H 243.

[135] Cf. R. Harder, *Kleine Schriften* (Munich 1960), 248-9: "Die ganze Ilias dreht sich um einen Rechtshandel; und in der Schildbeschreibung kristallisiert sich das friedliche Stadtleben für Homer in zwei Bildern, Hochzeitsfest und Gerichtsverhandlung. Aischylos hat in den 'Eumeniden' eine grandiose Gerichtsszene auf die Bühne gebracht ... Befremdlich wirkt es vielleicht auch, dass Prozessreden bei den Griechen zur ernsten Literatur rechnen. Jeder Rechtsfall ist ein Streit mit hohem Einsatz und unsicherem Ausgang, ein 'Wettkampf': daher das tiefe Interesse dieses streitlustigen, wettfreudigen Volkes an allen Gerichtsdingen". For Near-Eastern parallels cf. Walcot, *Near East*, 91.

passage also shows that Homer did not draw a sharp distinction between the local and the active aspects of the assembly (θῶκος has the same ambivalence). Similarly, in 29 the local aspect and in 30 the active aspect is more prominent. In both lines ἀγορή refers to the sitting of the court, just as at Hom. Σ 497 and μ 439 [136].

29: ἐπακουόν. For ἐπι- referring to an intention cf. 268 ἐπιδέρκεται, 448 ἐπακούσῃς, 767 ἐποπτεύειν, Hom. Γ 277 Ἥλιός θ' ὅς πάντ' ἐφορᾷς καὶ πάντ' ἐπακούεις, and ἐπερωτάω, ἐπιμένω, ἐπιμέλομαι, ἐπινοέω, etc.

30: ὥρη. 'Heed', 'concern' (cf. ὥραν ἔχειν τινος). The word ὀλιγωρία is here seen in *statu nascendi*. The reading ὥρη (e.g. Latt.) is a *lectio facilior*; it is not supported by Hom. λ 379 ὥρη μὲν πολέων μύθων, ὥρη δὲ καὶ ὕπνου, for ὥρα always means a fixed or fitting time [137], and this meaning is excluded by ὀλίγη [138].

30: γάρ τε. See above, on 21 τε.

30: ὀλίγη. Euphemism for 'no'. A. C. Moorhouse, CQ 41 (1947), 31-45, points out that "μικρός generally has affective or emotional connotations, and ὀλίγος nearly always has not".

30: πέλεται. We. rightly observes that this implies dissuasion. He compares 572, where σκάφος οὐκέτι is equivalent to οὐκέτι χρὴ σκάπτειν, but his explanation, "the derivation of 'ought not' from 'does not'" (cf. his note on 320 οὐχ ἁρπακτά: "The addition of a negative ... may in some cases be tantamount to a veto") seems to me misleading: the transition does not lie in the negative, but in the fact that ἔστι (explicit or implicit) may be equivalent to ἔξεστι, and that 'cannot' is an euphemism for 'ought not' (cf. Dutch 'er is geen denken aan' = 'it cannot be thought of' = 'it should not be thought of', 'it is out of the question') [139].

30: ἀγορέων. For the ending cf. Edwards, 126 ff.

31: βίος. 'Means of living' (LSJ II, *Lex.* II, 62.9 ff.). Homer uses βίοτος in this sense.

31: ἐπηετανός. Derived from ἐπ' ἀεί or from ἐπ' ἔτος, although in both cases εἰς is usual. We. thinks that the sense 'lasting all through the year' is "appropriate, though never necessary, in some places where the word occurs". But at 517 it is not appropriate, for it would imply that cows and goats loose their hair during the year. In such places as Hom. η 99 and θ 233

---

[136] C. B. Welles, GRBS 8 (1967), 14, wrongly interprets 30 ἀγορέων as 'gains of the market'. See further M. I. Finley, *The World of Odysseus* (Harmondsworth 1977), 78 ff., *Lex.*, 89-91, and *Less. pol.*, 90 ff. (where 30 is wrongly listed under 'luogo di adunanza').

[137] Cf. J. Gonda, *The Character of the Indo-European Moods* (Wiesbaden 1956), 25-6.

[138] This fact has been overlooked by Skafte Jensen (above, n. 38), 7, who translates 'the season for disputes and forensic quarrels is short', and by Troxler (11-2), who tries to disprove the existence of ὥρη. Col. rightly prints ὥρη, but translates 'breve è il tempo' (!).

[139] K. J. Dover, CR N.S. 5 (1955), 206, assumes a development of the meaning of ὥρη to 'the appropriate undertaking', but the explanation given above seems to me more natural.

'abundant' is the most obvious translation, and this seems to be the original meaning, whatever the etymology [140].

31: κατακεῖται. 'Lies stored up' (LSJ 3 a, cf. κατατίθημι II 4). Subjunctive (from κείεται: Chantr. I, 257), although μή with the indicative sometimes occurs in quasi-conditional relative clauses (226, *Th.* 387, Hom. B 302).

P. Rose, *Hist.* 24 (1975), 135, thinks that the numerous references to inadequate livelihood (230, 242-3, 298-302, 363, etc.) point to an agrarian crisis, but the emphasis put by Hes. on this point more probably has a didactic purpose [141].

32: ὡραῖος. 'Gathered at the right time': cf. Hdt. I 202, 1 καρποὺς κατατίθεσθαι ὡραίους. Hes. attaches much importance to this idea: cf. 307, 394, 409, 422, 617, 630, 642, 665, 694-5, 697. In spite of Hes.'s predilection for word-play (see above, on 3 διά), the assumption of an allusion to 30 ὥρη (Wil.) seems far-fetched.

32. τὸν ... ἀκτήν. This is not "mere padding" (We.), but an application of the principle χρήματα δ' οὐχ ἁρπακτά, θεόσδοτα πολλὸν ἀμείνω (320).

32: Δημήτερος ἀκτήν. 'Food consisting of corn': cf. Hom. Λ 631 etc. ἀλφίτου ἀκτή. For ἀκτή 'food', not 'corn' (LSJ), cf. Hsch. τροφή and Chantr., *Dict. étym.*, 52 [142]. For Δημήτηρ 'corn' cf. the oracle in Hdt. VII 141, 4 σκιδναμένης Δημήτερος ἢ συνιούσης, and the epic line in Plut. *Is.* 377 D (= Allen 149, fr. XV) τῆμος ὅτ' αἰζηιοὶ Δημήτερα κωλοτομεῦσιν. This use should not be called 'metonymy', for the goddess was believed to be present in the corn, just as Hephaestus was thought to be present in a fire (see above. on 11 Ἐρίδων) [143].

33: δῆριν. Used at 14 in the general sense of 'strife', here referring to a 'Rechtsstreit'. See further *Lex.* II, 280-1.

33: ὀφέλλοις. See above, on 14 ὀφέλλει. We. thinks that the strife is increased by the cries of the spectators. However, they may increase the noise, but not the strife as such, unless they would try to interfere in it, but this is not indicated in the text. Accordingly, We. is wrong in suggesting (37) that vv. 33-4 are ambivalent, referring both to following other people's quarrels and to starting a quarrel oneself.

Rz. reads ὀφέλλοι because σοὶ δέ at 34 implies a contrast, and We. thinks that he is perhaps right. But at 402 there is no contrast between σύ and other

---

[140] See further B. Forssman, *Untersuchungen zur Sprache Pindars* (Wiesbaden 1966), 121-4, whose explanation, "Immerwährendes (d.h. Dauer) dabei habend", seems to me less natural than 'for ever being'.

[141] Cf. also M. Detienne, *Crise agraire et attitude religieuse chez Hésiode* (Brussels 1963), and the review by P. Walcot, JHS 86 (1966), 172-3.

[142] Latt.'s 'the pride of Demeter' is a misguided attempt to poetize a seeming pleonasm.

[143] The phrases Δήμητρος καρπός (Hdt. I 193, 3) and Δηοῦς καρπός (Ar. *Plut.* 515) are to be understood in the same way. The showing of an ear of corn which formed the culmination of the Eleusinian mysteries (Nilsson, 662) may well have been imagined as an epiphany of Demeter.

persons. We. in his note on that passage writes: "the focus in χρῆμα οὐ πρήξεις was on the neighbours (as if it were οἱ μὲν οὐκέτι δώσουσι), and the pronoun marks its shift back to the beggar". He mentions some parallels, but does not refer to K.G. I, 657-8. There we find two explanations, viz. (1) the subject is contrasted with other persons implied in the context; (2) the contrast pertains to the predicates (actions) rather than to the subjects. The latter view is adopted by Schw. II, 188 and 208, Denn., LXXI, Leaf on K 238, Jebb on S. *El*. 448 (Bruhn, § 76, "zu erklären durch scheinbaren (nur formell vorhandenen) Gegensatz", is too vague). The first view seems to me less convincing: in 402, e.g., the implication of οἱ μὲν οὐκέτι δώσουσι in χρῆμα μὲν οὐ πρήξεις is far from obvious. There is a third possibility, suggested by Abicht on Hdt. VII 6, 4, which may be the most attractive explanation: "Treten zwei Handlungen desselben Subjekts in Gegensatz, so denkt sich der Grieche, dass auch das handelnde Subjekt mit sich in Gegensatz trete, und gebraucht daher ὁ δέ, obwohl dasselbe Subjekt bleibt". For the difference between σὺ δέ and σύ γε see below, on 246 ὅ γε.

34: ἐπ' ἀλλοτρίοις. Not "ambivalent, like ὀφέλλοις" (We.), for the fact that Perses' watching legal disputes is inspired by a bad Eris shows that he had some evil plan in mind (see above, on 28 ἀπ' ἔργου). We. argues that the existence and the nature of this plan remain obscure until 37 f. But it is hinted at by the phrase διακρινώμεθα νεῖκος (35), which reveals that ἀλλοτρίοις refers to Hes.'s property and that ἐπί does not mean 'over' (We., 37)[144] but 'with a view to gaining': cf. Hdt. I 66, 1 ἐχρηστηριάζοντο ἐν Δελφοῖσι ἐπὶ πάσῃ τῇ Ἀρκάδων χώρῃ, LSJ B III 2.

34: οὐκέτι δεύτερον ἔσται. Perses will not have a second chance to go to law, because he does not have the means to live on during a protracted lawsuit. Krafft (88-9) argues that Hes., by urging his brother to set to work, would enable him to earn sufficient means of living to venture a second lawsuit, and that the contradiction between 33-4a and 34b-5 is so flagrant that the quarrel between the two brothers cannot have been real. But 28-9 show that Perses is planning a next action (see above, on 28 ἀπ' ἔργου), so that ἔσται refers to the near future, and it is out of the question that Perses, even if he would accept Hes.'s advice, would become a rich farmer within a short time[145].

---

[144] Krafft (89) even thinks: "Er soll nicht mehr für fremde Leute und fremdes Gut auf der ἀγορή Prozesse führen — als eine Art Klient".

[145] Krafft (89 n. 4) takes δεύτερον to mean 'weiterhin' or 'später', but 37-8 show that the meaning is 'a second time'. Skafte Jensen (above, n. 38), 8, paraphrases "From now on you will have to work and will hardly find time for the agora", but this is too idealistic a point of view. M. Gagarin, TAPA 104 (1974), 106, who thinks that Perses' first action had failed (see below, on 38 ἐφόρεις), concludes that "Hesiod expects that a final settlement will leave Perses without the means to try again", but he has to admit that we then should expect τρίτον instead of δεύτερον, and his explanation (107), "that the present dispute seems to be treated by Hesiod both as

35: ὧδ' ἔρδειν. Here and at 760 retrospective, at 382 both retrospective and prospective (see note *ad loc.*), at Hom. ε 342 and ζ 258 prospective. For ὅδε referring back to something mentioned but still present to the mind cf. K.G. I, 647, Schw. II, 209.

35: αὖθι. Not 'once more' (Pal), nor 'here' (Ev., Si., Maz., Wil.), but 'at once' (Waltz)[146]. The meaning 'once more', which is known from Hellenistic literature, is excluded by the context: Pal. translates: 'Let us once more get our dispute decided (and this time) by an impartial award', but the words 'and this time' have no equivalent in the Greek text. The local meaning would imply that "Hes. wished to settle the matter in private with his brother" (Si.)[147], but this is improbable on account of the specifically judicial meaning of ἰθείῃσι δίκῃς (as appears from 221 and *Th.* 85-6), and of the fact that Hes. warns his brother against perjury (219, 282)[148]. The temporal sense 'forthwith' has developed from the local sense, just as in *ilico*, 'sur-le-champ', 'auf der Stelle', 'on the spot' (similarly αὐτόθι: LSJ II). D. Pinto, *Recherches de Philol. et de Ling.* 2 (1968), 139-46, has tried to show that the word always has a local meaning, but there are passages where the temporal aspect clearly predominates, e.g. Hom. Ε 553 τῷ δ' αὖθι τέλος θανάτοιο κάλυψεν (cf. 560 καππεσέτην ἐλάτῃσιν ἐοικότε ὑψηλῇσιν), Ζ 281-2 ὥς κέ οἱ αὖθι / γαῖα χάνοι (cf. Ameis-Hentze: "ehe er wieder hinaus auf das Schlachtfeld ginge"), σ 339 ἵνα σ' αὖθι διὰ μελεϊστὶ τάμῃσιν[149].

35: διακρινώμεθα. 'Let us get decided': cf. Thuc. IV 122, 4 δίκῃ ἕτοιμοι ἦσαν περὶ αὐτῆς κρίνεσθαι. For the causative force of the middle cf. K.G. I, 108, 113, 116, Schw. II, 232, Humbert, § 169, and my notes on Men. *Epitr.* 44 and 205, Mnem. IV 27 (1974), 20 and 26, and Pind. *I.* 2, 16, Mnem. IV 34 (1982), 17[150].

---

separate from the earlier dispute and also as part of one long dispute, which includes the earlier one", sounds rather sophistical. L. Lenz, in *Dialogos: Festschrift H. Patzer* (Wiesbaden 1975), 23-33, explains the phrase as follows: "wer aus freien Stücken um fremden Besitz einen Prozess führen will, sollte mindestens so vermögend sein, dass er gleich zwei führen könnte, um nicht alles auf eine Karte setzen zu müssen" (26): an unnecessary and artificial assumption.

[146] 'Finally' (Latt.) is obviously impossible.

[147] Similarly Maz. (I), 45: "une transaction à l'amiable"; Wil.: "daher bietet ihm Hesiod einen gerechten Vergleich an".

[148] Cf. Kühn, 275. This objection also rules out the suggestion that the διάκρισις takes place 'here' in the sense of 'in the first part of the poem', "in einer idealen Rechtsprechung", as it is called by Munding (above, n. 8), 23; similarly van Groningen, *Hés. et Persès* (above, n. 45), 4, Krafft, 90, Livrea, 471 ff.

[149] Cf. also σ 91 ὥς μιν ψυχὴ λίποι αὖθι πεσόντα with β 367 οἳ δέ τοι αὐτίκ' ἰόντι κακὰ φράσσονται. We. argues that "inherent in 'right there', 'in that very place', is the idea of 'before getting anywhere else'", but the latter idea is not always *inherent* in the former: accordingly, we have to accept a *transition* from a local to a temporal sense.

[150] Gagarin (above, n. 145), 107 n. 11, rightly observes that Pl. *Phil.* 46 b 4 (adduced by LSJ) is not a good parallel, and that the causative middle is relatively rare, but his translation 'let us now settle this dispute ourselves' is based on the impossible assumption that the δίκαι at 36 "are the pleas of the two disputants" (see also above, on 34 αὖθι).

35: νεῖκος. For the nature of the quarrel see above, on 28 Ἔρις. The term does not imply that Perses had already gone to law [151], for in that case Hes. would either have informed us about the issue of the lawsuit (if it had been to his advantage) or have been silent about it (if he had lost it) [152]. It has been suggested that the phrase τήνδε δίκην at 39 and 269 refers to an impending lawsuit [153], but δίκη in Homer and Hes. never has the meaning of 'lawsuit' [154]. It certainly was Perses' intention to go to law [155], but Hes. tries to deter him from such an action. To that end he embodies two deterrent terms in his proposal: (1) the decision has to take place 'at once', i.e., so that Perses will not have the means to bribe the judges, and (2) the judgment will be ἐκ Διός, i.e., it will be determined by the god whom nothing escapes (105, 249-60, 267) and who will notice and punish any possible further tricks of Perses [156]. The use of these deterrents does not imply, however, that Hes. feared a second lawsuit. Hays (20) argues that Hes. "in anxiety as to the result [of the second action brought against him by Perses] wrote the first part of the poem": he finds "an unmistakable attitude of anxiety" in 34 ff., 213, 248 ff., 275 [157], but the tone taken in these passages is one of self-confidence (and confidence in the justice of Zeus) rather than of anxiety. We should not even call the poem Hes.'s plea (see above, n. 45): his aim is warning, admonition, and exhortation, not self-defence.

36: ἰθείῃσι. 'Straight', hence 'straight-forward', 'just' (LSJ I 2): cf. above, on 7 ἰθύνει and 9 ἴθυνε.

36: δίκης. 'Judgements' (in the sense of judicial sentences). The phrase ἰθεία δίκη (cf. Hom. Σ 508, Ψ 579-80) supports the derivation of δίκη from

---

[151] Or even that Hes. had taken the initiative to go to law, as is assumed by Kühn, 276.

[152] Cf. Munding (above, n. 8), 15-8. Schm. (251) improbably suggests that the poem was finished before the trial had ended.

[153] E.g. by Wil. (72). See also the discussion after *Aufbau*, 160-2.

[154] As was already observed by Maz. (I), 47. Van Groningen, *Hés. et Persès* (above, n. 45), 7-8 n. 22, argues that δίκη may have an early sense of 'lawsuit' because δικάζομαι in the *Odyssey* (LSJ II) means 'to go to law'. But the proper meaning of δικάζομαι is 'to have oneself judged' (for this use of the middle cf. K.G. I, 113, 116, Schw. II, 232). See also above, n. 32, and *Aufbau*, 160-1. For τήνδε see below, on 39.

[155] Cf. Walcot, *Peasants*, 53: "That Perses should incline to a legal action rather than to a private settlement is far from surprising when it is noted that Campbell says of the Sarakatsanos that 'he prefers to go to law knowing in advance that he must pay double the costs of a private agreement. Any compromise would be an admission of weakness in a personal confrontation' (p. 309)".

[156] It has been objected by Krafft (90 n. 4) that Hes. could not threaten Perses with a lawsuit because he did not trust the judges (39). But the two conditions stipulated by Hes. will keep the judges straight.

[157] Similarly Maz. (I), 45-6: "Il n'est pas douteux néanmoins qu'Hésiode ne craigne quelque peu ce procès qu'il déclare impossible ..., car toute une partie de son poème (202-285) trahit l'inquiétude".

δείκνυμι: the judge points out the right way of action because his pointing is 'right' (cf. Dutch 'recht wijzen' = pronounce sentence)[158].

36: αἴ τε. Cf. 3 ὄν τε.

36: ἐκ Διός. 'Rendus au nom de Zeus' (Maz.) is too weak: the sentences are not only "sanctioned by Zeus" (We.), but they are actually directed by Zeus according to the principle of justice (9). Cf. *Th.* 94-6 ἐκ γάρ τοι Μουσέων ... / ἄνδρες ἀοιδοὶ ἔασιν ... / ἐκ δὲ Διὸς βασιλῆες, and my notes in Mnem. IV 25 (1972), 256-7, Hom. Α 238-9 δικασπόλοι οἵ τε θέμιστας / πρὸς Διὸς εἰρύαται, Ι 98-9 τοι Ζεὺς ἐγγυάλιξε / σκῆπτρόν τ᾽ ἠδὲ θέμιστας[159].

36: ἄρισται. Brachylogy for αἵ τ᾽ ἐκ Διός εἰσιν, αἱ δ᾽ ἐκ Διός εἰσιν, εἰσιν ἄρισται. For the contamination of the two senses of εἶναι cf. Thuc. V 2, 3 ὅτι οὐδὲ Βρασίδας ἐν τῇ Τορώνῃ οὔτε οἱ ἐνόντες ἀξιόμαχοι εἶεν.

37: ἤδη. Not "contrasting with the more satisfactory result now anticipated" (We.) but contrasting with ἄλλα ... ἐφόρεις.

37: μέν. Pal. (followed by Hays) translates: 'For we had just shared between us our patrimony, when you began to plunder'. But μέν ... τε never has the meaning of εὐθὺς ... καί or ἅμα ... καί. We may take μέν as preparing τε (cf. Denn., 374-6) or as emphasizing ἤδη (cf. Denn., 361), but Maz. is probably right in holding the view that "μέν correspond à une idée sous-entendu, qui reprendrait celle du v. 34". The μέν clause is sometimes contrasted with what precedes: cf. S. *Trach.* 350-1 σαφῶς μοι φράζε πᾶν ὅσον νοεῖς· / ἃ μὲν γὰρ ἐξείρηκας ἀγνοία μ᾽ ἔχει, and Denn., 377-8[160].

37: κλῆρον. The paternal estate (LSJ II 2). See further We. on 341.

37: ἄλλα. I.e., in addition to the part due to you. Hes. probably thinks of valuable parts of the furniture: see below, on 38 ἐφόρεις, and cf. P. Walcot, SO 38 (1963), 8-9, *Peasants*, 49. If ἄλλα referred to the property of other people[161], there would not be a quarrel among the brothers[162].

38: ἁρπάζων. The verb does not always imply the use of physical violence (as appears e.g. from Hom. Γ 444), but suggests unlawful appropriation. Similarly 320 ἁρπακτά, 356 ἅρπαξ, 684 ἁρπακτός.

---

[158] Cf. Latte (above, n. 25), 65 ff. = 235 ff. See also J. Gonda, Δείκνυμι (Amsterdam 1929), 224 ff., E. Benveniste, *Le vocabulaire des institutions indo-européennes* (Paris 1960), II, 107-10. The considerations put forward by M. Gagarin, CP 68 (1973), 81-94, are vitiated by the assumption that the original meaning is 'settlement', which he equates with 'legal process': see above nn. 32 and 150.

[159] We. writes that "the present phrase need not imply a royal arbitration rather than an 'out-of-court' settlement", but we have seen that the phrase ἰθείῃσι δίκῃς excludes the idea of a private settlement.

[160] Krafft (90 n. 2) thinks that "γάρ begründet die Anwendung der ἰθεῖαι δίκαι", an absurd consequence of his idea that the διάκρισις takes place in the poem itself (see above, n. 148).

[161] As is assumed by J. F. Latimer, TAPA 61 (1930), 76, Krafft, 90.

[162] Ev. reads ἀλλὰ τὰ πολλά, but τὰ πολλά cannot mean 'the greater share'. Besides ἄλλα τε πολλά is a Homeric phrase (ρ 422, τ 78).

38: ἐφόρεις. Refers to movable things: cf. φέρειν 'to carry away as booty' (LSJ A VI 1). That the imperfect does not have iterative force[163], appears from 34 οὐκέτι δεύτερον ἔσται (although Perses may have carried away things little by little before he went to law: see below, on 359 αὐτός). That it is not conative[164] either, appears from Hes.'s hostile attitude toward the judges, which implies that Perses' first legal action has been successful[165]. The action of the imperfect can be simultaneous with that of the aorist, although the two tenses do not have the same force: cf. K.G. I, 144, Chantr. II, 193-4, Humbert, § 238: "L'imparfait indique, de façon courante, que l'on s'intéresse au développement de faits passés. Aussi est-il constamment employé dans toute description détaillée et concrète, par opposition à l'aoriste, temps de la chronologie pure et du procès-verbal". See also Bakker, *Imperative* (above, n. 37), 24-7, who concludes that the imperfect expresses "a relationship with another verbal notion, a point from which, around which, or before which the speaker views the process in its perspective". Similarly 97 ἔμιμνε, *Th.* 532 τίμα, 563 ἐδίδου.

38: κυδαίνων. 'Feeding their pride' (We., who compares Hom. ξ 438 κύδαινε δὲ θυμόν), a sarcastic euphemism for bribing. Cf. Thuc. I 137, 3 ἐκεῖνόν τε ἐθεράπευε χρημάτων δόσει[166].

38: βασιλῆας. The nobles who ruled the country and acted as judges. For the title of βασιλῆες cf. Hom. α 394-5, θ 390-1. In Homer the administration of justice does not seem to be an essential part of the king's function[167]. It has been maintained that in Hes.'s time, too, "la jurisdiction n'était pas une fonction officielle des rois, inhérente à leur position. La partie lésée s'adressait à eux comme à des arbitres choisis de plein gré"[168]. The last sentence may be true, but the picture of the king in *Th.* 80-92 (espec. 85 πάντες ἐς αὐτὸν ὁρῶσι) suggests a more or less official function[169].

39: δωροφάγους. A stronger expression than δωροδόκους, modelled on Hom. ι 191 σιτοφάγος and Α 231 δημοβόρος βασιλεύς. It has been suggested

---

[163] As is held by Fränkel, *W.u.F.*, 89 n. 2, Krafft, 90 (whose explanation, "aus einer langen Tätigkeit als Klient", is based on a misunderstanding of 34 ἐπ' ἀλλοτρίοις: see above, n. 144), We.

[164] Van Groningen, *Hés. et Persès* (above, n. 45), 4, Gagarin (above, n. 145), 104 ff.

[165] As is observed by H. Diller, in Heitsch, 247 n. 16. Gagarin's reply (n. 9), that the expense of the regular court fees "could cause the frugal farmer to complain about the 'gift-devouring' kings even if they had decided in his favor", is hardly worth mentioning.

[166] I cannot believe that κυδαίνων refers to the applause given by Perses to the judges while trying his case, as is assumed by van Groningen, *Hés. et Persès*, 5, or to his praise of the judges during the indictment, as is suggested by Skafte Jensen (above, n. 38), 8.

[167] The phrases Λυκίην εἴρυτο δίκῃσι (Π 542) and εὐδικίας ἀνέχῃσι (τ 111) do not necessarily refer to jurisdiction. Cf. M. P. Nilsson, *Homer and Mycenae* (London 1933), 223-4.

[168] Van Groningen, *Hés. et Persès*, 5.

[169] See further We. *ad loc.*, and R. J. Bonner, CP 7 (1912), 17 ff., CP 40 (1945), 11 ff., R. J. Bonner - G. Smith, *Administration of Justice from Homer to Aristotle*, I (Chicago 1930), 45 ff., and the literature mentioned in *Lex.* II, 40-1.

that the word does not refer to corruptibility but to the fact that the princes did not return sufficient benefits for the regular presents they received [170], but Hes. associates it with σκολιαὶ δίκαι (221, 264). See further We. *ad loc*. and Walcot, *Peasants*, 100-2.

The picture of the kings given in the *W.a.D.* sharply contrasts with that presented in *Th*. 80-92. The difference does not necessarily imply, however, a change in Hes.'s attitude towards the judges (Walcot, *Peasants*, 100), nor need it be assumed that the two poems were recited before different audiences (We., *Th.*, 44). The two pictures complement each other, one being apotropaeic, the other protreptic: cf. the contrast between 264 σκολιέων δὲ δικέων ἐπὶ πάγχυ λάθεσθε and *Th*. 85-6 πάντες ἐς αὐτὸν ὁρῶσι διακρίνοντα θέμιστας / ἰθείῃσι δίκῃσι. See further my note on *Th*. 80 βασιλεῦσιν, Mnem. IV 25 (1972), 251-2.

39: τήνδε δίκην. Not 'this cause' (Ev., Wil., Marg, Nicolai 23 n. 20), for δίκη does not mean 'lawsuit' (see above, n. 154), nor 'dispense this kind of justice' (Si.; similarly Maz., Diller, in Heitsch, 257 n. 26) [171], for δίκην δικάζειν means 'to pronounce a verdict' (We.), δίκην being an internal object: cf. fr. 338 μηδὲ δίκην δικάσῃς, πρὶν ἄμφω μῦθον ἀκούσῃς, Hdt. V 25, 1 ἐπὶ χρήμασι δίκην ἄδικον ἐδίκασε [172]. We.'s explanation of τήνδε, 'this (known)' is too vague: the meaning is 'the kind of judgement as is known here': cf. τήνδε δίκην at 249 and 269 (although δίκη there means 'justice'), Thuc. II 42, 1 οἷς τῶνδε μηδὲν ὑπάρχει, rightly explained by Gomme as 'these good things we enjoy here in Athens'. See further H. Hunger, WS 65 (1950-51), 20 ff. This usage is akin to ὅδε used as equivalent to τοιόσδε: e.g. Hom. Θ 236-7 Ζεῦ πάτερ, ἦ ῥά τιν᾽ ἤδη ὑπερμενέων βασιλήων / τῇδ᾽ ἄτῃ ἄσας; γ 352 τοῦδ᾽ ἀνδρός (Stanford: "an odd use"), Archil. 7 D. = 13 W., 7 ἄλλοτε τ᾽ ἄλλος ἔχει τόδε [173].

39: ἐθέλουσι. Not 'love to' (Ev.), 'are eager to' (Si.), 'see fit to' (We.), or 'are willing to' (Latt.), but 'use to'. The verb is commonly used in this sense with reference to inanimate beings (LSJ II 2), but the subject can also be animate: cf. Hom. ρ 320-1 δμῶες δ᾽, εὖτ᾽ ἂν μηκέτ᾽ ἐπικρατέωσιν ἄνακτες, / οὐκέτ᾽ ἔπειτ᾽ ἐθέλουσιν ἐναίσιμα ἐργάζεσθαι, Tyrt. 9 D. = 12 W., 39-40 οὐ

---

[170] R. Hirzel, *Themis, Dike und Verwandtes* (Leipzig 1907), 414, 421. Similarly van Groningen, *Hés. et Persès*, 6, Detienne (above, n. 141), 27. Van Groningen quotes fr. 361 δῶρα θεοὺς πείθει, δῶρ᾽ αἰδοίους βασιλῆας, but we do not know whether this refers to jurisdiction.

[171] In *Aufbau*, 120 n. 4 and 137 n. 1, I wrongly adopted this view. It is true that at 249 τήνδε δίκην means 'this kind of justice', but this does not force us to assume the same meaning at 39.

[172] Gagarin (above, n. 145), 108 and n. 13, rightly translates δίκην δικάζειν by 'give a ruling', but wrongly equates this to 'judge a case', and then translates the present phrase by 'to give a ruling in this case'. He refers to Thgn. 543-4 χρή με ... τήνδε δικάσσαι / ... δίκην, but this probably (because we do not know the context) means 'to pronounce this judgment'.

[173] For a similar use of οὗτος cf. Alcm. 1, 57 Ἀγησιχόρα μὲν αὕτα, Pind. *O*. 4, 24 οὗτος ἐγὼ ταχυτᾶτι, Hdt. I 116, 2 ταῦτα ποιήσω ὥστε, II 135, 3 ποίημα ποιησαμένη τοῦτο τὸ μὴ τυγχάνει ἄλλῳ ἐξευρημένον.

δέ τις αὐτὸν /βλάπτειν οὔτ᾽ αἰδοῦς οὔτε δίκης ἐθέλει, Pind. *O*. 11, 8-9 τὰ μὲν ἁμετέρα / γλῶσσα ποιμαίνειν ἐθέλει (similarly, *O*. 13, 9, *P*. 1, 62, *N*. 7, 10, *N*. 11, 40), Pl. *Meno* 95 b 1 ἐθέλουσιν οὗτοι παρέχειν αὐτοὺς διδασκάλους, Thuc. II 39, 4 ῥᾳθυμίᾳ ... ἐθέλομεν κινδυνεύειν, Theophr. *Char*. I 2 τοῖς ἐχθροῖς ἐθέλειν λαλεῖν. See also below, on 136 ἤθελον [174].

40: νήπιοι. Hes. has been called "a refined Thersites, who has maintained his disposition to ἐριζέμεναι βασιλεῦσι" [175]. But Hes.'s admonitions are not inspired by rebellion, but by the self-confidence of a prophet [176]. The free and superior tone he takes with the rulers (cf. also 202-12, 248-66) seems to show that their position had become much weaker than it had been in Homeric times. If it is true that "about the middle of the eighth century the monarchies fell throughout the Greek world" [177], Hes. was born in the beginning of that century rather than in the middle (as is suggested by We., *Th*., 65) [178]. For the moral connotation of νήπιος see below, on 218 νήπιος.

40: οὐδέ. Similarly 456 (= Hom. E 406) νήπιος, οὐδὲ τὸ οἶδε, Hom. Φ 410 νηπύτι᾽, οὐδέ νύ πώ περ ἐπεφράσω, φ 28 σχέτλιος, οὐδὲ θεῶν ὄπιν ἠδέσατο [179]. In these and other cases οὐδέ has explanatory (specifying) force: cf. Hom. A 94-5 ὃν ἠτίμησ᾽ Ἀγαμέμνων, / οὐδ᾽ ἀπέλυσε θύγατρα, ν 111-2 εἰσὶ θεώτεραι, οὐδέ τι κείνη / ἄνδρες ἐσέρχονται, Hdt. I 109, 2 οὔ οἱ ἔγωγε προσθήσομαι τῇ γνώμῃ οὐδὲ ἐς φόνον τοιοῦτον ὑπηρετήσω, and my note on Semon. 7, 8, Mnem. IV 21 (1968), 135. For δέ introducing a specification see above, on 9.

40: πλέον. Thgn. 145-6 βούλεο δ᾽ εὐσεβέων ὀλίγοις σὺν χρήμασιν οἰκεῖν / ἢ πλουτεῖν ἀδίκως χρήματα πασάμενος and similar passages adduced by We. do not explain the use of πλέον. The meaning is: a man who unlawfully tries to get more than his due runs a risk of losing all he has (or all he has in view). The words were understood in this sense by Plato (*Rep*. 466 bc, *Leg*.

---

[174] P. von der Mühll (in Wackernagel I, 195) wrongly thinks that ἐθέλουσι is equivalent to a future (similarly Schw. II, 266). Rz. reads ἐθέλοντι δίκασσαν, but an ellipse of σοι is very improbable in this context.

[175] D. F. W. van Lennep, Hermeneus 25 (1953), 55. Similarly, W. Donlan, Hist. 22 (1973), 150, speaks of "the Hesiodic bias against aristocratic values in favor of a peasant system of values".

[176] Cf. E. Meyer, in Heitsch, 478-82, Si., Introduction, Ch. III. The plain terms in which Hes. criticizes the rulers resembles the tone of the Hebrew prophets, espec. Amos: cf. M. E. Andrews, Journ. of Rel. 23 (1943), 194-205, N. J. Richardson, JHS 99 (1979), 169. See also above, n. 47.

[177] A. H. J. Greenidge, *A Handbook of Greek Constitutional History* (London 1896), 17. See further P. Rose, Hist. 24 (1975), 132 ff., C. G. Starr, *Essays on Ancient History* (Leiden 1979), 129 ff. The decline of the power of the 'kings' begins in the *Odyssey*: cf. K. W. Welwei, Gymn. 88 (1981), 13 ff.

[178] For the problem of dating cf. also Edwards, 199 ff.

[179] These parallels show that P. Friedländer (in Heitsch, 233 n. 20) is wrong in maintaining that νήπιοι does not refer to the judges but that the phrase is equivalent to νήπιοί εἰσιν οἳ μὴ ἴσασι.

690 de)[180]. Accordingly, Maz.'s interpretation, "savoir vivre de peu est la vraie richesse"[181], is wrong: romanticism is beyond Hes.'s horizon, and lawful πλεονεξία is recommended by him: cf. 23-4, 313, 341[182].

For proverbs in Hes. see above, on 22 ὅς and 23 δέ τε, and below, on 317 and 367. Cf. also We. on 218, and A. Hoekstra, Mnem. IV 3 (1950), 89 ff., E. Pellizer, QUCC 13 (1972), 24-37, espec. 28, where he suggests that the original form of the present saying may have been πλέον δέ τοι ἥμισυ παντός.

For the oxymoron cf. 57-8 κακόν, ᾧ κεν ἅπαντες / τέρπωνται ... ἐὸν κακὸν ἀμφαγαπῶντες, and We. ad loc., Th. 585 καλὸν κακόν, We., Th., 76, Fehling, 289 ff.

41: μαλάχῃ. 'Mallow', food of the poor: cf. Ar. Plut. 543 σιτεῖσθαι δ' ἀντὶ μὲν ἄρτων μαλάχης πτόρθους.

41: ἀσφοδέλῳ. A liliacous plant, the seeds of which were roasted, while the stalk was fried and the bulb was pounded down with figs (Theophr. HP VII 13, 3). See further We. and Lex., 1466-7.

41: ὄνειαρ. 'A profitable thing' (Renehan, 346, who rightly observes that the separate meaning given by LSJ I 2 should be deleted). We. writes that the princes "will have no fear of being reduced to this diet, however honestly they deal. It looks as if Hesiod has been led on by one proverb to another that tended to be associated with it". He compares Instr. of Amen-em-Opet 9, 5-8 'Better is poverty at the hand of God than riches in the storehouse'. But Hes. does not preach modesty or simplicity as an ideal in itself[183], for his ideal is riches in the storehouse (e.g. 301, 307, 313, 363). His present point is that poor food is a boon as compared with no food at all[184]. Wil. rightly observes that this idea is relevant to Perses rather than to the princes (similarly Nicolai, 24-5). But (1) I have already remarked (above, on 10 Πέρσῃ) that Hes.'s admonitions often have a wider reference than that of the addressee; (2) Hes. likes to express his thoughts in drastic terms (e.g. the fable of the hawk and the nightingale, 203-12, is not strictly applicable to the rulers and their subjects); (3) the greediness of the judges is a form of ὕβρις (see below, on 213 ὕβριν), and ὕβρις may lead to famine striking a whole community (238-43).

---

[180] As was pointed out to me by Dr. K. J. McKay, who also referred to Dio Chrys. or. XVII 467 R. p. 250, Paroem. e cod. Bodl. 683 Gaisf., Suda s.v. νήπιος, Ael. fr. 112 Herch.

[181] Similarly, Krafft (91) speaks of the "Freude des Bauern über den an ihren Erträgen gemessen zwar halb so grossen, aber eigenhändig und ehrlich erarbeiteten Lebensunterhalt".

[182] See further Weber, Pleonexie (above, n. 117), 19-20.

[183] As is observed by R. Vischer, Das einfache Leben (Göttingen 1965), 33. Cf. also Quaglia, 45, and see above, on 40 πλέον.

[184] This point has been overlooked by Y. Gerhard, MH 34 (1977), 72-3, who suggests that "l'avantage qu'on peut tirer d'une relative pauvreté est d'éviter l'"Ερις κακόχαρτος", a very implausible idea.

The present line forms an impressive conclusion and at the same time leads the argument back to the theme of labour (see below, on 42 γάρ)[185].

42: κρύψαντες. *Scil.* in the earth, from which men must obtain it by tillage[186].

42: γάρ. Maz. thinks that this introduces the explanation of the general idea underlying 27-34a (of which 34b-41 is only an offshoot): in the long run one cannot live on litigation, but one has to work, for ...[187]. It may be admitted that this is the general trend of Hes.'s argument. Yet γάρ seems to refer to the immediately preceding words: apart from its proverbial function, viz. the recommendation of prudence, v. 41 evokes an association: mallow and asphodel are a real boon for the poor; yet the food itself is poor, too; if you want something better (viz. corn), you have to work for it, for ... (Wil.). Ar. *Plut.* 543 quoted above and Plut. *Sept. sap. conv.* 14, 157 DF show that the mention of mallow suggested the thought of bread as something better[188].

42: ἔχουσι. The phrase κρύψαντες ἔχουσι should not be regarded as a periphrasis of the perfect[189], but both verbs still have their proper force: 'they have hidden it and (try to) keep it', *scil.* away from men: cf. Hom. Ω 115 Ἕκτορ᾽ ἔχει ... οὐδ᾽ ἀπέλυσεν, ο 230-1 ὅς οἱ χρήματα ... / εἶχε.

41: θεοί. Not equivalent to Zeus (47): cf. above, on 16 ἀθανάτων.

42: βίον. Cf. 31.

43: γάρ. 'For otherwise': cf. Denn., 62-3.

43: ἐπ᾽ ἤματι. 'In one single day'. Similarly Hom. K 48, T 229, β 284. For ἐπί cf. Hom. N 234 ἐπ᾽ ἤματι τῷδε, Hdt. IV 112 ἐπ᾽ ἡμέρῃ ἑκάστῃ, LSJ B II 1. Leaf (on K 48) thinks that "there is much to be said for the conj. of Schrevelius, ἕν᾽ (= ἑνί), as we should expect the idea *one* to be expressed".

---

[185] This interpretation is called by Nicolai (26 n. 26) "zu naiv", but this judgement is based on his own preconception of the poem as a collection of 'blocks': cf. 26: "Die Blöcke sind Vortragseinheiten, in sich abgeschlossen, durch Pausen getrennt". See also above, n. 35.

[186] Cf. Th. Ph. Howe, TAPA 89 (1958), 60 n. 76, and We., who compares *H. Dem.* 306-7 οὐδέ τι γαῖα / σπέρμ᾽ ἀνίει· κρύπτεν γὰρ ἐυστέφανος Δημήτηρ. Krafft (97 n. 1) wrongly thinks that κρύψαντες refers to the creation of Pandora. His view has been elaborated by Neitzel, *Pandora*: see further below, on 95 ἐσκέδασε.

[187] Similarly Hays, Kühn, 277, Col., Quaglia, 49. We. assumes an ellipse of "the kings are wrong to uphold your rapacious claim: wealth must be won by work", which neglects the fact (observed by We. himself) that 40-1 are not primarily relevant to the kings.

[188] This association seems to me more natural than the reconstruction of the argument proposed by Si., "and no good food is to be despised, for ...", and Nicolai (26 n. 25), "v. 42 begründet den Wert von Asphodelos und Malve": in the eyes of a prosperous farmer like Hes. these plants hardly have any value. The ellipse assumed by Sellschopp (116), "Zeus lässt den, der dies [vv. 40-1] nicht beherzigt, die bösen Folgen schon fühlen", is equally artificial.

[189] As is done by Krafft (97 n. 1) and Col. The first evident examples of this construction are to be found in Sophocles and Herodotus: cf. W. W. Goodwin, *Syntax of the Moods and Tenses of the Greek Verb* (²London 1897), §47, K.G. II, 61-2, Schw. I, 812-3, Bruhn, §11, W. J. Aerts, *Periphrastica* (Amsterdam 1965), 128 ff.

But the idea left unexpressed is not 'one' but 'only': for the ellipse of 'only' cf. Hom. Θ 228 εἶδος ἀγητοί, Ψ 319 ἵπποισι καὶ ἅρμασιν οἷσι πεποιθώς, Ω 531 ᾧ δέ κε τῶν λυγρῶν δώῃ. See further my notes on A. *Prom.* 928, *Miscellanea ... Kamerbeek* (Amsterdam 1976), 469, and Ps. Pl. *Clit.* 407 b 6, Mnem. IV 35 (1982), 144, and the literature mentioned there.

43: ἐργάσσαιο. 'Earn by working': cf. Hdt. I 24, 1 ἐργασάμενον χρήματα μεγάλα, LSJ II 4.

44: ὥς τε. Consecutive ὥς τε is found only twice in Homer (I 42 and ρ 21: cf. Ruijgh, 615-6), and there is only one (possible) parallel in Hes. (*Th.* 831: cf. Ruijgh, 895). "Originally, no doubt, the consecutive relation is expressed by the infinitive alone, and ὡς means 'as' " (Denn., 527). The function of τε is complementary (see above, on 3 ὅν τε): it emphasizes the fact that the main clause and the consecutive clause belong together: cf. J. Gonda, Mnem. IV 7 (1954), 210. See also Ruijgh, 606 ff., who takes the force of τε to be 'digressive'.

44: κεῖς. For the crasis (καὶ εἰς) cf. We., *Th.*, 100 [190]. The meaning is 'for a full year': for the emphatic force of καί cf. Hom. Ψ 833 ἕξει μιν καὶ πέντε περιπλομένους ἐνιαυτούς, and Denn., 320. Sittl reads κ'(ε) εἰς (CE), but the potential seems less appropriate in this context.

44: ἔχειν. 'To have enough'. For the absolute use of the verb (see above, on 1 κλείουσαι) cf. S. *Ai.* 157 τὸν ἔχοντα, E. *Phoen.* 405 κακὸν τὸ μὴ ἔχειν, LSJ A I 1.

44: ἀεργόν. Cf. *Less. pol.*, 257-8.

45: πηδάλιον. We. thinks that corn was shipped to be sold elsewhere, but 393-5 points to a possible shortage of corn, so that merchandise may also have consisted of other products such as sheep, oil, wine.

45: ὑπὲρ καπνοῦ. In ordinary circumstances, to keep it dry: cf. 629, Ar. *Ach.* 279, *Av.* 711 (see further We.).

45: καταθεῖο. Hays argues that "the force of the preposition was no longer felt, as is shown by ὑπέρ". But κατα- suggests storing away for later use: cf. above, on 27 ἐνικάτθεο.

46: ἔργα βοῶν. In Homer (κ 98) the result, 'ploughed fields', here the labour itself.

46: δέ. For the postponement cf. Denn., 187-9.

46: βοῶν ... ἡμιόνων. Used to draw the plough: cf. Walcot, *Peasants*, 40.

46: ἀπόλοιτο. 'It would be all up with' (cf. Hom. K 186 ἀπό τέ σφισιν ὕπνος ὄλωλεν, LSJ B II), 'one could dispense with'.

47: ἔκρυψε. Scil. βίον. For the ellipse of the object cf. Hom. Z 124, K.G. II, 561-2, Schw. II, 708-9, and my notes on E. *Ba.* 97 and 148, Mnem. IV 34 (1981), 304 and 312.

---

[190] For κᾱς in Attic cf. Renehan, 346.

48: ἐξαπάτησε. At a sacrifice, by hiding the flesh and the inner parts of the victim, and by offering the bones 'wrapped up in shining fat' to the gods (*Th.* 538-41)[191]. For ἐκ- as a reinforcement (cf. 'extremely') see Wilamowitz on E. *H.F.* 155, Schw. II, 268, R. Renehan, *Studies in Greek Texts* (Göttingen 1976), 24 ff.

48: Προμηθεύς. Probably a pre-Greek name afterwards associated with μῆδος and μῆτις: cf. We. on *Th.* 510[192].

48: ἀγκυλομήτης. In Homer and at *Th.* 18 etc. this is an epithet of Kronos, who was a Titan like Prometheus. For the original meaning cf. We. on *Th.* 18, *Lex.*, 71-2, and *Less. pol.*, 67-8. The reference to craftiness seems to be based on the analogy of σκολιός. Sellschopp (19) may be right in suggesting that Hes. chose ἀγκυλομήτης instead of ποικιλομήτης (in Homer said of Odysseus) in order to emphasize the contrast between Prometheus and Zeus: the latter is μητιόεις (51), equivalent to the Homeric μητίετα. The motive behind Prometheus' deceit is supposed to be known from *Th.* 534 ἐρίζετο βουλὰς ὑπερμενέι Κρονίωνι.

49: ἄρα. 'As was to be expected': cf. K.G. II, 319, Schw. II, 558-9.

49: ἀνθρώποισιν. Fränkel (128) writes: "Die Menschen wollen es besser haben als es ihnen zukommt, und zum Entgelt machen ihnen die Götter das Leben sauer". But Hes. does not suggest that Zeus holds mankind co-responsible for the crime of Prometheus. He simply applies the principle that a whole community has to suffer for the evil done by one (or some) of its members: 240, 261. Similarly *Th.* 552. That Prometheus is imagined to belong to the party of mankind appears from the dative of interest ἀνθρώποισι at 51. This does not imply, however, that he is the personification of "der sich gegen Zeus auflehnende menschliche Verstand", as is suggested by Neitzel, *Pandora*, 402 n. 37.

49: ἐμήσατο. Μήδομαι and related words often denote the execution of a plan, or even the doing of things which have not been planned before: cf. e.g. Hom. Κ 48-52 τοσσάδε μέρμερ' ἐπ' ἤματι μητίσασθαι, / ὅσσ' Ἕκτωρ ἔρρεξε ... / ἔργα δ' ἔρεξε ... / ... τόσα γὰρ κακὰ μήσατ' Ἀχαιούς, Χ 395 Ἕκτορα δῖον ἀεικέα μήδετο ἔργα, Κ 497 διὰ μῆτιν Ἀθήνης ('through'),

---

[191] Neitzel (*Pandora*, 408-9) argues that ἐξαπάτησε is identical with ἔκλεψε (πῦρ) at 51, but this view is sufficiently disproved (1) by 50 αὖτις, which suggests a preceding move, and (2) by the analogy between 49 ἀνθρώποισιν and *Th.* 552 ἀνθρώποισι. Neitzel thinks that "der gescheiterte Versuch eines Betruges kann nicht mit ἐξαπάτησε umschrieben werden", but we may take the aorist to have ingressive force or (more probably) to denote the action as such irrespective of its completion. Similarly 50 κρύψε.

[192] See further L. Séchan, *Le mythe de Prométhée* (Paris 1951), Ch. II-III, K. Reinhardt, Eranos-Jb. 25 (1957), 241-60, W. Kraus, RE 45 (1957), 657-64, Fink, 45-53, J. Duchemin, *Prométhée* (Paris 1974), J. P. Vernant, *Mythe et société en Grèce ancienne* (Paris 1974), 177-94, id., Ann. Sc. Norm. Pisa, Lett. e Filos. 3, 7 (1977), 905-40, V. Schmidt, ZPE 19 (1975), 183-90, A. Casanova, *La famiglia di Pandora* (Florence 1979), M. Erren, in *Gnomosyne: Festschrift W. Marg* (Munich 1981), 155-9.

Z 97 μήστωρα φόβοιο ('originator'). The same holds good of νοέω (e.g. η 299-301) and μνάομαι (P 185 etc. μνήσασθε δὲ θούριδος ἀλκῆς, not only 'think of' but also 'use'). In archaic thought the spheres of thinking and acting were not clearly distinguished [193]. See also below, on 95 ἐμήσατο, 264 ἐπὶ ... λάθεσθε, 298 μεμνημένος.

49: κήδεα. The toil caused by the fact that Zeus ἔκρυψε βίον. This toil, though necessary and good in itself, is regarded by Hes. as an evil. Labour is sent by Zeus as a revenge, not as a means of educating men [194]. The idea of a permanent nobility residing in work [195] is far from Hes.'s mind [196]: pragmatism and hedonism are his principles (cf. 307-13).

50: κρύψε. We. observes that "one might have expected κρύπτε, since this κρύψις was frustrated by the thief", but cf. 48 ἐξαπάτησε (above, n. 191).

50: πῦρ. The fact that fire, after being stolen by Prometheus, is freely available to men, whereas the βίος remains hidden in the earth (although it can be recovered by labour), does not imply that the withdrawal of fire does not belong to the κήδεα λυγρά (Wil.): it forms the first but frustrated stage of Zeus' revenge. Hes. first states the final result (47 Ζεὺς ἔκρυψε) and the primary cause (48 ἐξαπάτησε Προμηθεύς) of the conflict, and then relates the details [197]. Accordingly, δέ has explanatory (specifying) force: see above, on 9 [198].

---

[193] Cf. Böhme, *Seele* (above, on 13 θυμόν), 62-3, Luther, 76 n. 2, Fränkel, 87-8, and my remarks in Lampas 5 (1972), 105-6. Hom. X 395 quoted above and H 478 show that We. is wrong in thinking that only the aorist is used in the sense of 'doing'. Neitzel (*Pandora*, 396 n. 26) maintains: "Dass ἐμήσατο immer planende Absicht impliziert ... wird durch Homer bewiesen", and he calls my contention (*Aufbau*, 125 n. 1) that the verb sometimes simply means 'to do' "unbeweisbar". But such actions as described at X 395 ff. are impulsive rather than planned.

[194] As is assumed by E. Vandvik, *The Prometheus of Hesiod and Aeschylus* (Oslo 1943), 11, 13, 19. Similarly, Quaglia (57) suggests that Zeus "illumina gli uomini che pure punisce, e indica nella Eris buona ed attiva il modo per procurarsi il βίος usando il fuoco seconda giustizia". The Greek text does not warrant such constructions.

[195] W. Jaeger, *Paideia*, I (Berlin 1934), 89 (= Engl. ed., Oxford 1945, 57): "so offenbart sich im Hesiod die zweite Hauptquelle der Kultur: der Wert der Arbeit"; 106 (= 71): "Im Schweisse seines Angesichts soll der Mensch sein Brot essen, aber das ist kein Fluch für ihn, sondern ein Segen"; Pohlenz, *Der hell. Mensch* (above, n. 117), 83: "die Arbeit gibt dem Leben seinen Sinn und Wert".

[196] Cf. J. Brake, *Wirtschaften und Charakter in der antiken Bildung* (Göttingen 1935), 43, C. B. Welles, GRBS 8 (1967), 9.

[197] This fact has caused a number of misunderstandings: cf. the difficulties created by W. Oldfather, RE 36:2 (1949), 543, W. Aly, in Heitsch, 333-4, K. von Fritz, in Heitsch, 402, Quaglia, 54-5, on the supposition that ἔκρυψε βίον and κρύψε πῦρ were simultaneous actions. Rudhardt (273) even maintains that "le feu symbolise tout ce qui est indispensable à la vie". On the other hand, Lendle (98) suggests that the formal similarity of the hiding of βίος and the hiding of fire tempted the poet to include the story of Prometheus in his poem. Nicolai (28) rightly calls 50 "den ersten Racheakt".

[198] This note is a correction of *Aufbau*, 123 in the following respects: (1) I now take κρύψε δὲ πῦρ to be a (partial) specification of κήδεα; (2) I am no longer inclined to put a full stop at the end of 49; (3) I prefer to leave open the question how man obtained fire before it was hidden by

50: μέν. We. thinks that this "prepares us for another development". He compares *Th*. 289, but the present sentence expresses another development rather than preparing it. Pal. takes μέν as emphasizing τό, but it is much simpler to take it as preparing 53 δέ (Sellschopp, 116).

50: αὖτις. 'In his turn': cf. Hom. σ 60 τοῖσ' αὖτις μετέειπε, *Th*. 169 αὖτις μύθοισι προσηύδα, *Lex*., 1616.5 ff. (where this use is wrongly called post-Homeric: cf. σ 60 τοῖσ' αὖτις μετέειπε), LSJ II 2. The translation 'again' (Ev., Marg) would imply that men had already possessed fire, but Hes. clearly suggests that it properly does not belong to the human world (see below, on 51 ἔκλεψε)[199].

50: ἐύς. Not 'noble' (Ev.)[200] but 'powerful' (Latt.).

51: ἔκλεψε. The idea that man got fire by theft is also found among other peoples: it is based on the belief "that fire does not belong on earth but in heaven, where are the burning sun and the bright sky (αἰθήρ), and from where the lightning breaks" (We., *Th*., 306)[201].

51: μητιόεντος. Homer has only φάρμακα μητιόεντα (δ 227), but Hes. thought of μητίετα Ζεύς (Edwards, 65).

52: νάρθηκι. 'Fennel' (*ferula communis*), the pith of which keeps glowing without burning the stalk. Fire was kept in this way in the Balkans till the 19th cent.: cf. Frazer, *op. cit.*, 195, We. on *Th*. 567.

52: Δία. Renehan (346) speaks of a polyptoton (see above, on 23 γείτονα γείτων), but it rather seems an emphatic repetition (see below, on 188 γηράντεσσι): it marks Prometheus' insolence in trying to deceive the highest god.

52: τερπικέραυνον. 'Taking delight in the thunderbolt', not 'hurling the thunderbolt' (Leaf on Λ 773), for τρέπω never means 'to throw'. For ι instead of ε cf. εἰλίπους, λαθικηδής, Schw. I, 444[202].

54: Ἰαπετιονίδη. A double patronymic: cf. Hom. Β 566 Ταλαϊονίδης, We. on *Th*. 528[203]. It has been suggested that the word "erinnert ihn

---

Zeus. *Th*. 563 suggests that it was elicited by friction of wood: cf. *H. Herm*. 108, Rzach, Zeitschr. f. österr. Gymn. 1898, 26-7, H. J. Rose, Harv. Theol. Rev. 51 (1958), 15 n. 23 (similarly We.). But (1) "it is not attested that the Greeks used ash-wood in particular for fire-making" (We.), and (2) "die Eschen sind weder zahlreich in Griechenland noch für den Baumbestand charakteristisch" (Wil., *Gl*. I, 190-1).

[199] Cf. Fuss, 33 n. 6, and K. Reinhardt, Eranos Jb. 25 (1957), 248 n. 6, who points out that Prometheus was regarded as the Fire-bringer (Πυρφόρος), not as the Fire-recoverer. See also F. Wehrli, in Heitsch, 415-7.

[200] And certainly not 'bienveillant', as is assumed by Vernant (above, n. 191), 919.

[201] See further J. G. Frazer, *Myths of the Origin of Fire* (London 1930), *passim*, J. A. K. Thomson, HSCP 31 (1920), 28 ff. Walcot's reference (*Near East*, 85) to a Sumerian myth about divine laws does not seem to me a convincing parallel.

[202] See further E. Risch, *Wortbildung der homerischen Sprache* (²Berlin 1973), 193-4.

[203] See further C. J. Ruijgh, Minos 9 (1968), 142.

höhnend an das Schicksal seines büssenden Vaters im Tartaros" [204], but it seems to have been chosen mainly for metrical reasons (cf. *Th.* 528, 614).

54: πάντων πέρι. Not 'about everything' (suggested as an alternative by Pal.) but 'above all others': cf. Hom. A 287 περὶ πάντων ἔμμεναι ἄλλων, B 831 περὶ πάντων ἤδεε μαντοσύνας, LSJ A III. Similarly 819.

54: μήδεα. We. on *Th.* 559 may be right in suggesting that this alludes to the name Prometheus (see above, on 3 διά). For προ- 'above others' cf. Hom. προβούλομαι, προλέγομαι, προφερής.

56: πῆμα. Consecutive apposition to the internal object implied in the preceding verbs: cf. Hom. Γ 48-50 γυναῖκ' ἐυειδέ' ἀνῆγες / ... / πατρί τε σῷ μέγα πῆμα, Ω 735 ῥίψει (*scil.* αὐτόν) ... λυγρὸν ὄλεθρον, K.G. I, 284-6, Schw. II, 617 (who wrongly believes that the original construction was in the nominative).

56: ἀνδράσιν. See above, on 49 ἀνθρώποισιν.

57: δέ. Has explanatory (specifying) force: see above, on 9.

58: ἀντί. Not 'to counter-balance' (We.)[205], for which there are no parallels, but 'in return for' (*scil.* the theft of): cf. LSJ A III 3. Similarly *Th.* 570.

57: δώσω. N. Loraux, Areth. 11 (1978), 73 n. 41, takes this to be "une référence claire au geste du père 'donnant' sa fille". I mention this as an illustration of the danger of introducing sociologism into classical scholarship.

58: τέρπωνται. The subjunctive has prospective force: cf. Hom. Δ 191 φάρμαχ', ἅ κεν παύσῃσι μελαινάων ὀδυνάων, Goodwin, *Moods* (above, n. 189), § 568, K.G. II, 426-7, Schw. II, 312, Chantr. II, 247, Gonda, *Moods* (above, n. 137), 68 ff. For the oxymoron see above, on 40 πλέον.

58: κατὰ θυμόν. Probably equivalent to θυμῷ (*Th.* 443, 446, Hom. λ 55), 'with all their heart'. Similarly 358.

58: ἑόν. Synonymous with σφέτερον: cf. *Th.* 71, and see above, on 2 σφέτερον.

58: κακόν. Hes.'s suspicious attitude towards women clearly appears from such passages as 78, 373-5, 699-705, *Th.* 590-3, but it would be misleading to call him a misogynist: (1) his appreciation of women is dominated by an economic point of view[206], (2) although he calls the race of women ὀλώιον

---

[204] Reinhardt (above, n. 199), 258-9.

[205] Similarly Hays: 'as an offset to', Vandvik (above, n. 194), 14, R. G. A. Buxton, *Persuasion in Greek Tragedy* (Cambridge 1982), 224 n. 28: 'as an equivalent for fire' (wrongly comparing this line with 705). Vandvik refers to Thgn. 343 δὸς δέ μοι ἀντὶ κακῶν καί τι παθεῖν ἀγαθόν, but there and in similar passages (e.g. E. *Med.* 1383) the meaning is 'in return for', not 'as a compensation for'. The connections between Pandora and fire imagined by Vernant, *Mythe et société* (above, n. 192), 188-9, are based on the misunderstanding of ἀντί as 'equivalent to'.

[206] Cf. Walcot, *Peasants*, 66-7, S. B. Pomeroy, *Goddesses, Whores, Wives and Slaves* (New York 1975), 48 ff. See also M. B. Arthur, Areth. 6 (1973), 24 ff., F. Brenk, CB 49 (1973), 73 ff., L. S. Sussman, Areth. 11 (1978), 27-41.

(*Th.* 591), he admits the occurrence of exceptions (*Th.* 609)[207], and (3) women's extravagance and ill-nature is a common theme in many myths[208].

58: ἀμφαγαπῶντες. Intentionally ambiguous: 'cherishing' (cf. Hom. ξ 381 ἤλυθ' ἐμὰ πρὸς δώματ', ἐγὼ δέ μιν ἀμφαγάπαζον) or 'embracing' (cf. *H. Dem.* 439), with a reference to the descent of the race of women from Pandora (*Th.* 590). It has been objected (Neitzel, *Pandora*, 411) that in that case the men of the golden age would have lived without women, but Hes. disregards the chronological connection between the story of Prometheus and the myth of the ages (see below, on 113 πόνων)[209]. Most interpreters think that in contradistinction to *Th.* 591 ff., where the first woman herself is the evil sent to mankind, Pandora's only function is to open the jar of evils. But the choice of the verb ἀμφαγαπάω and the use of the present participle show that it is also in her quality of being a woman that Pandora will become an evil[210]. The emphasis put on her bad qualities (67 and 78) points in the same direction. The poet does not say in which respect she will become an evil, apparently because he assumes his audience to be familiar with the corresponding passage in the *Th.*, where women are said to be no good but at eating up the fruits of their husbands' labour. This fact is of topical interest in connection with Zeus' intention to keep hidden from men the means of living. It now appears that the κήδεα λυγρά (49) do not only consist in the toil of labour but also in the wastage of its products.

59: ἐκ δ' ἐγέλασσε. 'Burst out laughing': cf. Hom. Z 471, π 354, σ 35. Similarly ἐκβοάω, ἐκδακρύω, etc. For the tmesis cf. 61 ἐν, 121 κατά, etc., Schw. II, 425.

60: Ἥφαιστον. It has been argued that pottery (61) is foreign to the function of Hephaestus[211], but it may be answered (1) that the proper patron of pottery, Prometheus could not be used in this context, (2) that 61-2 αὐδὴν /

---

[207] This may serve to answer Fränkel's objection (129 n. 9), "Manches im Text klingt zwar als ob mit Pandora das Weib überhaupt erschaffen wäre [and at *Th.* 591 she is explicitly called the first woman], aber es ist doch wohl nur die Frau als Luxuswesen gemeint; denn auf die Mägde (*WuT* 303 f.) passt die Pandorafabel durchaus nicht". See further P. A. Marquardt, CP 75 (1982), 177-86.

[208] Cf. G. S. Kirk, *Myth: Its Meaning and Functions* (Berkeley-Los Angeles 1970), 235 ff., *id.*, *The Nature of Greek Myths* (Harmondsworth 1974), 140 ff.

[209] His other objections (411-2) are logical quibbles rather than real difficulties. His own conclusion (413-5), that Pandora is not a real woman but a mythical image of the female character comparable to Semonides' images of women, and that her action is typical rather than historical, does not suit the mental outlook of Hes., who is not a satirist like Semonides, but a teller of true stories (10).

[210] Fink (39 ff.) rightly remarks that 58 cannot refer to the opening of the jar, but wrongly concludes that 54-69 cannot belong to the *W.a.D.* and should be inserted after *Th.* 559. Similarly, We. (*Th.*, 307) speaks of "narrative inconsistencies". M. Hofinger, in *Mélanges ... R. Fohalle* (Gembloux 1969), 205-17, seems to me wrong in denying that Pandora in the *W.a.D.* is the first woman. See also Quaglia, 68 ff.

[211] Erren, in *Gnomosyne* (above, n. 192), 158, who speaks of "eine ganz ungereimte Verleumdung".

καὶ σθένος is a reminiscence of Hom. Σ 419-20, so that Hephaestus acts as a miracle-worker rather than as a smith[212], and (3) that he is also the personification of fire (cf. Hom. B 426 σπλάγχνα ... ὑπείρεχον Ἡφαίστοιο) and as such prefigures Anaximander's theory of the origin of living beings from earth and water under the action of heat[213].

60: περικλυτόν. Cf. Hom. A 571 etc. κλυτοτέχνης, θ 345 κλυτοεργόν.

61: ὕδει. Cf. δόρει, οὔδει, and Schw. I, 548. For the production of a human being made out of earth and water cf. Hom. H 99 ὑμεῖς πάντες ὕδωρ καὶ γαῖα γένοισθε (rightly explained by Leaf as "may you all rot away to the elements of which you were made")[214], Xenoph. B 33 πάντες γὰρ γαίης τε καὶ ὕδατος ἐκγενόμεσθα, We. on *Th.* 571[215]. See also below, on 108 ὁμόθεν.

61: φύρειν. 'Mix and knead'.

61: αὐδήν. 'The faculty of human speech': cf. Hom. Τ 407 αὐδήεντα δ' ἔθηκεν (*scil.* the horse Xanthus) θεὰ λευκώλενος Ἥρη, ε 334 Λευκοθέη, ἣ πρὶν μὲν ἔην βροτὸς αὐδήεσσα, *Lex.*, 1540-4[216]. See also below, on 79 φωνήν.

62: σθένος. Clement of Alexandria has νόον, which is not "a better reading in itself" (Pal.), for Hes. had Hom. Σ 419-20 in mind, where it is said of the golden handmaidens of Hephaestus: τῆς ἐν μὲν νόος ἐστὶ μετὰ φρεσίν, ἐν δὲ καὶ αὐδὴ / καὶ σθένος, ἀθανάτων δὲ θεῶν ἄπο ἔργα ἴσασιν. We. thinks that the last clause of the Homeric passage "adapts words from 62 to the sense of 64". But that clause has closer parallels in the formula γυναῖκας ἀμύμονα ἔργα εἰδυίας (Ι 128 etc.) and such phrases as θεῶν ἄπο μήδεα εἰδώς (ζ 12).

It has been argued[217] that σθένος is "nicht die Kraft eines Einzelnen, sondern vielmehr die anlagebedingte Kraft einer Gruppe von Wesen, ja einer Gattung", and that Hes. "deutet den Unterschied der Kraft an, der zwischen Gott und Mensch besteht". But I do not believe that ἀνθρώπου should be taken with σθένος: there does not seem to be a fundamental difference between the present phrase and such passages as Hom. Λ 11 σθένος ἔμβαλ' ἑκάστῳ. I do not believe either that at Σ 420 σθένος includes "seelische

---

[212] Cf. M. Delcourt, *Héphaistos, ou la légende du magicien* (Paris 1957), 53 ff., 145 ff.

[213] Cf. W. K. C. Guthrie, *In the Beginning: Some Greek Views on the Origins of Life and the Early State of Man* (London 1957), 33-4.

[214] Interpreted by Loraux (above, on 57 δώσω), 73 n. 36, as "becoming women" (!).

[215] See further my remarks in Mnem. III 13 (1947), 288-9 (where more literature is mentioned), J. H. Loenen, Mnem. IV 7 (1954), 222-5, C. W. Müller, *Gleiches zu Gleichem* (Wiesbaden 1965), 168, M. M. Sassi, Dialoghi di archeologia 1 (1981), 33 ff., espec. 36. Walcot (*Near East*, 64 ff.) compares the Egyptian god Khnum, who shaped queen Hatshepsut on a potter's wheel.

[216] See further H. Fournier, *Les verbes 'dire' en grec ancien* (Paris 1946), 229-30, H. J. Krapp, *Die akustischen Phänomene in der Ilias* (Ph. D. diss. Munich 1964), 23-4, J. Clay, Hermes 102 (1974), 130-5.

[217] W. Schütz, Ἀσθένεια φύσεως (Ph. D. diss. Heidelberg 1964), 36-7.

Kräfte" and that in Hes. it "repräsentiert das menschliche Innere": it is true
that νόος and ἦθος at 67 denote mental faculties, but it does not follow that a
more general mental power must have been mentioned before.

62: ἀθανάτης. For the ending cf. Troxler, 106.

62: εἰς ὦπα. Similarly Hom. Γ 158 θεῆς εἰς ὦπα ἔοικεν, α 411 κακῷ εἰς
ὦπα ἐῴκει. The meaning is not 'in respect of face' (K.G. I, 317, Si., Krafft,
46) but *scil.* ἰδόντι, 'if one looks into the face': cf. Hom. Ι 373 etc. εἰς ὦπα
ἰδέσθαι.

63: παρθενικῆς. Properly 'belonging to the group of παρθένοι' (cf. Chantr.,
Dict. étym., 858), but here and at Hom. Σ 567, λ 39 used as a substantive (see
below, on 71 ἴκελον), probably to avoid the metrical difficulty of παρθένου.

63: καλόν. The short α is not "fatal to the genuineness of the verse" (Pal.),
for it reappears at *Th.* 585 and *H. Ven.* 29. Similarly, 752 is the only line
where ἴσος has a short ι: it is bracketed by Pal., but the short ι reappears at
Thgn. 678, Sa. 31, 1, etc. See further We., *Th.*, 82, Edwards, 107, Troxler,
48[218].

63: εἶδος. The digamma is neglected, just as at 714, Hom. Γ 224[219]. See
further above, on 28 ἀπ᾽ ἔργου. The object of ἐίσκειν is the mixture, εἶδος
being the predicate expressing the result. The construction is analogous to
ποιεῖν with a double accusative (K.G. I, 318-9), for ἐίσκειν does not mean 'to
fashion as something like' (Ev., Col.) but 'to make like' (cf. Hom. ν 313 σὲ
γὰρ αὐτὴν παντὶ ἐίσκεις). Krafft (46) takes εἶδος to be the object, but one
could hardly say 'to make a maiden-shape like to goddesses'.

63: ἐπήρατον. 'Lovely' is too weak, for the meaning is 'exciting desire':
cf. *Th.* 64-7, 908-11. Similarly ἐρατός: cf. my note on Pind. *I.* 2, 31, Mnem.
IV 35 (1982), 25. It has been observed that in epic and archaic lyric poetry
εἶδος is accompanied only by favourable epithets[220].

63: Ἀθήνην. It has been suggested that she is associated with Pandora
because she is a "déesse artificielle"[221], but in Hes.'s view she was conceived
by Metis and brought forth by Zeus (*Th.* 924 γείνατο), so that there is
nothing artificial about her.

64: ἔργα. The pregnant use (for weaving and spinning) is well-known from
Homer (LSJ I 2 b). Pal. suspects 63-4 because at 76 Athena is described as
arranging Pandora's ornaments, but cf. below, *ad loc.*

64: διδασκῆσαι. Cf. Pind. *P.* 4, 217 ἐδιδάσκησε. The form need not be a
Boeotism (as is supposed by Sittl and Wil.), for cf. ἐθέλησω, ἐμέλησε,

---

[218] Cf. also A. Hoekstra, *Homeric Modifications of Formulaic Prototypes* (Amsterdam 1965),
25 n. 3, J. C. Kamerbeek, Mnem. IV 20 (1967), 386-7.

[219] Unduly suspected by Leaf and Chantr. I, 142. At θ 169 τε should not be deleted, nor ἄρ᾽
at Ε 451.

[220] Cf. C. Sandoz, *Les noms grecs de la forme* (Neuchâtel 1971), 24-5, 27.

[221] G. Dumézil, quoted with approval by Loraux (above, on 57 δώσω), 48 and n. 43.

ἐδέησε, ἀλεξήσειε (γ 346), Troxler, 84, Schw. I, 752. Neitzel (28-32 and in Hermes 111, 1983, 372-4) defends the reading διασκῆσαι (D) by comparing *Th.* 580-1 ἀσκήσας ... / ... δαίδαλα and Hom. Ξ 178-9 ἑανὸν ... Ἀθήνη / ἔξυσ᾽ ἀσκήσασα, τίθει δ᾽ ἐνὶ δαίδαλα πολλά. His translation runs: 'Zeus befahl Athene, ihre Werke gründlich und kunstfertig zu verrichten, nämlich ein kunstvolles Gewand zu weben'. It may be objected, however, that in that case we should expect ἔργον instead of ἔργα. On the other hand, Neitzel objects to διδασκῆσαι that "lernte sie [Pandora] die Webkunst, besässe sie eine nützliche Fähigkeit und könnte nicht als κακόν bzw. πῆμα bezeichnet werden"[222]. But (1) such passages as Hom. υ 70-2 show that the command of Athena's 'works' is a stock element of the well-educated woman's character, and so adds to Pandora's attractiveness, and (2) the harmfulness of women is confined by Hes. (*Th.* 593, 599) to their gluttony and wastefulness[223].

64: πολυδαίδαλον. Cf. Hom. Ξ 179 quoted above[224]. The asyndeton has explanatory (specifying) force: cf. above, on 11 οὐκ.

65: ἀμφιχέαι. To be taken literally, because χάρις is a kind of substance: cf. Hom. ζ 232-5 ὡς δ᾽ ὅτε τις χρυσὸν περιχεύεται ἀργύρῳ ἀνὴρ / ... / ... / ὡς ἄρα τῷ κατέχευε χάριν κεφαλῇ τε καὶ ὤμοις[225]. Similarly ψ 156 κὰκ κεφαλῆς χεῦεν πολὺ κάλλος Ἀθήνη, σ 192 κάλλεϊ μέν οἱ πρῶτα προσώπατα καλὰ κάθηρεν[226], λ 433 οἵ τε κατ᾽ αἶσχος ἔχευε, μ 338 γλυκὺν ὕπνον ἐπὶ βλεφάροισιν ἔχευαν[227]. The difference between abstract and concrete notions was so vague that even glory and grief could be imagined as 'things': cf. Ω 110 κῦδος Ἀχιλλῆϊ προτιάπτω, Β 15 Τρώεσσι δὲ κήδε᾽ ἐφῆπται[228].

---

[222] His second objection, that Pandora's character as described at 67 and 78 excludes the willingness to learn, is much weaker. His final argument, that Pandora is unable to learn before she has been endowed with mental qualities (67 and 77-8), collapses if we assume that the order in which Zeus' instructions are given does not necessarily correspond with the order in which they will be carried out.

[223] Neitzel's defence (31-2) of the emendation διασκήσαιμι at *H. Dem.* 144 is not convincing either: he rejects διδασκήσαιμι because "Demeter will selbst arbeiten", but she can do so by supervising maid-servants, just as Euryclea says (χ 422): δμῳαί· τὰς μέν τ᾽ ἔργα διδάξαμεν ἐργάζεσθαι. Renehan (346) suggests that Hes., "by a typical false etymology, felt the presence of ἀσκέω in the form διδασκῆσαι ('teach the working of')". But at 662 and *Th.* 22 he obviously did not feel it.

[224] The term δαιδάλεος has been studied by F. Frontisi-Ducroux, *Dédale: Mythologie de l'artisan en Grèce ancienne* (Paris 1975), 39 ff., but her analysis is unsatisfactory: cf. H. Koenigs, Gnom. 51 (1979), 42-5. See further *Lex.* II, 195-6.

[225] This passage suffices to disprove the view put forward by M. Treu, *Von Homer zur Lyrik* (Munich 1955), 58-9, that χάρις has a concrete meaning in the *Iliad*, but an abstract meaning in the *Odyssey*.

[226] The scholiasts, followed by many modern commentators, wrongly explain κάλλος as a beauty cream: beauty itself may manifest itself as a kind of cream.

[227] For sleep conceived as a liquid cf. Onians, 31-3. Beauty could also be imagined as a kind of breath: cf. Hes. fr. 43 a, 74, *H. Dem.* 276, Onians, 73-4.

[228] Cf. also J. Gonda, *Ancient-Indian ojas, Latin *augos and the Indo-European Nouns in es/os* (Utrecht 1952), 72.

65: κεφαλῇ. Because "in questions of χάρις the head is especially important" (We.), but also because the head is the seat of life and may represent the whole person (Hom. Θ 281): cf. Onians, 96, 98.

65: χρυσέην. May refer to her radiant beauty (LSJ III 1), but more probably to her jewellery (Ameis-Hentze on Θ 337): cf. *H. Ven.* 61-5, 84-90 [229].

66: πόθον. Logically the longing and the cares belong to the beholder, but in archaic thought emotions are considered to seize or to enter a person from without (e.g. Hom. δ 596 οὐδέ κέ μ' οἴκου ἕλοι πόθος) and so may be imagined to issue from their objects: cf. *Th.* 910 τῶν καὶ ἀπὸ βλεφάρων ἔρος εἴβετο and We. *ad loc.* Similarly Hom. Ξ 198, where Hera asks Aphrodite δὸς νῦν μοι φιλότητα καὶ ἵμερον [230].

66: ἀργαλέον. Not 'difficult to contain' (Sittl) but 'painful': cf. e.g. Hom. τ 136 Ὀδυσῆ ποθέουσα φίλον κατατήκομαι ἦτορ.

66: γυιοκόρους. Not to be connected with κόρος (Proclus) but with κείρω in the sense of 'to devour': cf. Hom. λ 578 γῦπε ... ἧπαρ ἔκειρον, LSJ III. The reading γυιοβόρους (So., We.) is a *lectio facilior* (cf. Hom. Η 210 θυμοβόρος ἔρις). West, Phil. 108 (1964), 158-9, defends γυιοβόρους on the ground that "κείρω is not used in any sense appropriate to the effect of worry". But if κείρω can have the meaning of 'to devour' it is only a stronger expression for eating. Hes. preferred the stronger expression, just as Achilles at Hom. Α 243 σὺ δ' ἔνδοθι θυμὸν ἀμύξεις (cf. Ω 129 σὴν ἔδεαι κραδίην). Cf. also A. *Pers.* 161 με καρδίαν ἀμύσσει φροντίς, Theocr. 13, 71 χαλεπὸς γὰρ ἔσω θεὸς (love) ἧπαρ ἀμύσσει, and the similar use of δάπτω at Pind. *N.* 8, 23, A. *Prom.* 437, S. *O.R.* 682. The 'cares' are imagined as little monsters feeding on the human flesh: cf. Onians, 86-7. In the present case the worries obviously have an erotic character, and at *Th.* 121 Eros is called λυσιμελής, which implies a waste of vital liquid: cf. 586 κεφαλὴν καὶ γούνατα Σείριος ἄζει, and Onians 110-1, 187, 202-3.

For the difference between γυῖα and μέλεα cf. Snell, 16: "Gyia sind die Glieder, sofern sie durch Gelenke bewegt werden, Melca die Glieder, sofern sie durch Muskel Kraft haben". See further *Lex.* II, 183-4.

66: μελεδώνας. Not μελεδῶνας, for μελεδώνη, not μελεδών, is the older form [231]. The word is explained in the *Etym. Magn.* as αἱ τὰ μέλη ἔδουσαι φροντίδες, and Hes. probably intended to allude to this derivation: for his etymological speculations see above, on 3 διά.

---

[229] See further J. van Eck, *The Homeric Hymn to Aphrodite* (Ph. D. diss. Utrecht 1978), 40, who points out that her jewellery serves to arouse love. Latt. is obviously wrong in taking χρυσέην with χάριν, 'golden endearment'.

[230] For πόθος see further W. Vollgraff, *L'oraison funèbre de Gorgias* (Leiden 1952), 86 ff., G. Broccia, Λέξεις. *Ricerche di lingua e di stile* (Rome 1971), 37-46.

[231] Cf. W. Aly, in Heitsch, 91-2.

67: κύνεον. 'Impudent': cf. Hom. I 372-3 αἰὲν ἀναιδείην ἐπιειμένος· οὐδ᾽ ἂν ἐμοί γε / τετλαίη κύνεός περ ἐὼν εἰς ὦπα ἰδέσθαι, and κύων and κυνῶπις used as terms of abuse with reference to Helen, Clytemnestra, and the maids in the house of Odysseus [232].

67: νόον. 'Character', but considered from the intellectual point of view: 'way of thinking'. Cf. Γ 63 ἀτάρβητος νόος ἐστί 'not thinking of fear', LSJ I 3. See further K. von Fritz, CP 38 (1943), 83-4 = H. G. Gadamer (ed.), *Um die Begriffswelt der Vorsokratiker* (Darmstadt 1968), 256-7, and my note on *Th.* 37, Mnem. IV 25 (1972), 242.

67: ἐπίκλοπον. The original meaning of κλέπτω is 'to hide one's real intention': cf. Hom. A 132 μὴ κλέπτε νόῳ. See further Luther, 105 ff., 134. According to Plato (*Leg.* 781 a), the female sex is λαθραιότερον καὶ ἐπικλοπώτερον διὰ τὸ ἀσθενές [233]. For ἐπι- denoting an intention see above, on 29 ἐπακουόν.

67: ἦθος. In Homer 'usual dwelling-place', as at *Op.* 167, 525. In the present line and at 137, 222, 699 the word means 'habit', 'disposition' (cf. Pl. *Leg.* 792 e 2 τὸ πᾶν ἦθος διὰ ἔθος; similarly Arist. *EN* 1103 a 14). The translation 'character' is misleading, because (1) it suggests a fixed state of mind, whereas ἦθος is teachable (cf. 699 and Hdt. II 30, 5) and changeable (cf. Thgn. 213, E. fr. 1024, Arist. *Rhet.* 1331 b 31-2), and (2) it suggests a basic and all-embracing unity, whereas Pandora's ἦθος rather refers to a special habit [234]. On the other hand, Quaglia (61) rightly observes that the description of Pandora in the *Th.* is limited to her outer appearance, whereas in the present passage considerable attention is paid to her inner qualities. This is connected with Hes.'s growing interest in man's mental powers and reactions: cf. the use of θυμός (13, 28, 58, etc.) and νόος (260, 323, etc.). See also Sellschopp, 26-7.

The digamma of ἦθος is also neglected at 137 and Hom. Z 511 (where τε is unduly suspected by Chantr. I, 150).

---

[232] See further S. Lilja, *Dogs in Ancient Greek Poetry* (Helsinki 1976), 22 and 38, U. Dierauer, *Tier und Mensch im Denken der Antike* (Amsterdam 1977), espec. 10-1, and my critical remarks in Mnem. IV 34 (1981), 186. Cf. also Campbell, *Honour* (above, n. 106), 57, who observes that among the Sarakatsani "the female is a constant threat to the honour and integrity of the male".

[233] H. F. North, ICS 2 (1977), 45, points out that "in Old Comedy the thieving ways of women still constitute a commonplace, together with their reputation for sexual license". Cf. also Campbell, *Honour*, 277: "a natural predisposition to evil (κακία) is the most striking feature of the female character. She is above all cunning in the sense that her cunning involves the corruption of another, that is the man".

[234] Cf. Luther, 134 n. 1: "Wir dürfen in dem Singular keinen Beweis dafür sehen, dass hier die 'einheitliche Wesensart' gegenüber der Vielheit ihrer konkreten Auswirkungen schon für sich allein ins Auge gefasst ist. Für Hesiod fallen im ἐπίκλοπον ἦθος verstohlenes, verschlagenes 'Wesen' und 'Verhalten' zusammen". H. Diller, *Kleine Schriften zur antiken Literatur* (Munich 1971), 273, thinks that in Aeschylus ἦθος denotes "eine das ganze Wesen erfassende Anlage". He refers to O. Thimme, Φύσις, τρόπος, ἦθος (Ph. D. diss. Göttingen 1935), 43, but e.g. at *Ag.* 727 the word refers to a single trait of character, viz. bloodthirstiness.

68: Ἑρμείην. The god of trickery; cf. Hom. Ω 24, τ 396, Nilsson, 507, and Deichgräber (above, n. 84), 108 ff. For the Ionic form cf. We., *Th.*, 80 and 90 [235].

68: διάκτορον. The most obvious translation seems to be 'conductor' (cf. *H. Herm.* 392 Ἑρμῆν δὲ διάκτορον ἡγεμονεύειν), especially as ψυχοπομπός, but also more generally, as at Hom. Ω 333 ff.: cf. Wil., *Gl.* I, 162-3, Nilsson, 507-9, J. Chittenden, AJA 52 (1948), 24-33, R. Janko, Glotta 56 (1978), 192-5, *Lex.* II, 282-3.

68: Ἀργεϊφόντην. Hom. B 651 ἀνδρεϊφόντης is formed after Ἀργεϊφόντης, so that we may assume that Homer, just as Aeschylus (*Suppl.* 305), took it to mean 'Slayer of Argus'. See further *Lex.*, 1195-8 [236].

69: ὣς ἔφατο. After a speech reported indirectly: cf. Hom. I 688, Ψ 149, α 42, θ 570, *H. Dem.* 316, 448. Similarly Τ 130 ὣς εἰπών.

70: δέ. Has explanatory (specifying) force: see above, on 9.

70: γαίης. Water (61) is not mentioned here (and at *Th.* 571), because earth is the primary substance: cf. *Th.* 131 (Γαῖα) ἀτρύγετον πέλαγος τέκεν, Xenoph. B 27 ἐκ γαίης γὰρ πάντα. In Genes. 2, 6 a mist rises from the earth, and Xenoph. B 37 probably serves to illustrate the origin of water from earth.

70: Ἀμφιγυήεις. Probably 'handy': cf. γύαλον, ἐγγυαλίζω, and ἀμφιδέξιος (Hippon. 70, 2 D. = 121 W.). The translation 'with both feet crooked' (H. Vos, *Lex.*, 673-4, who compares Hom. Σ 371, Υ 270 κυλλοποδίων) is less appropriate, as the word is usually combined with (περι-, ἀγα-)κλυτός and so seems to be a laudatory name [237].

71: αἰδοίη. Not 'chaste' (Maz.), 'modest' (Ev.), 'decorous' (Latt.), but 'commanding respect' (Moschop. αἰδοῦς ἀξίᾳ): cf. 257: Dike is αἰδοίη θεοῖς. In Homer, too, αἰδοῖος always has this meaning, except at ρ 578 κακὸς δ' αἰδοῖος ἀλήτης. See further my remarks in Mnem. III 12 (1944), 47-60, IV 10 (1957), 250 [238].

71: ἴκελον. 'Something resembling'. We. on *Th.* 572 writes: "I am not sure whether this is neuter ... or (masculine for) feminine". But (ε)ἴκελος always has three endings, and the neuter singular of an adjective is more often used as a substantive than the masculine or feminine. For adjectives used as substantives cf. Hom. σ 132 κακὸν πείσεσθαι, Pl. *Phd.* 62 d 1 ἔοικεν τοῦτο ...

---

[235] The fact that Hes. occasionally uses forms with ᾱ where η might be expected (Edwards, 102) does not seem to me sufficient proof that he "deliberately strove to reproduce Homer's oscillation, exactly in the same manner as Antimachus and the Hellenistic epic poets did", as is suggested by G. Giangrande, JHS 92 (1972), 191.

[236] To the literature mentioned there may be added H. Koller, Glotta 54 (1976), 211-5, H. Herter, RhM 119 (1976), 210-1, We., 368-9.

[237] Cf. also H. Humbach, in *Studi ... V. Pisani* (Brescia 1969), 569-78.

[238] The fact that a woman may command respect shows that A. W. H. Adkins, *Merit and Responsibility* (Oxford 1960), 36-7, is wrong in thinking that Homer denies to women the competitive excellences. Similarly, Walcot (*Peasants*, 60) wrongly connects αἰδοῖος with the 'quiet virtues'.

ἀτόπῳ, K.G. I, 60, 268, and my notes on Pl. *Phdr.* 263 c 1, Mnem. IV 8 (1955), 283-4, and A. *Prom.* 871, *Miscellanea ... Kamerbeek*, 468 [239].

71: βουλάς. See above, on 16 βουλῇσιν.

72: κόσμησε. With a shining garment and an embroidered veil (*Th.* 573-5) [240]. This does not imply that Athena here anticipates the results of her teaching (64) [241]. It is only natural that the order to teach Pandora needlework and weaving is not executed at the very moment of her creation.

72: γλαυκῶπις. Whatever the original meaning of this epithet [242], Homer is unlikely to have associated it with 'owl': the goddess assumes the appearance of a vulture (H 59), a falcon (Υ 350), a sea eagle (γ 372), or a swallow (χ 240), but never of an owl (Wil., *Gl.* I, 144). The most obvious translation seems to be 'with gleaming eyes': cf. Υ 172 γλαυκιόων.

73: Χάριτες. Cf. *Th.* 907-11, where their erotic nature is emphasized. We. rightly rejects the suggestion put forward by C. Robert (in Heitsch, 354-5), that 73-5 are equivalent to 65-6 [243], but his explanation, that "Pandora must be made attractive ... in a new way", is insufficient. Hes. adapts his reminiscence of *Th.* 576-7, where Athena adorns Pandora with garlands of flowers, to the order of the instructions given at 65, where Aphrodite comes after Athena. The result is that golden necklaces (cf. 65 χρυσέην Ἀφροδίτην) are added to the garlands and that the adornment is executed by Aphrodite's attendants. This does not mean, however, that the instruction given to Aphrodite is not carried out: its execution is taken for granted, just as the conferment of αὐδή and σθένος (61-2) and the teaching of weaving (64). The lack of an exact correspondence between command and execution may be assumed to show the influence of writing on the technique of oral composition [244].

---

[239] Pal. wrongly assumes an ellipse of πλάσμα, Krafft (101 n. 8) of εἶδος. N. Loraux, Areth. 11 (1978), 49, argues that there was not yet a model for the creation of Pandora, but her paraphrase, "la femme apparaît sous l'espèce de la vierge", is based on the wrong assumption that "le mot *ikélos* n'établit pas toujours un lien de ressemblance entre deux objets". The obvious meaning is that Pandora resembled a being known to the present reader as a παρθένος.

[240] I fail to see why the fact that these objects are not mentioned here necessarily ("notwendig") gives the verb a causative sense, as is maintained by Krafft, 102.

[241] As is suggested by W. Aly, in Heitsch, 335; similarly Quaglia, 63. C. Robert (in Heitsch, 335) even thinks "dass die Göttin während des Anziehens die Pandora in die Geheimnisse der Weberei einweiht" (!). This is quoted with approval by Krafft (102), but his explanation, "hier stünde das Konkrete für das Abstrakte", leaves us in the dark.

[242] Cf. W. Brandenstein, Arch. Orient. 17 (1949), 84, M. Leumann, *Homerische Wörter* (Basel 1950), 142-52, W. Watson-Williams, G & R N.S. 1 (1954), 36-41 and Class. Med. 21 (1960), 7-14, W. Pötscher, Gymn. 70 (1963), 404-6, P. Chantraine, *Mélanges Carcopino* (Paris 1966), 193-204, P. G. Maxwell-Stuart, *Studies in Greek Colour Terminology*, I (Leiden 1981), 90-1 and the critical remarks made by M. M. Sassi in her review, RFIC 110 (1982), 311-3, and the literature mentioned in *Lex.* II, 161.

[243] Similarly Krafft (103), who maintains that "für πόθος steht Peitho" (!) and that "der Blumenschmuck der Horen bewirkt γυιοκόρους μελεδώνας bei den Männern (bes. im Frühling)" (!).

[244] As is suggested by P. Walcot, REG 74 (1961), 16-9.

73: θεαί. They had a cult in Orchomenus, Olympia, and other places[245], but apart from that they could be called 'goddesses' as divine powers: see above, on 11 Ἐρίδων. For their association with Aphrodite cf. Hom. E 338 and θ 364-6.

73: Πειθώ. She, too, has her own cult[246], but here acts as an attendant of Aphrodite: cf. Sa. 1, 18 (and my remarks in Mnem. IV 9, 1956, 102), 96, 29, Ibyc. 288, Pind. *P.* 9, 39, fr. 123, 14, A. *Suppl.* 1040. In the present context she embodies women's power to persuade men into love-making[247].

74: ὅρμους χρυσείους. Aphrodite wears ὅρμοι χρύσειοι when she appears before Anchises (*H. Ven.* 88-9). Apart from the attraction implied in the gold, the necklace has a magic power to bind the beholder[248].

74: χροΐ. The body as far as the surface is concerned: cf. Snell, 17[249]. For the construction οἱ ... χροΐ see above, on 28 σε ... θυμόν.

74-5: ἀμφὶ ... στέφον. See above, on 59 ἐκ δ' ἐγέλασσε.

75: Ὧραι. They make everything ripe (ὡραῖος), and hence beautiful. They dress and adorn Aphrodite (*H. Ven.* VI 5 ff.) and dance with her (*H. Ap.* 194-6)[250].

75: στέφον. For the imperfect synchronous with the aorist (ἔθεσαν) cf. above, on 38 ἐφόρεις.

75: εἰαρινοῖσιν. We. writes that "the Horai operate with the flowers that are their special concern", but this does not answer the question why they choose spring flowers. The obvious answer is that spring flowers are the most beautiful and the most abundant (cf. Hom. B 89).

76: κόσμον ἐφήρμοσε. This line has been rejected by many critics as being a repetition of 72[251]. But there is no repetition, for we should not translate 'Athena bedecked her form with all manner of finery' (Ev.; similarly Col.), but 'Athena adjusted the whole adornment to her body', i.e., she added the finishing touch[252].

---

[245] Cf. Farnell, *Cults* V, 427-31, Wil., *Gl.* I, 192-3, KP I, 1136.7 ff., Hamdorf, *Kultpersonifikationen* (above, n. 65), 45-6.

[246] Cf. Farnell, *Cults* II, 664, Hamdorf, *op. cit.*, 63-4, Buxton, *Persuasion* (above, n. 205), 31-6, H. Strohm, in *Festschrift R. Muth* (Innsbruck 1983), 495-506.

[247] Cf. Buxton, *op. cit.*, 37, who compares Pind. fr. 123, 1-2.

[248] Cf. Buxton, *loc. cit.*, who refers to A. *Cho.* 617-8.

[249] Krafft (38-9) wrongly thinks that in Hes. (even at 416) χρώς refers to the skin only.

[250] At *Th.* 901-3 they have a different function: cf. We. *ad loc.* See further Farnell, *Cults* IV, 130, Wil., *Gl.* I, 191-2, Hamdorf, *Kultpersonifikationen*, 39-40, KP II, 1215-6, Motte, *Prairies* (above, n. 88), 90.

[251] Solmsen suspects 72 in Gnom. 52 (1980), 216, but keeps it in the second edition of his text. Q. Cataudella, in *Mythos: Scripta in honorem M. Untersteiner* (Genova 1970), 121-6, proposes to read χρυσέη Ἀφροδίτη at the end of 72. His assumption that ζῶσε there refers to Aphrodite's κεστός is quite arbitrary.

[252] J. Kerschensteiner, *Kosmos* (Munich 1962), 7 n. 4, points out that when κόσμος refers to the adornment of goddesses it is "immer auf die gesamte Ausstattung bezogen, meist nach Aufzählung einer Reihe von Schmuckstücken" (cf. Hom. Ξ 187, *H. Ven.* 162, *H. Art.* 17). Krafft

77: ἄρα. 'As was to be expected' (on account of 67-8): see above, on 49 ἄρα.

78: ψεύδεα. "In dieser frühgriechischen Zeit wird noch nicht geschieden zwischen den einzelnen Fällen von Lügen und der dahinterstehenden einheitlichen Eigenschaft" (Luther, 134). Similarly Hom. Ψ 515 κέρδεσιν, β 118 κέρδεα.

78: αἱμυλίους. Usually translated either by 'wheedling' or by 'wily', but the meaning is 'wheedling by means of wiles'[253]. Similarly 374 αἱμύλα.

78: λόγους. "Non des mots, mais des idées" (Maz. I, who refers to στήθεσσι, but in II he translates 'mots trompeurs'). It is more correct to say that words and thoughts were not clearly distinguished: cf. Hom. Α 543 εἰπεῖν ἔπος, ὅττι νοήσῃς, Α 545-6 μὴ δὴ πάντας ἐμοὺς ἐπιέλπεο μύθους / εἰδήσειν, δ 676 μύθων, οὓς μνηστῆρες ἐνὶ φρεσὶ βυσσοδόμευον. At θ 177 νόος takes up ἀγορητύς (168) and ἔπεα (170, 175)[254]. It is well-known that φημί often means 'to think' (LSJ I b). In λόγος the blending of speaking and thinking came about the more easily because originally it did not denote the single word but an ordered combination of words, a 'tale'[255]. See further my remarks in Lampas 5 (1972), 103-4.

78: ἦθος. We. thinks that "an ἦθος is not localized within the body", but cf. 67 ἐν θέμεν, and Renehan, 347.

79: Διὸς βουλῇσι. The repetition (cf. 71 Κρονίδεω διὰ βουλάς) emphasizes the central position of Zeus. For the plural βουλῇσι see above, on 16 βουλῇσιν.

79: βαρυκτύπου. Just as conventional as ἐρίγδουπος and ἐριβρεμέτης (cf. Hom. Ο 377 μέγα δ' ἔκτυπε μητίετα Ζεύς). This would not have been pointed out if Krafft (106 n. 1) had not suggested that "diese Charaktereigenschaften [of women] werden ein 'schwerer Schlag' für ihre Männer sein, wie es die Absicht des Zeus ist" (!).

79: φωνήν. This line has been condemned by a number of critics because

---

(103-4) unnecessarily takes the verb to be used in a causative sense: 'achtet darauf, dass alles gut passt'. His suggestion (104 n. 1) that κόσμος here means 'das Passende' because "damit nicht eigentlich Genanntes umfasst wird", is equally unconvincing. C. J. Rowe, JHS 103 (1983), 129, argues "that Hesiod is describing the same thing from two different aspects. Looked at from the point of view of the connection of Pandora's beauty with her dress, the action belongs to Athena; from the point of view of the effect that her adornment will have, it is the gift of the Charites and Persuasion". This is correct except for the important fact that Athena does not do the same thing as the Charites and Peitho: the latter are concerned with the details, Athena with the whole.

[253] See further H. Boeder, Arch. f. Begriffsgesch. 4 (1959), 89-90. Krafft's translation (105 n. 4) 'interessante Erzählungen' is obviously wrong.

[254] Called by Ameis-Hentze a "störende Differenz".

[255] Cf. H. J. Flipse, De vocis quae est λόγος significatione et usu (Leiden 1902), 20-1, Fournier, Dire (above, n. 216), 217, and my remarks in Stud. Gen. 19 (1966), 103 and Phron. 11 (1966), 81-3.

at 61 Hephaestus is ordered to give her αὐδή[256]. There is, however, a difference between the two words: αὐδή is the articulate voice (cf. schol. Hom. ζ 125 αὐδηέντων· ἐνάρθρῳ φωνῇ χρωμένων) and φωνή the resonant voice (cf. the Homeric formula φωνήσας ... προσηύδα[257]). It is true that the difference is sometimes neglected[258], but this does not prove that it is not observed here. It is only natural that Hermes as herald of the gods makes her speech sounding (as is observed by Maz.)[259].

80: θῆκε. After this word a comma should be put, and the semicolon after βαρυκτύπου should be removed: just as 85 θεῶν ταχὺν ἄγγελον, the apposition indicates in which function the god is acting.

80: ὀνόμηνε. The naming is not an addition to the creation, but its completion. There is a wide-spread belief among ancient and primitive peoples that it is the name that makes a new-born baby an individual and real being[260]. We. thinks that Hermes is called θεῶν κήρυξ "not so much because Hermes is giving Pandora a voice as because he is about to proclaim her name. It justifies Hesiod in leaving her naming with Hermes instead of reverting to Zeus". This conclusion is far from obvious: it is more natural to assume that "the god of speech also interprets (ἑρμηνεύει) things by giving them their right names"[261].

80: τήνδε. We. argues that because retrospective ὅδε "is exceedingly rare in narrative", τήνδε "is best explained as a reflection of what Hermes would have said, ὀνομαίνω τήνδε γυναῖκα Πανδώρην". The usage is rather frequent, however, in Herodotus: cf. Stein on I 137, 1. See further above, on 35 ὧδε.

81: Πανδώρην. Not 'Endowed with everything', nor 'Endowed by all (the gods)', but 'Present of all (the gods)'. It has been argued that "the name Pandora emerges out of the description how 'all' — in truth more and more — gods contribute to her appearance and personality"[262]. But the repetition of δῶρον at 85 and 86 obviously refers back to the name Πανδώρη. It is true that the phrase δῶρον ἐδώρησαν in itself could mean 'they had given her each

---

[256] Danielsson (above, n. 97), 7, suggests ἧκε for θῆκε: 'and besides he raised his voice'. This is ingenious and inept at the same time.

[257] Cf. also Γ 161 ἐκαλέσσατο φωνῇ ('raising his voice') and the phrase φωνὴν ῥῆξαι (Hdt. I 85, 4, etc.). See further Fournier, *Dire*, 230, V. Pisani, in *Studi ... R. Cantarella* (Salerno 1981), 515-7. Krafft (48 n. 2) seems to me wrong in taking αὐδή to refer to the sound, and φωνή to the choice of words. Quaglia's suggestion (65) that the phrase αὐδή καὶ σθένος represents "lo spirito vitale" is equally unconvincing.

[258] E.g. at *Th.* 39 ῥέει αὐδή and Hom. φ 411 ἣ δ᾽ ὑπὸ καλὸν ἄεισε, χελιδόνι εἰκέλη αὐδήν (but not at T 407, as is held by We.: see above, on 61 αὐδήν).

[259] For Hermes as the god of speech cf. RE VIII, 781-2.

[260] Cf. Rank, *Etymologiseering* (above, n. 13), 18-20 and the literature mentioned there. See also P. Walcot, SO 33 (1957), 44-5, Th. Ph. Feldman, SO 46 (1971), 28 ff., F. Jouan, in J. Hani (ed.), *Problèmes du mythe et de son interprétation* (Paris 1978), 69 ff., espec. 81 ff.

[261] J. H. Waszink, in Entret. s. l'ant. class. 7 (1962), 162.

[262] Solmsen, *Hes.*, 79. Cf. Fink, 9-10.

a gift', but the fact that she became a πῆμ' ἀνδράσιν was not caused by her being endowed but by her being sent to men (as is pointed out by Quaglia, 67 n. 46).

Originally Πανδώρα was an epithet of Mother Earth, 'Giver of all' (Ar. *Av.* 971; see further We.), represented as a woman emerging from the earth [263]. Afterwards this woman was regarded as an envoy of Earth, and as Earth was the prototype of woman (Pl. *Mexen.* 238 a, Lucr. V 795-827) [264], Pandora became the first woman [265]. Hes. knew her only as such (cf. *Th.* 589), ignoring her connection with Earth (except 70 ἐκ γαίης) [266], and, in accordance with his inclination to etymological speculation (see above, on 3 διά), giving a new meaning to the word Πανδώρα [267].

82: δῶρον. Predicate: cf. on 81 Πανδώρην.

82: ἐδώρησαν. Not to be translated by a pluperfect [268], but by an imperfect. For the active form cf. Schw. II, 234.

82: πῆμα. Consecutive apposition: see above, on 56 πῆμα.

82: ἀλφηστῇσιν. 'Eating barley-groats' (ἄλφιτον), equivalent to σῖτον ἔδοντες (Hom. ι 89), σιτοφάγοι (ι 191), οἱ ἀρούρης καρπὸν ἔδουσιν (Ζ 142). For men ἄλφιτον is a condition of life (cf. β 290 ἄλφιτα, μυελὸν ἀνδρῶν and Onians, 113-4, 221-2), whereas the gods οὐ σῖτον ἔδουσι (Ε 341). The translation 'earning' (ἀλφάνω), 'enterprising' is less probable, for it is not true that the word is especially used of traders and seafarers (as is suggested by LSJ) [269].

The authenticity of 69-82 has been questioned by many critics [270]. The main objections have already been dealt with in the commentary. Two points

---

[263] Cf. C. Robert, in Heitsch, 342 ff., L. Séchan, Bull. Budé, April 1929, 3-36. See further W. A. Oldfather, RE XVIII 2 (1949), 529-48, Fink, 9 ff., C. Bérard, *Anodoi*, Bibl. Helv. Rom. 13 (Rome 1974), 161-4, We., 164-6.

[264] Loraux (above, on 57 δώσω), 76 n. 71, wrongly takes *Menex.* 237 e - 8 a to suggest "que la femme reproductrice est modèle pour penser la production des nourritures cultivées".

[265] Cf. Paus. I 24, 7 and Rudhardt, 276 n. 107.

[266] *Th.* 578-86 is another possible reminiscence: cf. Fink, 14-5. I cannot believe that Pandora's ἐπίκλοπον ἦθος is derived from the deceitful nature of Earth, who is a giver of good and evil, of life and death, as is suggested by W. B. Kristensen, Meded. Kon. Ned. Akad. v. Wet., Lett. 66 B 3 (1928), 19 ff. (similarly Fink, 13 and 31): Hes. does not refer to such an ambivalent character of Earth, and he obviously connects Pandora's character with that of Hermes himself.

[267] Neitzel (*Pandora*, 414-6) suggests that Hes. is playing with the ambiguous sense of the name because Pandora pretends to 'give everything', but this is not implied in her description.

[268] If this were the only possibility, as is assumed by Danielsson (above, n. 97), 8-10, Πανδώρη could not mean 'Present of all'.

[269] Krafft (106 n. 3) takes the word to refer to "das schwere Los der Menschen, im Gegensatz zu den Göttern (α 349) als ῥέα ζώοντες und den unbelasteten Phaiaken (ζ 8)", but ἀλφάνω does not imply hard work. See further S. L. Radt, *Lex.*, 589. Vernant (above, n. 192), 910 n. 11, calls Pandora "première épouse féminine" and concludes: "Sur ce plan déjà, le lien apparaît entre l'agriculture et le mariage" (!).

[270] E.g. by Wil. *ad loc.* and Lendle, 14 ff., 46 ff. See also Fink, 33 ff. and the reviews of Lendle's book by H. Erbse, Gymn. 66 (1959), 561-3, and J. H. Kühn, Gnom. 31 (1959), 114-23.

have to be added: (1) The fact that Hes. uses γυνή at 94 instead of Πανδώρη does not imply that she was anonymous to him[271]. (2) The fact that 70-72 repeat (with a slight variation) *Th.* 571-3 is not unparalleled: cf. 124-5 and 254-5, 149 and *Th.* 152, *Th.* 150-2 and 671-3.

83: δόλον. Walcot (*Near East*, 60) points out that "Epimetheus and Zeus fall victim to an identical trick, and Zeus, therefore, pays his enemies back in their own coin by an act of deceit which is comparable but much more crushing".

83: αἰπύν. We. in his note on *Th.* 589 writes: "Probably the sense of 'steep' was extended to that of 'hard to overcome'". This explanation is unsatisfactory. In Homer the word is an epithet of ὄλεθρος (Z 57 etc.), πόνος (Λ 601), φόνος (Ρ 365), χόλος (Ο 223). The usual translation, 'deep' ("death being regarded as the plunge from a high precipice", LSJ) neither suits the last passage nor the phrase ὑπεκφυγεῖν αἰπὺν ὄλεθρον, which rather points to a height than to a depth. This height is imagined as moving forward and coming down upon its victim, though the latter may try to escape from under its downfall or to keep it off (Σ 129 ἀμυνέμεν αἰπὺν ὄλεθρον). The metaphor has probably been taken from a rising wave. Accordingly, αἰπύς means 'unapproachable', 'irresistible'. It is true that α 37 αἰπὺν ὄλεθρον is followed by 46 ἐοικότι κεῖσθαι ὀλέθρῳ, but this seems to be a modal, not a local, dative (cf. Α 418 σε κακῇ αἴσῃ τέκον, and K.G. I, 435). The addition of ἀμήχανον to δόλον αἰπύν also shows that αἰπύς means 'hard to resist'. Cf. also Ν 317 αἰπύ ('difficult') οἱ ἐσσεῖται[272].

83: ἀμήχανον. *Th.* 589 is more explicit: ἀμήχανον ἀνθρώποισιν.

83: ἐξετέλεσσεν. For ἐξ- cf. above, on 48 ἐξαπάτησε.

84: εἰς. Chantr. II, 103-4, writes: "Une des originalités de la syntaxe homérique est l'emploi de εἰς avec des noms de personne (là où l'attique emploie ὡς, πρός, παρά)". It should be added (1) that εἰς is used with reference to persons if emphasis is put on the place where these persons are dwelling or staying (cf. K.G. I, 468, Schw. II, 459), (2) that the usage is also found in Attic, e.g. at Ar. *Plut.* 237 εἰς φειδωλὸν εἰσελθών (where van Leeuwen and Coulon unnecessarily read ὡς), (3) that the meaning is 'into' (the house of): cf. LSJ I 1.

84: Ἐπιμηθέα. For ἐπι- 'afterwards' cf. ἐπίγονος, etc.: see further Fink, 54

---

[271] Wil. also refers to a vase on which Pandora is depicted rising from the earth and receiving golden ornaments from a winged figure. But this is clearly a contamination of the Pandora-Earth tradition with the Hesiodic conception (Si.). The inscription Ἀνησιδώρα does not mean 'letting go the presents (from the jar)' (Danielsson, above, n. 97, 7 n. 4) but 'sending up gifts', which is an epithet of Earth (cf. Fink, 13 n. 4, 57 n. 2, We., 164-5).

[272] See further my remarks in Mnem. IV 6 (1953), 115, and G. van N. Viljoen, *Pindaros se tiende en elfde Olympiese odes* (Leiden 1955), 179-81. H. J. Koch, Glotta 54 (1976), 218, who proposes the translation 'headlong destruction', calls my arguments "not convincing", but does not discuss them.

n. 1, We. on *Th.* 511. We. (*Th.*, 307) plausibly suggests that Epimetheus was "invented by a poet (possibly Hesiod himself) who wished to connect the origin of women with Prometheus as the wages of his sin, but who regarded Prometheus himself as too clever to be deceived by the trick"[273]. On the other hand, I do not believe that Hes. intended to suggest an analogy between Epimetheus and Perses, as is assumed by Walcot, *Near East*, 62, who compares 293-7.

84: πατήρ. *Scil.* ἀνδρῶν τε θεῶν τε (59): cf. We. *ad loc.*

84: κλυτόν. We. rightly observes that the fact that Hermes is always called κρατὺς Ἀργεϊφόντης need not induce us to read κρατύν here. His conclusion, that Hes.'s choice of the epithet was influenced by 70 κλυτὸς Ἀμφιγυήεις and that "this is one of the processes by which the formulaic system evolved", should be modified by the observation that Hom. Υ 230 is the only place where Achilles is called κλυτός, and Ω 789 the only place where Hector is called κλυτός.

85: θεῶν. Not to be connected with δῶρον (Maz.) but with ἄγγελον: cf. 80 θεῶν κῆρυξ. It is true that at Hom. Ω 292 ταχὺν ἄγγελον is used without a qualifying genitive, but the original reading probably was ἑὸν ἄγγελον (cf. Leaf *ad loc.*, and see above, on 2 σφέτερον). It has been objected that a caesura after the second trochee is very unusual[274], but cf. e.g. 97 ἔνδον ἔμιμνε, Hom. Η 236 ἠὲ γυναικός, ξ 444 οἷα πάρεστι. See further We., *Th.*, 95[275]. The fact that θεῶν δῶρα is an epic phrase (Γ 65, Υ 265) need not induce us to take θεῶν both with δῶρον and with ἄγγελον (as is suggested by So. and Renehan, 347): the divine character of the gift has been sufficiently defined at 81-2.

85: θεῶν ταχὺν ἄγγελον. An example of the tendency of archaic poets to put the main things first and to append the details: see my note on *Th.* 519 κεφαλῇ, Mnem. IV 24 (1971), 2. Cf. also above, on 50 πῦρ.

86: ἐφράσαθ' ὥς. Not 'non si diede pensiero che' (Col.) but 'had not given heed to (the way of action) as told to him by Prometheus'.

88: κακόν. Not 'de crainte qu'il n'arrivât malheur' (Waltz; similarly Maz., Col.) but 'for fear it might prove to be something harmful' (Ev.): κακόν is predicate, and δῶρον is to be understood as the subject.

88: γένηται. The subjunctive is used instead of the optative because Hes. imaginatively puts himself in the place of Prometheus. Similarly Hom. Δ 229-30 τῷ μάλα πόλλ' ἐπέτελλε παρισχέμεν, ὁππότε κέν μιν / γυῖα λάβῃ

---

[273] At *Th.* 511-4 the connection between Epimetheus' character and his way of acting is less clearly indicated, but that does not imply that in Hes.'s first version of the story he did not play any part at all, as is assumed by Fink, 56 ff.

[274] Cf. Fink, 10 n. 1, who refers to Fränkel, *W.u.F.*, 107.

[275] It is true that δῶρον ἄγοντα does not satisfy the criteria of what Fränkel calls a "Wortbild", but these criteria seem to me rather arbitrary.

κάματος. See further Leaf on Δ 230, Goodwin, *Moods*, §§ 318-21, K.G. II, 555, Chantr. II, 269. For γίγνομαι 'turn out to be' cf. Hom. E 63 (νῆας) αἳ πᾶσι κακὸν Τρώεσσι γένοντο, and my notes on Hipp. *Aër.* 6, Mnem. IV 8 (1955), 16, Semon. 7, 36, Mnem. IV 21 (1968), 36, and Pind. *I.* 2, 33, Mnem. IV 35 (1982), 25-6.

89: δή. It is misleading to say that this "is equivalent to ἤδη" (We.): the meaning is 'precisely when', 'just when' (Denn., 219-20).

89: ἐνόησεν. 'Realized its true nature', 'saw through it': see above, on 12 νοήσας. The story points the same moral as 218 παθὼν δέ τε νήπιος ἔγνω and 295 ἐσθλὸς δ' αὖ κἀκεῖνος, ὃς εὖ εἰπόντι πίθηται[276].

90: ἐπὶ χθονί. A reminiscence of the formulaic use of ἐπιχθόνιος, but probably in the pregnant sense of 'all'. Similarly *Th.* 556, Hom. η 307 (cf. Edwards, 180-1). Cf. also 11 ἐπὶ γαῖαν 'everywhere'.

91: νόσφιν ἄτερ. For the pleonasm cf. Hom. Κ 416 νόσφιν ἀπὸ φλοίσβου, Β 305 ἀμφὶ περὶ κρήνην, K.G. I, 528-9, Schw. II, 428, 430, 540.

91: τε. Does not connect νόσφιν and ἄτερ (as is suggested by Sittl), but points forward to καί: for corresponsive τε ... καί in anaphora (ἄτερ) cf. Denn., 512.

91: καί. Has explanatory (specifying) force: cf. Hom. Δ 55 φθονέω τε καὶ οὐκ εἰῶ διαπέρσαι, Δ 308 ζωόν τε καὶ ἀρτεμέα. See further J. Gonda, Mnem. IV 7 (1954), 199, and my note on E. *Ba.* 43, Mnem. IV 33 (1980), 11.

91: ἄτερ. For the repeated preposition cf. 102 ἐφ' ... ἐπί, and We., *Th.*, 76.

91: πόνοιο. Wil. maintains: "Arbeit kann das nicht sein, auch nicht Schmerz, sondern allgemein Mühe, Plage". But this general trouble may include labour[277], and the repetition of 49 κήδεα λυγρά at 95 strongly suggests that it does[278]. It even must include labour, for the story of Pandora must include some explanation of the fact that man's βίος has been hidden by Zeus (47), as has been rightly observed by Neitzel (*Pandora*, 388). He concludes (389), however, "dass das Entlassen der Übel aus dem Fass keine Antwort auf die Ausgangsfrage sein kann, inwiefern Zeus den Menschen durch Pandora den βίος verborgen hat", for "was versteckt ist muss man suchen". It may be answered that labour is a form of seeking: man's means of living are no longer ready to hand, but they have to be unearthed. There is no difficulty in *Th.* 226 Ἔρις στυγερὴ τέκε μὲν Πόνον ἀλγινόεντα, for it appears from 22 that a corresponding good Ponos belongs to the good Eris. On the other hand, such a good πόνος could still be considered a necessary evil.

---

[276] Cf. Kühn, 271 ff., Fink, 75-6, H. Dörrie, *Leid und Erfahrung. Die Wort- und Sinn-Verbindung* παθεῖν-μαθεῖν *im griechischen Denken*, Abh. Akad. Mainz, Geistes- u. soz. wiss. Kl. 1956:5, espec. 11-2.

[277] G. Broccia, Par. Pass. 62 (1958), 300, wrongly concludes from 397-400 that labour and πόνος are opposites. See also Quaglia, 72.

[278] As is observed by J. H. Kühn, Gnom. 31 (1959), 122.

A πόνος brought over men by the action of a woman probably also includes man's suffering caused by women's gluttony and wastefulness (see above, on 58 κακὸν ἀμφαγαπῶντες). This is suggested by the fact that Pandora's beautiful appearance is intended to be deceptive (83 δόλον)[279], and it is confirmed by the correspondence between her αἱμύλιοι λόγοι (78) with 374 αἱμύλα κωτίλλουσα, τεὴν διφῶσα καλιήν. Neitzel (*Pandora*, 389-90) carries logic too far by concluding that in that case Pandora herself should be among the contents of the jar: the latter may very well contain the evil consequences of her behaviour without containing her whole nature.

92: νούσων. Maz. and Neitzel (*Pandora*, 399) think that these are the diseases caused by πόνος, but 102-4 show that all kinds of diseases are meant. See further G. Preiser, *Allgemeine Krankheitsbezeichnungen im Corpus Hippocraticum* (Berlin 1976), 91 ff.

92: τε. Introduces a further specification (see above, on 3 τε): 'and especially'. Similarly Pind. *O.* 3, 38-9 Ἐμμενίδαις / Θήρωνί τε, *O.* 7, 52, A. *Ag.* 514.

92: ἀργαλέων. The fact that ἀργαλέος is sometimes replaced by κακός (e.g. *Th.* 527 κακὴν ... νοῦσον) does not imply that "ἀργαλέων is for Hesiod a synonym of κακῶν" (We. on *Th.* 601), for ἀργαλέος means 'painful', 'grievous': cf. Hom. Ν 667 νούσῳ ὑπ' ἀργαλέῃ, and see above, on 66 ἀργαλέον. For the masculine ending -ων cf. Chantr. I, 201 n. 1, Edwards, 127 n. 15.

92: αἵ τε. Cf. above, on 3 ὄν τε.

92: κῆρας. Not 'cares'[280], but 'destruction' (cf. κηραίνω): cf. Hom. Β 352 φόνον καὶ κῆρα φέροντες, LSJ II 1. For the plural cf. Hom. Β 302 οὓς μὴ κῆρες ἔβαν θανάτοιο φέρουσαι, Μ 326 κῆρες ἐφεστᾶσιν θανάτοιο, Χ 210 δύο κῆρε τανηλεγέος θανάτοιο. These phrases may imply the conception of the κῆρες as maleficent beings who carry off the spirits of the dead to Hades, but the construction κῆρας ἔδωκαν shows that Hes. does not intend the word to be taken in this sense. The terms ἐξέπτη (98), ἀλάληται (100), and φοιτῶσι (103) suggest some personification, but the evils are not represented as ghosts[281].

---

[279] Cf. Kühn, *loc. cit.*, 120, who rightly points out that Pandora's adornment is a functional element in the story.

[280] Séchan (above, n. 263), 11: 'd'amers soucis'. J. Kroll, *Theognis-Interpretationen* (Leipzig 1936), 13, argues that at Thgn. 13 the word means 'misfortune'. He refers to Hom. Σ 535, *Scut.* 249, Emp. B 121, but in all these places (and at Thgn. 767) the word seems to be connected with death. The broader meaning is not found before A. *Ag.* 206 (cf. LSJ II 2).

[281] As is assumed by J. Harrison, JHS 20 (1900), 99-114, who in her *Prolegomena to the Study of Greek Religion* (Cambridge 1903), 169 n. 2, even proposes to read ἅς ... κῆρες. See further F. von Nägelsbach, *Homerische Theologie* (³Nürnberg 1884), 140-1, Rohde I, 239-40, E. Samter, *Volkskunde im altsprachlichen Unterricht* (Berlin 1923), 95-102, Nilsson, 222-5, W. Pötscher, WS 73 (1960), 14 ff., D. J. N. Lee, Glotta 39 (1960-61), 191-207, B. C. Dietrich, *Death, Fate and the Gods* (London 1965), 240-8, C. M. Dawson, YCS 19 (1966), 65-7, A. Parvulescu, Helikon 8 (1968), 277-310.

93. This line (= Hom. τ 360) was added by someone who read γῆρας instead of κῆρας at 92. We. argues that "originally the line must have been a comment on 113 f.", and that it is the source of the reading γῆρας (which is first found in a manuscript of 1466). But (1) recent manuscripts sometimes contain old readings, (2) a comment on γῆρας at 92 was much more urgent than one on 113-4, and (3) We. does not explain why the line was added after 92.

94: ἀλλά. Answers μέν at 90: cf. Denn., 5-6.

94: πίθου. Not 'box' (Si.) but 'jar'. These jars were used to store provisions[282]. There were two of them, one containing good and one containing evil, in the palace of Zeus (Hom. Ω 527-8). Yet Pandora is unlikely to have brought along the jar of ills from heaven, for Hes. would not have omitted describing such an important detail. According to Proclus, Prometheus had received the jar of ills from the satyrs and deposited it with Epimetheus, urging him not to accept Pandora. Maz. suggests that Prometheus probably had persuaded the satyrs to steal the jar of ills from Zeus, when the latter was about to pour them out over mankind. This may have been a familiar tale which Hes. thought unnecessary to relate[283].

94: μέγα. We. thinks that "the epithet is transferred from the jar", but Hes. probably intended to suggest that Pandora's action was directed by a super-human power (cf. 99).

94: ἀφελοῦσα. Neitzel (*Pandora*, 401 n. 36) wrongly thinks that 'taking off' implies "auf den Boden setzen": if we assume that Pandora put back the lid from sheer fright (see below, on 98 ἐπέμβαλε) she is more likely to have kept it a few seconds above the opening of the jar.

95: ἐσκέδασε. *Scil.* τὰ κακά (91). For parallels in other folktales cf. We., 155 n. 1. Neitzel (*Pandora*, 390-2) argues that σκεδάννυμι means 'to dissipate' a number of things which originally formed a unity and after their dissipation lose their function or effect, and that accordingly the object of ἐσκέδασε cannot be τὰ κακά[284]. But such a loss of function or effect does not always occur: for instance, when a meeting is broken up Homer says that Agamemnon λαὸν (not the assembled group) μὲν σκέδασεν κατὰ νῆας ἐΐσας (Ψ 162) or that Achilles ἄλλους μὲν ἀπεσκέδασεν βασιλῆας (Τ 309)[285]. Neitzel

---

[282] Cf. P. Girard, REG 22 (1909), 229, P. Roussel, BCH 51 (1927), 166, and We. *ad loc.*

[283] Jane Harrison's assumption of a connection with the festival of the Πιθοίγια has been definitely abandoned: cf. K. von Fritz, in Heitsch, 371-2, Fink, 20-1. The jar may have been a symbol of the womb of Earth (Fink, 23 ff.), but it seems doubtful whether such a reminiscence was still present to Hes.'s mind.

[284] He even thinks that χείρεσσιν goes with both ἀφελοῦσα and ἐσκέδασε, but Pandora is more likely to have lifted the lid out of curiosity.

[285] Neitzel further refers to Η 329-30 τῶν νῦν αἷμα κελαινὸν ἐύρροον ἀμφὶ Σκάμανδρον / ἐσκέδασ᾿ ὀξὺς Ἄρης, which he explains as follows: "er löst es aus der Verbindung mit dem Körper, in dem es allein wirken kann". But ἀμφὶ Σκάμανδρον shows that the meaning is 'he shed blood all around' (LSJ). In post-Homeric Greek, too, objects of σκεδάννυμι may continue to

(393-6) thinks that the object of ἐσκέδασε is πίθον, to be understood in the sense of 'the contents of the jar' (see below, on 368 λήγοντος), and that this view is confirmed by the fact that the κήδεα λυγρά, just as at 49, refer to the toil required to acquire one's food. He compares 364 κήδει, but this does not suffice to prove that the word must have such a narrow sense: at *Th.* 102 κηδέων does not have a special object, and there is no reason to assume that in the *W.a.D.* the word should have a kind of technical sense. It may further be objected (1) that the image of a jar containing food does not square very well with the idea suggested by 43-4 and supported by 117-8 that before the deceit committed by Prometheus the earth produced corn which only had to be reaped, and (2) that Neitzel is forced to assume (as had been done by Krafft, 110) that ἐλπίς means 'Hoffnung auf neue Vorräte', a specification which does not find the slightest support in the context [286].

95: δέ. Has consecutive force ('and thereby'): see above, on 18 δέ. Neitzel (*Pandora*, 392-3) argues that if τὰ κακά is taken to be the object of ἐσκέδασε the line becomes inconsistent: "bringt nun Pandora durch ein und dieselbe Handlung gleichzeitig sowohl alle Übel als auch einen Teil von ihnen über (bzw. unter) die Menschen". He concludes: "Der Widerspruch beweist, dass sich die zu den Übeln gehörenden Sorgen nicht als Folge der Verbreitung aller Übel einstellen können". I fail to see, however, why the fact that cares (included among the evils) are brought about (see next note) could not be represented as a consequence of the fact that all evils are spread among men.

95: ἐμήσατο. This does not imply that she acted from malice [287]. It is true that she had a shameless character (67), but the fact that she quickly put on the lid again (98) shows that she was "surprised and frightened by the results of her action. It was not her cunning or wiliness that prompted her to open the jar, but her curiosity" (K. von Fritz, in Heitsch, 370). On the other hand, Paley's emendation ἐλύσατο is unnecessary, because μήδομαι can have the meaning of 'to bring about': see above, on 49 ἐμήσατο.

95: κήδεα λυγρά. Repeated from 49. There they denote the unpleasant consequences of the fact that Zeus ἔκρυψε βίον, but here such a connection

---

function, e.g. at Hdt. IV 14, 2 ἐσκεδασμένου τοῦ λόγου ἀνὰ τὴν πόλιν. Neitzel's second argument (392), "πίθος heisst immer Vorratsfass ... Zeus teilt Güter und Übel (wie Vorräte) mit einem Mass zu, Pandora dagegen 'zerstreut' gewisse Vorräte", is not convincing either: stores can be spread or dispersed as well as dissipated.

[286] Conversely, Neitzel (395-6) objects that "hätte Hesiod sagen wollen, dass die Vorräte zufällig Übel waren, dann hätte er dies auch wie Homer geschrieben". But after 91-2 there can be no doubt that the jar contained evils. This simple observation carries more weight than Neitzel's structural analysis and logical reasoning (404 ff.). Cf. also the critical remarks made by F. Preisshofen, *Untersuchungen zur Darstellung des Greisenalters in der frühgriechischen Dichtung* (Wiesbaden 1977), 44 n. 115.

[287] As is assumed by C. Robert, in Heitsch, 358 n. 35, W. Oldfather, RE XVIII 2 (1949), 542, Latt. ('her design was'), Neitzel, *Pandora*, 392 (who speaks of "planende Absicht").

with the necessity of labour is much less evident[288]. It is true that πόνος (91) may include labour, but the only evils which are mentioned by name are the diseases (102-4). This seems to imply a shifting of Hes.'s point of view, viz. from the idea of labour to the other centre of his thinking, the idea of justice. Labour is a punishment inflicted on men by Zeus for the deceit of Prometheus. The penalty is augmented by the creation of woman, who wastes the fruits of man's labour (see above, on 58 κακὸν ἀμφαγαπῶντες). But now the punishment becomes still more comprehensive, including any kind of misfortune. See also below, on 105 οὕτως.

96: αὐτόθι. Serves to emphasize the location: cf. Hom. Ω 707 αὐτόθ' ἐνὶ πτόλεϊ, and R. Renehan, *Studies in Greek Texts* (Göttingen 1976), 122.

96: ἐλπίς. Hes. does not tell us why ἐλπίς remained in the jar. There is a vast number of modern explanations, of which I shall discuss only the most important ones. They may be divided into two classes according as they presume that the jar served (1) to keep ἐλπίς for man, or (2) to keep off ἐλπίς from man. In the first case the jar is used as a pantry, in the second case it is used as a prison (just as in Hom. E 387). Furthermore, ἐλπίς may be regarded either (a) as a good, or (b) as an evil. In the first case it is a comfort to man in his misery and a stimulus rousing his activity, in the second case it is the idle hope in which the lazy man indulges when he should be working honestly for his living (cf. 498). The combination of these alternatives results in four possibilities which we shall now briefly consider.

(1a) Ἐλπίς is good hope preserved for man (among others Pal., Wil., Maz.) or in the power of man[289]. But why and how did it come along with the evils? It has been argued that hope is the natural companion of misery[290]. But hope accompanies man in favourable as well as in unfavourable circumstances[291]. We might call hope the natural companion of man, but not the natural companion of misery. Quaglia (75-6) argues that Elpis would have become an evil if it had escaped from the jar, but that Zeus enabled man to keep it under control, and that this idea is symbolized by the fact that it stuck

---

[288] The attempts made by G. Broccia, Par. Pass. 35 (1954), 118-36 and 62 (1958), 296-309, to show that the sending of Pandora is identical with the κρύπτειν βίον are unconvincing. For instance, when he writes (1958, 304-5): "se dai vv. 498-501 risulta che la ἐλπίς si accompagna agli uomini quando questi sono sprovvisti di βίος ... e nei vv. 96-99 si dice che, con Pandora, è venuta in mezzo agli uomini la ἐλπίς, è da concludere che gli uomini, dopo l'invio di Pandora, sono sprovvisti di βίος", this is a mere fallacy.

[289] Cf. K. J. Dover, JHS 86 (1966), 44 n. 17: "Hesiod meant to say what Hermokrates says more sophistically in Th. VI 78, 2 οὐ γὰρ οἷόν τε ἅμα τῆς τε ἐπιθυμίας καὶ τῆς τύχης τὸν αὐτὸν ὁμοίως ταμίαν γενέσθαι. Man is ταμίας of his own hopes and fears, because he can choose to hope and fear, but he cannot choose when to be sick or well".

[290] Maz. Similarly M. Pohlenz (above, n. 117), 81, J. J. A. Schrijen, *Elpis* (Groningen 1965), 36 and n. 1.

[291] It is simply nonsense to maintain that hope is inconceivable without evil (Schrijen, *loc. cit.*).

under the lid. She admits that man is sometimes dominated by an idle hope (e.g. at 498-501), but this may be explained by the assumption that the jar "rimane agli uomini, nel senso che resta la possibilità individuale di lasciarne uscire dissennatamente la speranza" (n. 72). This seems to me extremely unlikely: the fact that Pandora replaced the lid under the influence of Zeus obviously means that the jar then remained closed for ever.

It has also been suggested that the jar contained not only all evils but also all goods. When Pandora lifted the lid, all goods flew back to heaven, except hope[292]. But apart from the fact that there is nothing of this in the text, it is very improbable that a single jar should have contained goods as well as evils. It is still more inconceivable that Hes., who had such a keen eye for the distinction of contraries[293], should have contaminated two different stories, one about a jar full of evils, and another about a jar full of goods[294]. The latter story is to be found in a fable by Babrius (58), in which it is told that Zeus put all goods into a jar which he deposited with man. Man in his curiosity lifted the lid, and all goods flew back to heaven, except hope which was caught by the lid. But (1) the idea that the gods sent a jar of goods to man suits the Stoic conception of divine providence rather than the archaic conception of the gods[295], and (2) a late author such as Babrius is more likely to have contaminated his sources than Hes. In the present case we can even reconstruct the contamination. Theognis (1135 ff.) tells us how the gods left the earth because of the wickedness of man; only Ἐλπίς remained behind and stayed with man. It seems that Babrius, or his source, combined this tale with the tale of Pandora[296].

(1b) According to this view the fact that ἐλπίς remained within the jar symbolizes the fact that man is himself responsible for the evil consequences of his blind hope[297]. But this implies "that, if Pandora had not opened the jar, men would still be subject to all evils and would also be responsible for all of them", which is an obvious absurdity[298].

---

[292] P. Girard, REG 22 (1909), 217 ff.

[293] Cf. Sellschopp, 93-9, Broccia, *Tradizione* (above, n. 8), 41 ff.

[294] P. Friedländer, *Herakles* (Berlin 1907), 39 ff. Similarly A.S.F. Gow, *Essays and Studies Presented to W. Ridgeway* (Cambridge 1913), 99 ff., M. Nilsson, Gnom. 4 (1928), 614, A. Lesky, WS 55 (1937), 21-6 = *Ges. Schriften* (Bern-München 1966), 327-30, and *Gesch. d. griech. Lit.* (²Bern 1963), 121, W. Oldfather, RE XVIII 2 (1949), 539-40, Fink, 70.

[295] Cf. K. Reinhardt, Eran. Jb. 25 (1957), 254-6 = *Tradition und Geist* (Göttingen 1960), 202-4.

[296] Later authors went still further. In an epigram from the 6th cent. A.D. (*Anth. Pal.* X 71) the jar containing the good gifts of the gods is opened, not by man in general, but by Pandora. See further D. and E. Panofsky, *Pandora's Box* (London 1956). The idea that the jar contained only good things has been revived by Krafft (108 ff.) and Neitzel (*Pandora*, 390 ff.): see above, on 95 ἐσκέδασε.

[297] S. M. Adams, CR 46 (1932), 196. Similarly Onians, 404, Lendle, 108-9.

[298] Cf. K. von Fritz, in Heitsch, 369. See also J. H. Kühn, Gnom. 31 (1959), 119 (against Lendle).

There is also a general difficulty affecting both 1a and 1b. Hes. stresses the fact that ἐλπίς remained within the jar (αὐτόθι — ἔνδον — οὐδὲ θύραζε). This is the same jar from which the evils escaped, and this escape accounts for the fact that they have spread among men (100). It is a strange thing that a container which was meant to prevent its contents from coming among men should at the same time help one of these elements to come among men [299]. In other words, Hes. is supposed to have confused the functions of a pantry and a prison. It is surprising to see how light-heartedly interpreters have treated this supposition which is hardly less than an affront to the poet's intelligence [300]. A feeble attempt to justify the confusion is the suggestion that the fact that ἐλπίς is caught by the lid symbolizes the fact that hope always desires to be realized but never is [301]. But it would be highly unrealistic — and Hes. is a realist to the backbone — to maintain that hope is never fulfilled. It could at most be said that hope as such is different from its realization, but this fact does not account for its inclusion in the jar of evils [302].

(2a) As neither 1a nor 1b leads to satisfactory explanations, it may be concluded that the jar was intended to prevent ἐλπίς from coming among men [303]. According to Si., the fact that ἐλπίς remains within the jar means

---

[299] Cf. Oldfather, *op. cit.*, 542: "Wenn die Übel, so lange sie im Pithos eingeschlossen bleiben, ohnmächtig sind, wie soll dann die eingeschlossene Elpis wirksam sein?".

[300] E.g. Wil.: "Also meint die Geschichte, dass die Hoffnung bei den Menschen bleibt, und weiter dürfen wir nicht denken"; von Fritz, *op. cit.*, 406: "the logical discrepancy that man has both the hope which is supposed to have remained in the box, and the evils which have escaped from it, passes unnoticed"; *id.*, Entret. s. l'ant. class. VII (1962), 35: "Es ist verschiedenes durcheinandergekommen"; We.: "we are in a myth, not a grocer's shop ... mythical jars have different uses in respect of good and in respect of evil contents ... It is of course illogical to make the same jar serve both purposes at once. But this is what Hesiod has done". In *Th.*, 307 n. 1 he argues that Hes. "does not mention Hope as being in the jar until all the ills have escaped; in other words, he does not have to speak or think of goods and evils being in the jar together"; Schrijen, *op. cit.*, 25: "Wanneer we wederom het beeld van het vat voor ons halen, kan het ons normaal voorkomen, dat men daarin iets opbergt, waarvan men vrij wil zijn, het als het ware gevangen zet, terwijl men van de andere kant daarin ook iets kan opbergen om er van tijd tot tijd gebruik van te maken".

[301] Fränkel, 163-4; *id.*, *W.u.F.*, 332-4. Similarly Reinhardt, *op. cit.*, 253 (= *Trad. u. Geist*, 201), Kerschensteiner, 161-2, Nicolai, 32-3.

[302] K. von Fritz, Entret. s. l'ant. class. VII (1962), 37, maintains: "Und wenn danach die Hoffnung immer noch an sich ein Gut sein müsste, so hat Hesiod doch den Widerspruch, dass sie im Fass mit den Übeln ist, nicht empfunden, weil er sehr wohl davon wusste, dass sie in jedem Fall ein zweifelhaftes und trügerisches Gut ist". But for Hes. there is a good ἔρις and a bad ἔρις (11 ff.), a good αἰδώς and a bad αἰδώς (317-9), a good ἐλπίς and a bad ἐλπίς (500). The idea of a paradoxical value, such as hope which is good in principle but may be bad in practice, does not suit his sphere of thought.

[303] Cf. P. Walcot, Herm. 89 (1961), 250: "Her jar is not a storage pot like the giant pithoi located in the magazines at Knossos, but a prison used to shut away what it contains. If we want an analogy from Homer, we must compare it to the bronze jar in which Otos and Ephialtes locked up the god Ares (*Il.* 5, 385-391). According to the *Erga* the rest escape but Hope is left behind in its ἀρρήκτοισι δόμοισιν (96). Homer uses the same adjective to describe the bronze chains with which Hephaestos traps the illicit love of Aphrodite and Ares (*Od.* 8, 274-275)". However, his own suggestion (251) that ἐλπίς is left behind because "it is only with Hope that we

that human life is hopeless, not in the sense that hope does not exist, but that our general condition is desperate. But this idea could never be expressed by means of the word ἐλπίς: ἐλπίς does not refer to an objective condition of life but to man's subjective reaction to that condition [304]. Besides, if ἐλπίς could mean 'hopefulness', it is a mystery why Zeus should have put it into the jar of evils. If it had been his original intention to make life hopeful, he would have neutralized the effect of evil; and if it had been his intention to withhold 'hopefulness' from men, he should not have put it into the jar.

(2b) It follows that ἐλπίς must be some kind of evil which Zeus at the last moment could not bring himself to pour over men (for Pandora acts βουλῆσι Διός, 99). Apparently this was an evil which would have made human life utterly unbearable and impossible. It has been argued that this was the deceptive illusion which would have induced men to neglect their work, if they had known it (Fuss, 35-6). But it is a fact that this illusion has come among men: Hes. himself warns men not to rely on idle hope and neglect their work (498-501).

There remains still one solution. According to Proclus, φησὶν οὖν Ἀρίσταρ-χος, ὅτι ἡ μὲν τῶν κακῶν ἔμεινεν, ἡ δὲ τῶν ἀγαθῶν ἐξῆλθεν. The second part of this explanation cannot be correct, because the ἐλπὶς ἀγαθῶν is a good, and the jar obviously contained mere evils. The words ἡ μὲν τῶν κακῶν ἔμεινεν imply that Zeus had put into the jar the evils as well as the expectation of these evils, this expectation being the worst of evils. It was his original intention that any evil which was to strike man should be expected by him. This continual expectation of evil would have made life a torture beyond bearing. Zeus therefore at the last moment altered his decision [305]: he made Pandora release the lid of the jar so that the ἐλπὶς τῶν κακῶν remained enclosed in it [306]. Now that this ἐλπίς has not spread among men, evil takes us by surprise. As an example Hes. mentions the diseases: they come αὐτόματοι and σιγῇ (103-4) [307]. It is true that we sometimes expect evil [308],

retain a degree of control so that we can make either a good or a bad thing of it", is inconsistent with the fact that it is shut away: in order to become a good or a bad thing, it would have to come out of the prison.

[304] As is pointed out by K. von Fritz, in Heitsch, 369-70. If a Greek should have to express the belief that our condition is desperate, he would use ἄσωτος or ἀνήκεστος, or something similar.

[305] O. Lachnit, Elpis (Tübingen 1965), 49, wrongly speaks of "nur ein Zufall". It is true that Pandora put back the lid from sheer fright, but her whole action is determined by Zeus (99 βουλῆσι Διός).

[306] This interpretation disposes of the objection raised by S. Østerud, Hermes 104 (1976), 20-1 n. 25, "Any interpretation to the effect that Hope is also an evil is bound to fail, because it would make it immaterial whether the jar was opened or not".

[307] This interpretation was first proposed by A. Lebègue, Ann. Fac. des Lettres de Bordeaux 7 (1885), 249-53 (whose translation 'prescience du malheur', however, is not quite correct: ἐλπίς is 'expectation', not 'foreknowledge'). See also Waltz (I), 56, and REG 23 (1910), 49-57. It has been defended by me in Mnem. IV 24 (1971), 225-31, and has been adopted by Péron, 279-80.

but this is an exception. In general evil comes unexpected, and that is a good thing too.

It has been objected that the meaning 'hope' is so prevalent in Greek literature that "no one, reading the story as it is told by Hesiod, could have understood ἐλπίς as 'expectation of evil' "[309]. But in a case like this one the prevalent use of a word is not the decisive point. It should be borne in mind that the original meaning of ἔλπομαι is not 'to hope' but 'to suppose'[310]. Ἐλπίς in the sense of 'hope' is only a specialization of the meaning 'expectation', which in its turn is a specialization of 'supposition'. There is ample evidence that the linguistic feeling of the Greeks was fully alive to this fact. Plato (Laws 644c) defines ἐλπίς as δόξα μελλόντων and Aristotle (Rhet. 1386 a 2) uses ἐλπίζειν as the opposite of μεμνῆσθαι. He calls the art of divination a ἐπιστήμη ἐλπιστική (De mem. 449 b 12).

Supposition and expectation may refer to something good or something bad. Plato divides ἐλπίς as δόξα μελλόντων into θάρρος and φόβος. Similarly, in the Rep. (330 e ff.) he contrasts a κακὴ ἐλπίς and a ἡδεῖα ἐλπίς. Aeschylus uses the expression φόβου ἐλπίς (Ag. 1434), where φόβου is a qualifying genitive defining the special kind of expectation which is meant here[311].

It must be admitted that Hes. does not define ἐλπίς in the same way as Plato's κακὴ ἐλπίς or Aeschylus' φόβου ἐλπίς. But this does not mean that it lacks any determination. The determination does not lie in an attributive word but in the whole context. Hes. makes it abundantly clear that ἐλπίς here belongs to a company of evils, and that these evils are no moral evils but misfortunes (91 κακῶν ~ 101 κακῶν, 95 κήδεα λυγρά ~ 100 μυρία λυγρά). This fact suffices to exclude a reference to the idle hope mentioned in v. 498. If, then, the present ἐλπίς is no moral evil, the only possibility left is that it denotes the expectation of evil[312].

F. Martinazzoli, SIFC 21 (1946), 15 = Ethos ed Eros nella poesia greca (Florence 1946), 111, wrongly maintains that the expectation of evil was intended to be useful to men. In that case it would not have been an evil itself. Lachnit (op. cit., 49) rightly explains ἐλπίς as 'expectation', but seems to me wrong in narrowing down this meaning to 'right expectation'. He argues that "im Gegensatz zu den menschlichen ἐλπίδες ist unsere Göttin nicht blind, sondern die immer richtige Voraussicht". But Hes. does not represent ἐλπίς as a goddess. It is human expectation conceived as a universal power. The question whether all human expectations were intended by Zeus to come true is irrelevant to Hes.'s picture. Lachnit wrongly projects the τυφλαὶ ἐλπίδες of A. Prom. 250 into our passage.

[308] K. von Fritz, in Heitsch, 369, Schrijen (above, n. 290), 21.

[309] K. von Fritz, loc. cit. Similarly We. ad loc.

[310] Cf. Hom. I 40, Π 281, Σ 194, and Lachnit, op. cit., 3 ff. See also ThWNT II (1935), 515-6, Schrijen, op. cit., 1 ff.

[311] This has been denied by Fraenkel, Denniston-Page, and Rose, but cf. Thuc. VII 61, 2 τὴν ἐλπίδα τοῦ φόβου, E. Or. 859 ἐλπίς, ἣν φοβουμένη ..., and Lachnit, op. cit., 98.

[312] Similarly, in A. Ag. 999 and S. O.R. 487, 771 the meaning of ἐλπίς as anxious foreboding is determined by the context. For ἐλπίζω, ἔλπομαι 'to expect anxiously' cf. Hdt. VIII 12, 2

There seems to be a reminiscence of this motif in the *Prometheus Bound*. Prometheus proudly declares that he has stopped mortals from foreseeing death (248). There is a variant of this tale in Plato's *Gorgias* (523d), where Zeus himself instructs Prometheus to deprive men of the foreknowledge of death[313]. Here a special part, perhaps the most important part, of the ἐλπὶς κακῶν is withdrawn from men. This limitation is foreshadowed by the prominent part played by fatal diseases in Hes.'s description (92).

96: ἀρρήκτοισι. The jar was probably made of bronze: cf. P. Walcot, Hermes 89 (1961), 250, and *Near East*, 61 (who compares Hom. E 385 ff., where Ares is kept a prisoner in a χάλκεος κέραμος). Similarly J. Anastassiou, *Lex.*, 1352.

96: δόμοισιν. We. concludes that "Hope is fully personified. The jar is her prison". But a personal goddess can hardly be imagined as living in a jar. The difficulty disappears if it is borne in mind that δέμω means 'to construct' and that δόμος can denote constructions not designed as dwelling-places: cf. Bacch. 3, 49 ξύλινον δόμον (pyre), E. *Alc.* 160 κεδρίνων δόμων (clotheschest). For the amplifying force of the plural see above, on 8 δώματα.

97: ἔμιμνε. This is better than ἔμεινε, which is a *lectio facilior*. It is not necessary that the tense is identical with that of ἐξέπτη (as is maintained by Wil.): cf. above, on 38 ἐφόρεις.

97: οὐδὲ θύραζε. Repetition in negative form is a very common form of emphasis in Greek: cf. Hom. Γ 59 κατ' αἶσαν οὐδ' ὑπὲρ αἶσαν, K.G. II, 586, Bruhn, § 208, Fehling, 272-3, We. on *Th.* 102-3, S. L. Radt, Mnem. IV 29 (1976), 33 and n. 1. Similarly 228-9.

98: ἐπέμβαλε. *Scil.* Pandora. The reading ἐπέλλαβε ('took her by surprise') is explained by We. as an instance of the common confusion of βαλ- and λαβ-, but it is more likely to be an attempt to remove a supposed contradiction between Pandora's own initiative (implied in ἐπέμβαλε) and the initiative of Zeus (βουλῇσι Διός). Some modern editors (e.g. Wil. and So.) have made a similar attempt by bracketing 99. For Hes., however, such a contradiction did not exist: in his view, everything was directed and determined by Zeus (cf. on 3 διά, 79 Διὸς βουλῇσι, 122 Διός). Pandora put back the lid from sheer fright, but such a spontaneous action was at the same time divinely planned. Similarly, at Hom. I 702-3 Achilles will fight again, ὁππότε κέν μιν/θυμὸς ἐνὶ στήθεσσιν ἀνώγῃ καὶ θεὸς ὄρσῃ.

99: αἰγιόχου. We. (366-8) plausibly argues that the second element must be connected with ϝέχω 'to move', but his speculations about a connection

---

ἐλπίζοντες πάγχυ ἀπολέεσθαι, IX 113, 1 ἐλπόμενος τί οἱ κακὸν εἶναι. See also Lachnit, *op. cit.*, 56, 62, 64-6, 76-8.

[313] It has been objected (Quaglia, 77) that Prometheus stops men from fearing death by giving them τυφλαὶ ἐλπίδες (A. *Prom.* 248-50). But I fail to see why one kind of expectation cannot be replaced by another kind.

between goats and storms are futile: the traditional explanation 'moving the aegis' is supported by Hom. Δ 167 σείω and P 595 τινάσσω. On the other hand, B 447 αἰγίδ᾽ ἔχουσα and O 308 ἔχε τ᾽ αἰγίδα suggest a connection with ἔχω: Homer apparently felt free to reinterpret the word. For the authenticity of 99 see preceding note. For the value of the testimonies of Ps. Plutarch, Origen and Stobaeus cf. We. and Krafft, 110 n. 2.

100: ἄλλα. Krafft (111 n. 3) argues that this means 'other things, viz.' (similarly Maz. 'mais, en revanche, des maux', Marg, We.), because the alternative would be 'another ten thousand', which is impossible in this context. But Homer frequently (e.g. A 22) uses ἄλλοι without article for 'the others', so that we should translate 'the other evils in infinite numbers'. This disposes of the objection raised by Neitzel (*Pandora*, 397-8), that in the traditional interpretation the text should run ἄλλα δὲ πάντα τὰ λύγρα. Neitzel further argues (396-8) that ἄλλα contrasts with κήδεα, not with ἐλπίς (see above, on 95 ἐσκέδασε). But (1) in that case we have to assume an exceptionally long parenthesis (96-9), and (2) there is an obvious contrast between ἔμεινε ... οὐδὲ θύραζε ἐξέπτη and κατ᾽ ἀνθρώπους ἀλάληται. Neitzel objects (1) that "wenn im Epos μοῦνος und ἄλλος in eine Antithese eintreten, dann immer in der Weise, dass der ἄλλος-Begriff vorangeht und die Form von μοῦνος (οἶος) folgt", and (2) that "Vorräte fliegen nicht, gleichgültig ob sie aus Korn oder aus Übeln bestehen". But (1) the idea of ἄλλα is implied in ἐσκέδασε (τὰ κακά) and is resumed, not introduced, at 100, and (2) in Babrius' fable 58 the goods escaped from a jar sent by Zeus fly back to heaven.

100: ἀλάληται. For the personification see above, on 92 κῆρας. Fränkel (130) points out that in Hom. Ω 527-31 Zeus takes special evils from the store jar and sends them to special people, whereas he now makes Pandora release all evils together and lets them go their own ways.

101: πλείη. The anaphora (see above, on 6 ῥεῖα) has pathetic force. Similarly 267 πάντα.

101: γαῖα ... θάλασσα. A polar expression for 'the whole world': cf. Hom. Ω 341-2 μιν φέρον ἠμὲν ἐφ᾽ ὑγρὴν / ἠδ᾽ ἐπ᾽ ἀπείρονα γαῖαν, κ 458-9, Fehling, 274-5.

102: νοῦσοι δέ. For the specifying force of δέ see above, on 9. Consequently, what is said of the diseases implicitly applies to the other κακά[314].

102: ἐφ᾽ ἡμέρῃ. Cf. Hom. Θ 529 ἐπὶ νυκτί, and above, on 43 ἔπ᾽ ἤματι. It has been argued that ἐφήμεροι (Ps. Plut.) is to be preferred as a *lectio difficilior*[315], but 'during the day' is ἐφημέριος (e.g. Pind. *N*. 6, 6 ἐφαμερίαν οὐκ εἰδότες οὐδὲ μετὰ νύκτας), not ἐφήμερος ('daily').

---

[314] As is rightly observed by Fränkel, *W.u.F.*, 333 n. 3. Cf. also Krause, Ἄλλοτε ἄλλος (above, on 5 χαλέπτει), 69-70.
[315] Forssman (above, n. 140), 13.

102: αἶ δέ. The pronoun is not "redundant" (Si.), for αἶ μέν has to be mentally supplied: cf. Hom. Χ 157 παραδραμέτην, φεύγων, ὁ δ᾽ ὄπισθε διώκων, K.G. II, 265-6, Gildersleeve, *Syntax*, 219-20, Denn., 166.

102: ἐπί. For the repeated preposition cf. above, on 91 ἄτερ.

102: νυκτί. The disjunction means 'at any time': similarly Hom. Ε 490, β 345, Thgn. 160, Pind. *N.* 6, 6, Ε. *Ba.* 187, Pl. *Tim.* 71 a 6, etc. See also above, on 101 γαῖα ... θάλασσα. The order 'day-night' (similarly 176-7) is a more recent conception than 'night-day': cf. *Th.* 124, and S. Accame, RFIC 89 (1961), 370.

103: αὐτόματοι. We. reads αὐτόμαται, which he thinks to be supported by 118 αὐτομάτη. The variation may be accepted, however, just as ἀθάνατος-ἀθανάτη in Homer (e.g. ε 218). See further Schw. II, 38, Troxler, 107 (who compares Hom. Ε 479 αὐτόμαται).

Wil. concludes from αὐτόματοι: "Er verwirft also jeden Versuch, die Erkrankung auf natürliche Ursachen zurückzuführen"[316]. But αὐτόματος means 'without external agency' (LSJ I 4), and this is not the same as 'without natural cause'[317]. On the other hand, Fränkel (589) speaks of "kräftige Ansätze zu naturwissenschaftlichem Denken" and thinks that from Hes. "leitet eine gerade Linie zur Theorie und Empirie eines Hippokrates" (131). In the next line, however, it is said that Zeus has deprived the diseases of their voice: this suggests that it is he who determines their occurrence, as is also apparent from 242-3. Fränkel (*W.u.F.*, 332) admits: "Gewiss hat auch Hesiod geglaubt, dass Gott auf den Lauf der Dinge einwirken kann und dass er es tut", but he immediately adds: "Aber er sieht nicht mehr hinter jedem eingreifenden Ereignis Gottes besondere Fügung". We have seen, however, that in Hes.'s view everything is determined by Zeus (above, on 98 ἐπέμβαλε). It might be objected that this would make Zeus the 'external agent', but Hes. obviously takes 'external agency' in the special sense of 'human influence'[318]. We have to conclude that Hes. leaves it undecided whether diseases spring from natural or supernatural causes[319]. He could not make such a decision

---

[316] Similarly Deichgräber, *Trug* (above, n. 84), 149, L. Edelstein, *Ancient Medicine* (Baltimore 1967), 378, Weinreich, *Studien* (above, n. 13), 62, S. Lanata, *Medicina magica e religione popolare in Grecia* (Rome 1967), 30.

[317] For αὐτόματος referring to events beyond the range of human production cf. P. H. Schrijvers, Mnem. IV 30 (1977), 20-1.

[318] R. M. Frazer, GRBS 13 (1972), 235-8, argues that the diseases coming of their own accord are implicitly distinguished from those sent by the gods to punish men (as at 242-7). But whatever the origin of the story (see above, on 94 πίθου), the context clearly shows that Hes. took the contents of the jar to serve as a punishment sent to man by Zeus.

[319] Cf. W. D. Smith, TAPA 97 (1966), 549: "As in the epic the divinities work on and through the natural elements to do what they do, so theurgic medicine addresses itself to the same phenomena of disease, similarly understood, as rational medicine, but enlists extraordinary powers". See also F. Kudlien, RhM 108 (1965), 293-300, and *id.*, *Der Beginn des medizinischen Denkens bei den Griechen von Homer bis Hippokrates* (Zürich 1967), espec. 151.

because the distinction between the natural and the supernatural was unknown at his time. A seeming exception is Hom. ι 411, where the frenzy of Polyphemus is called νοῦσος Διός by his fellow-Cyclopes. Stanford *ad loc.* remarks: "Actually the pious reference is out of character": he refers to ι 275 οὐ γὰρ Κύκλωπες Διὸς αἰγιόχου ἀλέγουσιν, but this phrase does not imply that they were atheists. On the other hand, the expression νοῦσος Διός does not imply that all other diseases were regarded as purely natural phenomena (cf. ε 395-6 ἐν νούσῳ κεῖται ... / ... στυγερὸς δέ οἱ ἔχραε δαίμων). It means that madness was regarded as pre-eminently divine, probably because it bears some resemblance to ecstasy. The term ἱερὰ νόσος, which came into use afterwards, has the same meaning: it does not imply that all other diseases are not 'sacred', but only that this disease is more 'sacred' than the others, as appears from the conclusion of the Hippocratic treatise Περὶ ἱερῆς νούσου[320].

103: φοιτῶσι. 'Come repeatedly' (LSJ II): cf. A. *Prom.* 598 κέντροισι φοιταλέοισιν, S. *Trach.* 980-1 φοιτάδα δεινὴν / νόσον, *Phil.* 807-8 ἥδε (*scil.* ἡ νόσος) μοι / ὀξεῖα φοιτᾷ.

104: σιγῇ. The dative has modal force, but properly denotes attending circumstances (*comitativus*): cf. Hom. Δ 412 σιωπῇ ἧσο, Γ 2 κλαγγῇ τ᾽ ἐνοπῇ τ᾽ ἴσαν, K.G. I, 435, Schw. II, 162, Chantr. II, 75. The meaning obviously is 'secretly' (LSJ II 2), not 'Und wenn der Mensch in seiner Qual verstummt', as is assumed by F. Dornseiff, in Heitsch, 131. For the difference between σιγάω ('be silent') and σιωπάω ('keep something quiet') cf. T. Krischer, Glotta 59 (1981), 93-107.

104: φωνήν. Cf. above, on 79 φωνήν.

104: ἐξείλετο. This does not imply that originally they did have φωνή, as is assumed by Krafft, 111 n. 4.

105: οὕτως. Introduces the moral of the story: cf. Hom. θ 167 οὕτως οὐ πάντεσσι θεοὶ χαρίεντα διδοῦσιν, Semon. 1, 20 οὕτω κακῶν ἄπ᾽ οὐδέν, Thgn. 788 οὕτως οὐδὲν ἄρ᾽ ἦν φίλτερον ἄλλο πάτρης. Hes. repeats the conclusion drawn at *Th.* 613, but it is misleading to say that "its reference is now less precise" (We.): we have already seen (above, on 95 κήδεα λυγρά) that in the course of the story Hes.'s interest shifts from the problem of labour to the problem of divine retribution. Similarly a Homeric simile may result in something different from its starting-point (e.g. M 145-59, O 618-29)[321].

---

[320] See further W. Nestle, *Griechische Studien* (Stuttgart 1948), 517 ff., G. Vlastos, Rev. of Rel. 13 (1949), 282 ff., H. W. Miller, TAPA 84 (1953), 1-15, W. D. Smith, TAPA 96 (1965), 403-26. The idea of the supernatural in a strict sense seems to have its origin in Hebrew thought: cf. R. M. Grant, *Miracle and Natural Law in Graeco-Roman and Early Christian Thought* (Amsterdam 1952). The study of Lanata (above, n. 316) is vitiated by a loose usage of the term 'magic'.

[321] See further H. Fränkel, *Die homerischen Gleichnisse* (Göttingen 1921), 6 ff., and my remarks in REG 73 (1960), 345 ff. Quaglia (81) tries to harmonize the two points of view by

105: τί πη. Stresses οὐ: cf. Hom. φ 219 οὐδέ τί πη δύναμαι. It depends on the context whether the indefinite force has a weakening or a strengthening effect: cf. K.G. I, 663-4, Schw. II, 215, LSJ τις A II 8 (who, under 14, are wrong in calling τι in such phrases as οὐδέν τι "pleonastic"). See also below, on 113 τι. The original meaning of πη seems to be 'über irgendeine Strecke hin' (Schw. II, 579). We. reads πη, which is the common form in Homer (cf. Schw. I, 550).

105: νόον. 'Purposeful intelligence' (We. on *Th.* 613, who compares Hom. Π 688 ἀλλ᾽ αἰεί τε Διὸς κρείσσων νόος ἠέ περ ἀνδρῶν). See further K. von Fritz, CP 38 (1943), 86, F. Zucker, *Verbundenheit von Erkenntnis und Wille im griechischen Sprachbewusstsein*, in *Semantica, rhetorica, ethica* (Berlin 1963), 48 ff.

105: ἐξαλέασθαι. For ἐξαλεύασθαι: cf. ἔχεα = ἔχευα, and Chantr. I, 159.

106: εἰ δ᾽ ἐθέλεις. This does not imply that ἕτερον refers to an alternative solution[322]. The phrase does not suggest a choice, but "is simply an appeal to the listener, calling attention to a new theme" (Si.). Similarly Hom. Y 213.

106: ἕτερον. Much speculation has been devoted to the connection between this story and the preceding section. The simplest solution is to deny any connection, as is done by We.: "Hesiod knows another story about man's passage from an original paradise-state to his present misery, and he determines to put this too into his poem"[323]. But Hes. is not a simple story-teller: the present addition must have a special purpose. We. observes that Hes. "does not attempt to reconcile it with the Prometheus-Pandora myth, with which it is in fact incompatible". It is true that Prometheus and Pandora cannot be chronologically fitted into the scheme of the five 'races' (see below, on 113 πόνων). It is equally true that "das Weib als Bringerin der Übel ist mit dieser allmählichen Entartung der Menschheit unvereinbar" (Wil.). But Hes.'s point of view is not a purely historical one: he tries to explain the origin of evil, not its development[324]. His present explanation has a supplementary function: the poet is going to show that divine punishment is caused not only by the individual behaviour of Prometheus but also by the general behaviour of men. The two causes are not clearly coordinated because (1) Hes. does not

---

concluding that "l'uomo giusto che sceglie il lavoro supera in realtà la condizione di chi non può sfuggire al νόος di Zeus, perché intelligentemente si adegua a questo νόος e si comporta secondo gli intendimenti di Zeus". But the Greek text says only that one cannot escape the intention of Zeus, not that complying with it means a kind of moral victory.

[322] As is assumed by W. Kraus, RE XIV (1957), 663. Schm. (274) even maintains that the poet offers two stories, "zwischen denen er mit einer gewissen Selbstironie (106 f.) die Wahl lässt".

[323] Similarly J. Fontenrose, CP 69 (1974), 5, thinks that Hes. introduces the story "as an alternative to the Prometheus and Pandora tales".

[324] Cf. Kühn, 272, Solmsen, *Hes.*, 89-90, Lenz, 237. On the other hand, Fontenrose (*loc. cit.*, 15) is wrong in calling the myth "a paradigm ... a synchronic scheme presented as history".

draw a sharp distinction between divine and human responsibility (see above, on 16 ἀθανάτων), and (2) the supplementary character of the story serves a practical rather than a historiographical purpose[325]: the story of Prometheus forms the introduction to the protreptic part of the poem (the exhortation to work), the story of the world-periods introduces the apotreptic part (the admonition to avoid wrongdoing)[326]. For this reason the last part of the myth, the description of the iron race, is painted in very strong colours[327].

106: λόγον. We. writes: "Hesiod presents the story not as an absolute truth but as something that people tell, worth serious attention". But all the things to which Hes. calls his brother's attention are truths (10 ἐτήτυμα)[328].

106: ἐκκορυφώσω. We. rightly explains, "the head of a story is what completes it", but wrongly translates 'state summarily' (similarly Pal., LSJ,

---

[325] Cf. C. J. Rowe, JHS 103 (1983), 132-4, who concludes that "in the end the business of explanation, in the sense of looking for causes, matters rather less to him than reflection of a different sort, and especially of a moralising sort". It should be added, however, that the moral is based on a causal analysis. See also next note.

[326] Similarly Solmsen, Gnom. 52 (1980), 214. Cf. also Kühn, 268 ff., who forces the parallelism, however, by assuming an analogy between the advice given by Prometheus to Epimetheus (85-8) and that given by Hes. to Perses (286 ff.).

Mazon (I), 68-70, proposes another reconstruction of the argument: man has to work — work is based on good Eris — bad Eris is destructive, as is shown by the history of the world.But (1) at the end of the story of Prometheus the idea of work falls into the background; (2) Hes. does not resume the connection between work and Eris; (3) Eris does not form the centre of the story of the five 'races': only at the end (195) ζῆλος appears, and Mazon (61) is forced to assume that "c'est dans les derniers vers du récit qu'il faut chercher l'intention du poète". Fontenrose (above, n. 323), 12, argues that the central thesis of the poem is that "injustice arises from trying to win livelihood and wealth without working for them" (cf. 14: "justice, of which work is the foundation"). This applies to Perses, but not to mankind in general: the primary cause of its destruction is injustice in the sense of failure of social cooperation, as appears from 134-5 and 182 ff. See further below, on 320, 342, and n.414. B. Peabody, *The Winged Word* (Albany 1975), 248, thinks that "106-108 relate, not to the close of the Pandora Myth, but to the Ἔρις associations of the Strife Passage". He refers to the fact that at Hom. Δ 442 κορύσσεται is said of Eris, but such 'parallels' (he even compares 108 ὁμόθεν with Δ 444 νεῖκος ὁμοίιον!) obviously do not have any value.

Jaeger (*Paideia*, I, 101-2) writes: "Die Geschichte von dem goldnen Weltalter und den folgenden sich immer mehr verschlimmernden Zeiten soll zeigen, dass die Menschen es wirklich ursprünglich besser hatten als jetzt und ohne Mühsal und Leiden lebten" (similarly Latt.: "the same thing may be said in a different way"). But the fact that formerly life was easier than nowadays is not the kernel of the story. T. G. Rosenmeyer (in Heitsch, 615-6) argues that Hes.'s aim is aetiological, but that "the bulk of the tale does not really fit this design", and that the result is rather historiographical. My comments will try to show that the details of the story have a symbolical rather than a purely historical meaning.

[327] Its apotreptic purpose is overlooked by We. when he writes (p. 49): "The reason why the myth goes in this direction is probably that this was the form in which Hesiod heard it. He ought to have tailored it to suit the argument he began in 42".

[328] Th. Horovitz, *Vom Logos zur Analogie* (Zürich 1978), 68, tries to deduce the intended truth of the story from the fact that this is the earliest example of λόγος used in the singular, but she forgets (1) that a single story does not always have "geschlossene Einheit", and (2) that even such unity does not guarantee truth. The truthful character of the story cannot be deduced from the meaning of λόγος either, as is suggested by Gatz (below, n. 341), 34, who writes: "der Dichter stellt eine Rechnung auf".

Latt., *Aufbau*, 163, Col., Marg, T. G. Rosenmeyer, in Heitsch, 621-2[329]). It is true that κορυφαί may be the main points of a story (e.g. Pind. *O*. 7, 68), but in Hippocr. *Morb*. IV 48 (579 L.) οὕτω δέ μοι ὁ λόγος οὗτος πᾶς ἐκκεκορύφωται the addition of πᾶς shows that the meaning is 'to bring to a conclusion', 'to tell from beginning to end'. So Tzetz. εἰς κορυφὴν αὐτὸν καὶ τέλος ἀγαγών. Cf. also A. *Cho*. 528 ποῖ τελευτᾷ καὶ καρανοῦται λόγος; Pl. *Gorg*. 505 d 2 ἀπόκριναι οὖν καὶ τὰ λοιπά, ἵνα ἡμῖν ὁ λόγος κεφαλὴν ἔχει, *Tim*. 69 b 1 τελευτὴν ἤδη κεφαλήν τε τῷ μύθῳ πειρώμεθα ἁρμόττουσαν ἐπιθεῖναι τοῖς πρόσθεν, Hsch. κορυφῶσαι· ἐκτελέσαι. The 'top' in this case denotes the end (conceived as the consummation[330]), not the culminating-point[331]. For ἐκ 'thoroughly' cf. above, on 48 ἐξαπάτησε.

107: εὖ καὶ ἐπισταμένως. Not 'pour obéir à la fois à la logique et aux règles de l'art' (Maz.; similarly Marg), but εὖ is 'competently' (cf. LSJ I 1; similarly 295), and καί has explanatory (specifying) force: see above, on 91 καί. Similarly Hom. υ 161 εὖ καὶ ἐπισταμένως κέασαν ξύλα. For ἐπισταμένως referring to the professional skill of the poet cf. Hom. λ 368 μῦθον δ' ὡς ὅτ' ἀοιδὸς ἐπισταμένως κατέλεξας[332]. For Hes.'s self-confidence cf. above, on 10 ἐγώ.

107: ἐνὶ φρεσὶ βάλλεο. Not 'bewege hin und her, erwäge' (Ameis-Hentze on Hom. A 297), for this is μετὰ φρεσὶ βάλλεο (see below, on 274), but 'take to heart'. For the dative emphasizing the state of rest resulting from a movement cf. Hom. A 585 ἐν χειρὶ τίθει, E 75 ἤριπε δ' ἐν κονίῃ, K.G. I, 541-2, LSJ II 6. For βάλλω 'to put' cf. LSJ II 6.

108: ὥς. To be connected with λόγον: the phrase σὺ ... σῇσιν is a parenthesis (see above, on 24 ἀγαθὴ ... βροτοῖσιν). Cf. also Quaglia, 126 ff., who compares Hom. μ 217-8 σοὶ δέ, κυβερνῆθ', ὧδ' ἐπιτέλλομαι· ἀλλ' ἐνὶ θυμῷ / βάλλευ, ἐπεὶ νηὸς γλαφυρῆς οἰήια νωμᾷς, but wrongly concludes that 108 is spurious (see below).

108: ὁμόθεν. Cf. Hom. ε 476-7 θάμνους / ἐξ ὁμόθεν πεφυῶτας, *H. Ven*. 135

---

[329] Whose conclusion, that the story of the five races, in contradistinction to that of Prometheus and Pandora, is 'history', is rightly criticized by Rowe (above, n. 325), 132-3.

[330] As is rightly pointed out by Diller, in Heitsch, 260. He compares "die Addition einer von unten nach oben geschriebenen Zahlenreihe", but does not give parallels for such a method of addition. Dem. 19, 18 has ἀναριθμέομαι, but καταριθμέομαι and καταλέγειν are more common. We find κεφαλή in the sense of 'sum', 'total' (LSJ IV 3), but this need not refer to a way of reckoning. See also Quaglia, 86-7 n. 2.

[331] As is assumed by Wil., Kerschensteiner, 166, Kühn, 268, Krafft, 113 and n. 5. Maz.'s translation, 'je couronnerai mon récit par un autre', is impossible. E. Vandvik, SO 24 (1945), 156 n. 1, 'bring the tale down from its high peak of wisdom', is equally wrong, and Gatz (below, n. 341), 35, 'Ich werde eine Rechnung ausgipfeln, d.h. Punkt für Punkt abwärtsschreitend aufstellen', is quite absurd.

[332] See further my remarks in Mnem. IV 36 (1983), 20-1. For ἐπίσταμαι 'to know how' cf. LSJ I 1, B. Snell, *Die Ausdrücke für den Begriff des Wissens in der vorplatonischen Philosophie* (Berlin 1924), 81 ff., id., *Der Weg zum Denken und zur Wahrheit* (Göttingen 1978), 40-1, and J. Gould, *The Development of Plato's Ethics* (Cambridge 1955), 7 ff.

σοῖς τε κασιγνήτοις οἵ τοι ὁμόθεν γεγάασιν. These parallels show that the word cannot be translated by 'aus denselben Lebensumständen' (Krafft, 114)[333]. The gods have originated from Earth (*Th.* 126 ff.) and the first men were created by the gods from earth (Pl. *Prot.* 320 d 2). Cf. also 563 γῆ πάντων μήτηρ and Pind. *N.* 6, 1-2 ἓν ἀνδρῶν, ἓν θεῶν γένος· ἐκ μιᾶς δὲ πνέομεν / ματρὸς ἀμφότεροι[334]. This seems to me a more natural explanation than the one proposed by Renehan (347), who refers to *H. Ap.* 335-6 Τιτῆνές τε θεοὶ ... / ... τῶν ἒξ ἄνδρες τε θεοί τε.

The authenticity of 108 has been suspected by Maz. and others, because (a) the idea of a common origin of gods and men is inconsistent with the fact that the first men are created by the gods (110), and (b) the common origin of gods and men is not the subject of the story as told at 109 ff. Maz. thinks that the line is an interpolation originally intended to explain 112. But the fact that the first men lived like gods is not very clearly explained by referring to a common origin. Si., who apparently takes σὺ ... ἄνθρωποι as a kind of parenthesis, suggests that Hes. wanted to emphasize the fact that his story of the creation of successive 'races' of men was not inconsistent with the traditional belief in the common origin of gods and men. But such a remark is out of place before the story has been told[335]. All difficulties disappear if the line is taken, not as a title[336] or a programme of the story, but as an introduction to the story. This introduction puts the degeneration of the human race in a special perspective, viz. in the perspective of a growing estrangement of men from the gods: they had the same origin as the gods[337],

---

[333] Similarly van Groningen, 288 n. 3 ('une condition égale, la félicité'), H. Diller, in Heitsch, 260, F. Solmsen, in Entret. s. l'ant. class. 7 (1962), 163. The translation proposed by Peabody (above, n. 326), 249, 'how men as well as gods differentiated (into dissimilarity and conflict)', is characteristic of his arbitrary handling of the text.

[334] See further A. Dieterich, *Mutter Erde* (²Berlin 1913), 36 ff., Nilsson, 458-61, S. Strebel, *Autochthonen. Die Vorstellungen der Griechen von der Herkunft der Menschen aus der Erde* (Ph. D. diss. Tübingen 1962). P. Walcot, REG 74 (1961), 6-7, wrongly thinks θεοί (108) to be identical with δαίμονες (122) and μάκαρες (141), and ὁμόθεν to refer to Zeus.

[335] The argument adduced by me in *Aufbau*, 128, that the phrase σὺ δ' ἐνὶ φρεσὶ βάλλεο σῇσιν always points back, is not correct: cf. Hom. A 297, λ 454. Wil. thinks that Hes. intended to draw a parallel between the succession of the races of men and that of the races of gods: "Er hätte nicht ὁμόθεν sagen sollen, sondern ὁμοίως ... Im Hinblick auf die Θεογονία hat er gesagt 'ihr Ursprung ist derselbe'". Apart from the fact that such a contamination would make the poet a muddle-head, it should be noted that the parallelism assumed by Wil. applies to the golden race only. We. maintains that the common origin of gods and men "is not relevant to the myth of Ages", but his explanation, "Hesiod means here that they started on the same terms", is far from clear.

[336] Cf. Marg *ad loc.*: "Die die Geschichte zusammenfassende Überschrift ist merkwürdig".

[337] The inconsistency assumed by Maz. does not exist: Sinclair, Gnom. 5 (1929), 627, rightly observes that "ὁμόθεν does not imply contemporaneous origin, only that the ultimate source of all life divine or human is one". It is surprising to see that E. des Places, *Syngeneia. La parenté de l'homme avec Dieu d'Homère à la patristique* (Paris 1964), 22, contents himself with the remark that 108 is suspect. Broccia, *Tradizione* (above, n. 8), 68, observes that the formula σὺ δ' ἐνὶ

originally men and gods lived together (*Th*. 535, 586, fr. 1, 6-7)[338], the men of the golden age lived like gods (112), but those of the silver age turned away from the gods (135-9), and this separation increased till finally the last gods living among men, Aidos and Nemesis, fled away from the earth (197-200)[339].

109: χρύσεον. It has been argued that the association of the first race with gold was invented by Hes.[340], but such parallels as the dreams of Nebukadnezar (Dan. II 31-40) and Zoroaster (cf. We., 174-5) point to a Near Eastern origin, although the particular character of Hes.'s models cannot be determined[341]. Another problem is the question whether 'golden' is to be taken in a literal sense. We. argues that "144 f. and 176 show that Hesiod does not conceive the metals as the physical substance of the races. They are more symbolic". The symbolic connotation of incorruptibility (both in a moral and in a physical sense) is no doubt intended, but this does not imply that the meaning is exclusively symbolic. It should be borne in mind that in

---

φρεσὶ βάλλεο σῇσιν always refers to a preceding utterance, but wrongly concludes that 106-7 must be "un vero e proprio circuito chiuso" (70).

[338] Hom. α 22-5 and η 201-6 are reminiscences of this stage. Cf. also Gen. 3, 8 and Cic. *Leg.* II 11, 27 *antiquitas proxime accedit ad deos*.

[339] This analysis shows that Wil. (141) is wrong in calling the story of the five races "eine Abschweifung, die erst zuletzt zu dem hinführt, worauf es ihm ankommt, zu der Schilderung der sittlichen Zerfahrenheit seiner Gegenwart".

[340] H. C. Baldry, CQ N.S. 2 (1952), 83-92. Similarly Nilsson, 622 n. 1.

[341] Cf. T. G. Rosenmeyer, in Heitsch, 627: "no good purpose is served by trying to discover what sort of a scheme Hesiod may have found ready-made, and what he added of his own accord ... the problem is the same as that of the Homeric question". See also J. Kerschensteiner, *Platon und der Orient* (Stuttgart 1945), 164 ff., and Walcot, *Near East*, 85-6: "as yet we have no really convincing analogy ... The Near East does not help us at the moment with the myth of the ages". Similarly Quaglia, 118.

For the general problem of Eastern influence on Hes. cf. J. G. Griffiths, JHI 17 (1956), 109-19, H. Erbse, Philol. 108 (1964), 2-28, B. C. Dietrich, Acta Class. 8 (1965), 17 ff., A. Lesky's review of Walcot, *Near East*, Gnom. 40 (1968), 225-30, We., 3 ff.

To the bibliography of the story of the five races given by We. (177) may be added A. Heubeck, in Heitsch, 545 ff., espec. 547-9, U. Bianchi, Stud. Mat. Stor. Rel. 39 (1963), 143-210, Dietrich, *Death* (above, n. 281), 352-7, G. S. Kirk, Eranos Jb. 40 (1971), 135 ff., K. E. Müller, *Geschichte der antiken Ethnographie* (Wiesbaden 1972), 60-4, J. P. Vernant, *Mythe et pensée chez les Grecs* (²Paris 1974), 13 ff., K. Matthiessen, Philol. 121 (1977), 177 ff. and in *Arktouros: Studies ... B. M. W. Knox* (Berlin 1979), 25-32 (criticism of Vernant's view), H. Schwabl, *Weltalter*, RE Suppl. XV (1978), 784-95, P. Smith, CW 74 (1980), 145-63 (whose interpretation of the myth as "a symbolic expression of personal growth" is unconvincing: the Golden Age, e.g., can hardly be "an unconscious memory of infancy and early childhood", nor the Iron Age a representation of "embittered maturity"), Rudhardt, 245 ff., M. Erren, in *Gnomosyne: Festschrift W. Marg* (Munich 1981), 159-66.

For the Golden Age in ancient thought cf. Guthrie, *In the Beginning* (above, n. 213), Ch. IV, B. Gatz, *Weltalter, goldene Zeit und sinnverwandte Vorstellungen* (Hildesheim 1967), 18 ff. (whose structural analysis of Hes.'s myth seems to me over-subtle and artificial), Schwabl, *Weltalter*, 784 ff., P. A. Johnston, *Vergil's Agricultural Golden Age* (Leiden 1979), 15 ff., W. Burkert, in D. Hellholm (ed.), *Apocalypticism in the Mediterranean World and the Near East* (Tübingen 1983), 244-6. See also Hasting's *Encycl.*, I, 183-210: 'Ages of the World'.

archaic thought metals were not conceived as purely physical substances, but at the same time as 'powers' resembling those of living beings. This appears from such phrases as Hom. B 490 χάλκεον ἦτορ and X 357 σιδήρεος θυμός, and from the fact that weapons have μένος and behave themselves as living beings: see further my remarks in Lampas 2 (1969), 97-9 and Janus 64 (1977), 25 ff.

109: γένος. 'Race' in the sense of collection of similar beings: cf. Hom. M 23 ἡμιθέων γένος ἀνδρῶν, B 852 ἡμιόνων γένος, LSJ III 1 a.

109: μερόπων. 'Mortal' seems to be the most obvious translation, although 'looking at death' can hardly have been the original meaning[342]. The contrast gods — μέροπες is also found at A. *Suppl.* 86-90. For the choice of μερόπων instead of θνητῶν (123, 253) cf. Edwards, 66.

110: ἀθάνατοι. It does not follow from 111 that they are the Titans[343], for (1) they are equivalent to Fate (see above, on 16 ἀθανάτων), and (2) 122 Διός shows that Hes. does not strictly observe chronological distinctions.

111. Solmsen, HSCP 86 (1982), 23, thinks that this line "interferes badly with the impression produced by the preceding line. For the ἀθάνατοι ... Ὀλύμπια δώματ' ἔχοντες (v. 110) who create this generation are those regularly so designated, and the god who decides about the fate after death of this generation is Zeus (v. 122)". But the ἀθάνατοι are virtually identical with Fate, and Zeus is the personification of the moral order of the world (see above, on 16 ἀθανάτων βουλῆσιν) without regard to strict chronology (see below, on 122 Διός).

111: οἵ. Does not refer to ἀθάνατοι (as is assumed by Nilsson, 516, and K. von Fritz, in Heitsch, 387) but to ἀνθρώπων.

111: μέν. Emphasizes οἵ: cf. K.G. II, 140, who call this use 'confirmative', Denn., 360-1. For μέν as a weak form of μήν cf. Schw. II, 570, M. Leumann, MH 6 (1949), 85 ff. = *Kleine Schriften* (Zürich 1959), 229 ff., Ruijgh, 198. I do not believe that in such cases (cf. 122, 137, 141, 152, 161, 170) μέν is used "in telling what happened to someone ... before passing on to a different subject" (We. on *Th.* 289; similarly C. J. Ruijgh, Mnem. IV 34, 1981, 286-7).

111: ἐπί. 'At the time of': cf. Hom. E 637 ἐπὶ προτέρων ἀνθρώπων, LSJ A II, K.G. I, 496-7, Schw. II, 471.

111: Κρόνου. Although Hes. does not say that Kronos caused the prosperity on earth, he may have thought of his well-known function as a harvest

---

[342] As is assumed by M. Runes, IF 52 (1934), 216. See further H. Koller, Glotta 46 (1968), 18 ff., Chantr., *Dict. étym.*, 687, V. Pisani, Acme 29 (1976), 5-7.

[343] As is assumed by Gatz (above, n. 341), 41, Rudhardt, 263, Fontenrose (above, n. 323), 5-7. Rudhardt (264) suggests that "du temps s'écoule entre le moment où cette race disparaît et celui où Zeus attribue un statut nouveau à ceux qui en furent les représentants", but this is an extremely artificial assumption.

god: cf. Nilsson, 512-3 (who at 516, however, suggests that the idea of a golden age derives from Hes.), W. Fauth, KP III, 356-7, We. on *Th.* 137[344].

112: ὥς τε. So. and We. read ὥστε, but cf. Hom. P 133 ὥς τίς τε λέων and ὡς εἴ τε. See further Ruijgh, 894.

112: δέ. For the postponement cf. above, on 46.

112: ἀκηδέα. Once used by Homer (Ω 526) in the sense of 'without cares' and said of the gods. The word marks the contrast between the original state of the human race and its present state, which is determined by κήδεα λυγρά (49).

113: νόσφιν ἄτερ τε. See above, on 91. The similarity of the two passages supports the explanation of the position of τε proposed by Denn., 518-9: ἄτερ has to be mentally supplied after καί. For parallels in Homer (e.g. A 417 ἅμα τ' ὠκύμορος καὶ ὀιζυρός) cf. Ruijgh, 830-1.

113: πόνων. We. thinks that πόνου is supported by the Homeric formula πόνος(ν) ... καὶ ὀιζύς(ν) and that πόνων is due to the influence of κακῶν at 91. But the singular is more likely to be an assimilation to ὀιζύος and to πόνοιο (91). Krafft (112 n. 4) rightly remarks: "Mit dieser Wiederholung soll nicht gezeigt werden, dass 'die Zeit vor Pandoras Fassöffnung ... eben die des Goldenen Zeitalters' ist (Ed. Meyer), sondern nur, dass es früher den Menschen besser ging. Die beiden Geschichten entsprechen sich nicht in ihrer zeitlichen Abfolge, es werden nur Zustände verglichen"[345]. For the meaning of πόνων see above, on 91 πόνοιο.

113: τι. According to We., this is "hardly more than a metrical stopgap", but see above, on 105 τί πη. For οὐδέ τι 'and not at all' cf. Hom. A 343, β 283. Similarly οὔτε τι (A 115, E 879) and οὔ νύ τι (H 352)[346].

113: δειλόν. Cf. *Th.* 224-5 Νὺξ ὀλοή ... τέκε ... / Γῆρας τ' οὐλόμενον. The misery of old age is often emphasized: it is specified as (1) loss of physical vigour (here and Hom. Θ 103, Ψ 623, Mimn. 1, 5-10), (2) loss of social position and honour (Ω 487-9, λ 496-503), or (3) lack of domestic care (331, 705, *Th.* 604-5, Hom. E 153-4, ω 249-50, Thgn. 271-8)[347].

114: ἐπῆν. 'Was present': cf. LSJ I 2 (who wrongly mention this passage under II: 'of Time, to be hereafter'). The word is usually translated by 'rest

---

[344] The explanation put forward by K. von Fritz, in Heitsch, 394, that Kronos is the ruler of the Golden Age because of his intelligence, is unconvincing. See also Quaglia, 95 n. 28, Solmsen, HSCP 86 (1982), 23 n. 75.

[345] Similarly, Fontenrose (above, n. 323), 2, points out that "there is no way of fitting the Prometheus and Pandora tales into the myth of the ages".

[346] We. changes νύ τι at 756 into νύ τε, because he wrongly thinks that νύ τι "makes the god's disapproval oddly half-hearted".

[347] See further W. Schadewaldt, Ant. 9 (1933), 290 ff. = *Hellas und Hesperien*, I (Zürich-Stuttgart 1970), 109-26, Schütz, Ἀσθένεια (above, n. 217), 66 ff., H. Herter, Würzb. Jbb. 1 (1975), 83 ff., Preisshofen, *Greisenalter* (above, n. 286), espec. 42-7, M. I. Finley, G & R 28 (1981), 156-71, M. Schmidt, γῆρας, *Lex.* II, 144-6.

on', 'press upon', but this does not suit the context of Hom. ν 59-60 εἰς ὅ κε γῆρας / ἔλθῃ καὶ θάνατος, τά τ' ἐπ' ἀνθρώποισι πέλονται, where the tone is perfunctory ('things that are inevitable') and not emotional[348].

114: αἰεί. Goes with τέρπονται (secundarily) and with ὁμοῖοι (primarily): cf. Pl. *Symp.* 173 d 4 ἀεὶ ὅμοιος εἶ, ὦ Ἀπολλόδωρε[349].

114: πόδας καὶ χεῖρας. In which old age is most strongly felt: cf. Hom. Ψ 627-8 οὐ γὰρ ἔτ' ἔμπεδα γυῖα, φίλος, πόδες, οὐδ' ἔτι χεῖρες / ὤμων ἀμφοτέρωθεν ἐπαΐσσονται ἐλαφραί, λ 497 οὕνεκά μιν κατὰ γῆρας ἔχει χεῖράς τε πόδας τε, τ 359-60 τοιόσδ' ἐστὶ πόδας τοιόσδε τε χεῖρας· / αἶψα γὰρ ἐν κακότητι βροτοὶ καταγηράσκουσιν. We. writes that in the last passage "it is their appearance that is in question, not strength and speed, and this is also what suits the θαλίαι here". But in order to participate in perpetual festivities strength counts more than outward appearance[350].

115: τέρποντ' ἐν θαλίῃσι. A reminiscence of Hom. λ 602-3 μετ' ἀθανάτοισι θεοῖσιν / τέρπεται ἐν θαλίης. See further below, on 231 θαλίης.

115: ἐν. Cf. Hom. λ 603 τέρπεται ἐν θαλίης, S. *Trach.* 1118 ἐν οἷς χαίρειν προθυμῇ, K.G. I, 465. The meaning is not identical with τέρπομαι with dative, for ἐν still has locative force, just as in λαβεῖν ἐν χερσί (K.G. I, 542).

116: ὕπνῳ. Sleep is a brother of Death (*Th.* 756, Hom. Ξ 231, Π 682). Death during sleep was regarded as the ideal form of death: cf. Hom. σ 201-2, Hdt. I 31, 3-5, Pind. fr. 2-3, A. *Ag.* 1451[351].

116: ἐσθλά. Not in a moral but in a practical sense: 'prosperity' (LSJ II 3), here especially referring to material goods: cf. Hom. κ 523 πυρὴν ἐμπλησέμεν ἐσθλῶν.

116: πάντα. 'Every kind of': cf. Hom. Ε 60 δαίδαλα πάντα, ν 292 ἐν πάντεσσι δόλοισι, and my notes on Semon. 7, 78, Mnem. IV 21 (1968), 149, Pind. *O.* 7, 51, Meded. Kon. Ned. Akad. v. Wet., Lett. N.R. 35:2 (1972), 21, A. *Prom.* 111, *Miscellanea ... Kamerbeek* (Amsterdam 1976), 454.

117: καρπόν. 'Corn' (cf. Hom. Ζ 142 ἀρούρης καρπὸν ἔδουσιν), but possibly also other fruits: cf. Hom. Γ 246 οἶνον εὔφρονα, καρπὸν ἀρούρης, ι 357 φέρει ζείδωρος ἄρουρα οἶνον[352].

117: δέ. Has specifying force: cf. above, on 9.

117: ζείδωρος. Such passages as Hom. ι 357 (quoted above) and ε 463

---

[348] I doubt whether the common translation of ἐπὶ ... πέλονται by 'come upon' is correct: ἐπιπλόμενον ἔτος (η 261; similarly *Th.* 493) has been created for metrical reasons on the analogy of περιπλόμενον and so does not seem to suffice as a parallel for πέλομαι 'to come'.

[349] See further A. W. Mair, *The Poems and Fragments of Hesiod* (Oxford 1908), 103-4, who rightly combats J. Adam's suggestion that the feet and hands resemble each other.

[350] Gatz (above, n. 341), 39-40, creates a good deal of confusion by connecting the present use of ὅμοιος with that at 144 and 182.

[351] For the further tradition of this idea cf. F. Schwenn, *Der junge Pindar* (Berlin 1940), 62 n. 152.

[352] For ἄρουρα see further Hofinger, *Études* (above, n. 104), 29 ff.

κύσε δὲ ζείδωρον ἄρουραν show that the meaning is practically equivalent to 'fertile'.

118: αὐτομάτη. See above, on 103 αὐτόματοι.

118: ἄφθονον. 'Plentiful', properly 'given without grudge' (see above, on 26 φθονέει). We. observes that the word is not found in *Iliad* or *Odyssey*: it should be added that it is prefigured by such phrases as ζ 68 οὔτε τοι ἡμιόνων φθονέω, τέκος, οὔτε τευ ἄλλου. See further B. Mader, *Lex.*, 1708-9.

118: ἐθελημοί. Wrongly explained by Wil.: "dass sie in Ruhe auf dem Lande lebten, war ihnen willkommen". We.'s paraphrase, "casually and unforcedly" is not satisfactory either, and his quotations of θελημός are unhelpful. I prefer the interpretation proposed by Maz. (II), 90: "*contents* ... les hommes de cette race sont *satisfaits* des biens qui leur sont accordés" (similarly, Quaglia, 96, writes: "l'ἐθελημοί rivela la partecipazione gioiosa, l'adeguarsi della loro volontà al cosmo in cui vivono"). He observes that ἐθελημοί contrasts with the ὕβρις of the silver race: cf. Ap. Rh. II 655-7 οὐδέ οἱ ὕβρις / ἤνδανεν, ἀλλ᾽ ἐθελημὸς ἐφ᾽ ὕδασι πατρὸς ἑοῖο / μητέρι συνναί-εσκεν. The transition from 'willing' to 'contented' seems easy if 'willing' is taken in the sense of 'disposed to consent' (German 'willig').

119: ἥσυχοι. Not 'without working' (Wil.) but 'without strife' (Maz.): Guthrie (above, n. 213), 71, rightly observes that "the keynote of the age of Kronos is not wealth and luxury, but a sufficiency of natural food in conjunction with high moral character and a complete absence of wars and dissension". For ἡσυχία as the opposite of ὕβρις and as a synonym of σωφροσύνη cf. Sol. 3 D. = 4 W., 8-10, Pind. *P.* 8, 11, *P.* 11, 55-6, *N.* 9, 48, Epich. 101 Kaib., Pl. *Charm.* 159 b 2-3 [353]. We. writes that "there is a general similarity to *Od.* 11. 184 f. ἀλλὰ ἕκηλος / Τηλέμαχος τεμένεα νέμεται", but it should be added that ἕκηλος means 'left in peace by others', whereas ἥσυχοι means 'keeping quiet'.

119: ἔργα. We. thinks that this term, "with its connotation of tillage, is not altogether apt" [354]. But ἔργα, originally 'products of agriculture', can have the meaning of 'food' without the implication that work was necessary to produce it: cf. Hom. δ 318 ἐσθίεταί μοι οἶκος, ὄλωλε δὲ πίονα ἔργα, where the last words do not refer to rich farms (Ameis-Hentze, Merry-Riddell) but to abundant food: for πίων 'abundant' cf. ι 35 πίονα οἶκον, Τ 179-80 δαιτὶ ... / πιείρῃ.

119: ἐνέμοντο. Not 'they dwelt upon their lands' (Ev.) or 'vollbrachten ihre

---

[353] For ἡσυχία as a political ideal cf. Sol. 4, 5-7 D. = 4c, 1-3 W., Pind. *P.* 1, 70; 8, 1; *O.* 4, 16. See further R. A. Neill, *The Knights of Aristophanes* (Cambridge 1909), 209, G. Vlastos, CP 41 (1946), 68 ff.

[354] Cf. E. Meyer, in Heitsch, 502: "obwohl die Erde alles von selbst gibt, kann Hesiodos sich den Menschen doch nur als Bauern denken"; Marg, 39: "Etwas arbeiten auch die Menschen des goldenen Geschlechts, aber ohne den Druck der Notwendigkeit".

Werke' (Marg; similarly Latt.), but 'dispensed to themselves', hence 'had enjoyment of' (Proclus ἀπέλαυον τῶν γιγνομένων). Cf. Hom. υ 336-7 ὄφρα σὺ μὲν χαίρων πατρῴϊα πάντα νέμηαι / ἔσθων καὶ πίνων, λ 185-6 τεμένεα νέμεται καὶ (explanatory) δαῖτας ἐΐσας / δαίνυται. Similarly Β 751, Μ 313, Υ 185 [355]. See also below, on 231 νέμονται.

119: σὺν ἐσθλοῖσιν πολέεσσιν. Not 'together with many nobles' (Meyer, loc. cit., Fränkel, 132), but 'attended with many goods'. For ἐσθλά see above, on 116. For σύν denoting attendant circumstances or results cf. Hom. Ρ 57 ἄνεμος σὺν λαίλαπι, Thgn. 50 κέρδεα δημοσίῳ σὺν κακῷ, Hdt. VII 9 β, 1 σὺν κακῷ μεγάλῳ οἱ νικῶντες ἀπαλλάσσονται, LSJ A 5-6, and my note on Pind. N. 11, 10, ICS 7, 1 (1982), 21.

120. Quoted only by Diod. Sic. and rightly bracketed by most editors. Th. G. Rosenmeyer (in Heitsch, 644) suggests that the line was condemned by the Alexandrians because the possession of sheep was considered to be a characteristic of the fourth race (163). But Diodorus has another additional line after 113 which is certainly spurious, and his variants (e.g. 118-9 ἐπὶ γαίῃ / εὔφρονες) do not inspire much confidence [356].

120: ἀφνειοί. See above, on 24 ἄφενος.

120: μήλοισι. We. observes that the genitive is more usual. It may be added that μήλοισι is a dative of limitation: cf. K.G. I, 317, 437-8, 440, and my notes on Men. Epitr. 590, Mnem. IV 27 (1974), 39, and Pind. N. 11, 13, ICS 7, 1 (1982), 23.

121: καὶ τοῦτο. Most editors follow Plato (Crat. 397 e) in reading δή, but this is a lectio facilior and, as we shall see, Plato's other variants in 121-3 are to be rejected. For καί pointing forward ('this race as well as the next races') cf. Hom. Ζ 476-7 δότε δὴ καὶ τόνδε γενέσθαι / παῖδ᾽ ἐμόν, ὡς καὶ ἐγώ περ, Xen. Cyr. II 2, 6 οὕτω δὴ καὶ ἐγώ, ὥσπερ καὶ οἱ ἄλλοι ἐποίουν, Denn., 324, Verdenius-Waszink on Arist. GC 320 b 22, and my note on Arist. Cael. 282 a 25, in I. Düring (ed.), Naturphilosophie bei Aristoteles und Theophrast (Heidelberg 1969), 275.

121: γαῖα. Wil. adopts Plato's reading μοῖρα (cf. Hom. Ε 553 τὼ δ᾽ αὖθι τέλος θανάτοιο κάλυψεν, Ε 68 θάνατος δέ μιν ἀμφεκάλυψε, A. Pers. 915-7 εἴθ᾽ ὄφελεν, Ζεῦ, κἀμὲ ... θανάτου κατὰ μοῖρα καλύψαι), but this seems to be an alteration intended to remove the presumed contradiction with 123 ἐπιχθόνιοι [357]. We should not think of a grave-mound as the place where the

---

[355] Cf. also E. Laroche, Histoire de la racine nem- en grec ancien (Paris 1949), 10-1, and B. Jordan, CSCA 3 (1970), 161 ff., who shows that νέμεσθαι at Hdt. III 160, 2, VIII 136, 1, Thuc. I 2, 2, etc. means 'to draw the revenues from', 'to enjoy the profit of'.

[356] Cf. also We. on 111-20, and C. del Grande, Filologia minore (Milan-Naples 1956), 49-52.

[357] As is observed by Rosenmeyer, in Heitsch, 641. I do not believe that "Plato unconsciously replaced the original text by a more philosophic idea", as is suggested by M. van der Valk, Researches on the Text and Scholia of the Iliad, II (Leiden 1964), 292-3.

δαίμονες (122) were worshipped[358], for κατὰ γαῖ᾽ ἐκάλυψε is a mere formula for 'died': cf. e.g. Hom. Z 464[359].

122: μέν. See above, on 111 μέν.

122: δαίμονες. Rohde (I, 99) suggests that originally deified ancestors were called δαίμονες, but there is no evidence for this assumption. Wil. (*Gl.* I, 366) points out that Hes. never calls the gods δαίμονες: "Er hat also damit angefangen, diesen Namen für göttliche Wesen niederen Ranges zu verwenden, während er ihn von den Olympiern fern hält". This does not mean that they were freely invented by Hes.: "Volkstümliche Vorstellungen werden von ihm benutzt sein". But we do not know anything about such popular conceptions. It may be suggested that the idea developed from the Homeric conception of outstanding persons as ἰσόθεοι or ἡμίθεοι (see below, on 160). Such persons were thought to keep their semi-divine character after death, but they could not be called θεοί, which would have given them too high a status. The word δαίμων seemed an appropriate term as this often has a less concrete character than a θεός[360]. After Hesiod, and perhaps under the influence of his work, prominent men such as Darius (A. *Pers.* 620, 641) and Alcestis (E. *Alc.* 1003), and even ordinary men (Emp. B 115, 5), after death could be called δαίμονες. At the same time the δαίμονες came to be regarded as a special class (cf. S. fr. 555, 2 οὔτε δαίμων οὔτε τις θεῶν, E. *Tro.* 55-6, *Med.* 1391) intermediary between gods and men (Pl. *Symp.* 202 e - 3 a)[361].

122: Διός. Although, strictly speaking, he was not yet reigning. Similarly, at *Th.* 465 Hes.'s belief in the universal power of Zeus makes him disregard the chronology of the generations of the gods. The 'immortals' (110) are here replaced by Zeus because the golden race now gets a moral function: see above, on 16 ἀθανάτων βουλῇσιν, and below, on 138 Ζεύς.

Wil. reads δαίμονες ἁγνοὶ ἐπιχθόνιοι (Pl. *Rep.* 469 a 1) καλέονται (Pl. *Crat.* 398 a 1)[362]. But Plato quoted from his memory and he obviously contaminated Hes.'s line with Pind. fr. 133, quoted by him at *Meno* 81 bc, ἐς δὲ τὸν λοιπὸν χρόνον ἥρωες ἁγνοὶ πρὸς ἀνθρώπων καλεῦνται (cf. Pl. *Rep.*

---

[358] As is done by Krafft, 115. Cf. Wil., *Gl.* I, 362: "Der Kultus nennt seine Götter nicht Dämonen, und ein Kult von Dämonen ist verschwindend selten" (cf. E. *Alc.* 995-1005, Pl. *Rep.* 469 ab).

[359] Cf. W. Ferrari, SIFC 16 (1939), 232 n. 1.

[360] Cf. Nilsson, 220: "Der Daimon hat keine echte Individualität, sondern verdankt seine Individualität dem Geschehnis, in dem er sich offenbart ... er ist ein dem gelegentlichen Geschehnis angepasster Teil der supranormalen Kraft". Similarly E. Brunius-Nilsson, Δαιμόνιε (Uppsala 1955), 126, G. François, *Le polythéisme et l'emploi au singulier des mots* θεός, δαίμων (Paris 1957), 331, 334. Cf. also Walcot, *Peasants*, 109-10.

[361] See further W. Kranz, Philol. 102 (1958), 76 ff. = *Studien zur antiken Literatur* (Heidelberg 1967), 324 ff., M. Detienne, *De la pensée religieuse à la pensée philosophique* (Paris 1963), 93 ff., 133 ff., François, *op. cit.*, 338, Dietrich, *Death* (above, n. 281), 14 ff.

[362] Similarly Ferrari (above, n. 359), 234 ff., whose arguments (e.g. that the position of ἐπιχθόνιοι between ἐσθλοί and φύλακες is unnatural) do not carry conviction.

469 a 8 καὶ τὸν λοιπὸν δὴ χρόνον ὡς δαιμόνων θεραπεύσομεν αὐτῶν τὰς θηκάς). The reading τελέθουσιν (*Rep.* 469 a 1) is a Homeric reminiscence (Ι 441, Ψ 589, δ 85, τ 328 at the end of the hexameter) used to complete the line, just as at *The.* 180 e 1 ἀκίνητον τελέθει for Parm. Β 8, 38 ἀκίνητόν τ᾽ ἔμεναι. Plato's carelessness also appears from the fact that at *Rep.* 469 a he reads ἐπιχθόνιοι, at *Crat.* 398 a ὑποχθόνιοι (a reminiscence of 141; cf. also A. *Pers.* 628 χθόνιοι δαίμονες ἀγνοί), at *Crat.* 398 a θνητῶν (123), at *Rep.* 469 a μερόπων (cf. 109, 143). Similar inaccuracies occur in Plato's quotations from Homer, e.g. *Rep.* 424 b 9 ἐπιφρονέουσι for ἐπικλείουσι (α 352)[363]. Wil.'s contention (*Ilias u. Homer*, 7 n. 1) that Plato's quotations from Hes. "enthalten einen sehr viel reineren Text"[364], should be emphatically denied[365].

123: ἐσθλοί. Not 'attivamente volti a volere il bene' (Quaglia, 97) but 'giving profit' (see above, on 116 ἐσθλά), 'favourable'.

123: ἐπιχθόνιοι. Wil. adopts Plato's ἀλεξίκακοι, but this reading is an epic reminiscence (cf. Κ 20, Panyassis 12, 13) prompted by the fact that Plato considered the divine φύλακες to be shepherds (cf. *Polit.* 271 cd, *Leg.* 713 cd[366]). We. rightly quotes Rohde's remark that ἐπιχθόνιοι is contrasted with θεοὶ ἐπουράνιοι, ὑποχθόνιοι (141) being a secondary contrast, but does not give a further explanation. The task of watching human justice is assigned by Homer to the gods themselves, who go round on earth disguised as strangers (ρ 485-7). Hes. could not adopt this conception because in his view of the present age all gods have left the earth (197-200). J. Adam, *The Religious Teachers of Greece* (Edinburgh 1908), 72, rightly called this "the earliest symptom of a tendency that afterwards became prominent in Greek philosophical thought — the tendency to remove the Supreme Being from direct and immediate participation in human affairs, by the hypothesis of an intermediate order of beings who are as it were the vehicles of communication between God and man" (he refers to the δαίμονες at Pl. *Symp.* 202 d - 3 a)[367].

124-5. Although these lines are missing in two papyri[368] and are not given

---

[363] J. Labarbe, *L'Homère de Platon* (Liège 1949), 202-5, tries to defend Plato's reading. But in Plato's context μᾶλλον ἐπιφρονέουσι does not mean 'they understand more easily' but 'they pay more attention to' (and this caused the change of ἀκουόντεσσι into ἀειδόντεσσι). The Homeric use of ἐπίφρων and ἐπιφροσύνη shows that ἐπιφρονέουσα (τ 385) means 'with circumspection', so that ἐπιφρονεῖν ἀοιδήν could not mean 'to pay attention to a song out of interest'. Labarbe generally underrates the arbitrary element in Plato's quotations. A more realistic approach is to be found in G. Lohse, *Untersuchungen über Homerzitate bei Platon* (Hamburg 1961). Cf. *id.*, Helikon 4 (1964), 3-28 and 5 (1965), 248-95.

[364] Echoed by Schm., 284 n. 10, Kerschensteiner, 168 n. 2.

[365] Cf. also We., *Th.*, 68, and the (too) extensive discussion by van der Valk (above, n. 357), 290-303.

[366] See further F. Solmsen in Entret. s. l'ant. class. VII (1962), 185 ff.

[367] This point has escaped Berres (below, n. 518), 268-9, who argues that ρ 485-7 are a simplification of *Op.* 252-5.

[368] Cf. H. Maehler, ZPE 4 (1969), 87.

by Plutarch, Proclus, and Macrobius[369], there is no sufficient reason to bracket them, as is done by most editors. They reappear at 254-5, but Hes. has more repetitions (see above, on 82 ἀλφηστῆσιν). The sequence φύλακες ... φυλάσσουσιν well illustrates Sellschopp's observation (107 n.165), "Hesiod, der sich eben von der Formel befreit, klammert sich an das Wort, so dass das Wort Einheit und Fortgang der Rede bestimmt"[370].

Maz. concludes from πλουτοδόται (126) that in the original text the φύλακες were meant to be benefactors, not punishers. But in Hes.'s view prosperity and justice are closely connected: cf. 238-43 (similarly Hom. τ 111-2). Accordingly, We. is wrong in thinking that 124-5 "break the connection between 123 and 126": the watchers give wealth because they maintain justice.

124: ῥα. 'As may be expected' from φύλακες: see above, on 49 ἄρα.

124: τε. The position of τε suggests that another φυλάσσουσιν is to be mentally supplied after καί: cf. Denn., 519. See also above, on 113 ἄτερ τε.

124: δίκας. 'Judgments': see above, on 36 δίκης[371].

124: σχέτλια. See above, on 15 σχετλίη.

125: ἠέρα. 'Mist', used by the Homeric gods to make things invisible: see further above, on 18 αἰθέρι. Here "the invisibility of the δαίμονες must receive special emphasis since they are ἐπιχθόνιοι"[372].

125: φοιτῶντες. See above, on 103 φοιτῶσι.

126: πλουτοδόται. We. rightly observes that "in Hesiod's time 'wealth' was conceived primarily in terms of corn". He refers to 21-4 and to 306 f./312 f., but 22 φυτεύειν and 308 πολύμηλοί τ' ἀφνειοί τε show that 'wealth' was a more comprehensive idea.

126: καὶ τοῦτο. To be givers of wealth as well as watchers of jurisdiction[373]. For the specifying force of the asyndeton see above, on 11 οὐκ ἄρα.

126: βασιλήιον. Cf. Hom. τ 111-2 (a good king) εὐδικίας ἀνέχῃσι, φέρῃσι δὲ γαῖα μέλαινα / πυροὺς καὶ κριθάς, and below, 232-7. M. P. Nilsson, *Homer and Mycenae* (London 1933), 220, observes that "at the bottom there is the old primitive conception of the power of the king to influence the course of Nature", but he rightly adds: "The old idea has been deflected and modernized by the reference to the righteousness of the king as the cause of

---

[369] E. K. Rand, AJP 32 (1911), 138, n.2, points out that this does not carry much weight.

[370] Van der Valk's reference (op. cit., 302) to the "catalogical character" of archaic poetry is a very weak explanation.

[371] Krafft (80-1) argues that 124-5 do not suit the context because δίκας must have an abstract meaning, but this presupposition is wrong.

[372] T. G. Rosenmeyer, in Heitsch, 645.

[373] Rosenmeyer (loc. cit.) argues that τοῦτο refers to φυλάσσουσι δίκας rather than to πλουτοδόται, which "is to be understood as an apposition to the juridical activity". But although the giving of wealth is the consequence of the watching of jurisdiction (see above), the two activities are different.

the abundant supply". Accordingly, it is misleading to use the term 'magic' in this connection [374]: the good ruler is θεουδής (τ 109), and Homer and Hes. explain the reaction of nature in terms of recompense.

127: αὖτε. Ev. is certainly wrong in taking 122-6 as a parenthesis (similarly 141-2): for μὲν (109) ... αὖτε cf. Hom. A 237, LSJ αὖτε II 2, Denn., 376.

127: χειρότερον. Cf. λωΐτερος, ἀσσότερος, Chantr. I, 259, Schw. I, 539 [375].

127: μετόπισθεν. The idea of the degeneration of mankind is occasionally found in Homer (e.g. β 276-7 παῦροι γάρ τοι παῖδες ὁμοῖοι πατρὶ πέλονται, / οἱ πλέονες κακίους), but it is always conditioned by a momentary impulse and a special purpose, whereas Hes. emphasizes the general character and the steadiness of the decline [376].

129: φυήν. Not 'body' (Ev.) but 'stature' (cf. German 'Wuchs'): cf. Hom. Γ 208 ff., where φυήν is explained by στάντων κτλ. and στάσκεν κτλ. See also Krafft, 42-3.

129: νόημα. 'Way of thinking': cf. above, on 67 νόον.

130: ἔτεα. For the metrical lengthening at a caesura cf. We. on *Th.* 803, Chantr. I, 104-5.

130: μητέρι. Proclus suggests that the weakness of these men was mainly due to their being brought up by women (similarly Si., We.), but the Homeric parallel κ 8 αἰεὶ παρὰ πατρὶ φίλῳ καὶ μητέρι κεδνῇ shows that the meaning is simply 'in their parental home'.

131: ἀτάλλων. For the lengthening of the α cf. We., H. W. Nordheider, *Lex.*, 1474.41 ff., and Renehan, 347, who compares Alcman 80 ἐπᾱλείψα-σα [377]. The meaning is not 'growing up' (LSJ) but 'frolicking': cf. Hom. Z 400, Σ 567, and B. Mader, *Lex.*, 1473-5 (ἀταλάφρων and ἀταλός) [378]. The participle expresses a more important idea than the main verb: cf. K.G. II, 98-9, Schw. II, 389, and my notes on Men. *Epitr.* 219-20, Mnem. IV 27 (1974), 27, and Pind. *N.* 11, 5, ICS 7, 1 (1982), 18. See also Moorhouse (above, n. 21), 254-5.

131: νήπιος. Cf. Hom. Z 400 ἀταλάφρονα, νήπιον αὔτως. We. rightly observes that their long youth "was evidently part of the traditional myth, and originally represented a blessing", but the sequel, "Hesiod has lost the

---

[374] As is done by R. Mondi, Areth. 13 (1980), 204-5.

[375] See further A. C. Moorhouse, AJP 73 (1952), 298-301, M. Wittwer, Glotta 47 (1969), 54-110.

[376] Cf. Schütz, Ἀσθένεια (above, n. 217), 166-8. F. J. Teggart, JHI 8 (1947), 52 ff., argues that "the poet offers, not the picture of a continuous series, but examples of conduct designed to illustrate a moral principle". Similarly K. von Fritz, in Heitsch, 385, M. I. Finley, *The Use and Abuse of History* (London 1975), 16. It is true that "each race of men does not evolve into the next; it is destroyed and replaced by a new creation" (Finley), but the word μετόπισθεν clearly implies a succession of historical periods.

[377] See also K. Meister, *Die homerische Kunstsprache* (Leipzig 1921), 34 ff.

[378] See further C. Moussy, *Mélanges P. Chantraine* (Paris 1972), 157 ff.

sense of this, giving them a long childhood instead of a long ἥβη", is insufficient: the addition of μέγα to νήπιος (cf. the phrase μέγα νήπιε Πέρση, 286, 633) shows that the change was intentional: the words ᾧ ἐνὶ οἴκῳ repeat the idea already expressed by παρὰ μητέρι κεδνῇ, and this repetition contains the point of the description (We. only observes that after ἀτάλλων "the line is filled out with formulae"): while the golden race lived in perfect concord, the silver race is unfit for communal life: as soon as they leave the shielded condition of the domestic circle and enter society, things go wrong: their silliness passes into ὕβρις (134): for the moral overtone of νήπιος see below, on 218 νήπιος. Their inability to develop into social beings is grotesquely expressed by an endless childhood (similarly Quaglia, 98). Their lasting immaturity sharply contrasts with the undelaying maturity of the golden race [379]. It is this immaturity, both physical and moral (129 φυὴν ... νόημα), that increases the distance between gods and men. The absence of old age is the only link connecting this race with the gods.

131: ᾧ. For the neglect of the digamma cf. A. Hoekstra, Mnem. IV 10 (1957), 206-7.

132: ὅτ᾿ ἄρα. Both ὅτ᾿ ἄν and ὅτ᾿ ἄρ᾿ are possible, but the iterative optative without ἄν (κεν) is much more common in epic poetry: cf. Chantr. II, 225, 260 [380]. Maz. and Col. read ἀνηβῆσαι, but the only example of the meaning 'to attain to ἥβη᾿ is Callim. H. 1, 56 [381]. We. thinks that ἄρα "acknowledges that the happening is an expected one", but the particle does not belong to ἀλλά (as is assumed by Denn., 42) but to ὅτε and is more likely to express "a lively feeling of interest" (Denn., 33).

132: ἡβῆσαι τε. Wil. reads ἡβήσειε (E), "weil ein τε hier unpassend ist, denn mannbar werden und in das Mass, die Periode der Mannbarkeit, gelangen, sind zwei progressive Stadien". But there is a progress e.g. in Hom. Α 367 τὴν δὲ διεπράθομέν τε καὶ ἤγομεν ἐνθάδε πάντα. On the other hand,

---

[379] E. Meyer (in Heitsch, 502) suggests that Hes. wishes to show that the all too easy life of the golden race must result in degeneration, but there is nothing in the Greek text to support this point of view. K. von Fritz (in Heitsch, 384) regards Hes.'s description as "a humorous exaggeration of the way in which, in any 'progressive' era, bright and precocious children look upon their parents", but the social immaturity of the silver race has a fundamental character and has nothing to do with contempt of old-fashioned manners. Fontenrose (above, n. 323), 7, argues that they were wont to be nourished by their mothers (131), and "when their mothers died ... neither knew how to work nor wanted to work": accordingly, when they became hungry they naturally resorted to force or theft, and they did not sacrifice to the gods "because they produced nothing to sacrifice" (at p. 13 he gives a similar explanation of 336). But τρέφω is 'to rear' rather than 'to nourish'. It is true that ἀτάλλων implies 'not working', but Hes. does not emphasize this implication. Fontenrose certainly goes too far when in 136 ἤθελον οὐδ᾿ ἔρδειν he hears an overtone of 'they were unwilling to work'.

[380] We. writes that ὅτ᾿ ἄρα is "confirmed by fr. 205.2 = Il. 11. 225 αὐτὰρ ἐπεί ῥ᾿ ἥβης ... ἵκετο μέτρον", but 'supported' would be a more appropriate term.

[381] Wil. prints ὅτ᾿, but see above, on 22 ὅς.

in the present case no progress is meant, but τε καί has explanatory (specifying) force: see above, on 91.

132: μέτρον. Not the beginning (Maz.) but the full measure: cf. Hom. σ 217 μέγας ἐσσὶ καὶ ἥβης μέτρον ἱκάνεις, Sol. 1 D. = 13 W., 52 σοφίης μέτρον, 16, 1-2 γνωμοσύνης ... μέτρον[382].

133: παυρίδιον. For the suffix cf. Troxler, 131-2.

133: ζώεσκον. We. thinks that "the plural is awkward after 130-2", but a transition from (collective) singular to plural is very common in Greek: cf. Hom. τ 40 ἤ μάλα τις θεὸς ἔνδον, οἳ οὐρανὸν εὐρὺν ἔχουσιν, Sol. 1 D. = 13 W., 47-8 ἄλλος ... τοῖσιν, K.G. I, 86, Chantr. II, 21, Verdenius-Waszink on Arist. *GC* 322 a 19, Reinhard (above, on 11 ἔην), 132 ff., 149 ff.

133: χρόνον. Fränkel (*W.u.F.*, 2 and 15) observes that in the epic χρόνος is mostly used in a context which has a negative value[383]. For Hes., see also 326, 754.

134: ἀφραδίης. Used in a moral sense: cf. Hom. E 649 (cf. 650 ἠνίπαπε), β 281-2 μνηστήρων ἀφραδέων. Similarly ἄφρων (E 761 Ares), ἀφραίνω (B 258 Thersites), ἀφροσύνη (ω 457 the suitors)[384]. For the plural see above, on 16 βουλῇσιν, and below, on 146 ὕβριες.

134: ὕβριν ἀτάσθαλον. At Hom. π 86 said of the suitors (cf. the formula ὑβρίζοντες ἀτάσθαλα μηχανόωνται, γ 207 etc.). See further Kaufmann-Bühler, 267 ff., who points out that "die Vorstellungen und sprachlichen Ausdrücke, unter denen das Treiben der Freier in der Odyssee erscheint, sind genau dieselben wie für das Unrecht bei Hesiod: Leben von fremdem Besitz, Hybris und Bia, schliesslich Verlust der αἰδώς, auch hier begegnen ἀτασθαλίαι / ἀτάσθαλος".

134: ὕβριν. The opposite of δίκη: see below, on 213 ὕβριν.

134: ἀτάσθαλον. 'Reckless'. Derivation from ἄτη and θάλλω is doubtful, especially because θάλλω is not used in an unfavourable sense before Sophocles. See further Chantr., *Dict. étym.*, 132, H. W. Nordheider, *Lex.*, 1483-8[385].

135: ἀλλήλων. Not to be connected with ὕβριν (Si., Latt.) but with ἀπέχειν: cf. ἀπέχεσθαί τινος 'to hold oneself off a thing' (LSJ II 2).

135: θεραπεύειν. "An un-Homeric use of the word" (We.). It may be

---

[382] LSJ (3 b) seem to me wrong in distinguishing ἥβης μέτρον ἱκέσθαι 'the term which is puberty' and ἥβης μέτρον ἔχειν (438, Thgn. 1119) 'full measure of youthful vigour'.

[383] ξ 193 seems to be an exception, for it can hardly be maintained that "wahrscheinlich dominiert dieser negative Begriff der Musse" (Fränkel, 15). See further S. Accame, RFIC 89 (1961), 359 ff.

[384] See further Hoffmann, 54 ff. H. W. Nordheider in *Lex.* insufficiently acknowledges the moral aspect of these words, e.g. 1715.36 on E 649, 1729.59 on θ 209. Krafft (68) thinks that in Homer ἀφραδίη always implies ignorance and that in the present passage it means 'wissentlicher Frevel'. But the question whether an ἀφραδής acts knowingly and willingly lies outside the scope of the meaning of the word.

[385] Cf. also O. Andersen, SO 49 (1973), 21 ff.

added that the use is prefigured in θεράποντες Ἄρηος (Β 110) and θεράποντε Διός (λ 255).

136: ἤθελον. Does not refer to ill-will (as is assumed by Quaglia, 98), for nobody ordered them to worship the gods. The meaning is 'they used': see above, on 39 ἐθέλουσι.

136: ἔρδειν. Used absolutely, like Homeric ῥέζειν (Β 400). This might be taken to indicate the time when gods and men separated and sacrificial rules had to be established (*Th.* 535 ff.), but Hes. refrains from coordinating the story of the five races with the story of Prometheus (see above, on 106 ἕτερον).

137: ἥ. Rz. and Maz. read ᾗ, but there is no evidence for ᾗ used in the sense of ὡς [386]. LSJ and So. read ἥ, but ἥ in the sense of ὡς does not occur before Aeschylus. We. (on *Th.* 396) rightly explains ἥ as anticipating the gender of θέμις: cf. Hom. Ι 134 ᾗ θέμις ἀνθρώπων πέλει, τ 43 αὕτη τοι δίκη ἐστὶ θεῶν, K.G. I, 76-7, Schw. II, 606, Chantr. II, 19 [387].

137: θέμις ἀνθρώποισι. Their indifference with regard to cultic traditions is another expression of their ὕβρις: they ignore the limits between men and gods (Quaglia, 98). They continue to 'live like gods' (112) though they no longer possess the maturity required for it.

137: κατ' ἤθεα. Rz., Wil., Si., So. adopt Bentley's emendation ἀνθρώποις κατὰ ἤθεα (cf. We.: "Bentley may have been right"), but 67, 699, and Hom. Ζ 511 show that the digamma of ἦθος could be neglected (cf. also Edwards, 133, 135). The meaning is not 'wherever they dwell' (Hays, Ev.), 'having fixed dwelling-places' (Maz.), 'varying according to their dwelling-places' (Wil., Si., Col., Marg, We.), but 'according to their customs' (LSJ), as appears from *Th.* 416-7 ὅτε πού τις ἐπιχθονίων ἀνθρώπων / ἔρδων ἱερὰ καλὰ κατὰ νόμον ἱλάσκηται (cf. Pind. *O.* 8, 78 κὰν νόμον ἐρδόμενα) [388]. See also above, on 67 ἦθος. Krafft (115-6) wtrites: "Hesiod differenziert θέμις noch mit κατ' ἤθεα, der Ausdruck allein hat für ihn nicht mehr seine volle Bedeutung". But the meanings of the words are different: θέμις denotes a custom as something established (τίθημι), ἦθος as something varying from case to case.

138: μέν. See above, on 111 μέν.

138: Ζεύς. The gods (110, 128) are replaced by Zeus, not because he is "in der Zwischenzeit an die Macht gelangt" (Nicolai, 39) but because now moral decline begins: see above, on 16 ἀθανάτων, and for the idea of divine retribution, Kaufmann-Bühler.

138: ἔκρυψε. 'Made disappear': cf. *Th.* 730, Hom. Σ 397.

---

[386] Vos, Θέμις (above, on 9 θέμιστας), 33, refers to Cret. and Lac. ἥ 'where' or 'how', but this cannot be used to explain epic diction.

[387] For the reading of the MSS. ᾗ cf. S. R. Slings, RhM 115 (1982), 189 n. 6.

[388] We. writes that *Th.* 416-7 and fr. 322 "are comments on the local nature of cult", but ἀρχαῖος (fr. 322) shows that the emphasis is on the traditional, not the local, character.

138-9: οὕνεκα ... θεοῖς. This does not imply that "sovvertire questo rapporto [viz. between men and gods] porta fatalmente con sé anche il sovvertimento d'ogni principio morale nei rapporti umani" (Quaglia, 99 n. 34). Their social offences apparently punished themselves, but were not heavy enough to lead to mutual destruction, as in the case of the bronze race (152-3).

139: ἔδιδον. The MSS. have ἐδίδων (adopted by Col.), for which there are no close analogies. Pal. adopts ἐδίδουν from a quotation by Porphyry (cf. 225 διδοῦσιν and Chantr. I, 299), but this is not found before the Koine (Schw. I, 688). The Doric form ἔδιδον also occurs in *H. Dem.* 327 (and probably 437), perhaps in imitation of Hes. For Doric forms in Hes. cf. Schw. I, 108, We., *Th.*, 83 ff., A. Morpurgo Davies, Glotta 42 (1964), 138-65, Edwards, ind. s.v. Doric, G. Giangrande, JHS 92 (1972), 191.

141: μέν. Cf. above, on 111 μέν.

141: ὑποχθόνιοι. They get the position commonly assigned to the local heroes (cf. Nilsson, 184 ff.), i.e., they do not go to Hades, as the bronze race (153), but stay just under the surface of the earth. They are one stage further away from the gods than the golden race, which stays on the surface of the earth (123). The same sequence is found in Pl. *Rep.* 392 a 4 περὶ γὰρ θεῶν ὡς δεῖ λέγεσθαι εἴρηται, καὶ περὶ δαιμόνων τε καὶ ἡρώων καὶ τῶν ἐν Ἅιδου (cf. *Leg.* 717 b). Hes. does not call the silver race ἥρωες because he reserves this term for the fourth race (159). The latter could not be identified with the silver race because of their warlike spirit[389], but the local heroes could, because many of them were anonymous[390].

141: μάκαρες θνητοί. Peppmüller's conjecture θνητοῖς (adopted by Rz., Maz., Ev., Latt., LSJ) is unnecessary. It has been argued[391] that "le datif donne la réplique à 122: ne voulant attribuer à Zeus l'institution du culte rendu à ces 'génies inférieurs', il se contente de la rapporter à la tradition des 'mortels'". But Rohde (I, 100-1) rightly points out that Hes. tries "diese dem Homer nicht bekannte Classe der Wesen mit einem dem homerischen Sprachvorrath, auf den sich der Dichter angewiesen sah, entlehnten Ausdruck treffend und deutlich zu bezeichnen ... Man nannte später solche *gewordene* Unsterbliche 'Heroen'. Hesiod, der dies Wort in diesem Sinne noch nicht verwenden konnte, nennt sie mit kühnem Oxymoron: sterbliche Selige, menschliche Götter. Den Göttern ähnlich sind sie in ihrem neuen Dasein als ewige Geister; sterblich war ihre Natur, da ja doch ihr Leib sterben musste". Rosenmeyer (in Heitsch, 646) compares Pl. *Crat.* 397 de ἀνθρώπους δαίμονας. Cf. also E. *Rhes.* 971 ἀνθρωποδαίμων. Krafft (115) and Quaglia (100 n. 38) take μάκαρες as the attribute of θνητοί, but μάκαρ could also be said of

[389] As is rightly observed by K. von Fritz, in Heitsch, 374.
[390] Cf. von Fritz, *loc. cit.*, 376, and We. *ad loc.*
[391] V. Goldschmidt, REG 63 (1950), 35 n. 2.

a living man (e.g. Hom. Γ 182) and so would be unsuited to define a deified man[392].

141: καλέονται. 'They are the so-called': cf. Hom. Λ 757-8 Ἀλεισίου ἔνθα κολώνη / κέκληται, A. *Pers.* 1-2 τάδε ... / ... πιστὰ καλεῖται ('we are the so-called πιστοί'), Hdt. III 115, 1 οὔτε γὰρ ἔγωγε ἐνδέκομαι Ἠριδανόν τινα καλέεσθαι πρὸς βαρβάρων ποταμόν ('that there is a river called E. by the barbarians'). See further D. Tabachovitz, Eran. 58 (1960), 9-11, Verdenius, Maia 15 (1963), 125. The phrase does not imply that they were already known under this name, for it is Hes. who gives them the name[393].

142: δεύτεροι. Krafft (115 and n. 1) reads ἐπιχθόνιοι at 141 and argues that "der Zusatz δεύτεροι zeigt m.E. deutlich, dass das zweite Geschlecht ebenso wie die Menschen des Goldenen Zeitalters jetzt als ἐπιχθόνιοι aufgefasst wird". But ἀλλ᾽ ἔμπης shows that δεύτεροι means 'inferior' (LSJ II 1).

142: τιμή. Rohde (I, 99) writes: "im Sinne nicht einer einfachen Werthschätzung, sondern als thätige Verehrung"[394]. But the parallel in 126 shows that τιμή does not refer to the fact that they are worshipped by men, but to the fact that they have a special function, a privilege (apparently to protect the country where they are buried), just as every god has his τιμή (*Th.* 393, 462, 491, 885, Hom. O 189). It is true that to have a τιμή implies that one is honoured, but the honour comes from the authority who confers the privilege: cf. *Th.* 398 τὴν δὲ Ζεὺς τίμησε, Hom. P 251 ἐκ δὲ Διὸς τιμὴ καὶ κῦδος ὀπηδεῖ (*scil.* the leaders), ε 335 θεῶν ἐξ ἔμμορε τιμῆς (*scil.* of being a goddess).

It seems illogical that men who have led a guilty life receive a privilege after death (cf. Quaglia, 99 ff.), but we should not try to show that their afterlife is an appropriate answer to their life on earth[395]. The fact that Hes. leaves their function undefined shows that he simply included the local heroes in his scheme (see above, on 141 ὑποχθόνιοι).

142: ὀπηδεῖ. Goods and evils imparted to man are said to 'accompany' him because they are imagined as semi-divine powers: for ὀπηδέω cf. 230, 313, 326, Hom. P 251 (quoted above), for ἕπομαι cf. Hom. Δ 415, I 513. See further Becker, 178-9.

143: ἄλλο. 'Furthermore' (properly 'another race as the third'). For the

---

[392] C. de Heer, Μάκαρ – εὐδαίμων – ὄλβιος – εὐτυχής (Amsterdam 1968), 21, refers to the fact that at Hom. σ 306 and λ 483 μάκαρ is applied to the dead. But the present context asks for a definition, not a beatification. Cf. also A. Schoele, Acta Ant. Acad. Scient. Hungar. 8 (1960), 255-63.

[393] E. Meyer (in Heitsch, 500) wrongly concludes that not only their name but also their being was invented by Hes.: we have seen above that Hes. alludes to the worship of the local heroes.

[394] Similarly Latt., Dietrich, *Death* (above, n. 281), 55, and We., who compares Hom. λ 302 (where τιμήν is explained by 304 τιμὴν δὲ λελόγχασιν ἶσα θεοῖσιν).

[395] As is done by Quaglia (103), who quite arbitrarily calls their happiness (141 μάκαρες) "infeconda come i lunghi anni della loro fiacca infanzia".

quasi-adverbial use of ἄλλος cf. Hom. B 191 αὐτός τε κάθησο καὶ ἄλλους ἵδρυε λαούς, LSJ II 8, K.G. I, 275, Bruhn, §182, and my note on Pl. *Phd.* 110 e 5, Mnem. IV 31 (1978), 96[396].

144: οὐκ ... ὁμοῖον. Called by We. "a cramped counterpart of 129", but Maz. (I), 62, rightly observes that Hes. emphasizes the fact that there is a gradual difference (127 χειρότερον) between the golden race and the silver race, but a fundamental difference (οὐδὲν ὁμοῖον) between the silver race and the bronze race. Rosenmeyer (in Heitsch, 624) thinks that "the strong warriors of the bronze age are hardly to be regarded as inferior to the impious weaklings of the silver γένος"[397]. But they add warlike acts (145-6) to the ὕβρις already existing in the silver race (134), and this is certainly a further and serious degeneration. Cf. also Péron, 286-8, who points out a progressive concretization in the description of ὕβρις at 134-5, 145-6, and 191-2.

144: ἀργυρέῳ. For the synizesis combined with correption We. compares 583 δενδρέῳ (= Hom. Γ 152, wrongly called by Leaf "intolerable"), 640 ἀργαλέῃ, Hom. A 15 χρυσέῳ. Renehan (347) adds Λ 606 χρεώ.

145: Μελιᾶν. We. argues that Hes. uses the Aeolic/Doric ending (cf. Troxler, 61-2, Edwards, 103, and see above, on 139 ἔδιδον) because "he is thinking of the Meliai nymphs", but in that case the word should be capitalized, just as the Μελίαι at *Th.* 187. We. writes that the idea of the origin of men from ash-trees (implied in sch. T Hom. Χ 126, Palaeph. 35, and Hsch. μελίας καρπός) "is essentially the same as being born from tree-nymphs", but this explanation is too easy. Ash-tree-nymphs do not occur in other sources[398], and in the epic formula ἀπὸ δρυός ... ἀπὸ πέτρης referring to the origin of man (Χ 126, τ 164)[399] no nymphs are involved. It may also be asked why Hes. did not choose the more common Hamadryades[400] as the mothers of the bronze race. The answer is suggested by the fact that the Meliai of *Th.* 187 are related to the Erinyes and the Giants (*Th.* 185): this

[396] Cf. also W. Havers, *Handbuch der erklärenden Syntax* (Heidelberg 1931), 34-5, 217-8, E. L. Löfstedt, *Syntactica*, II (Lund 1933), 189.

[397] Similarly K. von Fritz, in Heitsch, 381, Fontenrose (above, n. 323), 8, Quaglia, 89-90.

[398] Melia, mother of Phoroneus, the first man, is an Oceanid (Apoll. II 1), and so is Melia, mother of Ismenius (Pind. *P.* 11, 3, Paus. IX 10, 5), so that the connection of this name with the ash-tree is at least doubtful.

[399] Cf. Virg. *Aen.* 8, 314 *gensque virum truncis et duro robore nati*, Juv. 6, 12 *homines ... rupto robore nati*. See further L. Preller, *Die Vorstellungen der Alten vom Ursprung des menschlichen Geschlechts*, Philol. 7 (1852), 1-60, espec. 11-4, Seeliger in Roscher's *Lex. d. gr. u. röm. Myth.* VI, 500-1, Samter, *Volkskunde* (above, n. 281), 17-9, G. Nagy, in *Antiquitates Indogermanicae: Gedenkschrift H. Güntert* (Innsbruck 1974), 113-21, R. S. Shannon III, *The Arms of Achilles and Homeric Compositional Technique* (Leiden 1975), 40 ff.

[400] First mentioned in *H. Ven.* 257 ff. See further Süss, RE VII, 2287-92, H. von Geisau, KP II, 928. The idea of nymphs living in trees seems to be later than the notion of animated trees such as the ἀγλαόκαρποι ἐλαῖαι at *H. Cer.* 23. Cf. A. Rivaud, Rev. Anthrop. 21 (1911), 167. On the other hand, I do not believe that Wil. (*Gl.* I, 189) is right in concluding from *H. Ven.* 264-72: "Dann hat also jeder Baum eine Seele".

implies that they have a fierce character, which corresponds with the bellicose nature of the bronze race. This character, and perhaps their whole being, seems to have been created by Hes. on the basis of an association with the epic ash-spear[401].

145-6: Ἄρηος ἔργα. We. mentions some epic parallels, but does not give a translation. 'Deeds' is better than 'works' (Ev.), and the context (ἔμελε and ὕβριες) shows that human deeds are meant. These human deeds can be called Ares' deeds because the power of the god is present in the human acts of war: see above, on 11 Ἐρίδων. Similarly 521 ἔργα Ἀφροδίτης.

146: ἔμελε. Refers to a natural tendency: cf. Hom. Β 338, ζ 270, μ 216, H. Ven. 6. Similarly 231, 531 μέμηλε. Hes. perhaps alludes to the name Μελίαι: see above, on 3 διά.

146: ὕβριες. We. writes: "it is difficult to decide between this and Ὕβριος, which I conjected in Philol. 108, 1964, 161 and which has since appeared in a papyrus ... Hesiod wanted to say ὕβρις ... The question is whether, to make it into a dactyl, he turned more easily to the plural or to the genitive". However, it is not a question of metrical ease, but a question of idiom: ἔργα στονόεντα is natural with Ares (cf. Hom. Γ 132 πολύδακρυν Ἄρηα, Δ 445 στόνον ἀνδρῶν, Θ 159 βέλεα στονόεντα) but not with Hybris[402]. The plural ὕβριες is not found anywhere else in early epic, but similar abstract nouns are used in the plural by Homer (e.g. Ν 108 μεθημοσύνῃσι, Χ 104 ἀτασθαλίῃ-σιν) and Hes. (e.g. 330 ἀφραδίῃς, 372 πίστεις, Th. 102 δυσφροσυνέων); see further K.G. I, 16, Schw. II, 43. For ὕβρις = ὕβρισμα cf. Hom. Α 214 ὕβριος εἵνεκα τῆσδε, LSJ II. The plural ὕβρεις is found e.g. at E. Ba. 247, H.F. 741, Pl. Leg. 884 a 7, Arist. Rhet. 1373 a 35. For the meaning of ὕβρις see below, on 213 ὕβριν.

146: οὐδέ τι. See above, on 113.

146: σῖτον. The contrast ἀλλ' ἀδάμαντος κτλ. shows that Hes. thinks of the Homeric characterization of civilized men as σῖτον ἔδοντες (θ 222, ι 89, κ 101) or σιτοφάγοι (ι 191). See further We. ad loc. Cf. also above, on 82 ἀλφηστῆσιν[403].

---

[401] As is suggested by Sittl (on Th. 137), Maz. (I), 66, who observes that 145 ὄβριμοι recalls the epic ὄβριμον ἔγχος, Si., and Shannon, op. cit., 47 (his far-reaching conclusions about Achilles' ash-spear, however, are to be rejected: cf. A. H. M. Kessels, Mnem. IV 31, 1978, 315-8). On the other hand, Latt. goes too far in translating 'they came from ash spears'. Nilsson (246) thinks that the Meliai are "nicht speziell Eschennymphen, sondern Baumnymphen überhaupt". This view has been adopted by We. (on Th. 187), but his argument, "if he had meant the nymphs of ash-trees in particular, he would have been bound to tell us about the nymphs of other sorts of trees too", is obviously invalid. Cf. also Rudhardt, 255.

[402] As a parallel for Ὕβριος We. quotes Sol. 1 D. = 13 W., 16, but there ὕβριος should be written (as is done by We. himself in his Iambi et Elegi Graeci): cf. 41 πενίης ἔργα and LSJ s.v. ἔργον II 1.

[403] Fontenrose (above, n. 323), 8, interprets the fact that they did not till the earth to produce bread as equivalent to the idea that "they did not do the work that Zeus intended for mankind".

147: ἀδάμαντος. Probably "a pre-Iron word for iron" (We. on *Th.* 161): it is πολιός (*Th.* 161) just as iron (Hom. I 366). See further *Less. pol.*, 152-4. We. suggests that "their endurance of a breadless diet was part of their general grim strength". This is wrong because (1) οὐδέ τι σῖτον ἤσθιον symbolizes their uncivilized nature, and (2) ἀδάμαντος symbolizes their grimness rather than their strength. Hes. is inspired by the Homeric phrase ἦ γὰρ σοί γε σιδήρεος ἐν φρεσὶ θυμός (Χ 357, ψ 172), but he avoids the word 'iron' because he is describing a bronze race. The θυμός can be said to be made of ἀδάμας because metals were imagined to possess vital powers: cf. above, on 109 χρύσεον.

148: ἄπλαστοι. Troxler (185-6) defends ἄπλητοι (C and Proclus read ἄπλατοι), but in the parallel passage *Th.* 151 all MSS. have ἄπλαστοι. The meaning is not 'unformbar' (Fränkel, 133) or 'unshapen', 'rough' (We., whose parallel 'unpolished' is too weak), but 'unapproachable' (Tzetzes ἀπροσπέλαστοι): cf. E. *Med.* 151-2 ἀπλάστου κοίτας ἔρος (where ἀπλήστου, given by some MSS., is rightly rejected by Page), S. fr. 387 ἄπλαστον ἀξύμβλητον ἐξεθρεψάμην, A. *Prom.* 371 ἀπλάστου (F¹) ... ζάλης, 716 πρόσπλαστοι ξένοις, *Eum.* 53 οὐ πλαστοῖσι φυσιάμασιν. These forms are usually emended to forms of ἄπλατος etc.[404]. Although in minuscule writing the confusion of τ and στ is rather common[405], ἄπλαστος may be kept if we assume that it was formed under the influence of ἐπελάσθην[406]. It may be added that the corruption ἄπληστος is easier to explain from ἄπλαστος than from ἄπλατος.

148: ἄαπτοι. H. Vos, Glotta 34 (1955), 292-4, plausibly argues that the word is to be derived from ἄπτομαι, so that the meaning is equivalent to that of ἄπλα(σ)τος: properly 'Hände, die man nicht auf freundschaftliche Weise fassen kann': cf. Hom. Κ 377, Ω 508 χειρῶν ἄπτεσθαι[407].

149: ἐπέφυκον. Cf. Hom. Ε 504 ἐπέπληγον, ι 439 ἐμέμηκον, Μ 125 etc. κεκλήγοντες, Κ.Β. ΙΙ, 118-9, Schw. Ι, 777, Chantr. Ι, 397, 438-9, Troxler, 91.

But this intention is not manifest in the story of the five ages, as is assumed by Fontenrose (who admits, p. 11, that "Hesiod does not tell us explicitly that the primary fault of the silver, bronze, and iron man is their failure to work for their livelihoods"). Accordingly, he is certainly wrong in taking ἔργα at 146 to have an ironic sense.

Rudhardt (274) thinks that they could not eat bread because they did not have fire. But fire is more essential to the preparation of meat. For the independent chronology of the story of the five races see above, on 106 ἕτερον. Smith (above, n. 341), 146 n. 5, suggests that they "had neither interest nor need for even the most necessary respite from fighting", but this weakens the contrast with the sequel.

[404] Cf. R. D. Dawe, *The Collation and Investigation of Manuscripts of Aeschylus* (Cambridge 1964), 118-9, who compares ἄκλαυστος for ἄκλαυτος (e.g. *Sept.* 696, *Eum.* 565).

[405] Cf. e.g. A. *Ag.* 142 φιλομάτοις, 556 κακοτρώτους, 1099 μαστεύομεν, Pl. *Rep.* 407 c 2 διαστάσεις, 546 a 4 ἕκαστον.

[406] This seems to me more likely than that the σ originated from a confusion of ἄπλητος and ἄπληστος, as is suggested by E. M. Voigt, *Lex.*, 1027.

[407] A. Amory Parry, *Blameless Aegisthus* (Leiden 1973), 160 n. 1, suggests 'powerful in grasping' (a spear, for example), or 'powerful in smiting', but the word is not used in special connection with spears. See further *Less. pol.*, 2-5.

149: ἐπὶ στιβαροῖσι μέλεσσι. We. rightly keeps 148-9, although they are modelled on *Th.* 151-2 and 673 (for repetitions in Hes. see above, on 82), but thinks that ἐπὶ στιβ. μέλεσσι "no longer makes sense": cf. his note on *Th.* 152: "while μέλεα can mean the body as a whole, it cannot mean the body as distinct from the arms". But We. himself (in his note on 540) observes that Homer uses μέλεα and γυῖα for the body "as a repository for energy and strength" (for a more accurate definition see above, on 66 γυιοκόρους), i.e., μέλεα does not express a purely quantitative notion. It may be added that even in modern languages 'body' is used for the trunk. Aeschylus does the same at *Pers.* 991 βοᾷ μοι μελέων ἔντοσθεν ἦτορ. Hes. could do so the more easily as in archaic thought there does not exist a clear conception of the body as a whole and of the soul as a whole: cf. Snell, 17-8, and my remarks in Lampas 3 (1970), 101 ff. For Hes.'s conception of the body cf. Krafft, 35 ff., whose conclusion (39), "Hesiod sah den 'Körper' schon als innere Einheit", goes much too far.

150: τεύχεα. We. writes: "since bronze was just as much the metal for armour in Hesiod's time as it had ever been, he is probably using the word to mean 'weapons', as in *Od.* 24.534". We get more support from such passages as Χ 112-3 and 125, Ψ 798-800, χ 109-10, which show that τεύχεα may include shields and spears; these were not commonly made of bronze in Hes.'s time, and even in the *Iliad* bronze is not the main material of shields (cf. Μ 295-7).

150: χάλκεοι. For the anaphora see above, on 6 ῥεῖα.

150: οἶκοι. In Homer bronze buildings are confined to divine and semi-divine beings, such as Hephaestus (Σ 371), Aeolus (κ 3), and Alcinous (η 86).

151: εἰργάζοντο. This cannot refer to tilling (cf. 145-6)⁴⁰⁸, but must denote working on such materials as wood and stone: cf. Xen. *H.G.* III 3, 7 ὅπλα ... ὁπόσοις ἄνθρωποι καὶ γῆν καὶ ξύλα καὶ λίθους ἐργάζονται⁴⁰⁹.

151: μέλας. We. adopts the explanation of sch. vet., 'imagining it rusty', because "otherwise in epic, iron is πολιός or αἴθων". But another scholium refers to the fact that in Homer the sea is called both πολιός and μέλας, and water both δνοφερός and ἀγλαός. It may be added that wine is called both μέλας (ε 265, ι 196) and αἶθοψ (Δ 259, β 57). These qualifications obviously depend on the circumstances in which the object is viewed⁴¹⁰. In the present passage iron is called 'dark' as compared with bronze. There may be an additional suggestion of gloom, pointing forward to the fifth race: cf. Hom. μέλας θάνατος, LSJ III 1⁴¹¹.

---

⁴⁰⁸ As is observed by Maz. (I), 66 n. 4, who in II, however, translates 'ils labouraient'. See also A. Doudelet, Rech. de Philol. et de Ling. 3 (1972), 119-25.

⁴⁰⁹ Latt.'s 'they worked as bronzesmiths' is obviously wrong.

⁴¹⁰ This also explains the fact that in Homer the sky is called both χάλκεος (Ρ 425, γ 2) and σιδήρεος (ο 328).

⁴¹¹ See further S. Fogelmark, *Studies in Pindar* (Lund 1972), 28-31, E. Irwin, *Colour Terms in*

151: δέ. Has explanatory (motivating) force: see above, on 13.

152: μέν. See above, on 111 μέν.

152: σφετέρῃσι. 'One another's': cf. ἑαυτῶν for ἀλλήλων (K.G. I, 573-5, LSJ III).

153: εὐρώεντα. 'Rusty' (Wil.) is too special, "as a place of physical decay" (We. on *Th.* 731) is too general, 'moisi' (Maz.), 'dank' (Ev.), 'mouldry' (LSJ) are correct.

153: κρυεροῦ. We. gives some parallels, but fails to note that the meaning is 'chilling', 'shuddering', 'gruesome', just as in Hom. N 48 κρυεροῖο φόβοιο, Ω 524, δ 103 κρυεροῖο γόοιο (cf. I 2 φόβου κρυόεντος, E 740 κρυόεσσα ἰωκή)[412].

154: νώνυμνοι. This does not mean that they do not get a honourable title like the two preceding races (which in fact is true)[413], but that their name does not live on either in their fame (cf. Hom. M 70, ω 93-4) or in their posterity (cf. α 222-3).

154: δέ. See above, on 151 δέ.

155: μέλας. See above, on 151 μέλας. We. rightly observes that the position of the word marks the contrast with λαμπρόν. Cf. 182 πατὴρ παίδεσσιν, 497 λεπτῇ δὲ παχύν, 538 παύρῳ πολλήν, *Th.* 942 ἀθάνατον θνητῇ, Hom. Z 236 χρύσεα χαλκείων, Λ 802 ἀκμῆτες κεκμηότας. Antithetic juxtaposition became especially popular in tragedy, as appears from such extreme cases as A. *Sept.* 695-6 φίλου γὰρ ἐχθρά μοι πατρὸς ... / ... προσιζάνει, E. *El.* 1026 ἔκτεινε πολλῶν μίαν ὕπερ. See further Bruhn, § 220, Fehling, 281 ff.

157: αὖτις ἔτι. A seeming pleonasm (cf. Hom. I 375 ἔτ᾽ αὖτις and LSJ II 1 πάλιν αὖτις): αὖτις is 'again', 'next', and ἔτι is 'further', 'in addition' (cf. Schw. II, 564).

157: ἄλλο. See above, on 143.

157: ἐπὶ χθονί. See above, on 90.

158: δικαιότερον. In so far as they did not destroy one another at random, but for clearly defined reasons (163, 165): see below, on 161 κακός[414].

Greek Poetry (Toronto 1974), 173-5, H. Dürbeck, *Zur Charakteristik der griechischen Farben-bezeichnungen* (Bonn 1977), 153-4.

[412] Cf. N. Zink, *Griechische Ausdrucksweisen für Warm und Kalt im seelischen Bereich* (Heidelberg 1962), 24-6. Waltz (II) *ad loc.* wrongly thinks of the fact that sunshine does not penetrate the underworld.

[413] As is assumed by Rohde I, 102-3 (similarly M. Schmidt, *Lex.*, 1699.35). Vernant, *Mythe et pensée* (above, n. 341), 277, is equally wrong in concluding that according to Hes. the dead in Hades lose their individuality.

[414] Fontenrose (above, n. 323), 9, again insists on his assumption that the myth of the ages is dominated by the idea of work (see above, n. 403) by suggesting that Hes. considered the epic heroes to be more just because some of them plowed their fields, cultivated their vineyards, or tended flocks. He even thinks that 158 πουλυβοτείρῃ has the pregnant sense of 'that they would make productive', and that they continued their labour (but now "painless" and "easy") on the

158: καὶ ἄρειον. Maz. (I), 67, and We. rightly observe that it is δίκη which makes them better. For καί 'and therefore' cf. K.G. II, 248, and my note on Men. *Epitr.* 114, Mnem. IV 27 (1974), 23, and the references given there.

158: ἄρειον. The basic meaning is 'superior' in a general sense: the context gives it moral (here), social (193), physical (207), or another, force. See further J. Anastassiou, *Lex.*, 1223-6.

The question why Hes. interrupted the degeneration in his series of races by inserting a 'better' race has been answered in the simplest and most satisfactory way by Reitzenstein[415]: "Der Gegensatz zwischen Heroenzeit und Gegenwart beherrscht das Denken des Rhapsoden; aus der Heroenzeit leitet sich der Adel der Gegenwart her" (cf. 160 προτέρη γενεή)[416]. It may be added that Hes. wants to confront his contemporaries, and especially the 'kings', with a contrasting picture: war was not absent from the generation of the heroes, but as a whole they were 'more just', and the disappearance of justice is the most serious danger to the future of the present world.

159: ἀνδρῶν ἡρώων. We. writes that "in epic generally the phrase seems to mean much the same as ἀνδρῶν αἰχμητάων". But even the singer Demodocus and the herald Moelius are called ἥρως (θ 483, σ 423). The word does not refer to special abilities, but serves to denote the lofty character of the 'heroic' age[417].

159: θεῖοι. Because the heroes, although mortal, are θεοείκελοι (θεοειδέες, ἀντίθεοι, ἰσόθεοι)[418].

159: καλέονται. See above, on 141.

160: ἡμίθεοι. We. quotes a number of texts to show that "the word refers to their parentage (cf. ἡμίονος, and our 'half-brother')", but in Homer (M 23) and Hes. the heroes are not said to be of semi-divine descent, and in the epic tradition this certainly was not the rule. The original meaning of the word seems to be 'almost gods' (cf. ἡμιθνής). Leaf (on M 23) thinks that the use of the word "is totally inconsistent with Homer's idea of the heroes, who, though of divine descent and stronger than men of his own day, are yet no

---

Isles of the Blest, because "if the fields produce three times a year [173], then, though unusually rich, they have to be worked" (!).

[415] R. Reitzenstein, *Studien zum antiken Synkretismus* (Leipzig-Berlin 1926), 62. Cf. also K. Matthiessen, Philol. 121 (1977), 176-88, and in *Arktouros* (above, n. 341), 31-2.

[416] It is certainly wrong, however, to conclude that Hes. assumed the whole iron race to descend from the heroes, as is suggested by Rudhardt, 248-9. Hes. does not mention the creation of the iron race because he takes it for granted (it seems to be implied in 180). See also below, n. 434.

[417] Cf. W. Pötscher, RhM 104 (1961), 329 ff., who proposes the etymology 'der (zur Ehe) reife Mann'. See also Nilsson, 184 ff., 382, Dietrich, *Death* (above, n. 281), 24 ff. We. (pp. 370-3) argues that the later, religious sense did not develop from the epic use, but cf. Rohde I, 155, Nilsson, 185-6, Pötscher, *op. cit.*, 336-7.

[418] We. also notes that "they were descended from gods", but in Homer even Odysseus, Oileus (N 694), and Thoas (Ξ 330) are called θεῖος.

more than men"[419]. But apart from the immortality of the gods there was no sharp dividing-line between gods and men[420], but only a gradual difference: cf. I 498 τῶν (the gods) περ καὶ μείζων ἀρετὴ τιμή τε βίη τε. Just as the gods in their actions and feelings may sink to the human level, prominent men may conversely rise to the level of the gods: cf. e.g. E 78 etc. θεὸς δ᾽ ὣς τίετο δήμῳ, Μ 312 θεοὺς ὣς εἰσορόωσι, Χ 394 ᾧ Τρῶες κατὰ ἄστυ θεῷ ὣς εὐχετόωντο, Ω 258 θεὸς ἔσκε μετ᾽ ἀνδράσιν[421]. The anthropomorphism of the gods is complemented by the theomorphism of the heroes[422].

160: προτέρη γενεή. At Hom. Ψ 790 'an older generation', here 'the race before ours'. For this use of γενεά cf. Hdt. III 122, 2 τῆς δὲ ἀνθρωπηίης λεγομένης γενεῆς.

160: κατά. We. observes that in the epic ἐπ᾽ is more usual, but he does not explain the difference: ἐπὶ γαῖαν is 'everywhere on earth' (cf. above, on 11 ἐπὶ γαῖαν), κατὰ γαῖαν 'in many places on earth' (cf. Hom. ρ 418 ἐγὼ δέ κέ σε κλείω κατ᾽ ἀπείρονα γαῖαν).

160: ἀπείρονα. Not to be taken literally, for the earth has πείρατα (168), but 'very large' (cf. 'immense').

161: μέν. See above, on 111 μέν.

161: κακός. See above, on 14 κακόν. We. rightly says that Hes. puts their fighting in a more favourable light than that of the bronze race. He refers to M. van der Valk (above, n. 357), 298-9 n. 121, who observes that the poet "on purpose diversifies the expressions [152 and 161] and does not attribute the end of the fourth generation to its own members, but to 'War' and 'Strife'". It should be added that the more favourable aspect of their fighting lies in the fact that they have clear motives for their combats, whereas the bronze race was moved by a native (146 ἔμελε) pugnacity only (cf. Quaglia, 105-6).

162: ὑπό. Not necessarily "on the lower ground outside the wall" (We.), for the position marked by ὑπό is low as compared with the height of the walls.

162: ἑπταπύλῳ. A traditional epithet: cf. Hom. Δ 406, λ 263.

162: Θήβῃ. The Theban war is mentioned first, because it was considered the older, and perhaps because Hes. was nearer to Thebes (We.).

---

[419] Similarly E. Bethe, *Homer*, II (Leipzig 1922), 303-6, who argues that M 23 is an imitation of Hesiod. But the priority of M 23 is successfully defended by Krafft (117-9), although not all his arguments are equally convincing.

[420] E 441-2 οὔ ποτε φῦλον ὁμοῖον / ἀθανάτων τε θεῶν χαμαὶ ἐρχομένων τ᾽ ἀνθρώπων is not a theological axiom, but an incidental utterance prompted by the dramatic situation.

[421] Odysseus' question put to Nausicaa (ζ 149), θεός νύ τις ἢ βροτός ἐσσι; (where many editors wrongly print ἤ), is not a mere compliment, but a real dilemma. Cf. Ζ 123-8, π 183-7.

[422] See also J. Adam, *The Vitality of Platonism* (Cambridge 1911), 124, Rohde I, 152 n. 2, Ehnmark, *The Idea of God* (above, n. 65), 3, W. F. Otto, *Die Götter Griechenlands* (³Frankfurt 1947), 231-2, who is wrong, however, in considering the theomorphism of man to be the basis of Greek religiosity.

162: Καδμηίδι. Used like Hom. Α 254 Ἀχαιῗδα γαῖαν (We.). It has probably been added to distinguish Boeotian Thebes from Egyptian Thebes (Hom. Ι 383, δ 126).

162: γαίῃ. We. compares E. *Phoen.* 245 ἑπτάπυργος ἅδε γᾶ. For γῆ referring to a city LSJ (II 2) quote E. *Tro.* 868 as illustrating a use frequent in tragedy: cf. e.g. A. *Ag.* 338-9 τοὺς πολισσούχους θεοὺς / τοὺς τῆς ἁλούσης γῆς (Troy). It may be added that conversely πόλις often includes the surrounding country: cf. 227-8 τέθηλε πόλις ... / εἰρήνη δ᾽ ἀνὰ γῆν κουροτρόφος, Hom. Ξ 230 Λῆμνον δ᾽ εἰσαφίκανε, πόλιν θείοιο Θόαντος, LSJ II.

163: μήλων. Usually taken to refer to the whole of Oedipus' property (cf. κτῆνος), but more probably referring to the war between the Thebans and the Minyans (Apollod. II 4, 11, *FgrH* 3, 95, l. 16; cf. also Hom. Ψ 679 δεδουπότος Οἰδιπόδαο)[423]. Wars often began with cattle-raiding (cf. Hom. Α 154, Λ 761 ff., Σ 520 ff., ι 405, λ 289-90, υ 51, φ 18, and Walcot, *Peasants*, 97-8, and Hist. of Rel. 18, 1979, 326 ff.), and Renehan (347) rightly points out that "it is the epic convention to give a concrete, specific cause in such ἕνεκα phrases".

164: δὲ καί. Equivalent to δ᾽ αὖ: cf. Denn., 305.

164: ἐν νήεσσιν. We. rightly observes that "the great sea journey is for Hesiod a striking part of the story", but I do not believe that death at sea "may be at the back of his mind".

164: μέγα λαῖτμα θαλάσσης. For this formula as a metrical equivalent of ἰοειδέα πόντον (*Th.* 844) cf. Edwards, 59.

165: ἀγαγών. According to We., "a less natural verb for πόλεμος". He thinks that Hom. Β 834 κῆρες γὰρ ἄγον μέλανος θανάτοιο is not comparable, but war was probably imagined as a demonic power: cf. its στόμα (Hom. Κ 8, Τ 313, Υ 359) and Ρ 737 ἄγριος.

166. Bracketed by So.: in AJP 103 (1980), 22-4, he argues that all heroes went to the Isles of the Blest. But τοὺς μέν and τοῖς δέ might refer to the same persons: cf. Hom. Ρ 193-5 ἤτοι ὁ μὲν τὰ ἃ δῶκε φέρειν προτὶ Ἴλιον ἱρὴν / Τρωσὶ φιλοπτολέμοισι, ὁ δ᾽ ἄμβροτα τεύχεα δῦνε / Πηλεΐδεω Ἀχιλῆος. Solmsen observes that 166 is missing in two papyri and is disregarded by the ancient commentators, and concludes: "In cases of this kind the chances are far better that the line was interpolated than that it was omitted". But We. rightly points out that the line may have been omitted "to purge the passage of an apparent contradiction" or to adapt it to the later idea that more or all heroes went to the Isles. See further below, on 167 τοῖς.

166: ἤτοι. Not ἦ τοι (most editors), for 'truly' would add too much emphasis: cf. C. J. Ruijgh, Mnem. IV 34 (1981), 272-87, espec. 272-3, who

---

[423] Cf. L. Deubner, *Oedipusprobleme*, APrAW 1942:4, 31 ff., E. L. Cock, Acta Class. 4 (1961), 8-10, W. Pötscher, Eran. 71 (1973), 23-5.

also points out (espec. 286) that the word is practically equivalent to μέν and that it introduces a specification rather than a correction (as is held by R. M. Frazer, Mnem. IV 34, 1981, 265-71).

166: θανάτου τέλος. A Homeric phrase (Γ 309 etc.) properly meaning 'fulfilment (realization) of dying': cf. F. M. J. Waanders, *The History of* τέλος *and* τελέω *in Ancient Greek* (Amsterdam 1983), 49-51.

166: ἀμφεκάλυψε. Not a metaphor, for cf. Hom. Π 350 θανάτου νέφος ἀμφεκάλυψεν (similarly E 68, Π 333-4, Υ 417). See further Onians, 421 ff. (who is wrong, however, in concluding that τέλος means 'band' or 'bond').

167: τοῖς. For the construction cf. S. L. Radt, Mnem. IV 32 (1979), 295: "Ein sowohl zum Verbum finitum wie zu einem damit verbundenen Partizip gehöriges (Pro)nomen wird normal zum Verbum finitum konstruiert ... zu dem Partizip nur wenn dies vorangeht". He refers to Krüger, *Gr. Spr.*, § 60, 5, 2; cf. also K.G. II, 562-3.

In Homer (δ 561-9) only Menelaus and Rhadamantys obtain this privilege, but Hes. obviously thinks of a larger number of heroes[424]. He does not specify their names, for that would have involved him in the difficulty that some morally outstanding heroes, such as Patroclus and Hector, did not escape death. Many interpreters assume that all heroes go to the Isles of the Blest (e.g. Pal., Sittl, Wil., *Aufbau*, 131, Nicolai, 45, Quaglia, 106-12, Solmsen, AJP 103, 1980, 22-4). Solmsen argues (1) that "as a glance at the account of the golden and silver generation shows, death is the prior condition for an elevated status", and (2) that justice demands the same fate for all. But (1) many epic heroes did not die, and (2) Hes. could hardly disregard the Homeric view that the persons going to the Isles of the Blest did not die (δ 560-1). It is true that Pindar (*O.* 2, 57 ff.) has a different view, but this is closely connected with his belief in rebirth, and such a belief can hardly be attributed to Hes. Consequently, his account seems to be a compromise between the demands of justice and those of the epic tradition.

167: βίοτον. Not 'a living' (Ev., Latt.; similarly Maz. 'une existence') but 'means of living', 'substance': cf. 172-3, and *Lex.* II, 63. 29 ff.

167: καὶ ἤθεα. For the observance of the digamma cf. A. Hoekstra, Mnem. IV 10 (1957), 220-1.

168: ἐς πείρατα. We. prints ἐν πείρασι, the reading of a papyrus published by H. Maehler, MH 24 (1967), 63 ff., who thinks that ἐς πείρατα stems from Hom. δ 563-4 ἀλλά σ' ἐς Ἠλύσιον πεδίον καὶ πείρατα γαίης / ἀθάνατοι πέμψουσιν. This is true, but the borrowing should be ascribed to Hes. himself: his description of the race of heroes is especially full of Homeric phrases (cf. Wil. on 161, Krafft, 119). The reading of the papyrus is a *lectio*

---

[424] As is observed by We., who does not notice, however, that the extension of the number is one of the points telling against his assumption that *Iliad* and *Odyssey* are post-Hesiodic: cf. N. J. Richardson, JHS 99 (1979), 170.

facilior: cf. e.g. *Th*. 329, Pind. *P*. 5, 70-1. We. suggests that the construction with εἰς may be a later use (cf. καθίζω τινα εἰς), but Homer has both κατατίθημι ἐν (Π 683, ν 135) and κατατίθημι εἰς (ν 230, π 285, τ 17, υ 96).

For πεῖραρ 'boundary' cf. Onians, 310 ff., A. L. T. Bergren, *The Etymology and Usage of* πεῖραρ *in Early Greek Poetry* (University Park, Pa. 1975). Oceanus was conceived as not only encircling but even 'binding' the earth: cf. *Th*. 790-1 and Onians, 316-7.

169. Belongs to the interpolation 173 a-e: see We. *ad loc*. For Kronos as a ruler of the Isles of the Blest (incompatible with *Th*. 717, 729-33, 851) cf. also M. Pohlenz, RE XI (1922), 2007-8.

170: μέν. Cf. 161 τοὺς μέν, and see above, on 111 μέν.

170: ἀκηδέα θυμὸν ἔχοντες. Repeated from 112. Similarly 172-3 is a reminiscence of 117-8[425].

171: ἐν μακάρων νήσοισι. We. observes that "μάκαρες unqualified in the poetic language almost always means 'the gods'" (e.g. above, 136). He concludes that these islands may originally have been 'isles of the gods', but his arguments are too vague to carry conviction. For μάκαρες denoting semi-divine beings cf. 730 μακάρων τοι νύκτες ἔασιν, which refers to 'spirits' like the δαίμονες of 122 ff. rather than to the Olympians[426]. The conception of Isles of the Blest may have Near-Eastern and/or Minoan origins[427], but the description as a paradise is so general that a more precise localization does not seem to be necessary[428].

171: παρά. We. thinks that "the preposition suits a shore better than islands", but it appears from *Th*. 790-1 that Hes. assumed an area of 'ordinary' sea between the shore of the earth and the (river) Oceanus, and it may be in this sea that the islands are situated[429].

171: Ὠκεανόν. According to Homer (Ω 246), Oceanus is 'the origin of everything' (γένεσις πάντεσσι): its eternal self-movement (βαθυδίνης)[430]

---

[425] As is observed by P. Walcot, REG 74 (1961), 5, who is wrong, however, in speaking of ring-composition: cf. Rudhardt, 281 n. 114, who points out the differences between the golden race and the race of heroes. See also V. Goldschmidt, *Questions platoniciennes* (Paris 1970), 166-70.

[426] As is suggested by C. de Heer, Μάκαρ (above, n. 392), 23, who seems to me wrong, however, in thinking (22) that these δαίμονες "might have their headquarters on the island".

[427] Cf. F. Hommel, *Die Insel der Seeligen in Sage und Mythus der Vorzeit* (Munich 1901), L. Malten, JAI 28 (1913), 35 ff., Nilsson, 325-6, P. M. Schuhl, *Essai sur la formation de la pensée grecque* (²Paris 1949), 103-5, Motte, *Prairies* (above, n. 88), 255-8, C. Froidefond, *Le mirage égyptien* (Aix-en-Provence 1971), 40-1.

[428] See further Rohde I, 68-90, E. Norden, *Aeneis, Buch VI* (³Leipzig 1926), 18 ff., 295 ff., A. Schulten, Geogr. Zeitschr. 32 (1926), 229 ff., H. Wagenvoort, *Studies in Roman Literature, Culture and Religion* (Leiden 1956), 274 ff., Dietrich, *Death* (above, n. 281), 345 ff., H. von Geisau KP III, 908-9, H. Thesleff, in *Gnomosyne* (above, n. 192), 34-6.

[429] A. Lesky, *Thalatta* (Vienna 1947), 70-1, can hardly be right in locating the Isles "jenseits des Okeanos", for in that case they would not be islands.

[430] Cf. also the epithets βαθυρρείτης, βαθύρροος, ἀψόρροος, and A. *Prom*. 139 ἀκοιμήτῳ

expresses its power as the source of universal life[431]. Its nearness may well have exercised a vitalizing influence on the inhabitants of the Isles[432].

172: ὄλβιοι. 'Happy on account of god-given abundance': cf. Hom. ρ 419-20 οἶκον ... ἔναιον / ὄλβιος ἀφνειόν, de Heer (above, n. 392), 15, 20-2, Richardson on *H. Dem.* 480.

172: τοῖσιν. For ὄλβιος, ὅς as a formula of μακαρισμός cf. Richardson, *loc. cit.*

172: μελιηδέα. We. rightly observes that καρπόν refers to corn in the first place (just as at 117), but it should be added that in this case the word does not denote a sweet flavour but means 'delicious': cf. Hom. Κ 569 μελιηδέα πυρόν, Θ 188 μελίφρονα πυρόν, ω 489 σίτοιο μελίφρονος[433].

173: τρίς. May be lengthened before the initial digamma of ἔτεος (LSJ), but at 596 "the frequency with which the word stands before a consonant, especially in the emphatic position at the beginning of the line (21 × *Il.* out of 30 occurrences, 9 × *Od.* out of 13), has caused Hesiod to use it as a heavy syllable in its own right" (Edwards, 79-80), and this may be the case here, too.

'Thrice' as a symbol of abundance (similarly δ 86) is based on 'three' as a symbol of completion and perfection: cf. Hom. ε 306, ζ 154 τρὶς μάκαρες, Θ 488 τρίλλιστος, and many similar compounds. See further my note on E. *Ba.* 123 τρικόρυθες, Mnem. IV 34 (1981), 306-7, and the literature mentioned there.

173: ζείδωρος. See above, on 117 ζείδωρος.

174: μηκέτι. Hes. uses μή because ὤφελλον μετεῖναι is equivalent to an optative: cf. K.G. I, 207, Wackernagel I, 228. The parallels adduced by We. to explain ἔτι are irrelevant: Hes. did not live during the preceding ages. Pal., Maz., Si. take the sentence to mean 'Next there came another age, in which I am living, but would that I might no longer live in it', but the phrase πρόσθε θανεῖν shows that the meaning is 'would that I had never lived in it'. The force of ἔτι seems to be purely rhetorical, lending emphasis to μή: cf. Hom. κ 297 ἔνθα σὺ μηκέτ' ἔπειτ' ἀπανήνασθαι θεοῦ εὐνήν (there has not been a previous opportunity to accept such a contact), Pind. *O.* 1, 5-6 μηκέτ' ἀελίου σκόπει / ἄλλο θαλπνότερον (the poet is not yet looking out for the brightest star). See also my note on Tyrt. 6-7 D., 14, Mnem. IV 22 (1969), 345.

ῥεύματι. See further J. Rudhardt, *Le thème de l'eau primordiale dans la mythologie grecque* (Bern 1971), 27-8, 75.

[431] Cf. Pl. *The.* 152 e, 180 cd, Arist. *Met.* 983 b 30, Virg. *Georg.* 4, 382, Rudhardt, *op. cit.*, 35-45, and my essay *De adem Gods*, Meded. Kon. Ned. Akad. v. Wet., Lett. N.R. 36:8 (1973), 17-24, espec. 20.

[432] Homer mentions the cooling winds issuing from the Oceanus, but the verb ἀναψύχειν might have the overtone of 'reviving': cf. N. 84 ἀνέψυχον φίλον ἦτορ and ω 348 ἀποψύχοντα 'fainting'.

[433] Where Ameis-Hentze seem to me wrong in thinking that σίτοιο includes wine. I even doubt whether μελιηδής said of wine means 'sweet' in a literal sense: wine, too, is called μελίφρων (Ζ 264, η 182, ν 53), just as sleep (Β 34).

174: πέμπτοισι. This race is not especially created by the gods because it consists of the descendants of the men who had lived in the heroic age: see above, on 158 ἄρειον and 160 προτέρη [434].

175: ἔπειτα. This has been taken to allude to a return of the golden age (e.g. by Pal., Hays, Si., pp. 15-6) or to a sixth age better than the fifth (Krafft, 116, Quaglia, 91), but there is no trace of a cyclic view of world history in Hes. [435]. Others have suggested that ἔπειτα refers to a time in the present age when some improvement will have been achieved [436], but such an improvement will not set in without his own present activity. Consequently, the wish to be born later cannot be meant seriously: it forms a rhetorical complement to πρόσθε θανεῖν (see above, on 9 ἰδών), and the whole phrase means that Hes. would have preferred to live at any time but the present one (Maz.).

This does not imply, however, that Hes. was a pessimist [437]. He would never have agreed with the view that 'the best thing of all is not to have been born' (Thgn. 425) [438]. Hes. solemnly declares (180 ff.) that mankind approaches its own destruction, but this is not an expression of despair [439]. The fact that he profuses in good advice and exhortation betrays his belief that things might take a turn for the better [440]. This also appears from such positive prospects

---

[434] This does not imply that the whole present population is descended from the heroes (see above, n. 416): Fontenrose (above, n. 323), 10, points out that "Hesiod knew very well that in the time of the Trojan and Theban wars the population in general did not consist of heroes". He is wrong, however, in concluding that the heroic age "is not a separate age, but the first part of the fourth and final age of iron": it appears from 180 that the iron race is one separate age. It may be added that Hes. does not mention the common people living in the heroic age because in the literary tradition the heroes put their stamp upon that age.

[435] For the meaning of *Th.* 38 τά τ' ἐσσόμενα cf. my remarks in Mnem. IV 25 (1972), 238-9. Walcot (*Near East*, 81-2) thinks that the myth of the ages ends at 173 and so consists of an ascending pair and a descending pair, but 174 πέμπτοισι and 176 γένος clearly show that the iron race belongs to the series. Quaglia's assumption (91-2) of three pairs of ages, the first descending, the second and the last ascending, does not make sense either in Hes.'s argument. For the theories proposed by V. Goldschmidt and J. P. Vernant cf. the critical remarks made by K. Matthiessen, in *Arktouros* (above, n. 415), 25 ff.

[436] E.g. Kerschensteiner, 175: "Wenn die tätige Überwindung der Not erreicht ist". Similarly Rudhardt, 281. Rosenmeyer's explanation (in Heitsch, 633), that Hes. expresses his aversion from the present situation but leaves the prospect of the future open, is too vague.

[437] As is held e.g. by H. Frisch, *Might and Right in Antiquity* (Copenhagen 1949), 86: "The deepest element in Hesiod's poetry is his pessimism". Similarly W. Nestle, Neue Jbb. 24 (1921), 83.

[438] Parallels are quoted by Greene, *Moira* (above, n. 80), 42 n. 189.

[439] As is assumed by J. Burckhardt, *Griechische Kulturgeschichte* (ed. by J. Oeri, Berlin-Stuttgart), II, 384, who ascribes to Hes. a "völlige Verzweiflung wegen Gegenwart und Zukunft". Similarly A. J. Festugière, *L'idéal religieux des Grecs et l'Évangile* (Paris 1932), 162.

[440] Wil. rightly remarks (154) that Hes. "hat die mutige Bejahung des Lebens darum nicht aufgegeben, dass das Leben Mühe und Arbeit ist". V. 418 κηριτρεφέων ἀνθρώπων might be adduced as an indication of fundamental pessimism, but such translations as 'born to misery' (LSJ) are misleading: the word means 'growing up for destruction', i.e. destined to die, and the context shows that the risk of fatal diseases is meant (cf. 92). Cf. also Schütz, Ἀσθένεια (above, n. 217), 170-1. On the other hand, H. Diels, *Der antike Pessimismus* (Berlin 1921), 7, goes too far when he calls Hes. the first "Überwinder des Pessimismus" and "ein wahrhaft faustischer

as 225-37 and 285. Accordingly, 174-5, just as 271-2 and Hom. β 230-4, is not a real wish but a rhetorical sigh, and 180 ff. is not a real prediction but a warning presented as a description of the consequences which will follow if the warning should be neglected[441]. See further below, on 179.

176: σιδήρεον. We. writes that "this time the name of the metal evidently has a built-in emotive value". He refers to *Th.* 764 σιδηρέη μὲν κραδίη, χάλκεον δέ οἱ ἦτορ, and in his note on that line he suggests that "Death is tireless as well as merciless". But in the Homeric parallels σιδήρεος, just as χάλκεος (B 490), more often refers to stubbornness and steadfastness than to mercilessness (ε 191), and never to moral insensibility, which is the characteristic of the iron age (185 ff.)[442]. Hes. chose iron simply because it came into general use later than bronze (151)[443].

176: οὐδέ. Cf. Denn., 193: "Kühner (II ii 294) observes that, when one οὐδέ is followed by another, the two never stand in reciprocal relation, like οὔτε ... οὔτε: but that either (*a*) the first is adverbial, the second connective: or (*b*) both are connective". The present case is an obvious example of (*b*), but it should be added that the first οὐδέ has explanatory (specifying) force (see above, on 40 οὐδέ), while the second gives the effect of climax ('and not even'), just as οὐδέ after οὔτε (Denn., 193).

176: ἦμαρ. Adverbial, properly an acc. of time: cf. Hom. E 490 νύκτας τε καὶ ἦμαρ, K.G. I, 314.

177: παύσονται. Wil. and Ev. read παύονται, but the sequel shows that a future is necessary. Rosenmeyer (in Heitsch, 634-5) suggests that this future denotes a necessary rather than a purely temporal prospect (cf. K.G. I, 175, Schw. II, 290-2)[444], but this explanation does not suit the futures at 179 and 184-96. We. thinks that οὐδέ ποτ' ... παύσονται καμάτου is equivalent to 'they suffer ills which will never end' and that "the futures in 178-9 follow by attraction". But that attraction can hardly extend to 182 ff. Pal. seems to me right in his view that Hes. regards his own lifetime as the beginning of a period in which matters will become worse and worse (similarly Hays,

---

Mensch": (1) pessimism did not yet exist in Hes.'s time, and (2) his optimism is based on his belief in Zeus (cf. 273).

[441] Cf. E. K. Rand, AJP 32 (1911), 142: "Both poets [Hes. and Horace] intend not an historical forecast, but moral denunciation, in the hope that it may prove a spur to moral activity. The pessimism of the moment is sincere, but in neither case is it incompatible with a temperament essentially courageous and urbane". Similarly Solmsen, *Hes.*, 89, Rudhardt, 281, Quaglia, 112-3.

[442] This distinction has been neglected by Quaglia (112 n.64), who thinks that the metaphorical use "ha gran peso" in the present context.

[443] Although Wil. (140) calls it "selten und neu": it is mentioned 52 times in Homer, and it was already used in Mycenaean times. See further A. Lang, *The World of Homer* (London 1910), Ch. X, P. Cauer, *Grundfragen der Homerkritik* (³Leipzig 1921), 311 ff., H. L. Lorimer, *Homer and the Monuments* (London 1950), 111 ff., R. J. Forbes, *Studies in Ancient Technology*, IX (²Leiden 1972).

[444] Similarly B. A. van Groningen, *In the Grip of the Past* (Leiden 1953), 118-9.

Nicolai, 47)[445]. If this interpretation is accepted, We.'s reference to an oriental model (in his note on 179-81) becomes superfluous.

177: καμάτου. 'Suffering', probably including the fatigue caused by hard work (305, *Th.* 599, Hom. ξ 417). See above, on 91 πόνοιο[446].

177: τι. See above, on 113 τι.

178: φθειρόμενοι. We. reads τειρόμενοι "with some confidence", and Renehan (344) thinks that it "rightly belongs in the text". Solmsen has adopted it in his second edition, but it is an unnecessary *lectio facilior*. Similarly, Eusebius' στεινόμενοι and Clement's γινόμενοι (= γεινόμενοι) are no palaeographical errors (as is suggested by We.) but deliberate attempts at precluding a misunderstanding of φθειρόμενοι in the sense of complete destruction. For the meaning 'withering' cf. S. *El.* 1181, *O.R.* 1502.

178: δέ. Has explanatory (motivating) force: see above, on 13 δέ.

178: θεοὶ δώσουσι. Obviously in return for man's injustice described at 182 ff. This remark would be superfluous if it had not been suggested[447] that 176-9 refer to the present time, in which a mixture of good and evil falls to man as a fate, just as at Hom. Ω 529, whereas 182 ff. describe the future, in which man himself will be to blame for his misfortune. Such a distinction cannot be maintained, for (1) it does not account for the futures at 177-9, and (2) Hes. certainly did not believe that the miseries of the present lay outside man's own responsibility.

178: μερίμνας. I do not believe that this especially refers to νύκτωρ (We.): cf. Sa. 1, 25-6 χαλέπαν δὲ λῦσον / ἐκ μερίμναν, Thgn. 343 κακῶν ἄμπαυμα μεριμνέων, etc.

179: μεμείξεται ἐσθλά. *Scil.* if men pay heed to Hes.'s admonitions and abstain from injustice[448]. For ἐσθλός 'profitable' (not 'edel', as is assumed by E. Meyer, in Heitsch, 509-10) see above, on 116 ἐσθλά. We. thinks that 179-81 "seem to interrupt the train of thought inopportunely" (the lines are bracketed by Rz., Waltz, Ev., Hays)[449], but his own explanation, that the conception of life as a mixture of good and bad was "a tenet of popular

---

[445] Cf. also L. Edmunds, HSCP 79 (1975), 84, who speaks of "a tendency, of which the present may be as representative as the future".

[446] Fontenrose (above, n. 323), 11 n. 21, argues that "Hesiod's point is that iron men will *not* work". But after the deceit committed by Prometheus work has become a bitter necessity (42-6), and Hes. does not suggest that his contemporaries increasingly turn to crime and fraud *because* they increasingly abstain from work, as is assumed by Fontenrose (11).

[447] By Krause, Ἄλλοτε ἄλλος (above, on 5 χαλέπτει), 71-2.

[448] Krafft's interpretation (120), "Mühen und Plagen tragen auch Früchte, solange man sie auf sich nimmt", is incompatible with the context (178 φθειρόμενοι).

[449] Solmsen, HSCP 86 (1982), 21, thinks that "here a rhapsode unwilling to expose his audience to the unmitigated horrors of their moral decline tries to comfort them ... The place for which it was originally intended was perhaps some ten or twenty lines later where the description of sins rampant in the world has become truly unbearable". But the mere description of an unbearable situation cannot have an apotreptic effect, and such an effect has certainly been intended by Hes. (see above, on 106 ἕτερον).

wisdom" and that "179 makes clear the difference between the present and the terrible final stage", is rather poor. The optimistic note of 179 seems to be based on Hes.'s self-confidence as a moral preacher: the preceding story has shown a degeneration in the development of mankind, but also the possibility of escaping divine punishment. The permanent order of the world established by Zeus ties up the present to the past, but leaves open a margin of human choice which may modify the future[450]. Accordingly, Hes. is convinced that his argument might save his contemporaries from further degeneration, and he proleptically includes this perspective in his gloomy picture of the future (for a similar expression of confidence see below, on 273)[451]. But he immediately realizes that his assurance might tempt his audience to careless-ness, and he therefore adds another prolepsis, a hint at the ultimate conse-quences of a bad development, meant to reinforce his warning.

181: γεινόμενοι. 'As soon as they were born': We. compares *Th.* 82 and A. *Sept.* 664. In such cases usually εὐθύς or similar adverbs are added: cf. K.G. II, 82-3.

181: πολιοκρόταφοι. Greyness begins on the temples: cf. Gow on Theocr. 14, 68. It is misleading to say: "In dem Greisentum der Neugeborenen liegt, dass sie gar nicht lebensfähig sind, aber wir empfinden mit, dass die Jugend immer altklüger und aberweiser wird" (Wil.), for (1) the sequel suggests that they die from neglect (188) rather than from physical weakness, and (2) their intellectual precocity is less evident than their moral immaturity[452]. They form a counterpart to the endless childhood of the silver race: the latter never reach moral and social maturity (see above, on 131 νήπιος), but the men of the iron race will grow old at an increasingly early age: accordingly, their moral development will be hampered more and more by the rigidity of old age, and their state of mind will become so inflexible that they will be unable to adapt their behaviour one to another (see below, on 182 ὁμοίιος)[453].

181: τελέθωσιν. 'Turn out to be' (We.): cf. e.g. Hom. η 51-2 θαρσαλέος

---

[450] Cf. Fuss, 41 n. 1, H. Diller, in Heitsch, 263, Lenz, 231. Gatz (above, n. 341), 25, is too vague in speaking of "die allgemeine Hoffnung, dass einmal wieder bessere Zeiten heraufkommen werden".

[451] I do not believe that Hes., like an accurate historian, feels obliged to record the few good things which always exist in bad times, as is suggested by Rosenmeyer, in Heitsch, 633.

[452] E. Meyer (in Heitsch, 510) writes: "gesteigerte Individualisierung und rücksichtsloser Egoismus sind die Ergebnisse des intellektuellen Fortschritts". This could be written in 1910, but not in Hes.'s time.

[453] Krafft (120 n. 1) suggests "dass die Jugend schon mit Ansprüchen auftritt, die erst ein Greis nach arbeitsamem Leben stellen kann: sie meint, diese Mühen nicht auf sich nehmen zu brauchen", but the idea of arrogant laziness is foreign to the context. Kirk, *Myth* (above, n. 208), 233-5, rightly considers progressive immaturity to be the leitmotiv of the History of the Ages, but does not sufficiently emphasize its moral and social character. He further wrongly adopts Vernant's division of the races into three pairs. The Indian and other parallels adduced by Reitzenstein (above, n. 415), 52 ff., 63, 67, and We. do not carry us much further.

γὰρ ἀνὴρ ἐν πᾶσιν ἀμείνων / ἔργοισιν τελέθει, and the similar use of γίγνομαι (above, on 88 γένηται).

182: οὐδὲ ... οὐδέ. See above, on 176 οὐδέ. The first οὐδέ now seems to have motivating rather than specifying force (179-81 being a kind of parenthesis): cf. Hom. A 124, Σ 126, γ 23, and my note on Men. *Epitr.* 302, Mnem. IV 27 (1974), 30.

182: πατὴρ παίδεσσιν. For the contrast cf. Fehling, 282.

182: ὁμοίιος. Different from ὁμοῖος (cf. We. and A. N. Athanassakis, RhM 119, 1976, 4-7), but here used as a synonym. The sequel shows that the meaning is equivalent to ὁμόφρων: cf. especially 184 φίλος and Arist. *EN* 1165 b 17 τὸ ὅμοιον τῷ ὁμοίῳ φίλον. Renehan (348) compares Hom. ρ 217-8 κακὸς κακὸν ἡγηλάζει, / ὡς αἰεὶ τὸν ὁμοῖον ἄγει θεὸς ὡς τὸν ὁμοῖον[454]. For conflicts between fathers and sons cf. S. Bertman (ed.), *The Conflict of Generations in Ancient Greece and Rome* (Amsterdam 1976), espec. 22, where M. Reinhold suggests "that in the period when Homer wrote ... age-old patterns of social cohesion were breaking apart, and that the stories of Phoenix and Meleager reflected contemporary dislocations".

182: τι. See above, on 177 τι. The fact that sons disagree with their father is more alarming than that a father disagrees with his sons.

182: παῖδες. *Scil.* πατρί. For the brachylogy cf. K.G. II, 566, Schw. II, 708-9. For the polyptoton see above, on 23 γείτονα γείτων. For Hes.'s love of drastic expressions see above, on 39 δωροφάγους, 41 ὄνειαρ, 66 γυιοκόρους.

183: ξεῖνος. For the importance of guest-friendship cf. Bolkestein, 214 ff., M. I. Finley, *The World of Odysseus* (Harmondsworth 1967), 115 ff., H. J. Kakridis, *La notion de l'amitié et de l'hospitalité chez Homère* (Thessaloniki 1963), 86 ff. See also below, on 225 and 327.

183: καί. We. compares *H. Dem.* 94-5 οὐδέ τις ἀνδρῶν / εἰσορόων γίγνωσκε βαθυζώνων τε γυναικῶν, but it should be added that here "τε steht in keiner Beziehung zu οὐδέ, sondern zu ἀνδρῶν (= ἀνδρῶν γυναικῶν τε)" (K.G. II, 293). In the present passage καί is to be explained in the same way.

183: ἑταῖρος. "Anyone who shares with another in a companionable activity ... Often it becomes a close, emotional relationship, in which mutual

---

[454] For ὁμόνοια in Greek ethics and politics cf. J. Ferguson, *Moral Values in the Ancient World* (London 1958), Ch. VII, F. Zucker, *Semantica, Rhetorica, Ethica* (Berlin 1963), 137 ff., B. Snell, *Dichtung und Gesellschaft* (Hamburg 1965), 33 ff., W. Fauth, KP II, 1209-10, G. J. D. Aalders, *Die Theorie der gemischten Verfassung im Altertum* (Amsterdam 1968), 23 n. 74, J. de Romilly, in *Mélanges P. Chantraine* (Paris 1972), 199 ff. and Rev. Phil. 46 (1972), 7 ff., Fraisse, *Philia* (below, on 183 ἑταῖρος), Index s.v. Communauté d'idées, E. Lévy, *Athènes devant la défaite de 404* (Paris 1976), 209 ff.

Neitzel (79-82) argues that general inferiority is meant and that after παῖδες not πατρί but παίδεσσιν is to be understood. But the idea of a progressive degeneration does not suit the context (even if φίλος is taken to be the predicate of both 183 and 184). Neitzel's objections to the traditional interpretation, (1) that it would require οὔτε τι instead of οὐδέ τι, and (2) that πατρί cannot be supplied after παῖδες, are refuted by the references given *ad loc.*

trust plays an important part" (We.). See further J. P. A. Eernstman, Οἰκεῖος, ἑταῖρος, ἐπιτήδειος, φίλος (Groningen 1932), 26 ff., J. C. Fraisse, *Philia. La notion d'amitié dans la philosophie antique* (Paris 1974), Index s.v. camaraderie.

184: κασίγνητος. At 707 the tie between brothers is assumed to be closer than that between ἑταῖροι. Similarly Thgn. 97-9. At Hom. Ω 47 a brother and a son are mentioned in the same breath as objects of affection. Cf. also Walcot, *Peasants*, 53, 78-9. It is not necessary to assume that Hes. is especially thinking of Perses (as is done by Kühn, 268).

184: φίλος. *Scil.* κασιγνήτῳ. Affection need not be absent from φιλία, but the primary meaning is a close relationship based on common interests: cf. 353, 370. See further Eernstman (above, on 183 ἑταῖρος), 76 ff., Bolkestein, 83-5, 120, M. Landfester, *Das griechische Nomen Philos und seine Ableitungen* (Hildesheim 1966), Fraisse, *Philia*, 46 ff., Dover, 276-7, and my note on Semon. 7, 62, Mnem. IV 21 (1968), 146.

185: αἶψα. "Probably not with the participle" (We.): this is correct in so far as the parents are not supposed to 'grow quickly old' (Ev.), but the meaning may be 'as soon as they grow old': see above, on 181 γεινόμενοι[455].

185: ἀτιμήσουσι. For the idea that respect has to be paid to parents cf. 331-2, Hom. β 130-4, Thgn. 277, 821-2. See further Bolkestein, 79-80, 118-9, Vollgraff (above, n. 230), 71-3, Dover, 273-5, 302, Preisshofen (above, n. 286), 44-6, Reinhold (above, on 182 ὁμοίιος), 25-7. J. W. Hewitt, AJP 52 (1931), 30-46, rightly points out that the sentiment is more often inspired by a sense of duty than by gratitude.

186: μέμψονται. Quarrels were likely to occur when parents and sons stayed living in the same house. Cf. Bolkestein, 282: "Staatliche Massregeln zur Versorgung alter Leute im allgemeinen sind uns nicht bekannt".

186: δέ. Has explanatory (specifying) force: see above, on 9 δέ.

186: ἄρα. 'As one can imagine': see above, on 49 ἄρα. For δ' ἄρα cf. Denn., 33-5.

186: χαλεποῖς. 'Harsh', properly 'hard to deal with'. Similarly Hom. Β 245 χαλεπῷ ἠνίπαπε μύθῳ, Γ 438 χαλεποῖσιν ὀνείδεσι, and χαλεπαίνω.

186: βάζοντες. Properly 'to talk', but practically synonymous with ἀγορεύω, λέγω: cf. R. van Bennekom, *Lex.* II, 1. For the construction with dative cf. Hom. κ 34 ἐπέεσσι πρὸς ἀλλήλους ἀγόρευον, A. *Sept.* 571 κακοῖσι βάζει πολλὰ Τυδέως βίαν. The latter parallel shows that in the present passage τούς may belong both to μέμψονται and to βάζοντες.

187: σχέτλιοι. 'Hard-hearted': see above, on 15 σχετλίη.

187: οὐδέ. Wil. keeps οὔτε given by all MSS., but his argument that οὐδέ

---

[455] I doubt whether Hom. Π 354-5 οἱ δὲ ἰδόντες / αἶψα διαρπάζουσιν is a parallel, as is assumed by H. Erbse, *Lex.*, 399.72: here αἶψα seems to intensify διαρπάζουσιν.

κεν ... δοῖεν is equivalent to οὔτε τοκήων is based on the wrong assumption that ὄπιν εἰδότες means 'having respect for' (see next note). For the formulaic character of σχέτλιος, οὐδέ cf. Hom. I 630, δ 729, φ 28 (σχέτλιος, οὐδὲ θεῶν ὄπιν ἠδέσατ' οὐδὲ τράπεζαν), ψ 150. Similarly νήπιος, οὐδέ (having specifying force): see above, on 40 νήπιοι, οὐδέ.

187: θεῶν ὄπιν. Not 'respect for the gods' (Wil.) or 'fear of the gods' (Maz., Ev.), but 'divine vengeance' (properly the regard paid by the gods to human affairs[456]): cf. 251, 706, *Th.* 222, Hom. Π 388, ξ 82 and 88, υ 215. Only at Tyrt. 6-7 D. = 10 W., 12 and afterwards ὄπις is used as a human sentiment[457]. Wil. (on 327) writes: "Der πατραλοίας ist verfehmt; aber welche Steigerung, wenn ein böses Wort gegen die alten Eltern eine Sünde ist, die Gott nicht verzeiht. Eine jede reformatorische Ethik muss weiter gehen als das Leben verträgt". But to pay respect to one's parents was generally felt as a religious duty: the honour due to parents was called ἰσόθεος (Aeschin. 1, 28, Men. fr. 600), and that this was not a mere hyperbole appears from Xen. *Mem.* II 2, 14 σὺ οὖν, ὦ παῖ, ἂν σωφρονῇς, τοὺς μὲν θεοὺς παραιτήσῃ συγγνώμονάς σοι εἶναι, εἴ τι παρημέληκας τῆς μητρός, μή σε καὶ οὗτοι νομίσαντες ἀχάριστον εἶναι οὐκ ἐθελήσωσιν εὖ ποιεῖν[458].

187: εἰδότες. 'Caring about': cf. Hom. Ε 761 οὔ τινα οἶδε θέμιστα, Ζ 351 ἤδη νέμεσίν τε καὶ αἴσχεα πόλλ' ἀνθρώπων. Krafft (80 n. 1) thinks the use of the participle "befremdlich": it may be explained as an assimilation to the participle βάζοντες.

187: μέν. Most editors reads κεν, but We. rightly observes that the potential particle may be omitted: cf. Hom. Τ 321 οὐ μὲν γάρ τι κακώτερον ἄλλο πάθοιμι, and Chantr. II, 216-8. We. translates 'nor again' and refers to Denn., 362, but Denn. himself admits that "far more probably μέν is emphatic" rather than progressive: for emphatic μέν see above, on 122 μέν.

188: γηράντεσσι. From aor. ἐγήραν: cf. Hom. Ρ 197, Chantr. I, 380, Jebb

---

[456] Cf. Porzig, *Die Namen für Satzinhalte im Griechischen und im Indogermanischen* (Berlin 1942), 352. W. Burkert, MH 38 (1981), 198 ff., explains the original meaning of ὄπις as equivalent to ὄπισθεν, but his arguments are insufficient: (1) it may be true that ὄπις cannot mean 'Auge' or 'Blicker' (198), but I do not see why it cannot mean 'look' (and hence 'regard'); (2) Burkert (199) calls ὄπιν οὐκ ἀλέγοντες (251 and Hom. Π 338) "eine syntaktische Anomalie" and thinks (200) that ζ 268 ὅπλα ... ἀλέγουσιν "ist etwas anders gelagert, insofern hier ein sehr direktes Objekt der Hantierung bezeichnet ist", but he forgets ν 23 δαῖτ' ἀλέγυνον (said of guests).

[457] Cf. my note in Mnem. IV 22 (1969), 344. I do no longer believe that at Hom. ξ 82 ὄπιν refers to a human sentiment: the word is defined by the next line (οὐ μὲν σχέτλια ἔργα θεοὶ μάκαρες φιλέουσιν), just as at *Th.* 221-2 it is defined by the context. Kaufmann-Bühler (285 ff.), who argues that ξ 83-4 are an interpolation, thinks that ὄπις at 82 and 88 refers to the fear of the vengeance of the victims, but such a usage would be unparalleled. He further observes (285 n. 3) that elsewhere the outer objects of φρονεῖν are adjectives or pronouns, but I do not think that this constitutes a difficulty. There is no difficulty either in φρονέοντες ('having in mind') having an external as well as an internal object.

[458] On the other hand, Bolkestein (119 and n. 1) is wrong in thinking that parents are called by Plato θεοὶ ζῶντες.

on S. *O.C.* 870, M. Schmidt, *Lex.* II, 146. We. maintains: "The repetition of 'aging parents' is clumsy, and suggests that Hesiod has taken over the line ready-made". But the repetition is emphatic: growing old is the central idea of this passage. Cf. 219 σκολιῇσι δίκῃσιν, 221 σκολιῆς δὲ δίκης, 227 τέθηλε, 236 θάλλουσιν, 284-5 γενεὴ μετόπισθε, 301 βιότου δὲ τεὴν πιμπλῇσι καλιήν, 307 βιότου πλήθωσι καλιαί, 302 ἀεργῷ, 303 ἀεργός, 305 ἀεργοί, 514, 516, 517, 519 διάῃσι, *Th.* 25 κοῦραι Διὸς αἰγιόχοιο, 29 κοῦραι μεγάλου Διός (Hes.'s consecration as a poet is implicitly sanctioned by Zeus), We. on *Th.* 429 ff. (whose comment, "We see again the limited range of Hesiod's expression", is misleading), Sellschopp, 113, and my notes on *Th.* 67, Mnem. IV 25 (1972), 248-9, and 551 γνῶ, Mnem. IV 24 (1971), 4. See also below, on 205 ὀνύχεσσι.

188: ἀπὸ ... δοῖεν. For the tmesis see above, on 59 ἐκ δ' ἐγέλασσε.

188: θρεπτήρια. 'Return for rearing', θρέπτρα in Homer, τροφεῖα in Attic. See further Bolkestein, 80, 160-1. Jaeger, *Paideia*, I (Engl. ed.), 415-6, observes that this passage refers to the three main ἄγραφοι νόμοι, respect for parents, gods, and strangers, although their formulation as a tripartite code is not found before Aeschylus (*Suppl.* 701-9)[459].

188: δοῖεν. An urbane expression for 'they certainly will ...': see above, on 10 μυθησαίμην.

189. Bracketed by many editors[460], but defended by We., who argues that "the repayment of the debt owed to one's parents has a strong connotation of τὸ δίκαιον, what is fair and equal. These people are χειροδίκαι, might is their right. This idea leads easily to that of inter-state aggression, and then to δίκη within the state". But the paraphrase "might is right" is too weak: χειροδίκαι is 'passing sentence with their hands', i.e., deciding disputed questions by violence instead of by argument (see below, on 192 δίκη δ' ἐν χερσί), and it obviously refers to people who take possession of something, not to sons who withdraw from paying their due to their parents. Secondly, the transition from misconduct within the family to inter-state conflicts seems to be intolerably harsh. On the other hand, χειροδίκαι gives the impression of being a truly Hesiodic formation (cf. 230 ἰθυδίκῃσι). The best solution seems to be to put the line after 181, as has been proposed by A. Pertusi, Aevum 26 (1952), 220 ff.: πολιοκρόταφοι are still able to wage wars.

189: ἕτερος. We. remarks that "the singular suits monarchs", but the word is more likely to have a collective sense: cf. Thuc. II 51, 4 ἕτερος ἀφ' ἑτέρου ἀναπιμπλάμενοι, and K.G. I, 286-8.

---

[459] See further R. Hirzel, Ἄγραφος νόμος, Abh. Sächs. Ges. d. Wiss. 20 (1901), 1-98, *id.*, *Themis, Dike und Verwandtes* (Leipzig 1907), 359-410, Greene, *Moira* (above, n. 80), 227-8, F. Heinimann, *Nomos und Physis* (Basel 1945), 124-5, 166-7.

[460] Wil. withdraws his rejection in Hermes 63 (1928), 389.

189: ἐξαλαπάξει. For the intensifying force of ἐξ- see above, on 48 ἐξαπάτησε.

190: εὐόρκου. Fidelity to oaths is the most convincing proof of moral integrity: cf. e.g. 219, 282, Thgn. 1139, Pind. *O.* 2, 66, E. *Med.* 439, Ar. *Plut.* 61. Perjury seems to have been a weakness of the Greeks, as appears from the self-imprecation which often accompanied the oath (e.g. Hom. Γ 300-1)[461]. Cf. also below, on 219 Ὅρκος. For the substantival use of the adjective ('a man who keeps his oath') see above, on 71 ἴκελον.

190: χάρις. 'Appreciation' (properly 'favourable disposition'): cf. Hom. δ 695 οὐδέ τις ἔστι χάρις μετόπισθ' ἐυεργέων.

190: οὐδέ. Rightly preferred by So. and We. to οὔτε: it may have consecutive force (see above, on 28 μηδέ).

191: οὔτε. Rightly kept by We.: for single οὔτε used simply to add something cf. K.G. II, 289, Denn., 509-10, and my note on Pl. *Meno* 91 c 2, Mnem. IV 17 (1964), 273.

191-2: ὕβριν ἀνέρα. Ev. reads ἀνέρες αἰνήσουσι, but the phrase is a combination of two rather common idioms, viz. (1) the use of a substantive as an attribute (originally an apposition, or more properly, a 'parathesis'[462]) of another substantive: cf. Hom. Α 358 παρὰ πατρὶ γέροντι, Ι 477 φυλακάς τ' ἄνδρας δμωάς τε γυναῖκας, K.G. I, 271-3, Schw. II, 614, Wilamowitz on E. *H.F.* 466, Renehan, 348[463]; (2) the use of *abstractum pro concreto*: cf. Hom. γ 49 νεώτερός ἐστιν, ὁμηλικίη δ' ἐμοὶ αὐτῷ, Λ 216 ἀρτύνθη δὲ μάχη, Ζ 145-6 τί ἢ γενεὴν (my descent) ἐρεείνεις; / οἵη περ φύλλων γενεή (a generation), τοίη δὲ καὶ ἀνδρῶν. These examples show that We.'s paraphrase, 'He is Hybris incarnate' (similarly Col.), is wrong[464]. See further K.G. I, 10-1 (who wrongly speak of 'metonymy', for the idiom is no artificial figure of speech: cf. the transition from abstract to concrete at Ζ 145-6). I do not know an exact parallel for the combination: Eup. 376 ὄλεθρος ἄνθρωπος is different, for there ὄλεθρος does not denote a quality but the man's effect on others (see n. 464). For the meaning of ὕβρις see below, on 213 ὕβριν.

192: τιμήσουσι. For the idea that honour is paid to those who do not

---

[461] R. S. Bluck, *Plato, Meno* (Cambridge 1961), 74 n. 8, rightly remarks: "A particularly severe attitude to perjury would be appropriate in an age when there were no written contracts" (one might add: "so that the temptation of perjury could easily arise"). See further R. Hirzel, *Der Eid* (Leipzig 1902), 142 ff., Samter, *Volkskunde* (above, n. 281), 32 ff., Rohde I, 65, K. Latte, *Meineid*, RE XV 1 (1931), 346, Luther, 90 ff., *id.*, *Weltansicht und Geistesleben* (Göttingen 1954), 86-8, E. Benveniste, Rev. hist. d. rel. 134 (1947-8), 81-94, Kaufmann-Bühler, 268 n. 3, E. Berneker, KP II, 209-10, Dover, 248-50.

[462] Cf. B. A. van Groningen, Mnem. III 9 (1941), 268-71.

[463] The usage is even found in inscriptions, e.g. δάφνῃ στεφάνῳ, θαλλῷ στεφάνῳ: cf. G. Daux, REG 54 (1941), 218-9.

[464] He is also wrong in comparing such cases as Hom. Π 498-9 σοὶ ... κατηφείη καὶ ὄνειδος ἔσσομαι, for ὕβριν denotes the man's quality, not his effect on others.

deserve it cf. Hom. I 319, υ 132-3, Thgn. 665-6, 1111-2, and my remarks in Lampas 5 (1972), 113.

192: δίκη δ' ἐν χερσί. An explanation of 189 χειροδίκαι. The meaning of δίκη is not 'justice' in the sense of 'right', but 'judicial sentence': cf. 230 ἰθυδίκῃσι μετ' ἀνδράσι and above, on 9 δίκη. For χείρ denoting physical violence cf. Hom. υ 267 ἐπίσχετε θυμὸν ἐνιπῆς καὶ χειρῶν, Xen. *Cyr.* I 5, 13 ἄρχοντες ἀδίκων χειρῶν, LSJ IV. For the use of *concretum pro abstracto* see below, on 267 ὀφθαλμός. For the plural of abstract notions see above, on 146 ὕβριες.

There is no difficulty in supplying ἔσται from 193 οὐκ ἔσται: copulative and existential εἶναι were not sharply distinguished, as appears e.g. from the use of adverbs with εἶναι: cf. Hom. H 424 διαγνῶναι χαλεπῶς ἦν, Hdt. IV 134, 2 ἀσφαλέως ἡ κομιδὴ ἡμῖν ἔσται, K.G. I, 43, Chantr. II, 9, LSJ C I, and Ch. H. Kahn, *The Verb 'Be' in Ancient Greek* (Dordrecht-Boston 1973), 150-6[465]. Accordingly, no semi-colon should be put after χερσί[466].

192: αἰδώς. Often misunderstood as 'sense of honour', 'sense of duty' (e.g. Wil.) or 'conscience' (Maz., Péron, 266, 272). In Mnem. III 12 (1944), 47-60, I have tried to show that the basic meaning is 'shrinking back' (German 'Scheu'), 'self-restraint' inspired by respect or reverence for some superior power. Cf. also my remarks in Lampas 5 (1972), 114, and my note on Pind. *N.* 11, 45 ἀναιδεῖ, ICS 7, 1 (1982), 35[467]. In so far as αἰδώς abstains from another's prerogative, it forms a complement to δίκη, which gives the other his due. The two terms are coupled again at Thgn. 938 (cf. 291-2), Pl. *Prot.* 322 c 2.

193: βλάψει. Properly 'thrust aside': cf. H. W. Nordheider, *Lex.* II, 64-5.

193: δέ. Has consecutive force: see above, on 18 δέ.

193: ὁ κακός. We. gives some examples of the article added to contrasted terms, but his last quotation, Hom. ρ 218 τὸν ὁμοῖον ἄγει θεὸς ὡς τὸν ὁμοῖον, shows that the article is used in contrasts because it has a generalizing function: cf. Chantr. II, 165. It should be added that its generalizing function

---

[465] Cf. also the critical remarks made by J. Klowski, Gnom. 47 (1975), 737-46, and C. J. Ruijgh, Lingua 48 (1979), 55-83, who take 'to be there' to be the basic meaning of εἶναι.

[466] Wilamowitz, Hermes 63 (1928), 389, withdraws his punctuation after χερσί and argues that ἐν χερσί ... ἔσται means 'will be at hand', 'will be there', but such parallels as ἐν χερσὶν ἔχειν τὸν γάμον (Hdt. I 35, 1), ἦν ἡ μάχη ἐν χερσί (Thuc. IV 43, 2) still show the literal sense of χείρ. We. reads ἐσσεῖται instead of οὐκ ἔσται, but Solmsen, Gnom. 52 (1980), 217, rightly remarks that "αἰδὼς ἔσται would be the opposite of what Hesiod wants to say, and αἰδὼς ἐν χερσίν makes no sense"; similarly, N. J. Richardson, JHS 99 (1979), 170, Renehan, 348.

[467] R. Harder, *Kleine Schriften* (Munich 1960), 210, is certainly wrong in taking αἰδώς in a passive sense as "die Respektzone, die den 'besseren Mann' umgibt". The definition proposed by A. Beil, Altspr. Unt. 5 (1961), 54, "die Regung der Befürchtung einer Entblössung", is equally impossible. A. Cheyns, Rech. de Phil. et de Ling. 2 (1968), 33, rightly observes that αἰδώς is "une sorte de retenue que le guerrier se garde de paraître lâche à ses compagnons", but still translates the word by 'sentiment de l'honneur'.

is based on its determinative force: cf. Schw. II, 22. The meaning of κακός, just as that of ἀρείονα (see above, on 158 ἄρειον), seems to be predominantly social: see below, on 213 Πέρση.

193: φῶτα. Synonymous with ἀνήρ: cf. my note on Pind. *I.* 2, 1, Mnem. IV 35 (1982), 1-2.

194: σκολιοῖς. See above, on 7 σκολιόν. The phrase refers to legal action: cf. 262.

194: ἐνέπων. The original form: cf. Chantr., *Dict. ét.*, 350. Properly 'telling', but here 'speaking': cf. LSJ 2, Fournier (above, n. 216), 47 ff.

194: ἐπί. In addition to his claim, rather than 'on it' (We.). Similarly Hom. I 274 ἐπὶ δὲ μέγαν ὅρκον ὀμεῖται, Φ 373 ἐγὼ δ᾽ ἐπὶ καὶ τόδ᾽ ὀμοῦμαι [468]. See also below, on 282.

194: ὀμεῖται. For the explanation of the future cf. Chantr. I, 451.

195: Ζῆλος. In a bad sense, as contrasted with 23 ζηλοῖ. The next line shows that the word should be capitalized: it is a superhuman power, just as bad Eris: see above, on 11 Ἐρίδων γένος. Cf. also Walcot, *Peasants*, 90, and *Envy* (above, on 23 ζηλοῖ), 13.

196: δυσκέλαδος. Not 'causing commotion' (We.) but 'foul-mouthed' (Ev.): cf. κέλαδος used of persons quarrelling at Hom. I 547, Σ 530, σ 402. At Hom. Π 357 δυσκέλαδος refers to cries of fear.

196: κακόχαρτος. See above, on 28, where the word is used of bad Eris.

196: ὁμαρτήσει. A semi-personification: see above, on 142 ὀπηδεῖ.

196: στυγερώπης. Not 'horrible' (LSJ) but 'with a malicious look': στυγερός always has a passive sense, but στυγνός is used both in an active and in a passive sense: cf. e.g. S. *Aj.* 561 στυγναῖσι λώβαις.

197: εὐρυοδείης. Not 'with broad ways' (LSJ) but 'with widely extending ways'. Similarly εὐρυάγυια: see my note on E. *Ba.* 87 εὐρυχόρους, Mnem. IV 34 (1981), 303.

198: λευκοῖσιν. Cf. Irwin (above, n. 411), 180: "Similarly, it was apparently their priestly office that prompted the prophets of Zeus in Crete to wear white (Eur. fr. 472, 16-19)".

198: φάρεσσι. Col. reads φαρέεσσι with the MSS., but the α is always long in Homer and still in Aeschylus.

198: καλυψαμένω. We. compares Thgn. 579 καλυψαμένη, but χρόα, which refers to the whole body, prevents us from thinking that they pull their cloaks over their heads, as is done by Odysseus (θ 85 and 92, κ 53). They apparently wrap their cloaks round themselves in order not to be defiled by the human world (Wil.). For the male ending of the participle cf. We. and K.G. I, 73-4, Schw. II, 35 n. 1, Troxler, 111 n. 4.

---

[468] We. thinks that these phrases support Leumann's explanation of ἐπίορκος, but not every ὅρκος is a false oath. See further below, n. 507.

198: χρόα. See above, on 74 χροΐ and 149 μέλεσσι.

200: Αἰδώς. See above, on 192 αἰδώς. A cult of Aidos cannot be dated with certainty before the 4th century (cf. Dem. 25, 35)[469], but the personification is certainly based on the feeling that she is a superhuman power: see above, on 11 Ἐρίδων γένος.

200: Νέμεσις. 'Decency' (Latt.) is too vague, and 'conscience collective' as opposed to αἰδώς 'conscience individuelle' (Péron, 269) is still more misleading: the meaning is 'public disapproval', properly 'distribution of what is due' (LSJ). See further Gruber, *Abstrakte Begriffe* (above, n. 54), 65 ff., J. C. Turpin, REG 93 (1980), 352-3 (whose own analysis, 353 ff., which results in the translation 'respect du devoir', seems to me unacceptable). The word is coupled with αἰδώς at Hom. N 121-2 ἀλλ' ἐν φρεσὶ θέσθε ἕκαστος / αἰδῶ καὶ νέμεσιν, where Ameis-Hentze explain νέμεσιν as "Entrüstung über das eigene Tun". This view may be supported by P 254 νεμεσιζέσθω δ' ἐνὶ θυμῷ and β 64 νεμεσσήθητε καὶ αὐτοί. But there is a closer parallel at P 93-5 μή τίς μοι Δαναῶν νεμεσήσεται ... / αἰδεσθείς (cf. also Z 351 ὃς ἤδη νέμεσιν τε καὶ αἴσχεα πόλλ' ἀνθρώπων, I 459-60 ὅς ῥ' ἐνὶ θυμῷ / δήμου θῆκε φάτιν καὶ ὀνείδεα πόλλ' ἀνθρώπων). It may be concluded that αἰδώς is the respect felt for public opinion, and especially for moral criticism publicly expressed[470]. That Hes. attached much weight to public opinion appears from 760-5. It is true that at *Th.* 223-4 he calls Nemesis a daughter of Nyx and πῆμα θνητοῖσι βροτοῖσι, but she is an ambivalent power, just as Aidos (cf. 317-8, and Sellschopp, 94)[471]. Her dark side even developed into a spirit of fateful revenge (Pind. *P.* 10, 44, A. fr. 266 N. = 244 M., S. *El.* 792), and as such she was worshipped in later times together with Adrasteia (cf. W. Fauth, KP IV, 1972, 48-9). The present personification is to be explained in the same way as that of αἰδώς (see above): this would be a superfluous remark if Péron (269) had not written that Hes. considers νέμεσις "dans ses rapports avec la divinité, comme l'incarnation de l'opinion ... de cette dernière", a warning example of the projection of modern concepts ("la divinité") into archaic texts.

200: τά. Not "those described above" (We.), but pointing forward and explained by ἄλγεα: cf. Hom. A 420 τοὺς δὲ κατὰ πρύμνας τε καὶ ἀμφ' ἄλα ἕλσαι, Ἀχαιούς, Δ 20 αἵ γ' ἐπέμυξαν, Ἀθηναίη τε καὶ Ἥρη, Φ 13 τὸ δὲ

---

[469] See further Hamdorff, *Kultpersonifikationen* (above, n. 65), 65.

[470] D. B. Claus, TAPA 107 (1977), 79, wrongly concludes from a comparison of N 121-2 with O 561 and Z 351 that αἰδώς is used "as both 'blame' and 'shame'". For the important role played by public opinion in Greek life cf. Burckhardt, *Griech. Kulturgesch.* (above, n. 439), II, 354 ff., J. Hornyansky, *Die Idee der öffentlichen Meinung bei den Griechen*, Acta Acad. Sc. Univ. Ungar. 1 (1922), 1-36, A. Zimmern, *The Greek Commonwealth* (⁵Oxford 1931), 59 ff.

[471] Péron (269 n. 4) is certainly wrong in thinking that she became an evil power as a result of her leaving the earth.

φλέγει, ἀκάματον πῦρ, K.G. I, 658, Schw. II, 21-3, Chantr. II, 160-1. Similarly 220 τῆς, 256 ἡ, 469 ὁ.

200: οὐκ ἔσσεται ἀλκή. For the problem of human responsibility see above, on 16 ἀθανάτων βουλῇσιν.

202-12. We. writes: "This little fable continues the theme of Dike and Hybris, and the series of stories", and refers to p. 49: "As he has just told two stories, it seems a suitable place to bring out another story". This can hardly be called an explanation. We should rather take the fable as an illustration of the basic principle underlying the characterization of the present age, viz. δίκη ἐν χερσί (192). The heroes were 'better' because they were more just (158), the present rulers are 'better' (207) because they are stronger (210). Accordingly, the myth of the five races and the fable form the general background to the admonitions addressed to Perses (213 ff.) and to the judges (248 ff.) (Kühn, 268). It should be admitted that the two stories are not exactly parallel: in the myth of the iron race both the evil-doers and their victims suffer ἄλγεα (200), in the fable the brute triumphs and the weak suffers ἄλγεα (211). We should not try to explain away this divergence[472], but rather accept it as a difference of accent. It may be added that the triumph of the hawk is no real victory, because animals do not know δίκη (278), so that the principle δίκη δ᾽ ὑπὲρ ὕβριος ἴσχει (217) does not apply to them. On the other hand, the fact that the fable is addressed to the judges suggests that they are forgetting the demands of δίκη to such a degree that they come to resemble wild animals, i.e. subhuman beings[473]. In this respect

---

[472] As is done by Skafte Jensen (above, n. 38), 20-2, who takes 210 to refer to the ἀφραδίη of the silver race (134) and of Epimetheus (86), and thinks that the hawk represents Zeus and that 211 is "not concerned with the nightingale but with the judges and Perses: they may think they are to win the case, but Hesiod has justice and therefore Zeus on his side, and in the end they will not only lose their victory, but will have made fools of themselves too" (she apparently forgets 202 φρονέουσι taken by her to mean that the judges "unlike the poor silly Perses ... are not committing injustice from not knowing any better"). Similarly, C. B. Welles, GRBS 8 (1967), 19, concludes that "the men of Iron, and the nobles too, are in the grip of forces greater than they ... Even the kings are subject to the will of Zeus". V. A. Rodgers, CQ N.S. 21 (1971), 290-4, too, argues that the fable implies that "when Zeus has them [the judges] in his claws he will have the upper hand" (291); in his opinion, 192 ff. mean that "men will no longer respect the power of the stronger" (292). It is astonishing that such fantasies could appear in print (cf. also the critical remarks made by S. Østerud, Hermes 104, 1976, 21-2). They are outrivalled, however, by Peabody (above, n. 326), 251-2, who concludes that "the whole passage is a magical prediction of the epiphany of the righteous victor in contest, Odysseus the eagle [τ 548]".

[473] Dierauer, *Tier und Mensch* (above, n. 232), 17, who compares Arch. 94 D. = 177 W. and concludes: "Hesiod hat somit sehr konsequent mit der alteingewurzelten anthropomorphen Tierbetrachtung gebrochen". P. Walcot, SO 38 (1963), 20, observes that when the hawk appears in Homeric similes (N 62-5, O 237-8, Π 582-3, X 139-42 and 308-10) it serves to glorify the aggressor. These texts show that M. Puelma, MH 29 (1972), 90 n. 20, goes too far in maintaining: "Der Habicht ist allgemein griechisches Symbol für Tyrannei, Raub, Rechtsbruch". The sub-human character of the hawk has been overlooked by L. W. Daly, TAPA 92 (1961), 45 ff., who concludes (50) that "the only paradigmatic value he [Hes.] intends it [the fable] to have is as an illustration of the ruthless exercise of might". Similarly, We. thinks that the kings "might more

Hes.'s fable distinguishes itself from the traditional fable: it contains a hidden moral which is opposed to the moral expressed in the story itself[474]. See further below, on 202 νοέουσι.

202: νῦν. "In passing to a new section" (We.), properly 'in the present circumstances': cf. my notes on Men. *Epitr.* 346, Mnem. IV 27 (1974), 32, Pl. *Phd.* 107 c 4, Mnem. IV 31 (1978), 94, Pind. *I.* 2, 43, Mnem. IV 35 (1982), 32. See also below, on 270 νῦν.

202: αἶνον. 'Tale with a hidden meaning': cf. Hom. ξ 508, Arch. 89 D. = 174 W., 1, 81 D. = 185 W., 1 ('fable'), Sellschopp, 84-6[475].

202: βασιλεῦσιν. See above, on 38 βασιλῆας.

202: ἐρέω. For the synizesis see above, on 5 ῥέα.

202: νοέουσι. This reading, found in a Berlin papyrus (H. Maehler, ZPE 15, 1974, 199 and 206) and given by a number of testimonies, is to be preferred to φρονέουσι because there is no parallel for φρονέω used in the sense of 'to be wise' (Maz., Si.)[476], and the meaning 'to know', 'to understand' does not seem to occur before Sophocles (*Aj.* 942, *Trach.* 1145, *O.C.* 1741)[477]. On the other hand, νοέω is often used in the sense of 'to understand the real situation' (see above, on 12 νοήσας). This is the sense of the verb in the Homeric parallels Α 577 καὶ αὐτῇ περ νοεούσῃ, Ψ 305 νοέοντι καὶ αὐτῷ, π 136 νοέοντι κελεύεις. In these phrases the participle has concessive force, and the same seems to be obvious in νοέουσι[478]. The Homeric phrases are expressions of urbanity intended to draw the addressee's special attention to

---

aptly have told the tale to Hesiod". Palumbo Stracca (above, n. 96), 43, rightly feels that the fable forms an anticlimax after the preceding stories if it does not contain a moral different from the one expressed at 210, but his suggestion, "è possibile che Esiodo abbia voluto sottolineare questo contrasto", is a lame excuse.

[474] As is pointed out by Puelma (above, n. 473), 86-7. A useful survey of the various interpretations of the fable is given by Quaglia, 131 ff.

[475] See further E. Hofmann, *Qua ratione* ἔπος, μῦθος, αἶνος, λόγος ... *in antiqua Graecorum sermone adhibita sint* (Ph. D. diss. Göttingen 1922), 49 ff., Puelma (above, n. 473), 86 n. 2, 88 n. 10, Diller, in Heitsch, 264 n. 38. Jaeger, *Paideia*, I (Engl. ed.), 433 n. 41, wrongly tries to derive the use of the word for 'fable' from 'praise': both 'praise' and '(allusive) tale' are special cases of the basic meaning 'weighty utterance': cf. Chantr., *Dict. étym.*, 35. Cf. also Luther, *Weltansicht* (above, n. 461), 67: "Es handelt sich jeweils um eine Rede mit ganz bestimmten Intentionen".

[476] At Hom. Ψ 304 and 343 φρονέων seems to mean 'deliberately', 'consciously'.

[477] These arguments, put forward by me in Mnem. IV 28 (1975), 190, seem to me stronger than those presented by Palumbo Stracca (above, n. 96), 40, although he is right in adding that φρονέουσι is the *lectio facilior*. At Hom. π 136 γιγνώσκω, φρονέω the latter verb does not mean 'I understand' but 'I am already considering the question'.

[478] Wil. takes φρονέουσι to have motivating force: "Wenn sie Einsicht haben, werden die Könige keiner Deutung bedürfen", but this presupposes an impossible ellipse of 'which I need not explain'. This seems to me a more decisive objection than the considerations put forward by Palumbo Stracca, 40-1. On the other hand, he convincingly refutes (41-2) the objections against the concessive interpretation raised by E. Livrea, Giorn. Ital. di Filol. N.S. 1 (1970), 1 ff., and the latter's own interpretation. Quaglia (134 n. 16) wrongly thinks that νοέουσι does not have concessive force because περ is absent: cf. Hom. Ψ 305.

the message[479]. In the present case, however, the situation is more complicated: Hes. can hardly be supposed to have felt a genuine respect for the rulers (see above, on 39 δωροφάγους), so that his urbanity is not genuine either. Furthermore, it should be borne in mind that νοέων does not refer to the fact that the addressee will understand the message, but that he already knows the situation on which the message has a bearing. The judges certainly do not have a full knowledge of the situation described at 182 ff.: otherwise the admonition καταφράζεσθε (248) would be superfluous. But the mock-heroic use of the formula νοέουσι καὶ αὐτοῖς and the sarcastic way in which the explicit moral of the fable summarizes the present situation will shake them up and make them realize that the fable contains an ulterior moral pointing to the bestial nature of their own behaviour[480].

203: ἴρηξ. The starting-point for the use of animals in fables is the epic custom of comparing warriors to lions, boars, mules, vultures, etc.: cf. Waltz I, 118-9[481]. "The hawk might have been selected for the role of aggressor because of its association with bird-omens, so that Hesiod might underline the solemnity of his message" (Walcot, *Peasants*, 115, who refers to Hom. O 237-8 and o 525 ff.). It should be added that the solemnity is mock-heroic: see above, on 202 νοέουσι.

203: ἀηδόνα. We. rightly observes that "the hawk's standard prey in Homer is the dove" and that "Hesiod prefers a nightingale because it stands for himself": see below, on 208 ἀοιδόν.

203: ποικιλόδειρον. Does not tally with the nightingale's real colour, but it is supported by Nonn. 47, 31 αἰολόδειρος ἀηδών: cf. Puelma (above, n. 473), 90 n. 22 (who rightly rejects the interpretation ποικιλόγηρυς proposed by LSJ). Van Lennep[482] suggests that Hes. has the *luscinia maculata* (nowadays called *luscinia luscinia*) in mind, "in cuius flavescenti pectore, praesertim, si annosae sunt aves, hic illic fuscae apparent maculae ac striae, quales etiam in albo collo observantur", but these spots are not conspicuous[483]. We. thinks that the description of the nightingale may have been contaminated with that of the thrush, but I prefer to assume a contamination with the swallow: (1) the epithet perfectly suits the *hirundo rustica* (and possibly the *hirundo daurica*), and (2) in Ovid's tale of Procne and Philomela the remnants of the

---

[479] Cf. We. and Palumbo Stracca, 42-3.

[480] Nicolai (53) writes: "indem die Könige ganz auf das Machtprinzip festgelegt werden, bieten sie eine Blösse, gegen die sich dann der Angriff der Parainese (248 ff.) richten kann". This is correct but insufficient: the self-characterization of the rulers is so inhuman that it contains an implicit criticism.

[481] See also L. Giangrande, *The Use of Spoudaiogeloion in Greek and Roman Literature* (The Hague-Paris 1972), 20. For Near-Eastern and Aesopic parallels cf. P. Walcot, REG 75 (1962), 17-20, *Near East*, 90, and We., 204-5.

[482] D. J. van Lennep, *Hesiodi Opera et Dies* (Amsterdam 1847), *ad loc.*

[483] I owe this information and that about the swallow to Dr. W. K. Kraak.

blood-spatters caused by the murder of Itys are still visible on the swallow, and probably on the nightingale, too (*Met.* 6, 669-70).

205: ἐλεόν. Synonymous with ἐλεεινόν, found only here and Hsch. ἐλεώτερον. See further Troxler, 172-3.

205: ἀμφί. Wrongly taken as an adverb by Wil. ("die Krallen bohren sich rings ein"): cf. Hom. A 465 ἀμφ' ὀβελοῖσιν ἔπειραν, where Leaf's explanation, "so as to make the spits project on both sides", is refuted by the parallel μ 395 κρέα δ' ἀμφ' ὀβελοῖσι μεμύκει. See further We., who rightly remarks: "when a spike is stuck into you, you are round it".

205: ὀνύχεσσι. We. observes that "the Greeks were less sensitive than we to the repetition of a word at a short interval". In the present case, however, the repetition may be intentional, serving to heighten the pathos of the scene. See above, on 188 γηράντεσσι.

206: δέ. Omitted by most editors, but We. rightly observes that it marks "a simple narrative progression ... abandoning the structure begun in 203".

206: γε. Enlivens the picture: cf. Denn., 123-4.

206: ἐπικρατέως. In Homer 'with overwhelming might', here 'in a harsh victorious tone': cf. Hom. A 25 κρατερὸν δ' ἐπὶ μῦθον ἔτελλεν.

207: δαιμονίη. We. contents himself with the remark that "this form of address is studied by Elisabeth Brunius-Nilsson, ΔΑΙΜΟΝΙΕ (Diss. Uppsala, 1955)", but the view proposed in that book, viz. that this vocative strikes a note of intimacy, which establishes a closer contact between the speaker and the person addressed, thus giving greater insistence to the speaker's appeal, is untenable: see my review, Mnem. IV 12 (1959), 147. In Homer the word always expresses astonishment or criticism: cf. Leaf on A 561, who is wrong, however, in thinking that at Z 407 it indicates "tender remonstrance" (similarly Ameis-Hentze: "ein milder Vorwurf"), for Andromache is μαινομένη ἐικυῖα (389). The literal meaning is 'possessed by a δαίμων', i.e. by an unidentifiable divine power. See further B. Mader, *Lex.* II, 198, who refers to σ 406-7 δαιμόνιοι, μαίνεσθε ... / ... θεῶν νύ τις ὔμμ' ὀροθύνει.

207: λέληκας. Used at Hom. Χ 141 of a falcon, but never of a nightingale: the present use is obviously sarcastic, the hawk treating his victim as a serious adversary[484]. For the intensifying force of the perfect cf. K.G. I, 148-9, Schw. II, 263. It need not express continuous noises, as is suggested by We.: cf. e.g. A. *Prom.* 743.

207: ἀρείων. In a physical sense: see above, on 158 ἄρειον. Cf. Hom. Φ 487-8 ὄφρ' ἐὺ εἰδῇς / ὅσσον φερτέρη εἴμ', ὅτι μοι μένος ἀντιφερίζεις. The hawk's whole speech has a mock-heroic ring in so far as it resembles the boasts of the Homeric warriors (including the gods) before or after a

---

[484] As is suggested by Puelma (above, n. 473), 93 n. 33, who compares 210 ἀντιφερίζειν. We. suggests that in an earlier version of the fable the verb may have been used of the hawk, but this does not explain anything.

combat[485]. For Hes.'s anti-heroic (or rather, a-heroic) attitude see above, on 15 οὗ ... φιλεῖ.

208: εἶς. Hom. εἶσθα, Attic εἶ: the ς has been added on the analogy of φέρεις, ἵστης, etc.: cf. Schw. I, 659, Troxler, 88, Edwards, 114.

208: ἤ σ' ἄν. We. suggests that the word-order "betrays the influence of Hesiod's home dialect", but this has been disproved by Edwards, 109[486]. K. J. McKay, SO 36 (1960), 18, argues that "by the combination of reiterated syllables (η–εις–ης; εγω–αγω) and the accumulation of harsh vowels, the wild screech of the hawk is graphically portrayed in all its power. But at the end of the verse the music ironically changes, for the number and variety of vowels in καὶ ἀοιδὸν ἐοῦσαν create a lyrical note". The effect may be intentional (cf. Hom. ζ 122 ἀμφήλυθε θῆλυς ἀϋτή, where Stanford thinks that the repetition of the υ "perhaps represents the high pitch of the girls' voices"), but this is difficult to prove: O. J. Todd, CQ 36 (1942), 29 ff., points out that assonance and alliteration do not always have an expressive function.

208: περ. "Determinative ... to the exclusion of other things" (Denn., 482).

208: καί. 'Even though': for the omission of περ cf. Hom. Υ 87 τί με ταῦτα καὶ οὐκ ἐθέλοντα κελεύεις;, LSJ B 9, and see below, on 360 καί τε.

208: ἀοιδόν. Cf. Wackernagel II, 15, Schw. II, 31. We have already seen (above, on 203 ἀηδόνα) that the choice of the nightingale as the hawk's prey implies that Hes. alludes to his own profession. This view is corroborated by the fact that Bacchylides (3, 98) and other poets call themselves nightingales: cf. W. Richter, KP III (1969), 1555.47 ff.[487]. The concessive clause certainly implies that "a singer is a person of standing" (We.), but this cannot be the whole story: 210 refers to a contest, but this does not mean that Hes. by proclaiming his conception of justice competes with the rulers and their treatment of justice[488]. It is true that at *Th.* 80 Hes. draws some parallels between the good judge and the good poet, but this does not imply a competition[489]. It is equally true that Hes. does not shrink from reading the judges a lesson (e.g. at 40), but this does not alter the fact that the nightingale has lost the contest (211). That cannot but remind us of the fact that Hes. lost the legal contest with his brother[490]. It has been objected that his opponent

[485] Cf. Kaufmann-Bühler, 280, Fränkel, 134, Puelma, 89, 93 and n. 32.

[485] See also R. Renehan, *Greek Lexicographical Notes*, I (Göttingen 1975), 191.

[487] The derivation of Hes.'s name from ἵημι ᾠδήν is almost certainly wrong: cf. Wilamowitz, *Sappho und Simonides* (Berlin 1913), 9 n. 1: "Der Bauer, der seinen Sohn Hesiodos nannte, wusste wirklich nicht, dass die Musen ihn von der Herde wegrufen würden". F. Bechtel, *Die historischen Personennamen des Griechischen* (Halle 1917), 29, explains ὁ τὴν αἰσίαν ὁδὸν πορευόμενος, based on the Aeolic form Αἰσίοδος.

[488] As is argued by Puelma, 92 ff.

[489] Puelma (94 and n. 37) wrongly calls this passage a "agonaler Synkrisis von βασιλῆες und ἀοιδός ... mit dem Anspruch auf Gleichwertigkeit ihrer Funktion".

[490] Wil.'s paraphrase, "so wird es dem H. ergehen, wenn sein Prozess vor die Könige kommt", is incompatible with Hes.'s self-confidence.

in that lawsuit was Perses, not the jury [491], but by letting themselves be bribed by Perses they virtually form one party together. Sellschopp (84) objects: "Durch die Einsicht in seine Schwäche und das offene Geständnis seiner Hilflosigkeit würde sich Hesiod den Königen rückhaltlos in die Hände liefern". But Hes. is confident that his plea for justice will be successful, and that Zeus will not allow an unjust man (like Perses) to get more than his due (again) (272-3).

209: δεῖπνον. We. (p. 383) wrongly maintains that "δεῖπνον is used only of humans' meals in Homer": cf. B 383. See further *Lex.* II, 239-40.

209: δέ. We. observes that "Mitscherlich's σ' would be an easy change", but it should be added that ellipse of the object (to be supplied from the context) is very common: see above, on 47 ἔκρυψε.

210-1. For the fact that the moral of the fable is expressed by one of the characters see We.

210: ἄφρων. Here without moral connotation (see above, on 134 ἀφραδίης), for the hawk speaks from a purely pragmatic point of view, and certainly does not intend to point out "la legalità del suo agire", as a "giudice che guarda oggettivamente alla situazione" (as is assumed by Quaglia, 135). He rather argues like a Homeric god or hero: cf. A 581 and 589, O 180-1, Y 368, Φ 481-2, and Kaufmann-Bühler, 279. See also above, on 207 ἀρείων.

210: δέ. Has explanatory (motivating) force: see above, on 13 δέ.

210: ἐθέλῃ. We. 'chooses to', but rather 'makes bold': cf. Hom. B 247 ἴσχεο, μηδ' ἔθελ' οἶος ἐριζέμεναι βασιλεῦσιν, I 353, γ 121, Hdt. III 52, 2, E. *Ba.* 1311.

210: κρείσσονας. For the generalizing force of the plural cf. We.

210: ἀντιφερίζειν. See above, on 207 ἀρείων [492].

211: νίκης. The asyndeton has explanatory (motivating) force: cf. *Th.* 533 (where We. wrongly takes the sentence to specify τιμή: in reality it motivates 528-9), Hom. Δ 204, χ 307, A. *Suppl.* 180, K.G. II, 344. See also my notes on Semon. 7, 75 and 97, Mnem. IV 21 (1968), 148 and 152, Men. *Epitr.* fr. 2, Mnem. IV 27 (1974), 17-8, and A. *Ag.* 36, in *Actus: Studies ... H. L. W. Nelson* (Utrecht 1982), 439.

211: πρός τ' αἴσχεσιν. We. rightly rejects Merkelbach's πρός τ' ἄλγεσιν αἴσχεα, but his defence of the transmitted text is insufficient: πρός τ' αἴσχεσιν has a mock-heroic ring: the hawk attaches more importance to the

---

[491] E.g. by Daly (above, n. 473), 48, Skafte Jensen (above, n. 38), 21, Puelma (above, n. 473), 92. Other objections are mentioned and rightly refuted by Puelma, 91 n. 26. Skafte Jensen further argues that 205-6 ἐλεόν ... μύρετο cannot refer to Hes. because he never applies for pity: but this is a picturesque detail serving to bring out the brute character of the hawk.

[492] There is no need to assume that in an earlier version of the fable the nightingale boasted to surpass all other birds by her song, as is suggested by Daly (above, n. 473), 48.

shame of defeat than to the pains⁴⁹³. For the amplifying force of the plural see above, on 96 δόμοισιν.

212: τανυσίπτερος. At Hom. ε 65 and χ 468 'extending their wings', but here and at *Th.* 525 'with extended, i.e. long, wings': cf. 516 αἶγα τανύτριχα, Hom. τανύπεπλος, Pind. *O.* 2, 26 τανυέθειρα. Similarly τανύπτερος (*Th.* 523, *H. Cer.* 89, etc.), τανυπτέρυξ (Hom. M 237).

213: ὦ. See above, on 27 ὦ.

213: Πέρση. We. writes: "Perses is substituted for the expected kings, to whom Hesiod could only say, 'There, you are like that'. To Perses he can say 'But don't you be like that, it doesn't suit your station' ". This view is open to the following objections: (1) δέ does not have adversative force (see next note); (2) Hes. does not only say to the rulers, 'There, you are like that', but his fable contains an implicit criticism of the fact that they abuse their superior power (see above, on 202-12); (3) the address to Perses soon passes into a consideration of the consequences of ὕβρις committed by the higher classes (214 οὐδὲ μὲν ἐσθλός ...)⁴⁹⁴. The reason why he still begins by addressing his brother is a manifold one: (1) we have seen that the fable implicitly refers to Perses (210 ἀντιφερίζειν); (2) from a personal point of view Hes. is more concerned with Perses, but from a social point of view the judges are more important; (3) when Perses gained the lawsuit he belonged to the κρείσσονες (210), but by wasting his profit he got into low water. He is now planning a second action, but he does no longer have the means to bribe the judges again (cf. 31-5). Hence he may be expected to have recourse to the means used by the lower classes during the iron age: crooked arguments and perjury (193-4). But this method will not pay in the end (214 κακή). Hes. postpones the explanation till 282-4, for he thinks it more urgent first to dwell upon the ὕβρις of the rulers, the consequences of which far outweigh those of his brother's behaviour.

213: δέ. Wrongly explained by We. as 'But you, Perses, listen (not to the hawk but) to Righteousness': for δέ after an apostrophe see above, on 27 δέ.

213: ἄκουε. Wil. reads ἄιε, but see We. For the meaning 'give ear to' cf. Hom. η 11 θεοῦ δ' ὣς δῆμος ἄκουεν, LSJ II 1-2. For the use of the present imperative see above, on 9 ἴθυνε.

213: Δίκης. 'Righteousness': see above on 9 δίκη⁴⁹⁵. For the personifica-

---

⁴⁹³ Similarly K. J. McKay, Hermes 90 (1962), 250.

⁴⁹⁴ Consequently, Quaglia (136) is wrong in maintaining that 213ff. "non riguarda i sindici".

⁴⁹⁵ Cf. also Dickie (above, n. 32), 98-101, who convincingly combats Gagarin's interpretation of δίκη as 'legal process' and 'settlement', and Rodgers' view that δίκη and δίκαιος "carry the meaning not of what is right or wrong in principle but of what is prudent in the light of material consequences".

tion cf. 220-3, 256-60, *Th.* 902, Pind. *O.* 13, 7, E. Berneker, KP II (1967), 25.23 ff.[496]

213: ὕβριν. 'Overstepping one's limits', especially by encroaching upon the domain of others. As such it is the opposite of δίκη, which gives others their due[497]. For the contrast δίκη–ὕβρις cf. 190-1, 217, 225 and 238, Hom. ζ 120, Thgn. 291-2, 378-80, 751.

214: γάρ τε. See above, on 21 γάρ τίς τε.

214: κακή. 'Harmful', 'disadvantageous' (LSJ A II), explained at 282-4. Hays (58) rightly emphasizes the fact that Hes.'s conception of justice is "purely utilitarian. Do right, for it will pay you, is the gist of Hesiod's advice". See, however, above, n. 111.

214: δειλῷ. 'Socially inferior': cf. Thgn. 57-8 οἱ δὲ πρὶν ἐσθλοὶ / νῦν δειλοί, Bacch. 1, 160-1 πλοῦτος δὲ καὶ δειλοῖσιν ἀνθρώπων ὁμιλεῖ. At 686 Hes. uses the Homeric formula δειλοὶ βροτοί (as contrasted with the gods) in its traditional sense, but in the present passage he gives it a new meaning[498]. This has been denied by Hoffmann, 105 n. 1, who thinks that Hes. uses the singular for metrical reasons. He argues that the poet never looks down upon common people. It may be answered (1) that ὕβρις is equally harmful to the gods (e.g. to Aphrodite in Hom. E, where 428 οὔ τοι, τέκνον ἐμόν, δέδοται πολεμήϊα ἔργα, is a disguised reproach of ὕβρις), and (2) that Perses is despised by Hes. not only because of his moral behaviour but also because of his poverty (cf. 31, 299-301, 312-4). At 713 δειλός is used in a predominantly moral sense. The various shades of meaning can be easily explained if we take 'weak' to be the basic meaning, but in that case the common etymology (connection with δείδω and δέος) will have to be abandoned. See further Hoffmann, 8-9, Luther, 141-2, R. van Bennekom, *Lex.* II, 233-4. Cf. also W. Donlan, QUCC 27 (1978), 105.

214: ἐσθλός. For the social sense cf. Hom. Ζ 489, ζ 189, Thgn. 57 (quoted above), Alc. 360, 2. See further Hoffmann, 79 ff., 132 ff.[499]

215: φερέμεν. *Scil.* ὕβριν: see above, on 47 ἔκρυψε. The idea seems to be

---

[496] For cultic worship of Dike cf. Hamdorf (above, n. 65), 52-3.

[497] As δίκη is 'righteousness', the original meaning of ὕβρις cannot be 'die konkrete Kränkung' or 'Gewalttat', as is assumed by Kaufmann-Bühler (270-1), but must be a moral quality, although this quality can manifest itself in concrete acts (see above, on 146 ὕβριες). See further C. del Grande, *Hybris* (Napels 1947), espec. 26 ff., R. Lattimore, *Story Patterns in Greek Tragedy* (London 1964), 22 ff., Weber, *Pleonexie* (above, n. 117), 20 n. 3, Dover, 54, 110-1, 147, J. T. Hooker, ABG 19 (1975), 125-37, D. M. MacDowell, G & R 23 (1976), 14-31, N. R. E. Fisher, *ibid.*, 177-93, 26 (1979), 32-47.

[498] This does not imply, however, that the use of βροτῷ instead of ἀνδρί is "unstylish" (We.): cf. e.g. 15, 487, 760.

[499] Kaufmann-Bühler (271) takes ἐσθλός to be "der Starke, der sich eine Gewalttat ... kraft seiner Stärke erlauben kann", but his parallels do not refer to strength but to excellence in special fields, e.g. fighting (Hom. Υ 434 etc.) or running (O 283).

that he is so much dominated by it (see above, on 16 βαρεῖαν) that he is helpless when confronted with evil consequences.

215: βαρύθει. Cf. Hom. Π 519 βαρύθει δέ μοι ὦμος ὑπ' αὐτοῦ (Edwards, 78, observes that there, too, βαρύθει is preceded by δύναται).

215: δέ. Has explanatory (specifying) force: see above, on 9 δέ.

216: ἐγκύρσας. We. writes: "The idea seems to be of ruffians encountered on the road"; accordingly, he capitalizes ἄτησιν. But the literal meaning is no more present than in 'to meet with': cf. 691 πήματι κύρσαι, Hom. Ω 530 ἄλλοτε μέν τε κακῷ ὅ γε κύρεται, ἄλλοτε δ' ἐσθλῷ, Archil. 68, 3 = 132 W. καὶ φρονέουσι τοῖ' ὁποίοις ἐγκυρέωσιν ἔργμασιν.

216: ἄτησιν. Not 'delusions' (Ev., Latt.) but 'disasters': cf. 231, Hom. μ 372 εἰς ἄτην 'leading to my ruin', LSJ II 2. See further J. Stallmach, *Ate* (Meisenheim a.Gl. 1968) and the review by H. Vos, *Mnem.* IV 24 (1971), 408-9 (where literature published between 1950 and 1963 is mentioned), Gruber, *Abstr. Begriffe* (above, n. 54), 56 ff., R. D. Dawe, HSCP 72 (1967), 97 ff., espec. 99 n. 19, J. M. Bremer, *Hamartia* (Amsterdam 1969), 102 ff., B. Simon, *Mind and Madness in Ancient Greece* (Ithaca, N.Y. 1978), 66 ff., W. F. Wyatt, AJP 103 (1982), 247-76, whose suggestion that the basic meaning is 'over-indulgence' does not seem to me convincing: the fact that the word is used in an objective and in a subjective sense ('disaster', 'ruin' and 'delusion', 'infatuation') is most naturally explained if we start from 'harm' (cf. Chantr., *Dict. étym.*, 3, who compares Hsch. ἀασιφόρος· βλάβην φέρων and ἀάσκει· βλάπτει). H. Roisman, Hermes 111 (1983), 491-6, argues that the meaning 'ruin' is post-Homeric and post-Hesiodic, but (1) she overlooks μ 372, and (2) she thinks that in the present passage the aorist participle ἐγκύρσας must refer to an action prior to βαρύθει: "It is the falling into ἄται—lack of careful thought—that promotes hybristic conduct, not the reverse". But (1) the action denoted by the aorist participle is often contemporaneous with that of the main verb (cf. K.G. I, 199, Schw. II, 301, Barrett on E. *Hipp.* 289), and (2) the obvious meaning is 'he is weighed down by her when he meets with disaster'. There is no sufficient evidence for the spelling ἀάτησιν (Rz., Maz., Wil., Si.): cf. We. on *Th.* 230.

216: ἑτέρηφι. In Homer 'with the other hand', here 'by the other way'. For the various meanings of -φι (instrumental, local, etc.) cf. Chantr. I, 234 ff., Schw. I, 551, Troxler, 70-3, L. Deroy, AC 45 (1976), 40-74. See also below, on 359 ἀναιδείηφι.

216: παρελθεῖν. Si. adopts Pal.'s interpretation, 'the road to pass in the other direction is better, that towards justice', but there is no parallel for παρελθεῖν ὁδόν. Pal. therefore reads μετελθεῖν (C), but this is obviously a *lectio facilior*. We., who translates 'pass by', apparently follows the explanation given by Becker (87), 'Es ist aber ein Weg auf der anderen Seite, der geschickter ist daran [the ἄται] vorbeizukommen, der führt zum Gerechten', but in that case we should not expect a comparative (κρείσσων). If we take παρελθεῖν ἐς to mean 'to arrive at', 'to reach' (cf. Dem. 9, 24 π. εἰς τὴν δυναστείαν), the construction seems to be the product of a contamination of the following sentences: (a) κρεῖσσον ἐστι παρελθεῖν ἐς τὰ δίκαια, (b) ἑτέρηφι παρέλθοις ἂν ἐς τὰ δίκαια, (c) αὕτη ἡ ὁδὸς κρείσσων ἐστιν.

217: τὰ δίκαια. Similarly 280. For the determinative use of the article cf. Schw. II, 23. See also above, on 193 ὁ κακός.

217: δίκη. Not 'Rechtshandel' (Wil.) but 'righteousness': see above, on 9 δίκη.

217: δέ. Has explanatory (motivating) force: see above, on 13 δέ. The particle introduces the reason why κρεῖσσον ἐστι παρελθεῖν ἐς τὰ δίκαια.

218: ἐς τέλος ἐξελθοῦσα. This cannot mean 'in the end coming out into the open' (We.; similarly Maz. 'quand son heure est venue'), for ἐξελθοῦσα needs some qualification[500]. We. thinks that 'coming out into the open' implies "where everyone can judge", but his parallels (S. *Phil.* 97, fr. 105, 2, E. *Alc.* 640) show that in that case εἰς ἔλεγχον is added[501]. The obvious translation is 'when it comes to fulfilment' (cf. LSJ I 1 'issuing in fulfilment, execution'): cf. Pl. *Rep.* 530 e 5 τι ἀτελὲς ... καὶ οὐκ ἐξῆκον ἐκεῖσε ἀεί, οἷ πάντα δεῖ ἀφήκειν[502].

218: παθών. For the absolute use of verbs see above, on 1 κλείουσαι. Homer (P 32, Υ 198) has ῥεχθὲν δέ τε νήπιος ἔγνω, which seems to be the original form of the proverb: ῥεχθέν refers to an action the true nature of which is realized by the agent, whereas the idea of suffering is expressed in the form of a warning preceding the proverb (πρίν τι κακὸν παθέειν). Hes., on the other hand, starts from the assumption that suffering will take place (216), and he therefore includes it in the proverb[503]. For the history of the idea of πάθει μάθος (A. *Ag.* 177) cf. H. Dörrie, *Leid und Erfahrung*, Abh. Akad. Mainz 1956: 5, espec. 13-4, and the review by Solmsen, *Kleine Schriften*, I (Hildesheim 1968), 191-7.

218: δέ τε. Introduces the application of a proverb: see above, on 23 δέ τε.

218: νήπιος. In Hes. this word always has a strongly moral connotation (see above, on 40 νήπιοι and 131 νήπιος), in Homer at α 8 and χ 370.

---

[500] Becker (87) explains, "Dike geht durch das ganze Geschehen hindurch bis zu seinem Ende", but such an ellipse is impossible. 'When she comes at length to the end of the race' (Ev.) and 'setzt am Ende sich durch' (Marg) are equally improbable. Neitzel (50 n.9) explains, "schliesslich kommt Dike doch immer wieder zum Vorschein, wenn der Frevler zu Schaden kommt", but Hes. does not suggest that Dike before her victory was hidden.

[501] D. Holwerda, Mnem. IV 16 (1963), 343-4, maintains that τέλος is equivalent to ἔλεγχος: this is quite arbitrary.

[502] After Hes. τέλος δίκης means the decision of a lawsuit: cf. A. *Eum.* 243, Pl. *Leg.* 767 a 4, LSJ I 4. See also Waanders (above, on 166 τέλος), 65, who rightly observes that 664 ἐς τέλος ἐλθόντος θέρεος means 'when summer has come to its peak' (not 'its end').

[503] This seems to me a clearer explanation than Krafft's suggestion (123) that in Hes.'s version suffering and learning coincide (see further below, on ἔγνω).

Similarly ἄφρων (e.g. Ε 761), ἀφραδίη (see above, on 134 ἀφραδίης), οὐ νοήμων (β 282, γ 133, ν 209)[504].

218: ἔγνω. Not to be taken in an absolute sense (Krafft, 123), but 'he realizes' that ὕβρις leads to ruin. Dörrie (above, on παθών), 16, rightly observes that in Homer's version of the proverb the object of ἔγνω is a special action, but in Hes. a general rule. For γιγνώσκω 'to realize the true nature' of a thing, a person, or a fact cf. Snell, *Ausdrücke* (above, n. 332), 21 ff., *id., Der Weg zum Denken* (*ibid.*), 22-6, J. H. Lesher, Phron. 26 (1981), 9-12, B. Mader, *Lex.* II, 155-60.

219: αὐτίκα. Because the false verdicts of the judges, just as the false accusations of the plaintiff (194), make them perjurers. For the oath taken by the jury cf. Kaufmann-Bühler, 293 n. 1.

219: γάρ. The self-imprecation implied in the oath (see above, on 190 εὐόρκου) leads to ruin.

219: τρέχει. Hes. expresses the epic conception that goods and evils 'accompany' man (see above, on 142 ὀπηδεῖ) by means of τρέχω in order to emphasize the quickness of the destruction. He may have been inspired by the Homeric image of the running Ate (Ι 505-7)[505].

219: Ὅρκος. A personification—but in the sense of a truly divine embodiment (see above, on 11 Ἐρίδων γένος)[506]—of the conditional curse which the oath-taker lays upon himself (see above, on 190 εὐόρκου). He is a πῆμ' ἐπιόρκοις (804), and a son of Eris, who is herself a daughter of Night (*Th.* 225-32)[507]. Péron (269-70) argues that the *Th.* emphasizes the negative aspect of Horkos, and the present passage his positive aspect, because "le premier texte se place du point de vue du parjure, et le second de celui de l'offensé". This is incorrect, for 219 explains 218 παθών.

219: σκολιῇσι. 'Crooked', hence 'unjust': see above, on 7 σκολιόν.

219: δίκῃσιν. 'Verdicts', 'sentences': see above, on 39 δίκην.

220: τῆς. Probably demonstrative and pointing forward to Δίκης: see above, on 200 τά.

---

[504] I do not believe that νήπιος at α 8 and χ 370, and οὐ νοήμων at β 282 and γ 133 refer to "die unkluge Missachtung der drohenden Strafe", as is suggested by Hoffmann, 57.

[505] We. compares Aesch. Ctes. 233 ὁ μὲν ὅρκος ὃν ὀμωμοκὼς δικάζει συμπαρακολουθῶν λυπεῖ, and adds the remark, "though that refers to the juror who has sworn to judge fairly": this is misleading because Hes., too, speaks about judges.

[506] Cf. also H. J. Rose, Harv. Theol. Rev. 51 (1953), 16-7, who points out that Dike and Horkos obviously operate under the supervision of Zeus, as appears from 225 ff. Kaufmann-Bühler (293) observes: "Der Meineid war immer so sehr Bereich der göttlichen Sanktion, dass er nie unter die staatliche Gesetzgebung fiel".

[507] A false oath and a perjurer are called ἐπίορκος, 'subject to the curse': cf. Hirzel, *Der Eid* (above, n. 461), 152, Maz. (I), 78, R. Strömberg, *Greek Prefix Studies* (Göteborg 1946), 86 ff., H. Forster, *Zur Geschichte der griechischen Komposita vom Typus* ἐπίχρυσος (Ph. D. diss. Zürich 1950), J. Bollack, REG 71 (1958), 32 n. 1, Fränkel, *W.u.F.*, 25 n. 2.

220: Δίκης. 'Righteousness': see above, on 9 δίκη. The personification is based on her divine power, just as that of Αἰδώς, Νέμεσις, Ὅρκος, etc.[508]

220: ῥόθος. Not the cries of Dike (Maz., Col.), for ῥόθος does not issue from a single person (Wil.). Most commentators and translators follow Wil. in taking the word to refer to the murmur of protest expressed by the public attending the lawsuit (cf. the parallels given by We.), but 222 ἤθεα λαῶν shows that the offence is general. The word probably refers to the tumultuous atmosphere in which the lawsuits take place (cf. 196 δυσκέλαδος), as is assumed by LSJ.

220: ἑλκομένης. Suggests rape: cf. Hom. Z 465, X 62 and 65, λ 580. For the drastic expression see above, on 182 παῖδες.

220: ᾗ κ᾽ ἄνδρες ἄγωσι. A reminiscence of 208 (We.). In a just society Dike goes her own way (as is implied in 262 παρκλίνωσι).

221: δωροφάγοι. See above, on 39 δωροφάγους.

221: σκολιῆς δὲ δίκης. For the emphatic force of the repetition (219) see above, on 188 γηράντεσσι. For δέ introducing the specification of 220 see above, on 9 δέ.

221: κρίνωσι. No longer governed by ᾗ (K.G. II, 432-4), but the mood of ἄγωσι persists: cf. Hom. χ 469-70 ὡς δ᾽ ὅτ᾽ ἂν ἢ κίχλαι τανυσίπτεροι ἠὲ πέλειαι / ἕρκει ἐνιπλήξωσι—τὸ δ᾽ ἐστήκη ἐνὶ θάμνῳ—and Ruijgh, 466. For κρίνω 'decide as a judge' cf. Hom. Π 387, μ 440, LSJ II 2 a. Similarly διακρίνω: Th. 85, Pind. O. 8, 24, Hdt. I 100, 1[509].

221: θέμιστας. 'Judgements', 'sentences': see above, on 9 θέμιστας. For the internal accusative cf. e.g. Hdt. II 129, 1 δίκας ... δικαιοτάτας κρίνειν. The combination δίκης ... θέμιστας is slightly pleonastic, but the two words denote different aspects of the activity of the judge: he points out (δείκνυσι) and establishes (τίθησι) guilt and innocence[510].

222: ἕπεται. Although she is being dragged: cf. Hom. M 395 ἐκ δ᾽ ἔσπασεν ἔγχος· ὁ δὲ σπόμενος πέσε δουρί, LSJ I 5.

222: κλαίουσα. We. maintains that "she is not an angel weeping for the sins of the world but a victim of rape weeping on her own account". Accordingly, he takes πόλιν to be an accusative of direction (similarly Ev.) and thinks that "Hesiod is rather awkwardly changing the picture to that of a

---

[508] Ehrenberg, *Rechtsidee* (above, on 9 δίκη), 68, argues that the deification of Dike was Hes.'s work. But the personification would not be convincing if δίκη was not generally felt to be a divine power. The representation of Dike as a woman on the chest of Cypselus (Paus. V 18, 2) and on a vase of about 530 B.C. (Beazley, *Attic Redfigure Vasepainters*, 13) cannot be based on Hes. alone. For cultic worship of Dike cf. Farnell, *Cults* V, 444 ff.

[509] Vos, Θέμις (above, on 9 θέμιστας), 10, suggests that κρίνειν θέμιστας originally meant 'Rechtsregeln wählen', but at Π 187 σκολιὰς κρίνωσι θέμιστας the first word can hardly mean "die für den konkreten Fall nicht passend sind". Besides βίη in the same line does not suit the translation 'wählen'.

[510] Krafft (79) explains σκολιῆς δίκης by "unter falscher Verwendung des Rechts", which is obviously impossible (see also above, n. 32).

vengeful spirit wandering across the earth, visiting the city from outside".
But such a change is extremely improbable, especially at this point in the
metre. In addition We. has to admit that at 224 the picture changes back into
that of a victim being driven out. The common interpretation is supported by
Arat. 116 ποθέουσα παλαιῶν ἤθεα λαῶν.

222: καί. Has explanatory (specifying) force: see above, on 91 καί.

222: ἤθεα. Not 'dwelling-places' (Maz., Si., Ev., Latt., We.) but 'habits'
(see above, on 67 ἦθος), 'mental attitude': cf. Isocr. 2, 31, Dem. 20, 14 τὸ τῆς
πόλεως ἦθος. V. 260 νόον seems to refer back to ἤθεα.

222: λαῶν. Not only the judges are guilty, but injustice extends more or
less to the whole population: cf. 190 ff., 269. The idea that a community
which tolerates the wrongdoings of some of its members is a party to their
guilt is prefigured at Hom. β 66-7: cf. Kaufmann-Bühler, 292-3.

223. Composed of elements taken from 103 and 125. The line is bracketed
by Maz. and Si. (followed by me in *Aufbau*, 136 n. 2), because (1) "it is odd to
speak of a departing divinity bringing evil to a city" (Si.), and (2) it is Zeus,
not Dike, who brings punishment to men (Maz.). But We. rightly remarks
that "the context requires mention of punishment", and that λαοί cannot be
the subject of ἔνειμαν. The best solution seems to be (1) to take ἠέρα
ἐσσαμένη (which can hardly be simultaneous with her being dragged) as
subordinate to φέρουσα: cf. K.G. II, 104, Schw. II, 406; (2) to take φέρουσα
in a desiderative sense: cf. K.G. I, 140, Schw. II, 258-9; (3) to consider that
κακὸν φέρουσα need not imply that she brings about the punishment herself:
as soon as she has been driven out of the city she will imperceptibly fly to
heaven and report the maltreatment to Zeus, who will effect the punishment
(258-62).

224: ἐξελάσωσι. We.'s reason for preferring the short-vowel form of the
subjunctive (-σουσι) does not seem to me cogent: he admits that Homer has
both types (Chantr. I, 454-6). See also my note on *Th.* 81 τιμήσωσι, Mnem.
IV 25 (1972), 252. The phrase is a reminiscence of Hom. Π 387-8 οἵ βίῃ εἰν
ἀγορῇ σκολιὰς κρίνωσι θέμιστας / ἐκ δὲ Δίκην ἐλάσωσι θεῶν ὄπιν οὐκ
ἀλέγοντες. The authenticity of these lines has been doubted by some
critics[511], but their arguments are far from decisive (see below, on 251
ἀλέγοντες). It has also been suggested that both poets drew upon the same
stock of traditional material[512], but the similarities are so specific that a
direct influence seems to be more probable.

224: καί. Has explanatory (specifying) force: see above, on 91 καί.

224: οὐκ. Goes with ἰθεῖαν, not, however, "because otherwise μή would be

---

[511] E.g. Leaf, Maz. (I), 81 n. 1, Ehrenberg, *Rechtsidee*, 69-70, P. von der Mühll, *Kritisches
Hypomnema zur Ilias* (Basel 1952), 247, H. Munding, Philol. 105 (1961), 166-8.
[512] P. Walcot, SO 38 (1963), 17-20.

required" (We.) (see below, on ἔνειμαν), but because ἰθεῖαν is the negated idea.

224: ἰθεῖαν. 'Straight': see above, on 9 ἴθυνε. The phrase δίκη οὐκ ἰθεῖα seems paradoxical, because righteousness is always right, but in Hes.'s imagination the divine power of righteousness is disfigured by the σκολιαὶ δίκαι of the judges. The predicate is equivalent to an adverb: cf. Hom. υ 242 ἀριστερὸς ἤλυθεν ὄρνις, K.G. I, 274 ff. (who wrongly explain the adjective as attributive), Schw. II, 178-9.

224: ἔνειμαν. The transition from subjunctive to indicative is well explained by We.: "What begins as a generic description gains definition so that the types become like individuals". See further Chantr. II, 354-6. The phrase 'they dispensed justice' shows that δίκη is not only the quality of righteousness (see above, on 9 δίκη) but also its result, one's due: cf. Hom. Τ 180 ἵνα μή τι δίκης ἐπιδευὲς ἔχησθα [513]. Similarly, βουλή is the ability to take counsel (e.g. Hom. Α 258), but also its product, a counsel or plan [514], and κάματος is used for 'product of labour' (305). See also below, on 239 and 271 δίκην.

It seems strange to us that the personification of Dike is abandoned in the middle of the sentence [515]. There is a parallel in Pind. *O.* 8, 21-2 Σώτειρα Διὸς ξενίου / πάρεδρος ἀσκεῖται Θέμις, where Themis is first viewed as a divine person, but then practised (ἀσκεῖται) as a principle. Conversely, at 763-4 rumour is first described as a human utterance (λαοὶ φημίξωσι), but then called a θεός. Such transitions [516] are possible because deification and 'reification' are different aspects of one and the same thing. See further above, on 11 Ἐρίδων γένος. Cf. also my note on Pind. *N.* 11, 8 Θέμις, ICS 7, 1 (1982), 19-20.

225-47. We. mentions some parallels from other countries, but he certainly goes too far in maintaining that Hes.'s picture "has a Semitic appearance" [517]: Hes.'s main model was Hom. τ 109-14, as has been pointed out by Neitzel, 56 ff., espec. 69-71 [518].

---

[513] The discussion of δίκη by E. Wolf, *Griechisches Rechtsdenken*, I (Frankfurt 1950), is vitiated by the assumption that the basic meaning is 'one's due' (148: "δίκη ist, wie anfänglich, das dem Wesen eines jeglichen Seienden Zukommende").

[514] Becker (180) translates ἔνειμαν by 'gelenkt haben'. He refers to Hom. μ 218 οἴηα νωμᾷς, but although the basic meaning of νέμω is 'to move to and fro' (cf. M. Pohlenz, *Kleine Schriften*, II, Hildesheim 1965, 335 ff.), we should distinguish the rudder (which is moved) from the ship (which is steered).

[515] Ehrenberg, *Rechtsidee*, 68, wrongly concludes: "Es ist, als zögerte Hesiod, Dike zur Göttin, zur Olympierin zu machen".

[516] Cf. also E. fr. 20 μὴ πλοῦτον εἴπῃς· οὐχὶ θαυμάζω θεόν, / ὃν χὠ κάκιστος ῥᾳδίως ἐκτήσατο, Ar. *Plut.* 237-8 (Plutus speaks) ἢν μὲν γὰρ ὡς φειδωλὸν εἰσελθὼν τύχω, / εὐθὺς κατώρυξέν με κατὰ τῆς γῆς κάτω.

[517] Cf. the critical remarks made by F. Solmsen, Gnom. 52 (1980), 215, but see also Walcot, *Near East*, 72-3.

[518] Th. Berres, Hermes 103 (1975), 257 ff., advocates a converse relationship, but his arguments do not carry conviction: e.g. such contentions as "Was Hesiod sich noch erkämpfen

225: ξείνοισι. See above, on 183 ξεῖνος.

225: ἐνδήμοισι. Not 'belonging to the δῆμος' (Wil.) but 'living in the country'. Similarly Thgn. 793-4 ξείνων ... ἐνδήμων.

225: διδοῦσιν. For διδόω = δίδωμι cf. Chantr. I, 299.

226: μή τι. See above, on 113 οὐδέ τι.

226: παρεκβαίνουσι. Based on the image of leaving the right road and walking beside it: cf. Hom. Κ 349 παρὲξ ὁδοῦ, δ 348 παρὲκ εἴποιμι, and Becker, 86.

226: δικαίου. Equivalent to δίκης. Snell (205-6), who thinks that general notions could not be formed without the use of the article (cf. 217 τὰ δίκαια), translates 'Gerechtes' ('something just': cf. Hom. δ 237 Ζεὺς ἀγαθόν τε κακόν τε διδοῖ, and above, on 71 ἴκελον), but παρεκβαίνουσι suggests that the transgression of a general principle is meant. Schw. II, 22 n. 2, rightly declares: "Das Generelle hängt nicht am Artikel"[519].

227: τοῖσι. *Dativus sympatheticus*: cf. Schw. II, 147-8.

227: τέθηλε. For the intensifying perfect see above, on 207 λέληκας.

227-8: πόλις ... γῆν. See above, on 162 γαίῃ.

227: δέ. Has explanatory (specifying) force: see above, on 9 δέ.

227: ἀνθεῦσιν. Cf. Hom. Ν 484 ἔχει ἥβης ἄνθος. For the chiastic word order see above, on 10 μυθησαίμην[520].

228: δέ. Has explanatory (motivating) force: see above, on 13 δέ.

228: κουροτρόφος. At Hom. ι 27 said of Ithaca. The epithet, combined with 227 τέθηλε, explains *Th.* 902 Εἰρήνην τεθαλυῖαν. See further W. Fauth, KP II (1967), 216-7.

228: οὐδέ. Equivalent to καὶ οὐ: cf. K.G. II, 293: "in der attischen Prosa nur nach vorangegangenem Gliede ... bei den Ioniern und in der Dichtersprache auch nach einem positiven Gliede". See further Denn., 190-2.

228-9: οὐδέ ... πόλεμον. For the repetition of the same idea in negative form see above, on 97 οὐδὲ θύραζε.

229: ἀργαλέον. Cf. Hom. Λ 4, 78, Ξ 87, Ρ 544. See further above, on 92 ἀργαλέων.

229: τεκμαίρεται. 'Marks out', hence 'assigns' (LSJ I).

229: εὐρύοπα. Originally accusative (Hom. Η 206), but used as a nominative and a vocative (Π 241) on the analogy of μητίετα and similar nominatives: cf. Chantr. I, 199-200. For εὐρυ- 'widely extending' see above, on 197 εὐρυοδείης.

---

musste, steht dem Odysseus zur bequemen Disposition" (265-6) and "die schon weiterentwickelte Begrifflichkeit des Odysseus" (268) are nothing but subjective impressions.

[519] This also applies to Attic: cf. K.G. I, 608, and my note on Ar. *Plut.* 578, Mnem. IV 8 (1955), 206.

[520] Berres (above, n. 518), 260, grossly exaggerates in maintaining: "Die poetische Gestaltung des Verses stellt wohl das Äusserste dar, was einem archaischen Dichter möglich war".

229: Ζεύς. Who sends war as a punishment (239): see above, on 16 ἀθανάτων βουλῇσιν.

230: ἰθυδίκῃσι. Cf. 189 χειροδίκαι and 224 ἰθεῖαν.

230: μετά. Waltz unnecessarily reads μέν: cf. Hom. Σ 234 μετὰ δέ σφι ποδώκης εἴπετ' Ἀχιλλεύς.

230: Λιμός. A child of Eris (*Th.* 226-7). For the personification cf. 299-300 and We. on *Th.* 227.

231: οὐδ' Ἄτη. Neitzel (56) translates 'noch sonst ein Schaden', apparently because ἄτη (see above, on 216 ἄτῃσιν)[521] may be considered to include λιμός[522]. But (1) there does not seem to be a parallel for δέ 'and generally' (a frequent sense of καί) and (2) Ate, just as Limos, is a child of Eris (*Th.* 230).

231: θαλίῃς. 'On the occasion of feasts': for this use of the dative (a special case of the locative use) cf. *H. Herm.* 56 θαλίῃσι, Pind. *O.* 1, 50 τραπέζαισι, *O.* 10, 76 θαλίαις, *P.* 1, 47 μάχαις, S. *Trach.* 268 δείπνοις, Ar. *Plut.* 1013 μυστηρίοις, K.G. I, 445 (who do not clearly distinguish this use from the dative denoting attendant circumstances). Attempts to connect θαλίῃς with μεμηλότα have not led to satisfactory results. Sittl reads Θαλίῃς, taken by him to be spirits of abundance, but Hes. knows only one Θαλίη (*Th.* 909). Neitzel (59-61) argues that θαλίη in Homer and Hes. always means 'prosperity', 'abundance', and translates 'vom Gedeihen umsorgte Felder', taking the plural to have amplifying force (cf. 211 αἴσχεσιν). But in archaic and classical Greek μέλω 'to be a care to' is never construed with abstractions but always with personal beings[523]. Hom. λ 603 τέρπεται ἐν θαλίῃς obviously refers to the ever-lasting feasts of the gods (cf. e.g. A 601-4). The θαλίαι of the golden race (115) resemble those of the Olympians, and the feasts of the just rulers resemble those of the golden race, with the important restriction that they have to work to acquire the ingredients (see below, on μεμηλότα).

231: μεμηλότα. 'On which they have bestowed care', i.e., for which they have had to work.

231: ἔργα νέμονται. Not 'they tend the field' (Ev.) or 'they do their work'

---

[521] Berres (262) wrongly translates 'Verblendung'. Wyatt (above, on 216 ἄτῃσιν), 265-6, translates 'overindulgence', but his reference to Hdt. VIII 115 and Panyassis fr. 13, 7-9 and 14, 5-6 K. insufficiently supports his interpretation.

[522] Latt.'s 'inward disaster' is obviously wrong.

[523] Pind. *Dith.* 4, 35 and fr. 155, 3, taken by Neitzel (60) to be exceptions, confirm the rule. The "poetical inversion" assumed by Pal. (who is certainly wrong in translating ἔργα by 'farms', apparently taken to be equivalent to 'farmers') is first found at Callim. fr. 75, 76 πρέσβυς ἐτητυμίῃ μεμελημένος. Cf. also IG XII (5), 911 (second cent. B.C.) σχήμασιν εὐτάκτοισιν μεμαλότες ἄκρον ἔφαβοι, *AP* X 10, 3 (first cent. B.C.) μέλω ... κύρτοις, Nonn. *Dion.* 37, 135 παντοίαις ἀρετῇσι μεμηλότες εἰσὶ μαχηταί. At Pind. *O.* 1, 89 ἀρεταῖσι μεμαότας the Byzantine variant μεμαλότας is wrongly defended by Forssman (above, n. 140), 66 ff.

(Latt.) [524], but 'ils jouissent du fruit des champs' (Maz.): see above, on 119 ἐνέμοντο. Hes. perhaps alludes to Eunomia, the sister of Dike and Eirene (*Th.* 902) [525].

232-7. For the idea that just rulership brings about fertility of soil, cattle and women see above, on 126 βασιλήιον. The same triad is mentioned at Hom. τ 111-4 (cf. Neitzel, 64 ff.), A. *Suppl.* 674-7, Hdt. III 65, 7, VI 139, 1, S. *O.R.* 25-7 [526].

232: βίον. 'Means of living': see above, on 31 βίος.

233: ἄκρη. Not 'on its outer surface' (We.) but 'on its upper part' as opposed to the trunk. Similarly τὰ ἄκρα 'heights', not necessarily tops: Hdt. VI 100, 2, etc. Cf. also ἀκρόδρυα 'hard-shelled fruits' as opposed to ὀπώρα (LSJ 1).

233: βαλάνους. For the consumption of acorns and chestnuts cf. We.

233: μελίσσας. Bees nesting in hollow trees are also mentioned by Ps. Phocyl. 173 and Virg. *G.* 2, 452-3. I do not believe that the present line is a rationalization of the mythological tradition of honey flowing from oaks in the Golden Age, as is suggested by We.: Hes. wrote as a farmer for farmers who knew where bees were to be found.

234: εἰροπόκοι δ' ὄιες. A Homeric phrase: cf. E 137, ι 443.

234: μαλλοῖς. A dative of limitation: see above, on 120 μήλοισι.

234: καταβεβρίθασι. Wil. writes: "die Wolle ist so reich, dass sie niederdrückt" (similarly Latt.), but κατα- is a generally intensifying prefix, the original meaning of which is more likely to be 'all over' than 'downwards': cf. Schw. II, 475-6, G. A. Cooper, GRBS 15 (1974), 415-6. For the intensifying force of the perfect see above, on 207 λέληκας.

235: ἐοικότα. For the neglect of the digamma cf. Edwards, 137. Wil.'s interpretation, "dass die Kinder gleichen Schlages wie die gerechten Eltern sind" (similarly Pal., who refers to 182), and We.'s first suggestion, "resembling their fathers and thus clearly legitimate", do not suit the context, which refers to prosperity in all its *physical* aspects (cf. also the counterpart at 244 οὐδὲ γυναῖκες τίκτουσιν). The wording shows that normal children, i.e. no monsters, are meant: cf. Aesch. *Ctes.* 111 ἐπεύχεται αὐτοῖς μήτε γῆν καρποὺς φέρειν μήτε γυναῖκας τέκνα τίκτειν γονεῦσιν ἐοικότα, ἀλλὰ τέρατα and the oath sworn by the Athenians before Plataea, ... καὶ γυναῖκες τίκτοιεν ἐοικότα γονεῦσιν· εἰ δὲ μή, τέρατα (Tod, *Gr. Hist. Inscr.* II, no. 204.39 ff.) [527]. Renehan (350-1) argues that general likeness is meant,

---

[524] And certainly not 'Geschäfte werden den Männern zugeteilt' (Troxler, 116).

[525] On the other hand, Neitzel (61) goes too far in calling 228-31 the 'social' or 'political' part of the description, and 232-5 the 'economic' part: 230 λιμός is an economic rather than a social notion, and θαλίαι and μεμηλότα belong to both categories.

[526] These parallels show that Ameis-Hentze are wrong in explaining τ 114 ἀρετῶσι δὲ λαοὶ ὑπ' αὐτοῦ as a transition from the physical to a neutral sense.

[527] See further L. Robert, *Études épigraphiques et philologiques* (Paris 1938), 307-8,

excluding the birth of monsters but also moral inferiority. He refers to Hom.
Ε 800 ἢ ὀλίγον οἳ παῖδα ἐοικότα γείνατο Τυδεύς and β 276-7 παῦροι γάρ τοι
παῖδες ὁμοῖοι πατρὶ πέλονται, / οἱ πλέονες κακίους, but this is a sentiment
characteristic of nobles who have to exert themselves to keep up (or raise) the
status of their families.

235: γονεῦσι. D has τοκεῦσι, but γονεῦσι is supported by a Berlin papyrus
(cf. H. Maehler, ZPE 15, 1974, 199). See further We. and *Lex.* II, 171.

236: θάλλουσιν. Refers back to 227 τέθηλε: the repetition marks the
central idea of the passage: see above, on 188 γηράντεσσι.

236: ἀγαθοῖσι. Dative of limitation: see above, on 120 μήλοισι. Similarly
Hom. Ρ 56 βρύει ἄνθεϊ λευκῷ, Pind. *I.* 7, 49 χρυσέα κόμα θάλλων. For
ἀγαθός 'profitable' see above, on 24 ἀγαθή.

236: οὐδέ. 'And therefore not': see above, on 28 μηδέ.

236: ἐπὶ νηῶν. See above, on 45 πηδάλιον. Krafft (121 n. 4) wrongly
suggests that Hes. is thinking not only of oversea trade but also of fishing (cf.
Hom. τ 113); Neitzel (69) is still more wrong in arguing that Hes. is aiming a
critical remark at fishery as presupposed in τ 113: see below, on 237 δέ.

237: νίσονται. Equivalent to νέονται. See further Schw. I, 287, 690,
Chantr. I, 171, 313, 440. The basic meaning is not 'to return' but 'to go
towards a definite goal': see my note on *H. Ap.* 472 νόστου, Mnem. IV 22
(1969), 195. For parallels cf. Leaf on Φ 48 νέεσθαι.

237: καρπὸν ... ἄρουρα. A reminiscence of 117: see notes *ad loc.*

237: δέ. Has explanatory (motivating) force (see above, on 13 δέ): oversea
trade is unnecessary because there is no need of import [528].

238-47. Wrongly called by Berres (above, n. 518) "ein untergeordneter
Abschnitt": 248 ff. continues the argument of 238-47, not of 225-37 (see
below, on 248 καὶ αὐτοί).

238: ὕβρις. The opposite of δίκη: see above, on 213 ὕβριν.

238: μέμηλε. See above, on 146 ἔμελε. For the perfect see above, on 207
λέληκας.

238: σχέτλια. See above, on 15 σχετλίη.

239: δέ. For δέ introducing an apodosis see above, on 23 δέ τε. Cf. also
Denn., 184, who rightly assumes that in Hes.'s time "duplicated δέ, as a
distinct idiom, had not yet been developed".

239: δίκην. Not 'punishment' (Ev.) or 'atonement' (We.), a sense not to be
found before Aeschylus and Herodotus, but 'justice' in the sense of 'result of

---

M. Delcourt, *Stérilités mystérieuses et naissances maléfiques dans l'antiquité classique* (Louvain
1938), Ch. II, Fraenkel on Hor. *C.* IV 5, 23, W. den Boer, *Private Morality in Greece and Rome*
(Leiden 1979), 133. It is misleading to quote Arist. *GA* 767 b 5 ὁ μὴ ἐοικὼς τοῖς γονεῦσιν ἤδη
τρόπον τινὰ τέρας ἐστίν, as is done by des Places, *Syngeneia* (above, n. 337), 22 n. 5, for the
meaning of that sentence is closely connected with a special theory.

[528] Waltz (I), 90 n. 2, wrongly suggests that navigation is avoided because it does not have
moral value.

righteousness': see above, on 224 ἔνειμαν. The fact that in the present case this result is destruction does not imply that "la notion de δίκη apparaît dans tout cela comme fondamentalement ambiguë" (Péron, 270).

239: τεκμαίρεται εὐρύοπα Ζεύς. An emphatic repetition of 229: see above, on 188 γηράντεσσι.

240: πολλάκι. The asyndeton has explanatory (specifying) force: see above, on 11 οὐκ. Berres (above, n. 518), 263, interprets the sentence as a corrective restriction: "nicht nur die Frevler selbst erhalten ihre Strafe (wie es 238 f. heisst), sondern oftmals ... wird ein einziger Frevler einer ganzen Stadt zum Verhängnis". But 239 obviously implies that the divine justice done to the unjust rulers also falls upon their subjects, just as the whole community benefits from the justice of the good ruler (227 ff.). Hes. here replaces the plurality of judges by one man in order to make his picture more impressive: for drastic expression see above, on 182 παῖδες, 220 ἑλκομένης.

240: πόλις. See above, on 162 γαίη.

240: ἀπηύρα. Si. reads ἐπαυρεῖ (cf. 419), because at *Th.* 423 and in Homer ἀπηύρα means 'he took away'[529]. But Aeschines has ἀπηύρα, and he certainly would have avoided that form if he had considered it abnormal (cf. his reading ὅς κεν for ὅστις at 241). That ἀπηύρα can have the meaning of 'he profited by' (in an ironical sense) appears from A. *Prom.* 28 ἀπηύρω (rightly defended by J. C. Kamerbeek, Mnem. III 13, 1947, 75-6), E. *Andr.* 1030, and perhaps Hom. X 489 ἀπουρήσουσιν (cf. K. Matthiessen, *Lex.*, 1022.20). The confusion was probably based on the analogy of ἀπολαύω. Wackernagel (I, 179) thinks that the aorist does not have gnomic but experiential force (cf. K.G. I, 159-60, who wrongly derive the former from the latter: cf. Ruijgh, 262-3), but We. rightly observes that "Hesiod's mind is not on past examples but on the universal principle". For the idea that a whole community may pay for the wrongdoing of one of its members cf. Hom. A 410 ἵνα πάντες ἐπαύρωνται βασιλῆος, Pind. *P.* 3, 35-6 γειτόνων / πολλοὶ ἐπηῦρον, ἁμᾶ δ' ἔφθαρεν, Pl. *Leg.* 910 b 5 πᾶσα οὕτως ἡ πόλις ἀπολαύῃ τῶν ἀσεβῶν[530].

241: ὅστις. Wil. wrongly adopts Aeschines' reading ὅς κεν: for the omission of ἄν or κεν cf. Hom. E 407, μ 66, K.G. II, 426.

241: ἀλιτραίνῃ. We. reads ἀλιτραίνει (all MSS.), because "this seems preferable to the subjunctive after the definite antecedent". But the antecedent is not definite: it is '*a* bad man', whose presence becomes harmful only *if* he commits an injustice. We. refers to the use of the indicative at 225 and 238 (cf. also 343, to which Troxler, 31 n. 4 refers), but there the indefiniteness pertains to the subject ('all those who'), not to the predicate (cf. K.G. II, 426 n. 2).

---

[529] Similarly E. Livrea, Helikon 6 (1966), 238-9.
[530] Cf. also G. Glotz, *La solidarité de la famille dans le droit criminal en Grèce* (Paris 1904), 557 ff., Kerschensteiner, 176 n. 2, Kaufmann-Bühler, 268 n. 1, 292.

The verb and cognate words (ἀλιταίνω, ἀλείτης, ἀλιτήριος, ἄλιτρος, ἀλιτήμων) often denote an offence against religious principles (see below, on 330 ἀλιταίνεται). Cf. Wil., *Gl.* II, 121-2, H. Vos, Glotta 34 (1955), 287-90, who concludes that "ἀλιτεῖν hat sich aus der τιμή-Ethik, wo es beleidigende Vergehen gegen Götter und Menschen bezeichnen kann, entwickelt zu einem Verb mit spezifisch religiöser Bedeutung in der mehr sittlich-rechtlich beding-ten Ethik"[531]. In the present case the 'bad man' offends against justice, but Dike is a divine power.

241: ἀτάσθαλα. Closely connected with ὕβρις (238): see above, on 134 ὕβριν ἀτάσθαλον.

241: μηχανάαται. Subjunctive with diectasis: cf. Hom. λ 110 ἐάᾳς, and Chantr. I, 75 ff. The meaning comprises planning and execution: see above, on 49 ἐμήσατο.

242: δέ. Has explanatory (specifying) force: see above, on 9 δέ.

242: οὐρανόθεν. Hes. may be thinking of torrential rain (cf. 555-6 οὐρα-νόθεν ... δεύσῃ) causing floods which destroy the crops, just as at Hom. Π 389-92 ποταμοὶ πλήθουσι ῥέοντες ... μινύθει δέ τε ἔργ' ἀνθρώπων.

243: λιμὸν ὁμοῦ καὶ λοιμόν. Similarly Hdt. VII 171, 2, Thuc. I 23, 3, and in later literature[532]. We. plausibly suggests that "malnutrition reduces resistance to disease"[533].

243: ἀποφθινύθουσι δὲ λαοί. A reminiscence of Hom. A 10 ὀλέκοντο δὲ λαοί and E 643 ἀποφθινύθουσι δὲ λαοί. For δέ having consecutive force see above, on 18 δέ.

244-5. Bracketed by Wil. and So., but (1) 244 forms the counterpart of 234-5 (see below on 244 οἴκοι), (2) the chiastic word order (cf. 227) and the assonance of -ινύθουσι (cf. Troxler, 6) are characteristic of Hes.'s style[534], (3) the emphasis laid on Zeus' supervision is characteristic of Hes.'s thought (see above, on 79 Διὸς βουλῇσι)[535].

244: οὐδὲ γυναῖκες τίκτουσιν. This is a disaster, because a son is needed to maintain the farm and to take care of his parents in old age: see below, on 378.

244: μινύθουσι δὲ οἴκοι. Not "from want of heirs" (LSJ; similarly Maz.), for οἶκος 'family' is not found before the 5th century (LSJ III), but 'supplies':

---

[531] See also W. H. P. Hatch, HSCP 19 (1908), 157 ff., *Lex.*, 466 and 491-2.

[532] Cf. Renehan, *Lex. Notes*, I (above, n. 486), 131.

[533] Delcourt (above, n. 527), 11 ff., argues that λοιμός does not mean 'pestilence' but 'disaster sent by the gods', and that in the present passage it refers to infertility of women and cattle. But at Hom. A 61 it is obviously a disease (sent by Apollo, who is also the oldest god of healing: cf. Nilsson, 540-1). Cf. also the phrase λοιμώδης νόσος (Thuc. I 23, 3, Hipp. *Acut.* 2), and see further G. Daux, REG 53 (1940), 97 ff.

[534] I do no longer believe that the barrenness of the women is a consequence of the pestilence, as I suggested in Mnem. IV 26 (1973), 411.

[535] The omission of the lines by Aeschines and their rejection by Plutarch are well explained by van der Valk (above, n. 357), 358-9.

see above, on 23 οἶκον, and cf. Hom. β 64 οἶκος ἐμὸς διόλωλε, δ 318 ἐσθίεταί μοι οἶκος, LSJ II. The phrase refers to 243 λιμόν, but at the same time forms an indirect counterpart of 234 in so far as the οἶκος includes the products of sheep[536].

245: φραδμοσύνῃσιν. Equivalent to βουλῇσιν (16, 79, 99). For φράζομαι 'plan' cf. LSJ II. For the plural see above, on 16 βουλῇσιν.

246: εὐρύν. See above, on 197 εὐρυοδείης.

246: ἤ. We. reads ἤ᾽, but the fact that ancient grammarians accentuated the second ἤ as ἦ (cf. LSJ II) shows that they accepted the absence of correption.

246: ὅ γε. Marks the identity of the subject in both parts of the sentence: cf. K.G. I, 656-7, Denn., 122. "It has the effect of giving more body to the clause that lacks the verb" (Nisbet-Hubbard on Hor. *C.* I 9, 16, quoted by We.): cf. Hom. Γ 409 σ᾽ ἢ ἄλοχον ποιήσεται ἢ ὅ γε δούλην, θ 488 ἢ σέ γε Μοῦσ᾽ ἐδίδαξε, Διὸς πάις, ἢ σέ γ᾽ Ἀπόλλων[537]. In the present case the destruction of a city-wall is more serious than that of an army.

247: ἀποτείνυται. Rz., Ev., Si. unnecessarily read ἀποαίνυται, for the ships are the penalty which Zeus makes them pay to himself: cf. Hom. Π 398 ἀπετείνατο ποινήν, ψ 312 ἀπετείσατο ποινήν.

248: ὦ. See above, on 27 ὦ. Chantr. (II, 37) observes that "on n'emploie pas ὦ en principe lorsqu'un homme s'adresse à une divinité ou un inférieur à un supérieur". This corresponds with the bold tone taken by Hes. with the rulers (cf. e.g. 39 δωροφάγους).

248: βασιλῆες. The MSS. have βασιλεῖς and βασιλῆς, but at 263 nearly all MSS. have βασιλῆες, and this form is supported by the metre at *Th.* 88 and 96. Wil., So., We. read βασιλῆς, but this form is not well attested before the fifth century (K.B. I, 449)[538]. The synizesis (see above, on 5 ῥέα) is less harsh than e.g. Hom. Ε 466 ἢ εἰς, and is paralleled by Hom. Λ 151 ἱππῆες[539] and *H. Dem.* 137 τοκῆες[540]. Cf. also 607 ἐπηετανόν.

248: δέ. See above, on 27 δέ.

248: καταφράζεσθε. Imperative, because the motivation (249 γάρ) refers to a required, not a factual, action. For κατα- 'thoroughly' see above, on 234 καταβεβρίθασι. For the use of the present imperative see above, on 9 ἴθυνε.

---

[536] Similarly Neitzel, 63. The phrase also occurs at Hom. P 738 (where οἶκοι means 'houses'). We. thinks that it is used "less aptly" there, but μινύθουσι may have the pregnant sense of 'they are destroyed': cf. Π 392 μινύθει δέ τε ἔργ᾽ ἀνθρώπων.

[537] This view has been called in question by Leaf on Γ 409 (and by me in Mnem. IV 33, 1980, 383): he refers to Μ 240 (but cf. 201 ἐπ᾽ ἀριστερά), β 327 (but cf. Ameis-Hentze: "Sparta, das nicht mit einfacher Seefahrt zu erreichen ist"), γ 214 (but resistance of the population would be a more alarming reason).

[538] It should be admitted that there are some rare contractions in Hes., e.g. 25 κεραμεῖ, 656 ἆθλος, *Th.* 84 ῥεῖ. Cf. Edwards, 139 n. 53.

[539] Where Leaf reads ἱππεῖς and Mazon ἱππῆς (accepted by Schw. I, 249 as a Ionism).

[540] Where Richardson prints West's emendation τοκῆς.

248: καὶ αὐτοί. *Scil.* for the gods are already observing it and will punish it.

249: τήνδε δίκην. Not 'meinen Rechtshandel' (Wil.): see above, on 39 δίκην. 'This custom', "namely the watching of Zeus and the spirits of justice" (Si.), is equally impossible. Ev. (followed by Quaglia, 137 n. 25) takes the phrase to refer to 239, but this leaves καὶ αὐτοί unexplained. Pal. compares 39 τήνδε δίκην and translates 'this kind of justice which you administer' (similarly We.), but δίκη cannot mean 'judging' (We.): it is the (quasi-) righteousness practised here, which in reality is identical with the ὕβρις mentioned at 238. For τήνδε see above, on 39 τήνδε δίκην.

249-51. Hes. no doubt adopted the idea from Hom. ρ 485-7 καί τε θεοὶ ξείνοισιν ἐοικότες ἀλλοδαποῖσιν / παντοῖοι τελέθοντες ἐπιστρωφῶσι πόληας / ἀνθρώπων ὕβριν τε καὶ εὐνομίην ἐφορῶντες. Cf. also ν 213-4 Ζεύς σφεας τείσαιτο ἱκετήσιος, ὅς τε καὶ ἄλλους / ἀνθρώπους ἐφορᾷ καὶ τίνυται, ὅς τις ἁμάρτῃ [541].

250: φράζονται. For the use of the simple verb after the compound We. refers to his note on *Th.* 803, but Renehan (350) refutes the idea that "the prefix would be more normally omitted when the verb is repeated". In the present sentence κατα- is not repeated because it is taken for granted that divine beings perceive sharply whatever they see.

251: ἀλλήλους τρίβουσι. "These sound like litigants, but perhaps in the gods' eyes litigants and judges are all much on a level, as mortals" (We.): not as mortals, but as belonging to the iron race: see above, on 222 λαῶν. For τρίβω 'to wear out' cf. Hom. Ψ 735 μηκέτ᾽ ἐρείδεσθον μηδὲ τρίβεσθε κακοῖσι.

251: θεῶν ὄπιν οὐκ ἀλέγοντες. A reminiscence of Hom. Π 388: see above, on 224 ἐξελάσωσι. For ὄπιν see above, on 187 ὄπιν. For ἀλέγω with accusative cf. Hom. ζ 268, Alcm. 1, 2, Simon. 543, 13-6, A. *Ag.* 1551, and ἀλεγύνω (always with accusative). Cf. also Schw. II, 109.

252: τρὶς ... μύριοι. 'Super-countless': cf. Emp. B 115, 6, Ar. *Av.* 1136, and τρίσμακαρ, τρισάθλιος *et sim.* Similarly at *Th.* 365 τρὶς χίλιαι denotes an indefinite large number. See further above, on 173 τρίς.

253: Ζηνός. 'Sent by Zeus': for the *genitivus auctoris* cf. Hom. υ 101 Διὸς τέρας, K.G. I, 332-3, Schw. II, 119. See also my notes on E. *Ba.* 8 πυρός, Mnem. IV 33 (1980), 2, Pind. *I.* 2, 34 Ἑλικωνιάδων, Mnem. IV 35 (1982), 26, *N.* 11, 27 Ἡρακλέος, ICS 7, 1 (1982), 28.

253: φύλακες. Probably identical with those mentioned at 122-5. We. refers to the spies of Mithra and concludes that "we are dealing here with a piece of Indo-European heritage". Whether this is true or not (cf. Kerschen-

---

[541] Divine supervision of human morality is much more emphasized in the *Odyssey* than in the *Iliad*: cf. e.g. β 66-7, γ 132-4, δ 806-7, ξ 83-4, ψ 63-4, ω 351-2.

steiner, 178 n. 1), it is more important to observe that in Hes.'s picture the gods no longer go round on earth themselves: see above, on 123 ἐπιχθόνιοι.

253: ἀνθρώπων. For two genitives depending on the same substantive cf. K.G. I, 337, Schw. II, 135, Bruhn, § 33, Wil. on E. *H.F.* 170.

254-5. See above, on 124-5.

256: ἡ ... Δίκη. Not 'Justice is a maiden' (Pal., Latt.), nor 'there is virgin Justice' (Ev.; similarly Maz.)[542], but 'and she is an unmarried woman, Dike'. For ἡ pointing forward see above, on 200 τά. We. wrongly thinks that ἡ points back to 220 ff.

256: παρθένος. The common translation 'virgin' seems to me unacceptable: justice is constantly violated in the present age (see above, on 220 ἑλκομένης), and the word cannot mean "that she is purer than most of her surroundings" (We.). Dike is an unmarried woman, so that when she is offended she cannot appeal to the help of a husband but has to apply to her father (259).

256: Διὸς ἐκγεγαυῖα. An 'etymology' of the name Δίκη: see above, on 3 διά. Similarly A. *Sept.* 662, *Cho.* 949-50. See further K. Deichgräber, KZ 70 (1951), 19-28.

257: κυδρή. Cf. the Homeric formula κυδρὴ παράκοιτις (Σ 184, λ 580, ο 26, *Th.* 328). Not 'honoured' (Ev., Maz.)[543] but 'majestic' (Marg 'hehr'), 'splendid' (Chantr., *Dict. étym.*, 595: "κῦδος ... exprime la force rayonnante des dieux ou celle qu'ils confèrent"): cf. Hom. Α 405 κύδεϊ γαίων, Φ 519 οἱ μὲν χωόμενοι, οἱ δὲ μέγα κυδιόωντες, Υ 42 ἐκύδανον ('were triumphant')[544]. See also below, on 313 κῦδος.

257: αἰδοίη. Cf. Hom. Σ 394 αἰδοίη θεά, *H. Dem.* 374 παρ' αἰδοίη Δημήτερι, Richardson on *H. Dem.* 190, and see above, on 71 αἰδοίη.

257: θεοῖς. Cf. Hom. ε 447 (a suppliant) αἰδοῖος μέν τ' ἐστὶ καὶ ἀθανάτοισι θεοῖσιν. Ev. and Si.[545] read θεῶν given by a papyrus, but there is no evident parallel for αἰδοῖος with genitive: δῖα θεάων is not comparable, for Dike is not an ordinary Olympian goddess. Cf. also Renehan, 350.

258: ῥα. As may be expected from a daughter of Zeus: see above, on 49 ἄρα. For καί ῥα cf. Denn., 43.

258: βλάπτῃ. See above, on 193 βλάψει, and cf. 262 παρκλίνωσι.

258: σκολιῶς. By means of σκολιαὶ δίκαι (221, 264).

258: ὀνοτάζων. 'Treating her scornfully' (cf. ὄνομαι). Solmsen, *Hes.*, 92-3,

---

[542] Maz. (I) translates 'il y a aussi la vierge', but in (II) 'il existe une vierge', without explaining ἡ.

[543] Latt.'s 'seemly' is obviously impossible.

[544] See further G. Steinkopf, *Untersuchungen zur Geschichte des Ruhmes bei den Griechen* (Würzburg 1937), 23 ff., M. Greindl, Κλέος, κῦδος ... (Ph. D. diss. Munich 1938), 38 ff., 95-7, H. Trümpy, *Kriegerische Fachausdrücke im griechischen Epos* (Basel 1950), 196, Gruber, *Abstr. Begriffe* (above, n. 54), 73-86, Fränkel, 88 n. 14, Benveniste, *Vocab. d. inst.* (above, n. 158), II, 57.

[545] Similarly A. Colonna in *Opere di Esiodo* (Turin 1977).

concludes that Dike is imagined as being personally offended, and that in this respect Hes.'s view of the gods is more primitive than that presented by Homer at Π 386-8 and χ 413-6 (cf. also I 510-2). But Dike does not complain to Zeus of injuries inflicted upon herself, but she reports (260 γηρύεται) the unjust mentality (260 νόον) of the judges. See also below, on 259 καθεζομένη.

259: πατρί. See above, on 84 πατήρ. We. thinks that "here following 256 we cannot help taking it as 'her father' ", but Διὶ πατρί is a formulaic phrase: cf. *Th.* 36, 580, and often in Homer.

259: καθεζομένη. We. compares Hom. Α 500 (Thetis) πάροιθ' αὐτοῖο (Zeus) καθέζετο, but Kühn (284-7) observes that the similarity is only superficial: Thetis asks for a personal favour, whereas Dike and Zeus are concerned with the principle of justice[546]. For Dike as a πάρεδρος of Zeus see We.

260: γηρύεται. We. writes: "in *Th.* 28 ἀληθέα γηρύσασθαι is on a par with ψεύδεα λέγειν", but the verbs are not synonymous: γηρύσασθα: is 'to proclaim' and γηρύεται is not 'tells him of' (Ev.) but 'svela ad alta voce' (Col.)[547].

260: ἄδικον. Rightly preferred to ἀδίκων by Pal., Ev., Latt., We., who compares Sol. 3 D. = 4 W., 7 δήμου θ' ἡγεμόνων ἄδικος νόος. Maz. argues that "le singulier témoignerait d'une certaine recherche, qui s'accorde mal avec le style du passage", but in reality it seems less pedantic than ἀδίκων (not all men are unjust). For ἄδικος cf. *Less. pol.*, 162-3.

260: νόον. 'Mental (and especially moral) attitude': see above, on 67 νόον. Homer pays more attention to the results of a moral action than to the mental attitude behind it: cf. W. Luther, *Weltansicht und Geistesleben* (Göttingen 1954), 88 ff., B. Snell, *Dichtung und Gesellschaft* (Hamburg 1965), 45 ff. See further below, on 282 ἕκων, 281 γιγνώσκων.

260: ἀποτείσῃ. According to the principle enunciated at 240.

261: δῆμος. 'The whole people', not as a political unit but as the inhabitants of the country: cf. H. Jeanmaire, *Couroi et Courètes* (Lille 1939), 44 ff.[548]. See also the literature mentioned by M. Schmidt, *Lex.* II, 275.

261: ἀτασθαλίας. Cf. 241 ἀτάσθαλα and above, on 134 ὕβριν ἀτάσθαλον.

---

[546] On the other hand, Jaeger, *Paideia*, I (Engl. ed.), 434 n. 46, rightly observes that "there is a remarkable contrast between this religious realism of Hesiod's belief in divine justice and Solon's idealistic concept of δίκη as a principle inherent in the social world of man as such and working automatically and organically" (3 D. = 4 W., 15 ff.).

[547] LSJ wrongly call νόον a cognate accusative.

[548] W. Donlan, PP 135 (1970), 385, maintains: "Here, as usual, δῆμος means the whole people exclusive of its leaders, but for the first time we have an intimation of oppression by the βασιλεῖς and an awareness of opposition on the part of the δῆμος". This view is not supported by the text: (1) δῆμος can equally well denote a people inclusive of its leaders (e.g. Hom. Γ 50 πῆμα πολῆϊ τε παντί τε δήμῳ), (2) injustice is not the same as oppression, (3) 240 ff. suggest that the leaders, too, will be struck by the calamity (cf. also 265).

261: βασιλήων. Most editors read βασιλέων: this is the regular form in Ionic and Doric (Schw. I, 575), but most MSS. have -ήων and this is the only form in Homer. For the synizesis cf. the Homeric ἤ οὐ (Chantr. I, 84) and see above, on 248 βασιλῆες.

261: λυγρά. 'Pernicious', 'baneful': cf. Hom. γ 303 Αἴγισθος ἐμήσατο οἴκοθι λυγρά, λ 432 (Clytemnestra) λυγρὰ ἰδυῖα, *Th.* 313 (Hydra) λυγρὰ ἰδυῖαν. At Hom. Ω 531 λυγρῶν is synonymous with κακῶν (528).

261: νοεῦντες. 'Having in mind': see above, on 260 νόον. The verb implies intention (cf. Thgn. 737-8 τὰ δίκαια νοεῦντες / ποιῶσιν), but not an evil intention: they do not intend ruin (for they intend their own advantage) but they intend things which turn out to be ruinous. See also below, on 286 ἐσθλὰ νοέων.

262: ἄλλη. 'In the wrong direction': this sense of ἄλλος reappears in Demosthenes and later authors (LSJ III 4) [549], but it is prefigured in Homer: cf. δ 347-8 ταῦτα δ᾽, ἅ μ᾽ εἰρωτᾷς καὶ λίσσεαι, οὐκ ἂν ἐγώ γε / ἄλλα παρὲξ εἴποιμι παρακλιδόν, ξ 124-5 ἄλλως, κομιδῆς κεχρημένοι, ἄνδρες ἀλῆται / ψεύδονται, τ 555-6 οὔ πως ἔστιν ὑποκρίνασθαι ὄνειρον /ἄλλη ἀποκλίναντα. In all these cases ἄλλος refers to untruth, and this also applies to the unjust judges [550].

262: παρκλίνωσι. Cf. Homeric παρακλιδόν and ἀποκλίναντα quoted above, and see above, on 226 παρεκβαίνουσι. The verb is probably used intransitively, just as at Hom. Ψ 424 and ἀποκλίναντα at τ 556 (cf. LSJ III 2) [551]: if we take δίκας as the object of παρκλίνωσι, the phrase σκολιῶς ἐνέποντες becomes redundant [552].

262: σκολιῶς ἐνέποντες. See above, on 194 σκολιοῖς ἐνέπων. For the use of the adverb (called unusual by Pal.) cf. Hom. Σ 508 δίκην (sentence) ἰθύντατα εἴποι.

263: βασιλῆες. See above, on 248 βασιλῆες. We. does not put the vocative between commas, but see my note on Ps. Pl. *Clit.* 407 a 5, Mnem. IV 35 (1982), 143.

263: ἰθύνετε. See above, on 9 ἴθυνε.

---

[549] Renehan (352) refers to Pl. *Prot.* 351 c 5, but this is not a certain example: cf. Adam *ad loc.* For ἕτερος used in a similar sense cf. LSJ III 2 (Hom. α 234, added by Renehan, *loc. cit.*, is not certain).

[550] We. compares Hom. A 120, but there the meaning is 'astray' in the sense of 'away' (cf. LSJ ἄλλως II 3), which is not relevant here.

[551] G. Arrighetti, SIFC 37 (1965), 158-60, tries to defend the reading of the MSS. παρακλίνωσι as a prosodic liberty based on a reminiscence of Hom. τ 556 ἄλλη ἀποκλίναντα and Ο 301 ἧκα παρακλίνας, but παρ- for παρα- is very common in epic language.

[552] Maz.'s comment, "la sentence est injuste, mais elle est en outre exprimée en formules tortueuses", is unconvincing.

263: μύθους. 'Words' (cf. 194), in this case 'sentences'. The unmetrical variant δίκας is due to 262 δίκας and 264 δικέων [553].

264: δωροφάγοι. See above, on 39 δωροφάγους.

264: σκολιῶν. So. reads σκολιέων given by a papyrus, but called by We. (*Th.* 83 n. 4) irregular: this seems far from certain, for cf. Chantr. I, 64-5, 69, 201. See also Edwards, 126-7.

264: ἐπὶ ... λάθεσθε. For the tmesis see above, on 59 ἐκ δ᾽ ἐγέλασσε (Schw. II, 427, seems to me wrong in connecting ἐπὶ πάγχυ). For the transition from 'forget' to 'neglect', 'omit' cf. Hom. Z 265 μή μ᾽ ἀπογυιώσῃς μένεος, ἀλκῆς τε λάθωμαι, K 98-9 μὴ ... / κοιμήσωνται, ἀτὰρ φυλακῆς ἐπὶ πάγχυ λάθωνται, Tyrt. 9 D. = 12 W., 17 αἰσχρῆς δὲ φυγῆς ἐπὶ πάγχυ λάθηται, Hdt. III 147, 1 τῶν ἐντολέων μεμνημένος ἐπελανθάνετο, We. on *Th.* 236 λήθεται, and see above, on 49 ἐμήσατο.

265-6. We. calls the proverbs (for which he gives some parallels) "not especially appropriate here" and thinks that they came into Hes.'s head by mental association (p. 47), but he does not explain the association. In my opinion, it can be explained, and in that case the lines become appropriate. Hes. realizes that 261 δῆμος might be taken to mean the people exclusive of its rulers, and that the present rulers will not care much about the evil which might befall their subjects. He therefore emphasizes the fact that the community punished by Zeus includes its rulers, and that the latter are even damaged most severely (266 κακίστη). Cf. also Quaglia, 138-9.

265: οἵ τ᾽ αὐτῷ. Pal., Wil., So. wrongly omit τε (which is also given by Arist. *Rhet.* 1409 b 28). Rz., Maz., Ev., Si. are equally wrong in reading γε: for τε introducing an explanation (motivation) cf. *Th.* 82, Hom. B 85, Archil. 7 D. = 13 W., 7 (where West wrongly omits τε). This seems to me a simpler explanation than the suggestions put forward by We. Ruijgh does not discuss the passage.

266: ἥ. Has generalizing force: see above, on 193 ὅ.

266: βουλή. 'Proposal', 'design': cf. Hom. I 74-5 ὅς κεν ἀρίστην / βουλὴν βουλεύσῃ, *Lex.* II, 82.

266: τῷ. Cf. Schw. II, 23: "ὅ bei Substantivierung, nicht als Mittel derselben, sondern zunächst nur determinierend".

267: πάντα. The asyndeton has explanatory (motivating) force: see above, on 211 νίκης.

267: ὀφθαλμός. For parallels cf. We. and C. Milani, RIL 103 (1969), 634-40. For the singular cf. LSJ II, West, BICS 24 (1977), 101, R. Renehan, *Greek Lexicographical Notes*, II (Göttingen 1982), 107 (ὄμμα). I do not believe that it is a reminiscence of the eye of the sun (as is assumed by Walcot, *Near East*,

---

[553] Wilamowitz, Hermes 64 (1929), 459, argues that at Hom. A 545 μύθους means 'sentences' in a jurisdictional sense, but the meaning more probably is 'thoughts': see above, on 78 λόγους.

92, and We.), but 'eye' is equivalent to 'look': for the use of *concretum pro abstracto* cf. Hom. A 77 ἔπεσιν καὶ χερσὶν ('deeds') ἀρήξειν, υ 266-7 ἐπίσχετε θυμὸν ἐνιπῆς /καὶ χειρῶν ('blows'), I 522-3 τῶν μὴ σύ γε μῦθον ἐλέγξῃς / μηδὲ πόδας ('coming'), τ 396 ἐκέκαστο κλεπτοσύνῃ ὅρκῳ τε ('swearing'). The 'look of Zeus' does not imply that in this case he does not need the help of 'watchers', as is suggested by Solmsen, *Hes.*, 94 [554].

267: πάντα. For the anaphora see above, on 101 πλείη.

267: νοήσας. We. writes: "The Homeric coupling of the verbs (*Il.* 10. 550, *Od.* 13. 318, 16.160) suggests that νοήσας means little more than ἰδών", but this is a wrong conclusion: see above, on 12 νοήσας.

268: νυ. 'In the present case': see above, on 202 νῦν.

268: αἴ κ' ἐθέλῃσι. Added in order to meet the objection that there is injustice on all sides, but divine punishment is not yet to be seen. For parallels cf. We. on *Th.* 28 εὖτ' ἐθέλωμεν. The form ἐθέλῃσι (We.; similarly 294 ἦσιν, 301 πιμπλῆσι) is defended by Renehan, 350.

268: ἐπιδέρκεται. For the intentional force of ἐπι- cf. Hom. ν 213-4 Ζεύς ... / ἀνθρώπους ἐφορᾷ καὶ τίνυται, ὅς τις ἁμάρτῃ, and see above, on 29 ἐπακουόν [555]. For δέρκομαι (properly 'look with shining eyes') 'look acutely' cf. Hom. P 674-5 αἰετός, ὅν ῥά τέ φασιν / ὀξύτατον δέρκεσθαι, Ψ 477 ὀξύτατον κεφαλῆς ἐκδέρκεται ὄσσε, Tyrt. 1 D. = 20 W., 10 τέρμ' ἐπιδερκόμενοι, A. *Suppl.* 408-9 δίκην κολυμβητῆρος ἐς βυθὸν μολεῖν / δεδορκὸς ὄμμα [556].

268: οὐδέ ἑ λήθει. Rightly taken as a parenthesis by Pal., Wil., Ev., Si., Col.: cf. Hom. A 561 αἰεὶ μὲν ὀΐεαι — οὐδέ σε λήθω —, K 279, Ψ 323, Ω 563 (see also above, on 24). For the repetition of an idea in negative form see above, on 97 οὐδὲ θύραζε.

269: δή. Cf. Denn., 218: "stressing the importance of the antecedent, or its exact identification with the consequent".

269: τήνδε δίκην. At 39 'the kind of judgement as is known here', at 249 and here 'the kind of justice practised here', where 'justice' does not mean 'jurisdiction' (Nicolai, 61 n. 101) but 'righteousness'. From a strictly grammatical point of view οἵην is predicate: cf. my paraphrase in *Aufbau*, 161: "Zeus weiss, welch eine Ungerechtigkeit die sogenannte Gerechtigkeit ist, die die Könige in dieser Stadt gewöhnt sind auszuüben". I do not believe that τήνδε δίκην refers to an impending or possible lawsuit (as is assumed e.g. by Wil. and Fränkel, 135): see above, on 35 νεῖκος [557].

---

[554] On the other hand, Krafft (53) goes too far in calling the look of Zeus "geistig".

[555] On the other hand, at *Th.* 760 and Hom. λ 16 ἐπιδέρκεται seems to mean 'reaches with his look'. Similarly Emp. B 2, 6 οὔτ' ἐπιδερκτὰ τάδ' ἀνδράσιν οὔτ' ἐπακουστά.

[556] In other contexts the verb denotes an expressive look, especially a look tinged with emotion: see my note on A. *Prom.* 248 προδέρκεσθαι, *Miscellanea ... Kamerbeek*, 458, and Snell, 13-4.

[557] Nicolai (*loc. cit.*) argues that τήνδε δίκην refers to the actual case of Hes. because "nur so

269: ἐντὸς ἐέργει. We. (on *Th.* 751) thinks that "ἐέργει in this phrase is no stronger than 'has'", but the context of the formula (Hom. B 617 etc.) suggests that the thing 'enclosed' fills the space completely. Accordingly, the present use implies that the injustice practised by the rulers extends to the whole town in so far as it is supported by the prevailing mentality of the inhabitants (see above, on 222 λαῶν).

270: νῦν. 'In these circumstances': see above, on 202 νῦν.

270: δή. Wil. reads δέ, but δή introduces the conclusion: cf. Denn., 237.

270-1: μήτε ... δίκαιος / εἴην. This wish has an ironical character, just as 174-5 (see above, on 175 ἔπειτα), and so does not point to "sentiments contradictoires" (Maz. II, 96 n. 2; similarly Fränkel, 135)[558].

270: ἐν ἀνθρώποισι. 'In my dealings with men' (We.): cf. S. *Ant.* 661-2 ἐν τοῖς γὰρ οἰκείοισιν ὅστις ἔστ᾽ ἀνὴρ / χρηστός, φανεῖται κἀν πόλει δίκαιος ὤν.

271: κακόν. 'Disadvantageous': see above, on 214 κακή. Col.'s translation 'è giusto che un uomo sia cattivo'[559] does not suit the context.

272: δίκην. 'Justice' as product of 'righteousness': see above, on 224 ἔνειμαν and 239 δίκην.

272: ἀδικώτερος. Equivalent to ἄδικος: for the comparative used in contrasts cf. K.G. II, 306, Schw. II, 183, M. Wittwer, Glotta 47 (1969), 54 ff., espec. 68 and 96-7[560].

273: οὔπω. In his commentary on *Th.* 560 We. declares: "I do not believe that οὔπω ever means 'not at all'". The same view has been defended by J. E. Fontenrose, AJP 62 (1941), 65-79, but the explanation of 'not yet' is difficult in such cases as Hom. Γ 306 and μ 208: cf. P. T. Stevens, AJP 71 (1950), 290-5. The transition from 'not yet' to 'not at all' has been convincingly explained by B. A. van Groningen, *In the Grip of the Past* (Leiden 1953), 13-4: "things which have not happened up to now cannot happen ... the lessons of the past are decisive". The negation probably goes with ἔολπα: cf. Hom. γ 226 οὔπω τοῦτο ἔπος τελέεσθαι οἴω (where Ameis-Hentze take οὔπω with τελέεσθαι).

273: ἔολπα. For the perfect see above, on 207 λέληκας. Not 'I hope' (Wil.) but 'I expect', 'I think': cf. *H. Dem.* 213, 227, and see above, on 96 ἐλπίς. For Hes.'s optimism see above, on 179 μεμείξεται ἐσθλά.

273: τελεῖν. Not 'bring to pass' (Ev.), for favours bestowed upon unjust

---

wird die Entrüstung der folgenden Verse (270 bis 273) verständlich", but he himself observes that these lines have a rhetorical character.

[558] Quaglia (140) explains: "Even if I should be willing to become unjust", "io ho fede che Zeus non avalla questa scelta", but τελεῖν does not mean 'to stand surety'.

[559] Approved by West, Gnom. 41 (1969), 120, but silently rejected in his commentary, where he quotes Trag. adesp. 528 κακὴ γὰρ αἰδώς, ἔνθα τἀναιδὲς κρατεῖ as a parallel.

[560] The juxtaposition of δίκην and ἀδικώτερος is of course ironical, but not for the reasons advocated by Claus (above, n. 470), 77-8.

people are a present fact, but 'bring to complete fulfilment': cf. Hom. γ 119 μόγις δ᾽ ἐτέλεσσε Κρονίων, and see above, on 218 τέλος. For Zeus as the god who brings fulfilment cf. 474, 669, Hom. A 523, Δ 160-1, Ψ 328, β 34, γ 119, δ 699, ρ 51. See further Nilsson, 206, 429, H. Schwabl, RE XV (1978), 1030-4.

274: Πέρση. Hes. turns back to Perses (see above, on 213 Πέρση) by means of a mental association: Perses is one of those ἄδικοι who always try to get μείζω δίκην (272): cf. 37-8.

274: μετά. Wil. reads ἐνί, because 'take to heart' (cf. 107) suits the context better than 'ponder over' (Hom. I 434-5, λ 428). But Perses is now able to weigh the advantages of injustice against the disadvantages. Similarly 688 (where Wil. wrongly reads ἐνί)[561].

274: βάλλεο. For the meaning of the present imperative see above, on 9 ἴθυνε.

275: καί. Has consecutive force: it introduces the conclusion of the pondering: see my note on Men. *Epitr.* 396 καί, Mnem. IV 27 (1974), 35, and the references given there.

275: νυ. See above, on 268 νυ.

275: ἐπάκουε. Pal.: "perhaps ὑπάκουε", but see above, on 213 ἄκουε Δίκης. For ἐπι- marking an intention see above, on 29 ἐπακουόν. Snell, *Dicht. u. Ges.* (above, on 260 νόον), 61, points out that in Hes. δίκη "ist nicht nur, wie bei Homer, das Fehlen von Hybris und Unrecht, sondern wird zu einem positiven Ziel, zu dem geistigen Band einer erstrebten Gesellschaft".

275: βίης. Not in a physical sense (as at 321) but 'violence': cf. Hom. Π 387 οἵ βίη εἰν ἀγορῇ σκολιὰς κρίνωσι θέμιστας, ο 329 τῶν (the suitors) ὕβρις τε βίη τε, *Lex.* II, 60.54 ff.

275: ἐπιλήθεο. See above, on 264 ἐπὶ ... λάθεσθε.

275: πάμπαν. Does not imply that Perses is already on the right road[562], but is purely emphatic, just as 264 πάγχυ.

276: νόμον. Wil. rightly observes that this is not a 'law' (Ev., Latt.): "Die Tiere treiben es nun einmal so, dass der Starke den Schwachen frisst". We. thinks that Ostwald (*Nomos*, 21) "surely goes too far in claiming that this νόμος of men is just 'a way of life' without prescriptive force. It is, as he goes on to say, a 'norm', not just what is usual but what is proper". This view[563] cannot be correct: (1) it does not apply to the world of animals (see above), (2) the human νόμος is recommended by Hes. on account of its advantage (279 ff.), not because it is an ordinance. It is a natural order, the validity of which is based not only on the fact that it has been determined by Zeus but

---

[561] Krafft's explanation (123), "Perses soll jetzt alles bei sich bedenken und seine bisherige Lebensführung *ändern*", is obviously impossible.

[562] As is suggested by van Groningen, *Hés. et Persès* (above, n. 45), 11.

[563] Wrongly approved by me in my note on 388 νόμος, Mnem. IV 33 (1980), 380.

also, and even primarily, on its being customary: cf. *Th.* 66 πάντων τε νόμους καὶ ἤθεα 'customary ways of acting and of thinking' (see my note in Mnem. IV 25, 1972, 248)[564].

276: διέταξε. 'Disposed': cf. *Th.* 74, LSJ 1.

277-9. Rightly called by Wil. "eine Antwort auf das Gleichnis vom Habicht": Hes. is the first Greek author who points out a fundamental difference between men and animals[565].

277: θηρσί. 'Land animals': cf. Hom. ω 291-2, Archil. 74 D. = 122 W., 7, Emp. B 21, 11.

277: οἰωνοῖς. 'Birds of prey' (LSJ I 1): used for birds generally first by Aeschylus (*Ag.* 563) and Sophocles (fr. 941, 11). Accordingly, ἀλλήλους is not quite logical in this case.

277: πετεηνοῖς. Cf. Hom. Β 459 ὀρνίθων πετεηνῶν. In both cases the epithet is not purely ornamental: large wings are characteristic of birds of prey, and Homer speaks of geese, cranes and swans ἀγαλλόμενα πτερύγεσσιν (462).

278: ἔσθειν. Some editors read ἐσθέμεν (Clem.), but cf. Hom. ε 197 ἔσθειν καὶ πίνειν, Ω 415 ἔσθουσι, and Chantr. I, 292 and 327.

278: ἐστὶν ἐν. The reading of the MSS., adopted by Pal., Rz. (ed. mai.), Waltz, Col., is unobjectionable: δίκη is 'righteousness' (see above, on 9 δίκη), and this is 'within their reach' (cf. Hom. Η 102, κ 69) or 'among' them (cf. Hom. Α 522, etc.).

279: ἀρίστη. 'Most profitable': cf. 281 and see above, on 24 ἀγαθή.

280: γίγνεται. I am not sure that So. and We. are right in reading γίνεται: the argument put forward by Von der Mühll (on β 320) and quoted with approval by We. on *Th.* 429, "apud Iones mature in usum venit, ideoque in Homero relinquendum est", does not carry much weight; cf. on the other hand Chantr. I, 13: "Il est impossible de déterminer vers quelle date cette orthographie s'est introduite dans notre vulgate". For the meaning 'turns out to be' see above, on 88 γένηται.

280: εἰ γάρ τίς κε. For the word-order see above, on 208 ἤ σ' ἄν.

280: ἐθέλη. 'Is in the habit of': see above, on 39 ἐθέλουσι.

280: τὰ δίκαια. See above, on 217 τὰ δίκαια.

280: ἀγορεῦσαι. 'Speak in public': cf. *Th.* 86. Hom. Β 250, etc. See further

---

[564] The basic meaning is not 'thing dispensed', as is argued by Heinimann, *Nomos und Physis* (above, n. 459), 61 ff., but is identical with that of νομός: 'moving to and fro' (cf. Hom. Υ 249 ἐπέων δὲ πολὺς νομὸς ἔνθα καὶ ἔνθα), espec. 'tending cattle', hence 'pasture', 'usual place' (cf. the combination νομός-ἤθεα at Ζ 511 and *Op.* 526-7), 'dwelling place', 'custom': cf. M. Pohlenz, *Kleine Schriften*, II (Hildesheim 1965), 333-40. For νόμος 'ordinance' We. refers to *Th.* 74, but the emendation νόμους cannot be correct: see my remarks in Mnem. IV 25 (1972), 249-50.

[565] Cf. Dierauer, *Tier u. Mensch* (above, n. 232), espec. 15-6, who is wrong, however, in interpreting the νόμος as a duty (16 n. 4). See further the review by H. Rahm, Gnom. 51 (1979), 713-7, and my remarks in Lampas 3 (1970), 99-101 and Mnem. IV 34 (1981), 185-7.

Less. pol., 83-90. The aorist is used, not because "Hesiod thinks in terms of a single occasion" (We.), but because: "l'infinitif aoriste s'applique à un fait, en dehors de toute considération de temps, à condition que, même s'il comporte effectivement de la durée, celle-ci n'entre pas en ligne de compte" (Humbert, 160). Cf. also Bakker, *Imperative* (above, n. 37), Ch. I.

281: γιγνώσκων. For the reading γινώσκων (So., We.) see above, on 280 γίγνεται. For the meaning 'consciously' see above, on 218 ἔγνω. For the importance attached by Hes. to mental attitudes see above, on 260 νόον.

281: μέν. The regular place would be after εἰ, but Hes. wants to emphasize the contrast between the apodoseis. For the same reason μέν and δέ are sometimes put both in the protasis and in the apodosis (Denn., 385-6).

281: τε. For apodotic τε cf. Denn., 534, whose explanation "generalizing" is less convincing than the alternative, "marking the correspondence between protasis and apodosis": see above, on 3 ὅν τε. The observation that the apodosis denotes a 'permanent' fact (Ruijgh, 899-900) seems to me less relevant.

281: ὄλβον. 'Abundance': see above, on 172 ὄλβιοι.

281: διδοῖ. See above, on 225 διδοῦσιν.

282: μαρτυρίησιν. The litigants gave evidence on oath: cf. Hom. Ψ 579-85. The dative expresses the occasion on which the oath is taken: see above, on 231 θαλίης.

282: ἑκών. Cf. *Th.* 232 (Horkos) πημαίνει, ὅτε κέν τις ἑκὼν ἐπίορκον ὀμόσσῃ. Hes. adds ἑκών (1) for the sake of clearness (at Hom. Κ 332 Dolon's oath is called ἐπίορκος although its falseness is not intentional), and (2) because, in contradistinction to Homer [566], he sets much value upon moral attitudes (see above, on 220 νόον). See further R. Maschke, *Die Willenslehre im griechischen Recht* (Berlin 1926), 10 ff., Luther, 143-4, *Less. pol.*, 241-50 (ἀέκων), A. Dihle, *The Theory of Will in Classical Antiquity* (Berkeley - Los Angeles 1982).

282: ἐπίορκον. *Scil.* ὅρκον. See further above, on 190 εὐόρκου and 219 Ὅρκος.

283: ψεύσεται. For the short-vowel subjunctive cf. We. on *Th.* 81 τιμήσουσι, and Chantr. I, 454.

283: ἐν. Adverbial, 'on the same occasion', 'similarly': cf. S. *Aj.* 675, *O.R.* 182, Hdt. I 74, 1 and often (Powell, *Lex.*, 120, E 1-2) [567].

283: βλάψας. Cf. 258 βλάπτῃ and see above, on 193 βλάψει.

283: νήκεστον. Goes with ἀάσθη: cf. *H. Dem.* 258 ἀφραδίῃσι τεῇς νήκεστον ἀάσθης. For the meaning cf. ἀκέομαι 'make amends' (LSJ II).

---

[566] For some exceptions (Ψ 585, χ 351) cf. G. Vlastos, *Plato's Universe* (Oxford 1975), 16 and 98.

[567] This use is not clearly distinguished by LSJ (C 2-3) from 'among them' and from Hom. ε 260, where ἐν points forward to ἐν αὐτῇ.

283: ἀάσθη. We. rightly prints the indicative: see above, on 224 ἔνειμαν[568]. The use of the passive form does not imply that he does not act on his own responsibility: cf. Hom. δ 503 ὑπερφίαλον ἔπος ἔκβαλε καὶ μέγ' ἀάσθη. See further *Less. pol.*, 5-7, and above, on 216 ἄτησιν.

284. Explains 214 κακή: see above, on 213 ὦ Πέρση.

284: δέ τε. Apodotic: see above, on 23 δέ τε.

284: ἀμαυροτέρη. 'Dim', 'obscure', 'unknown' (LSJ II 2), *scil.* because their wealth will diminish: cf. 313 and 325. For the comparative used in contrasted sentences see above, on 272 ἀδικώτερος.

284: γενεή. 'Offspring' (LSJ I 3): the self-imprecation connected with the oath included the juror's descendants: cf. Antipho 5, 11, Andoc. 1, 98.

284: μετόπισθε. 'In the future': cf. Hom. Γ 160 μηδ' ἡμῖν τεκέεσσί τ' ὀπίσσω πῆμα λίποιτο. The transition from 'behind' to 'in the future' is based on the fact that the Greeks generally imagined themselves to stand in the course of events their faces directed towards the past: cf. van Groningen, *In the Grip of the Past* (above, on 273 οὔπω), who, rather surprisingly, does not discuss the present idiom[569]. Hom. Α 343 οἶδε νοῆσαι ἅμα πρόσσω καὶ ὀπίσσω (cf. Γ 109, Σ 250, ω 452) does not mean 'das Vorige und das was hinterher kommt' (Ameis-Hentze) nor 'the immediate future and the more distant future' (Willcock), but 'the past and the future'. The adverb μετόπισθε is commonly taken with λέλειπται (cf. Hom. Υ 308 καὶ παίδων παῖδες, τοί κεν μετόπισθε γένωνται and, at the end of the line, Χ 334 μετόπισθε λελείμμην), but it may also, and even primarily, go with γενεή (cf. Sol. 1 D. = 13 W., 32 and Tyrt. 9 D. = 12 W., 30 γένος ἐξοπίσω, Hdt. V 22, 1 ἐν τοῖσι ὄπισθε λόγοισι): in that case the word serves to fix the meaning of γενεή (which can also mean 'race', 'descent').

285: γενεὴ μετόπισθε. For emphatic repetition of an important idea see above, on 188 γηράντεσσι. For repetition in contrasted sentences cf. We., *Th.*, 76.

286: δέ. Van Groningen (165 n. 3) thinks that "l'usage de δέ est absolument identique à celui du vers 202 νῦν δ' αἶνον βασιλεῦσιν ἐρέω: il relie à ce qui précède". But the word-order suggests that δέ is emphatic, just as δέ after an apostrophe (27, 213, 274). We. rightly observes that the section 286-319 "does for work what 212-85 did for Dike, and completes a chiastic sequence: work myth (47 ff.)—Dike myth—Dike protreptic—work protreptic. It is not that Hesiod likes to make patterns, it is that the end of the Age myth led him on to his sermon on Dike", but he continues with "and if he has more to say about work it must come afterwards": this should be replaced by "and

---

[568] G. Arrighetti, RFIC 37 (1965), 160-1, rightly defends ἀάσθη, but wrongly compares 218 παθὼν δέ τε νήπιος ἔγνω.

[569] LSJ (ὀπίσω II 1) suggest that "the future is unseen and was therefore regarded as *behind us*", but this explanation should be rather inverted: cf. van Groningen, *op. cit.*, 109 ff.

the end of the sermon on Dike leads him on to a sermon on work". The starting-point for the train of thought is v. 285, for this gives rise to the question whether justice is a sufficient condition in order to reach prosperity. The answer is that justice should be accompanied by work.

286: ἐσθλὰ νοέων. This cannot mean 'en homme qui veut ton bien' (Maz.), not because "νοεῖν ist noch auf das Erkennen beschränkt" (Wil., who overlooks e.g. Ψ 484 νόος ἀπηνής), but because ἐσθλός 'kindly disposed' is not found before the 5th century (e.g. S. *El.* 24). For ἐσθλά 'profitable things' see above, on 116 ἐσθλά, and Hom. Σ 313 ἐσθλὴν φράζετο βουλήν. Wil. takes the word with ἐρέω, but although νοέων may be used in an absolute sense (see above, on 12 νοήσας), it is more natural to take ἐσθλά both with νοέων and ἐρέω, just as at 280-1 τὰ δίκαια with ἀγορεῦσαι and γιγνώσκων. For the synizesis in νοέων see above, on 202 ἐρέω.

287: τήν. For the addition of the article to contrasted terms see above, on 193 ὁ κακός.

287: τοι. Frequent in gnomic utterances: cf. Denn., 542-4, who rightly explains it as "forcing the general truth upon the consciousness of the individual addressed". We. rightly rejects γάρ found in some testimonies.

287: κακότητα. Not 'vice' (LSJ I 2; Col.) but 'misery', 'misfortune', which is the opposite of the prosperity implied in 285 ἀμείνων.

287: καί. Cf. καὶ πολύς (Denn., 318) and καί with numerals (Denn., 320). See also above, on 44 κείς.

287: ἰλαδόν. Elsewhere (Hom. B 93, Hdt. I 172, 1) the meaning is 'in troops', 'in companies', and Wil. (followed by Becker, 57) thinks "dass diesen bequemen und kurzen Weg die Menschen scharenweise gehen". But ἑλέσθαι (not 'reach') shows that the word refers to κακότητα and means 'in quantities'. Pal. may be right in suggesting that it is "a metaphor from capturing animals in great numbers together": cf. 100 μυρία λυγρὰ κατ' ἀνθρώπους ἀλάληται.

288: ὀλίγη. Thus all MSS., a Berlin papyrus (cf. H. Maehler, ZPE 15, 1974, 201, 207), Proclus. Most editors adopt λείη from Plato, Xen., Plut., Arist. Quint., because "this reading avoids the tautology of ὀλίγη ... μάλα δ' ἐγγύθι ναίει, and provides an antithesis to ὄρθιος and τρηχύς" (We.). But this is tantamount to saying that λείη is a *lectio facilior*: cf. Hom. κ 103 λείην ὁδόν, Hdt. IX 69, 1 οἱ μὲν ... τὴν φέρουσαν ἄνω ... οἱ δὲ ... διὰ τοῦ πεδίου τὴν λειοτάτην τῶν ὁδῶν, Pl. *Phdr.* 272 c 1 ἵνα μὴ πολλὴν ἀπίῃ καὶ τραχεῖαν, ἐξὸν ὀλίγην καὶ λείαν. For ὀλίγος 'short' cf. also Hom. B 529. The tautology is only a seeming one, for ἐγγύθι ναίει (*scil.* κακότης) defines the end of the road. Hes. gives a more elaborate definition of the other road because that is the road which he recommends. Cf. also van der Valk, *Researches*, II (above, n. 357), 307-9.

289: ἀρετῆς. 'Prosperity', 'success': cf. Hom. ν 45, σ 132, and ἀρετάω.

Hes. thinks especially of "Wohlstand und geachtete Stellung in der Gesellschaft" (Wil., *Gl.* I, 346): cf. 313. See further Hoffmann, 118-20, Sellschopp,
102-3, Krafft, 94-5, Péron, 267 and n. 2, and my remarks in Mnem. IV 30
(1977), 79-80.

289: ἱδρῶτα. We. observes that "the graphic physical manifestation is
preferred to the abstract 'work' ", and compares 45-6. It may be added that in
the present passage 'sweat' still has its literal meaning, whereas at Simon. 579,
5 and Antipho Soph. B 49 it becomes equivalent to 'toil' [570]. Jaeger's
paraphrase (*Paideia* I, 106, Engl. ed., 71), "In the sweat of his brow shall he
eat bread — but this is not a curse, it is a blessing", is based on a serious
misunderstanding: in Hes.'s view the toil of agriculture is (1) a curse resting
on mankind as a consequence of the deceit committed by Prometheus, and
(2) not an end in itself, but a necessary means towards an end (viz.
prosperity) [571].

Sellschopp (102) writes: "Das grundsätzlich Neue der Ilias gegenüber ist
hier, dass die ἀρετή erarbeitet wird. Diese Zusammenstellung von Arbeit und
ἀρετή, ja die Abhängigkeit der ἀρετή von der Arbeit ist für die Helden
undenkbar: bei ihnen ist ἀρετή etwas Gegebenes, bei Hesiod aber gibt es einen
Weg zu ihr". It should be added (1) that the Homeric heroes, too, have their
work, viz. the ἔργον Ἄρηος (Λ 734; see further LSJ I 1), and that they have
constantly to 'work' in order to maintain their ἀρετή (cf. e.g. Z 479-81,
M 315-21), and (2) that the *Odyssey* shows a more positive evaluation of
manual labour [572]. For Hes.'s conception of work see also below, on 303
ἀεργός and 311 ὄνειδος [573].

289: θεοί. Nicolai (67) rightly observes: "es ist also göttlicher Wille, dass
die Menschen es schwer haben, arbeiten müssen; cf. 42 ff.".

290: δέ. Has explanatory (specifying) force: see above, on 9 δέ.

290: ὄρθιος. For the association of 'steep' with 'difficult' and 'laborious' cf.
Becker, 58, who compares Hom. N 317 αἰπύ οἱ ἐσσεῖται and Λ 601, Π 651
πόνον αἰπύν.

290: οἶμος. For the aspirate cf. We.

290: ἐς. This way leads 'into' the domain of ἀρετή, as appears from 292:
see above, on 84 εἰς.

---

[570] Cf. Zink, *Warm u. Kalt* (above, n. 412), 47. For the history of the idea of *per aspera ad
astra* cf. H. Hommel, *Symbola*, I (Hildesheim 1976), 274-89.

[571] Cf. Luther, 141 n. 2, and Wil., 138: "er verlangt die Arbeit nur, weil sie nötig ist, nicht weil
sie dem Leben erst Inhalt und Wert verleiht". It is misleading, however, to add (154) that in the
second part of the poem "das *labora* gibt dem Leben einen Inhalt". Waltz (I), 61, is equally
wrong in maintaining: "il avait assez vivement gout du travail pour l'aimer même avec
désintéressement".

[572] Cf. Luther, 141 n. 1, A. Aymard, Journ. de Psych. 41 (1948), 30-3. See further G. Glotz,
Le travail dans la Grèce ancienne (Paris 1920), 11 ff., Brake, *Wirtschaften* (above, n. 196), 44-8.

[573] Cf. also Brake, *op. cit.*, 52-6, Aymard, *op. cit.*, 36-8.

291-2. Pal. writes that "the spondaic followed by a dactylic verse seems intentionally to express laborious ascent and easy descent". But (1) Hes. has many lines with a spondaic beginning, and (2) 292 does not denote descent. On the other hand, Nicolai (67) may be right in suggesting that the dactyls emphasize the idea of ease: cf. Hom. P 458 ῥίμφ᾽ ἔφερον θοὸν ἅρμα [574].

291: εἰς ἄκρον. The image later becomes a metaphorical phrase: cf. Tyrt. 9 D. = 12 W., 43, LSJ II 1. For Hom. Ψ 339 ἄκρον ἱκέσθαι cf. Krafft, 94-5.

291: ἵκηται. The reading ἵκηαι (adopted by Maz., Wil., Si.) is a *lectio facilior*. The subject (the wayfarer) has to be supplied from the context: cf. K.G. I, 34-6 (who wrongly think that in such cases as Hom. X 199 ἐν ὀνείρῳ οὐ δύναται φεύγοντα διώκειν we should mentally supply τις), Schw. II, 245, who wrongly adopts Wackernagel's theory (I, 111-3) that the third person singular can express an indefinite personal subject [575]: see my note on Pl. *Meno* 79 b 5, Mnem. IV 10 (1957), 292-3.

292: ῥηιδίη. We. observes that "Hesiod reverts to the gender of ὁδός", but he does not explain why. Becker (57) takes ἀρετή to be the subject: as soon as the farmer has reached a sufficiently high level of prosperity, this is comparatively easy to maintain. The addition χαλεπή περ ἐοῦσα shows, however, that Hes. still has the image of the road in his mind. This road debouches into prosperity (see above, on 290 ἐς), so that the two ideas fuse (Hoffmann, 119), and this fusion manifests itself in the feminine gender.

292: δὴ ἔπειτα. Probably to be read with synizesis: see above, on 248 βασιλῆες.

292: ἐοῦσα. Not 'hard though it may still be' (Si., Maz.), but 'hard though it was before' (Ev., We.): for the imperfect participle cf. K.G. I, 200, Schw. II, 297, and my note on *Th.* 32 ἐόντα, Mnem. IV 25 (1972), 239 (where more literature is mentioned).

The confident tone of this passage and generally of Hes.'s advices shows that he was 'on top' himself: he was at least sufficiently well-to-do to afford the help of servants (405, 441) and slaves (470, 502, 573, 597, 608, 766) [576].

293-7. The logical place of these lines would be after 286. Wil. writes: "Hesiod weiss zwei ἐσθλά, wie es mit den beiden Wegen steht, und dass man zu nichts kommen kann, wenn man guten Rat verschmäht", but such a twofold recommendation is not indicated in the text. Hes. has postponed his admonition to listen to his advice to a point where it is more effective, and even necessary, from a psychological point of view, viz. the point where the advice has to be put into practice. Perses will no doubt pay kind attention to a general reflection about ways leading to failure and success. But now the

---

[574] See further W. A. Camps, *An Introduction to Homer* (Oxford 1980), 49-52.

[575] Similarly E. Benveniste, BSL 43 (1947), 1 ff., Chantr. II, 8.

[576] A. R. Burn, *The World of Hesiod* (London 1936), 32, calls Hes. "a substantial yeoman". See further G. Nussbaum, CQ N.S. 10 (1960), 213 ff.

moment has come that he will have to turn into the steep road and set to work, and Hes. foresees that this prospect will cause a strong resistance. He therefore sets the authority of his own long-range vision (294) against Perses' silliness (286 μέγα νήπιε). Becker (59) rightly observes that Hes. does not let his brother take his choice: he simply tries to enforce his compliance (295 πίθηται)[577].

293: οὗτος. Pointing forward: cf. K.G. I, 646, Schw. II, 209, Bruhn, §81, and my note on 388 οὗτος, Mnem. IV 33 (1980), 380.

293: αὐτός. So. prints αὐτῷ (here and at 296): this is the better attested reading, but it spoils the contrast with 295. Solmsen, CP 71 (1976), 252, argues that "for Hesiod himself, stylistic and logical considerations carry little weight". It is true that Hes.'s thought is not always strictly logical, but it is never illogical. Solmsen further (252-3) refers to Arist. *EN* 1141 b 34 τὸ αὐτῷ εἰδέναι, but the context (b 30 περὶ αὐτόν and 1142 a 7 τὸ αὐτοῖς ἀγαθόν) shows that αὐτῷ does not belong to εἰδέναι but that τὸ αὐτῷ means 'one's own interest'. Solmsen observes that "Hesiod too has practical advantage in mind", but that is not the point at issue[578]. For the *topos* of αὐτὸς νοεῖν as contrasted with listening to others cf. We. and see above, on 202 νοέουσι καὶ αὐτοῖς[579].

293: νοήσει. For the short-vowel subjunctive cf. We. and see above, on 283 ψεύσεται. For the meaning of νοέω see above, on 12 νοήσας.

294. Bracketed by Pal., Wil., but it is essential to the argument: Perses has always confined his attention to the advantage of the present moment and has neglected the consequences, and Hes. tries to impress upon him the necessity of a long-term view (cf. 284-5, 333, 394, etc.). Similarly Nicolai, 68 n. 119.

294: ἐς τέλος. 'In the end': cf. LSJ II 2 b.

294: ἀμείνω. 'More profitable': see above, on 19 ἀμείνω. The comparative is used instead of the superlative in implied contrasts: cf. Hom. Λ 469 ἀλεξέμεναι γὰρ ἄμεινον, K.G. II, 307, and see above, on 272 ἀδικώτερος.

295: κἀκεῖνος. We. prints καὶ κεῖνος, because Aristarchus preferred καὶ κει- in Homer, but Aristarchus even thought that Homer never uses ἐκεῖνος except under metrical compulsion (schol. α 177), and this may be a mere prejudice: cf. the harsh rhythm of O 94 οἷος κείνου θυμός and I 63 ἐστιν κεῖνος. See further Chantr. I, 276-7. Hes. uses ἐκεῖνος after οὗτος because "the second-best is further off" (We.): cf. K.G. I, 649.

---

[577] W. H. Race, *The Classical Priamel from Homer to Boethius* (Leiden 1982), 43 n. 24, points out that 293-7 is not a real priamel, because it begins with the superlative.

[578] The origin of the variant αὐτῷ (αὑτῷ) is difficult to explain. Wil. suggests that it was thought to belong to 294 φρασσάμενος, but it is also found in testimonies which do not have 294.

[579] Snell, *Dichtung u. Ges.* (above, n. 454), 58 n. 6, observes that Hes. is the first author who expresses the idea of mental concentration (cf. *Th.* 661 ἀτενεῖ νόῳ), but in the present phrase this is not expressed but at most implied.

295: εὖ. 'Competently' (see above, on 107 εὖ): the competent speaker is the same as the man described in the preceding lines.

295: πίθηται. Diller (in Heitsch, 267) suggests that Hes. may have found a model in Nestor's call (Α 274 ἀλλὰ πίθεσθε καὶ ὔμμες, ἐπεὶ πείθεσθαι ἄμεινον), but Nestor does not justify his authority except by his age.

296: νοέῃ. Used absolutely: see above, on 1 κλείουσαι.

296: ἄλλου. *Scil.* εὖ εἰπόντος.

297: ἐν θυμῷ βάλληται. 'Takes to heart' (see above, on 107 ἐνὶ φρεσὶ βάλλεο), *scil.* what the other says. For the choice of θυμῷ instead of φρεσί see above, on 27 θυμῷ.

297: δέ. Not because "the main clause as much as the relative protasis is contrasted with the preceding sentence" (We.), but apodotic: see above, on 239 δέ.

297: ἀχρήιος. 'Useless' (403), hence 'worthless': cf. A. *Prom.* 297, Thuc. II 40, 2, E. *Med.* 299, *Lex.*, 1778-9.

298: ἀλλά. Marks the transition from preliminary reflections to a call to action: cf. Denn., 14. Nicolai (69) wrongly thinks that 298 forms the beginning of a new 'block'[580].

298: ἡμετέρης. An instance of the *pluralis societatis*, a rhetorical trick used by superiors (commanders, teachers, etc.) to incite their inferiors (soldiers, pupils, etc.) to greater exertion by creating the illusion that they are cooperating on the same level. See further Wackernagel I, 42-3, 98-100 (whose explanation of the idiom as a form of urbanity does not seem to me convincing), K.G. I, 83-4, Schw. II, 243, Chantr. II, 33, H. Zilliacus, *Selbstgefühl und Servilität. Studien zum unregelmässigen Numerusgebrauch im Griechischen* (Helsingfors 1953).

298: μεμνημένος. With the intention of carrying it out: cf. 422, 616, 623, 641, 711, 728, and see above, on 49 ἐμήσατο and 264 ἐπὶ ... λάθεσθε.

298: ἐφετμῆς. Not 'command' (Marg) but 'urgent request or advice': cf. Hom. Α 495 Θέτις δ' οὐ λήθετ' ἐφετμέων παιδὸς ἑοῦ, Ω 300 ὦ γύναι, οὐ μέν τοι τόδ' ἐφιεμένη ἀπιθήσω.

299: ἐργάζευ. Not 'go on tilling your land' (Pal.), for Perses is an idler, but 'be a worker': for the use of the present imperative see above, on 9 ἴθυνε.

299: δῖον. The ancient explanation 'son of Dios' (accepted by Schm., 249 n. 1) is rightly rejected by We. He adopts Wil.'s interpretation: "Der zugewanderte Händler aus Kyme hatte sich den Bauern, die ihn unter sich aufgenommen hatten, als Nachkommen der Ritter vorgestellt, die einst aus Böotien nach der Äolis ausgewandert waren. Perses wird zugleich daran gemahnt, was er seinem Geschlechte schuldig ist" (similarly Renehan, 351).

---

[580] His assumption (69) of a "Einschnitt" after 319 seems to me equally wrong: see below, on 320 δέ.

But Hes. never assumes the air of a nobleman [581]. On the other hand, it may be assumed that Perses was not free of genteel manners (see below, on 311 ὄνειδος). Accordingly, the phrase δῖον γένος seems to be a mock-heroic allusion to διογενής. The irony is reinforced by an ambiguity: on the one hand, we may think of δῖος used in the epic of all kinds of men, on the other hand, the Homeric model of the phrase δῖον γένος (I 538) refers to a destructive boar sent by Artemis [582].

299: γένος. 'Descendant' (see above, on 11 γένος), hence 'creature': cf. Hom. Z 180, I 538, S. *Aj.* 784. For the use of *abstractum pro concreto* see above, on 191 ὕβριν.

299: Λιμός. See above, on 230 Λιμός.

300: ἐχθαίρῃ, φιλέῃ. For the chiasmus see above, on 10 μυθησαίμην. For ἐχθαίρω used of the gods cf. Hom. P 270, λ 560, τ 364.

300: ἐυστέφανος. Also used of Artemis, Aphrodite, etc. The crown does not seem to have a special function [583], but belongs to a beautiful woman: cf. 75, *Th.* 576, 578, Sa. 98 a.

301: αἰδοίη. See above, on 71 αἰδοίη and 257 αἰδοίη.

301: βιότου. 'Means of living' (see above, on 167 βίοτον), here 'corn': cf. *Lex.* II, 63.51 ff.

302: πάμπαν. Goes with σύμφορος.

302: ἀεργῷ. See above, on 44 ἀεργόν.

302: σύμφορος. 'The natural companion' (We.): cf. We. on *Th.* 593, Renehan, 351.

302: ἀνδρί. L. S. Sussman, Areth. 11 (1978), 27 ff., observes that Hes., in contradistinction to Semonides, does not speak about women neglecting their work. She suggests (31) that "Hesiod's exclusion of women from the economy" represents "a shift from an essentially pastoral economy featuring meat as a major dietary staple to an economy based largely on grain-raising". It is true that the Homeric warriors "eat a good deal of meat", but men in general are called ἀλφησταί and σῖτον ἔδοντες, and the earth is ζείδωρος.

---

[581] Walcot (*Peasants*, 112) suggests that "perhaps the poet is thinking back to the myth of the ages and the work of the Olympians or of Zeus in creating the first four races of mankind", but 'created by' is not identical with 'descending from'. Luther (142) thinks that Hes. alludes to the Homeric phrase πατὴρ ἀνδρῶν, to which he attributes a new, viz. anti-aristocratic, sense, but this seems rather far-fetched. Maz. compares the ironic use of ὦ θεῖε, ὦ δαιμόνιε, etc., but these parallels are anachronistic.

[582] Many editors think that the phrase denotes Artemis herself, but such parallels as Z 180, where the Chimaera is called θεῖον γένος οὐδ' ἀνθρώπων, and Ψ 346 Ἀρίονα δῖον suggest that the animal is meant and that δῖον means 'created by the gods'. Another example of mock-heroic language is *Th.* 543 ἀνάκτων: see my note in Mnem. IV 24 (1971), 3.

[583] As is assumed by D. Dickmann Boedeker, *Aphrodite's Entry into Greek Epic* (Leiden 1974), 27-8, who suggests that "the meaning of ἐυστέφανος, 'well-crowned, garlanded', may refer to the garlands often worn in the sacred dances performed for fertility goddesses".

In Hes.'s time peasant women certainly cooperated with their husbands, but his misogyny made him suppress this fact.

303: θεοὶ νεμεσῶσι. See above, on 200 Νέμεσις. Divine disapproval of human behaviour is also mentioned at 741, 756, Hom. Δ 507, Ε 872, Ν 119, ξ 284.

303: ἀεργός. For the repetition see above, on 188 γηράντεσσι. G. Nussbaum, CQ N.S. 10 (1960), 217, rightly observes that "it would be quite wrong to imagine that work is positively honourable to Hesiod. The need to work hard and to wring a living from the earth is part of the order of the Iron Age of the world". See further above, on 289 ἱδρῶτα. It may be added that work is honourable only in so far as its result, prosperity, increases one's prestige (313): see further below, on 311 ὄνειδος.

304-6. We. thinks that the simile is less apposite here than at *Th.* 594 ff., where it is applied to women. But it is misleading to say that "the idler of *Op.* does not feast on others' labours, he starves": even a starving idler sponges on the labours of his fellow-men.

304: κοθούροις. Probably 'without sting': cf. We. (see also Aly in Heitsch, 96).

304: ὀργήν. Not the whole character, but rather 'temperament': it is more dynamical and more emotional than φύσις, more intentional than θυμός. See further my note on Semon. 7, 11, Mnem. IV 21 (1968), 136-7.

305: κάματον. 'Product of labour': similarly *Th.* 599, Hom. ξ 417, and πόνος (LSJ III). See also above, on 224 ἔνειμαν.

306: φίλα. Predicate, the infinitive having consecutive force: cf. Hom. Α 107 αἰεί τοι τὰ κάκ᾽ ἐστὶ φίλα φρεσὶ μαντεύεσθαι, ρ 15 ἐμοὶ φίλ᾽ ἀληθέα μυθήσασθαι, Schw. II, 364, Chantr. II, 302.

306: μέτρια. Predicative with κοσμεῖν (Maz. wrongly construes ἔργα μέτρια). The word does not only denote the right quantity (Pal.), the right time (Maz.), or the right place (We.), but all these together.

306: κοσμεῖν. 'Arrange', 'keep and put in order' (LSJ I 2). Cf. Hom. χ 440 δόμον κατακοσμήσησθε.

307: ὡραίου. See above, on 32 ὡραῖος.

307: βιότου πλήθωσι καλιαί. For the repetition (cf. 301) see above, on 188 γηράντεσσι.

308: ἐξ ἔργων δέ. For the postponement of δέ cf. Denn., 185.

308: πολύμηλοι. Sheep were the most elementary productive animals: cf. Benveniste, *Vocabulaire* (above, n. 158), I, 35 ff., W. Richter, KP V (1975), 1-6.

308: ἀφνειοί. Not 'riches en or' (Maz.)[584] but more generally 'having

---

[584] Vernant, *Mythe et pensée* (above, n. 341), 130 n. 135, tries to defend Maz.'s translation by referring to Hom. α 392-3 δῶ ἀφνειόν and Β 570 ἀφνειόν τε Κόρινθον, but he forgets ρ 422-3

abundant means of living': cf. Hom. E 544, Z 14, Ξ 122 ἀφνειὸς βιότοιο. See further above, on 24 ἄφενος, and *Lex.*, 1711-3.

309: καί τε. Cf. 360, 371, 515-6, Denn., 529, Ruijgh, 900-2. For the neglect of the digamma of ἐργαζόμενος see above, on 28 ἀπ᾽ ἔργου. Maz. rightly explains: "l'homme qui travaille devient riche, parce que le travail en lui-même est agréable aux dieux; la richesse est le don des dieux (θεόσδοτα, 320)". For καί having explanatory (motivating) force cf. Hom. I 509 τὸν δὲ μέγ᾽ ὤνησαν καί τ᾽ ἔκλυον εὐχομένοιο, and my note on Men. *Epitr.* 120, Mnem. IV 27 (1974), 23.

309: ἐργαζόμενος. Maz., Ev., Si. read ἐργαζόμενοι, but this is a *lectio facilior*. For the participle used as a substantive see above, on 5 βριάοντα.

309: φίλτερος. *Scil.* than a man who does not work: see above, on 272 ἀδικώτερος.

310. Certainly spurious: " 'rich in flocks' goes with 'dear to the gods', not with 'dear to the gods and men', and the φιλεῖν/στυγεῖν axis is not appropriate to men's attitude towards the industrious and the idle" (We.).

311: ἔργον. Equivalent to ἐργασία: cf. Hom. σ 366, *H. Ven.* 10, Thuc. II 40, 1. For the use of *concretum pro abstracto* see above, on 267 ὀφθαλμός.

311: δέ. Introduces the counterpart to 309: working is first considered from the point of view of the gods, then from that of men.

311: οὐδέν. 'Not at all' (LSJ A III 1).

311: ὄνειδος. We. quotes G. Nussbaum, CQ N.S. 10 (1960), 217: "To Hesiod as to Homer physical work is not degrading. But it is interesting to find him saying so explicitly, as though he felt that some might think it was". It is still more interesting to ask who these 'some' might be. No doubt it was Perses, who thought himself superior to manual labour: see above, on 299 δῖον γένος, and Wil. on 299: "Wir stellen uns ... leicht vor, dass er das γυμνὸν σπείρειν, 391, für wenig standesgemäss hielt und aus falscher αἰδώς auf Abwege geriet".

311: ἀεργίη. Krafft (65-6) rightly combats the view proposed by Sellschopp (96), that this term was created by Hes., by pointing out that the contrast 'working–not working' is implied in Hom. ω 251. On the other hand, he wrongly thinks that ἀεργίη in Hes. has the moral connotation of 'laziness': the phrase ἀεργὸς ζώη (303-4) shows that ἀεργός denotes a fact and does not imply an evaluation [585].

311: ὄνειδος. Because idleness diminishes a man's wealth and hence his social status and reputation (313). This motivation shows that work is not an

---

ἦσαν δὲ δμῶες μάλα μυρίοι ἄλλα τε πολλά, / οἷσίν τ᾽ εὖ ζώουσι καὶ ἀφνειοὶ καλέονται and Hes. fr. 240, 1-2 Ἑλλοπίη ... / ἀφνειὴ μήλοισι καὶ εἰλιπόδεσσι βόεσσιν.

[585] Cf. Sellschopp, 101. The fact that ἀεργίη refers to a habit does not alter the situation, for a habit is not identical with "una posizione morale che nega radicalmente il lavoro", as is assumed by E. Livrea, Helikon 7 (1967), 83, whose view is elaborated in *Less. pol.*, 256.

"ethische Grundforderung Hesiods" (Hoffmann, 107)[586]. In Hes.'s view work is a necessity, not a duty: see above, on 289 ἰδρῶτα and 303 ἀεργός[587].

312: τάχα. " 'Quickly' implying 'readily', of what can easily be envisaged" (We., whose examples disprove LSJ's view that "Homer uses it only of time").

312: ζηλώσει. For the transition from 'envy' to 'admire' cf. LSJ I 2.

313: δέ. Has explanatory (motivating) force: see above, on 13 διὰ δέ.

313: ἀρετή. Not 'nobility' (Latt.) but 'prosperity', 'success': see above, on 289 ἀρετῆς.

313: κῦδος. See above, on 257 κυδρή. Krafft (128-9) thinks that κῦδος "eigentlich nichts mit 'Ruhm' zu tun haben kann" and concludes: "So kann auch Erg. 313 ἀρετή, das von anderen anerkannte Wohlergehen, neben κῦδος, dem eigenen Stolz über das Wohlergehen, stehen". This is a wrong distinction: the success denoted by ἀρετή need not be acknowledged by others, though it mostly is, and the glory denoted by κῦδος may include pride, but also fame. Walcot (*Peasants*, 6) translates the words by 'reputation' and 'prestige', but 'prestige' is too weak, and 'reputation' is too narrow, for the prosperity denoted by ἀρετή may include an easy life (cf. 476-8)[588].

The Homeric heroes, too, are inclined to regard wealth as a mark of general excellence: cf. e.g. λ 358-60, σ 125-7, 276. This appreciation has been explained as the survival of the peasant's point of view in a courtly society[589]. It has been added (Walcot, *Peasants*, 17-9) that the Homeric aristocrats "live much closer to the soil" than is commonly realized. We should not conclude, however, that the appreciation of wealth reflects a specifically rural mentality: it is based on a more generally 'primitive' attitude, which does not draw a sharp distinction between inner and outer values: see my remarks in Lampas 5 (1972), 107-10.

313: ὀπηδεῖ. See above, on 142 ὀπηδεῖ.

314: δαίμονι. 'Fortune', 'circumstances': cf. Thgn. 161 πολλοί τοι χρῶνται δειλαῖς φρεσί, δαίμονι δ᾽ ἐσθλῷ, S. *El.* 1306 ὑπηρετοίην τῷ παρόντι δαίμονι (where the religious aspect is more prominent: cf. 999 and 1266-70). The dative is not instrumental (Wil. 'wie du dich durch deinen δαίμων befindest') but limitative (Maz., We.): see above, on 120 μήλοισι.

---

[586] Similarly, Kühn (263) speaks of "Arbeitsethik" in Hes., and Vernant, *Mythe et pensée*, 200, maintains: "Le travail est pour lui une forme de vie morale".

[587] It is true that Campbell (quoted by Walcot, *Peasants*, 61) writes: "In the Sarakatsan view there must always be something morally wrong with a very poor man", but the sequel shows that "morally wrong" refers to his inability "to insist upon an equality in honour".

[588] Walcot (*Peasants*, 8) thinks that in this passage "the thought of personal prestige is very much in Hesiod's mind", but the predominant idea is pleasure (γηθήσειν) derived from ease. Walcot also refers to 482 θηήσαντο, but the pleasure of being admired is added to the pleasure of ease (481 χαίρων).

[589] Cf. H. L. Levy, TAPA 94 (1963), 145-53.

314: δέ. Not 'but' (We.) but 'therefore', introducing the conclusion: cf. Denn., 170 and my note on Men. *Epitr.* 332, Mnem. IV 27 (1974), 31 [590].

314: οἷος. Not 'however', i.e. rich or poor (Pal., Ev., Si., We.) or 'at whatever you have a talent for doing' (Latt.), but 'such as', i.e. poor. The line refers back to 28-34: a poor man cannot become rich by litigating but only by working.

314: ἔησθα. Pal. and We. read ἔῃσθα. We. rightly points out that Wil.'s and Maz.'s explanations of the imperfect as a past condition which continues into the present are unsatisfactory, because "only Perses' present or future condition is relevant to the necessity of his working now and in the future". But the imperfect may still be kept if it is taken to refer to something of which mention was made before, in this case Perses' poor condition indicated at 31-2. Cf. Hom. π 420 σὺ δ' οὐκ ἄρα τοῖος ἔησθα (*scil.* as I thought before), and see above, on 11 ἔην.

314: τό. Cf. Hom. υ 52 ἀνίη καὶ τὸ φυλάσσειν πάννυχον ἐγρήσσοντα. K.G. I, 579, Wackernagel I, 171, Schw. II, 20 n. 5, Chantr. II, 305, take τό as a demonstrative pronoun pointing forward to the infinitive (see above, on 200 τά), but it seems more natural to assume that the article has determinative force and that ἐργάζεσθαι is implicitly contrasted with the ἀεργίη mentioned in the preceding lines: see above, on 193 ὁ κακός.

314: ἄμεινον. 'More profitable': see above, on 19 ἀμείνω. For the use of the comparative in implied contrasts see above, on 294 ἀμείνω.

315-6. A specification of 314 ἐργάζεσθαι [591].

315: ἀπ' ἀλλοτρίων κτεάνων. A reminiscence of 34 κτήμασ' ἐπ' ἀλλοτρίοις.

315: ἀεσίφρονα. Wil., LSJ, H. J. Mette, *Lex.*, 4-5, Chantr., *Dict. étym.*, 3, think that ἀασίφρων (Apollon. *Lex.*, Phot.) is the correct form ('in den φρένες geschädigt', Mette). H. Vos, Glotta 34 (1955), 293-4, suggests "dass man an dem doppelten α Anstoss genommen hat" and that the original ἀασίφρων was changed into ἀεσίφρων. But ἀάατος and ἄαπτος remained unchanged, and there is no trace of ἀασίφρων in the MSS. Hom. φ 301-2 ὃ δὲ φρεσὶν ᾗσιν ἀασθεὶς / ἤιεν ἣν ἄτην ὀχέων ἀεσίφρονι θυμῷ is a playful collocation, not a serious etymology [592]. The ancient grammarians connected ἀεσίφρων with ἄεσα (ἰαύω), ἀείρω, or ἄημι (cf. *Less. pol.*, 259-61). Leaf (on Υ 183) rightly observes that the last explanation is the most plausible one:

---

[590] N. J. Richardson, JHS 99 (1979), 170, thinks that "this awkward line could be omitted. 315-16 make better sense after 313 than after 314, where they seem pleonastic". He has failed to see that 308-13 expresses a general truth, and 314 introduces the application to a special case.

[591] Quaglia (147 n. 43) doubts the authenticity of 314-6 because (1) the poor and the rich alike have to work, and (2) the lines contain a tautology. But (1) the lines are addressed to Perses, who is poor, and (2) Perses is so stupid that Hes. has to hammer the lesson into his head.

[592] Krafft (129) rightly disproves Sellschopp's view (71-2) that *Op.* 315 is prior to φ 302. Cf. also Edwards, 178-9.

cf. Hom. Φ 386 δίχα δέ σφιν ἐνὶ φρεσὶ θυμὸς ἄητο, Φ 395 θάρσος ἄητον ἔχουσα, Hsch. ἀεσίμαινα· ἡ τοῖς πνεύμασι τῶν ἀνέμων μαινομένη, θαλάσσης δὲ τὸ ἐπίθετον. For mental movement conceived as blowing cf. Onians, 46 and 52. Accordingly, the word refers to mental instability: it is a stronger expression than χαλίφρων, the opposite of ἐχέφρων (cf. also Z 352, σ 215 φρένες ἔμπεδοι).

316: ἔργον. See above, on 311 ἔργον.

316: τρέψας. Cf. Hom. Γ 422 ἐπὶ ἔργα τράποντο.

316: βίου. Equivalent to Hom. βιότου: see above, on 31 βίος. The genitive (also 443) on the analogy of μέλω and μέλομαι.

317: αἰδὼς δ᾽ οὐκ ἀγαθή. After having expressed his advice Hes. expects his brother to repeat his objection that manual labour does not befit a well-born man. He therefore anticipates such a reaction by naming the painful fact hinted at before (314): Perses may consider himself a well-born man, but he is poor, and a poor nobleman should not feel embarrassed to turn to labour, because that would testify to false shame. Cf. E. fr. 285, 14 (a poor nobleman) ὑπ᾽ αἰδοῦς δ᾽ ἔργ᾽ ἀπωθεῖται χερῶν.

317: αἰδώς. Not 'regard for others' (Si.) but 'reserve', 'aloofness': cf. 319 θάρσος and see above, on 192 αἰδώς.

317: δέ. Has explanatory (motivating) force: see above, on 13 διὰ δέ.

317: ἀγαθή. 'Profitable': see above, on 24 ἀγαθή. We. takes the word to be used predicatively, just as at Hom. ρ 347 αἰδὼς δ᾽ οὐκ ἀγαθὴ κεχρημένῳ ἀνδρὶ παρεῖναι (cf. 352 and for the construction of the infinitive see above, on 306 φίλα). Accordingly, he reads κομίζειν both here and at 500. But (1) κομίζει was probably assimilated to the infinitive in the Homeric line (where some MSS. have κομίζειν instead of παρεῖναι), and (2) Hes., who considers human life in terms of good and evil, adapts the Homeric line (or an existing proverb) to a new context, viz. the false shame of Perses[593]. Many commentators think that αἰδώς refers to a sense of inferiority characteristic of the poor (e.g. Maz., Si., Nicolai, 75 n. 148, Péron, 274, We.)[594], but (1) αἰδώς never means 'sense of inferiority', (2) a poor man is unlikely to be kept from working by a sense of inferiority, (3) Perses suffers from a sense of superiority

---

[593] Krafft (75) rightly defends the priority of ρ 347 against Sellschopp (59, 96-9)—cf. also K. J. McKay, AJP 84 (1963), 27, Edwards, 171—, but wrongly thinks that false shame "dazu führt, dass, wer sie anwendet, arm wird (κεχρημένος)".

[594] Similarly Bolkestein, 185-6, who compares Thgn. 177-8 καὶ γὰρ ἀνὴρ πενίῃ δεδμημένος οὔτε τι εἰπεῖν / οὔθ᾽ ἔρξαι δύναται, γλῶσσα δέ οἱ δέδεται, and K. J. McKay, AJP 84 (1963), 26, who speaks of "an inferiority complex" connected with "class consciousness". See also my discussion with Solmsen, Aufbau, 169. I omit a detailed discussion of this interpretation as well as of the views proposed by A. Hoekstra, Mnem. IV 3 (1950), 99-106, E. Livrea, Helikon 7 (1967), 83 ff., D. B. Claus, TAPA 107 (1977), 78 ff., because they do not seem to me to suit the context. Cf. also Quaglia, 147-9 n. 43.

rather than of inferiority, and (4) θάρσος is not 'self-confidence' as a consequence of prosperity but the 'courage' needed to acquire it (see below).

317: κεχρημένον. For the absolute use of the verb see above, on 1 κλείουσαι.

317: κομίζει. Not 'accompanies' (Maz., Si., Marg) but 'takes care of': cf. LSJ I 1 and Hoekstra (above, n. 594), 103-4, who rightly observes that the use of this verb has an ironic ring (because the result is idleness) and that such ironic expressions are characteristic of Hes.'s style (cf. e.g. 482 παῦροι δέ σε θηήσονται)[595].

318: αἰδώς. For the epanalepsis see above, on 8 Ζεύς. The line is identical with Hom. Ω 45, but there it is certainly spurious (cf. Krafft, 74 n. 4). It is bracketed by Maz., and transposed after 319 by Rz. and Si., but it clarifies the use of οὐκ ἀγαθή: Hes. has so far mentioned αἰδώς as a virtue (192, 200), and he now draws attention to the fact that, just as ἔρις, it has an ambivalent character (similarly 500 ἐλπὶς οὐκ ἀγαθή).

319: αἰδώς. For the anaphora see above, on 10 μυθησαίμην. The asyndeton has explanatory (motivating) force: see above, on 267 πάντα.

319: τοι. See above, on 287 τοι.

319: πρός. Usually taken to mean 'is a feature of' (We.), but αἰδώς does not mean 'inhibition' (We.) in the sense of an inherent feeling of inferiority: see above, on 317 ἀγαθή. The context suggests the translation 'is hard by', 'is close to' (LSJ B I 1), i.e. 'leads directly to': cf. 288 μάλα δ' ἐγγύθι ναίει.

319: θάρσος. Not 'self-confidence' (Ev., Maz.), 'pride' (Walcot, *Peasants*, 60), nor 'insolence' (Wil.), 'brazenness' (We.), but 'intrepidity': Perses has to take courage and forget his scruples[596].

319: ὄλβῳ. 'Abundance': see above, on 172 ὄλβιοι. For the antithesis see above, on 3 φατοί.

320: δέ. Courage is needed, but there is also a bad θάρσος, over-boldness which leads to unlawful appropriation. Nicolai (73) argues that after a section containing general admonitions ("Dikeparainesen 213-285, Arbeitsparainese 298-319") now follows a series of "Anweisungen", i.e. instructions about the ways how to act in special situations. But the admonition of justice and the exhortation to work are at the same time "Anweisungen", viz. indications of the right ways to attain prosperity, and 320-6 describe the wrong ways of trying to effect that purpose[597].

---

[595] Cf. also McKay (above, n. 594), 25-6. Claus (above, n. 594), 80, wrongly speaks of "heavy sarcasm".

[596] Hoekstra (above, n. 594), 102, argues that "pour Hésiode θάρσος est sans doute un vice ce que montrent encore clairement les vers 320-326". But 321-4 describe the bad kind of θάρσος implied in 320 ἁρπακτά.

[597] Nicolai is equally wrong in maintaining (74) that 320 "fasst die Lehre des ganzen Blocks 320-341 zusammen".

320: ἁρπακτά. See above, on 38 ἁρπάζων: Hes. speaks from experience[598]. For -τός equivalent to -τέος cf. Hom. ἀπόβλητος, νεμεσσητός, and Wacker-nagel I, 287-8, K.B. II, 288-90, A. Tovar, in *Serta Turyniana* (Urbana etc. 1974), 56-8. See also above, on 30 πέλεται.

320: θεόσδοτα. Formed on the analogy of διόσδοτος and used instead of θεόδοτος for metrical (rhythmical) reasons: cf. Schw. I, 239[599]. Waltz and We. rightly print a semi-colon after ἁρπακτά: Tzetzes and Moschopoulos assumed an ellipse of ἀλλά (taking both ἁρπακτά and θεόσδοτα to be construed attributively), but this seems to be unparalleled. The asyndeton has explanatory (specifying) force (see above, on 11 οὐκ ἄρα): 'god-given' is equivalent to 'lawfully acquired': cf. Thgn. 197-8 χρῆμα δ' ὃ μὲν Διόθεν καὶ σὺν δίκη ἀνδρὶ γένηται / καὶ καθαρῶς, αἰεὶ παρμόνιμον τελέθει, Sol. 1 D. = 13 W., 3 ὄλβον μοι πρὸς θεῶν μακάρων δότε and 7-8 ἀδίκως δὲ πεπᾶσθαι / οὐκ ἐθέλω[600].

320: ἀμείνω. See above, on 294 ἀμείνω. The meaning 'profitable' (see above, on 19 ἀμείνω) is specified in the next lines as 'durable'.

321: καί. We. translates 'even if' and refers to Denn., 300. But Denn.'s definition (299), "εἰ καί merely represents the fulfilment of the condition as immaterial, without conveying any effect of climax", does not suit the present argument. Denn., however, points out (302) that εἰ καί is sometimes used in the sense of καὶ εἰ, and that this "represents the condition as an extreme case, and does convey an effect of climax" (299): cf. 344, and K.G. II, 489. In the present sentence καί goes with μέγαν rather than with χερσὶ βίη: for the transposition of καί cf. Denn., 326-7.

321: χερσὶ βίη. Not a pleonasm: βία is not always used in a physical sense (see above, on 275 βίης). For the juxtaposition of an instrumental and a modal dative cf. A. *Pers.* 207-8 κίρκον εἰσορῶ δρόμῳ / πτεροῖς ἐφορμαί-νοντα, K.G. I, 441, Schw. II, 170.

321: ὄλβον. In normal circumstances ὄλβος is given by the gods: cf. 281 and see above, on 172 ὄλβιοι.

321: ἕληται. For the omission of ἄν cf. Schw. II, 313.

322: ὅ γε. See above, on 246 ὅ γε. This possibility gets more emphasis because it refers to the behaviour of Perses.

322: ἀπό. 'By means of': cf. LSJ A III 3, K.G. I, 458. The originally local

---

[598] Cf. Kühn, 264: "die immer wieder zum Ausdruck kommende Besitzfreude um des Besitzes willen (und nicht als Mittel zum Lebensgenuss) gewinnt vor dem Hintergrund der adeligen Lebensgewohnheiten des Perses erst seinen besonderen Aspekt".

[599] This seems a simpler explanation than that proposed by We. W. Aly (in Heitsch, 97) argues that the word has been derived from θεὸς δοτήρ: he refers to θεοσεχθρία, but that is a doubtful formation (cf. LSJ s.v. θεοισεχθρία).

[600] Renehan (351) argues that 320 means: "Goods are not just for the taking, but you have to work for them". This does not seem to me correct: the context (especially the connection with 319 θάρσος and 321 βίη) shows that the central idea is not 'work' but δίκη.

force is still apparent in such phrases as Hom. Θ 279 τόξου ἄπο κρατεροῦ Τρώων ὀλέκοντα φάλαγγας.

322: γλώσσης. *Concretum pro abstracto*: cf. LSJ I 2, and see above, on 267 ὀφθαλμός.

322: ληίσσεται. 'Acquires', probably in a neutral sense: cf. 702 ληίζεται and *Th*. 444 ληίδα. For the short-vowel subjunctive see above, on 283 ψεύσεται.

322: οἷα. Equivalent to ὡς: cf. Hom. λ 364 οἷά τε πολλούς, LSJ V 2.

322: πολλά. Properly 'in large numbers', but virtually equivalent to πολλάκις (LSJ III 1 a).

323: εὖτ' ἂν δή. 'Precisely when': cf. Denn., 219-20.

323: κέρδος. 'Desire of gain': cf. LSJ I 2.

323: νόον. Snell, *Dicht. u. Ges.* (above, n. 454), 57-8, argues that a νόος which can be deceived (similarly 373, *Th*. 537) "hat nicht mehr wie bei Homer die einfache Funktion das Wahre zu bemerken (wobei ihm natürlich etwas entgehen oder er 'blind' werden kann), sondern er kann zu falschem Urteil verleitet werden". He refers to K. von Fritz, CP 40 (1945), 226 = Gadamer, *Begriffswelt* (above, on 12 νοήσας), 284, who maintains that "the transition from a dulled to a deceived νόος ... creates, in fact, an entirely new concept". But (1) *Th*. 537 Διὸς νόον ἐξαπαφίσκων is paralleled by Hom. Ξ 160 ὅππως ἐξαπάφοιτο Διὸς νόον, and (2) desire of gain dulls the true insight into the consequences of wrongdoing, just as other emotions (sexual desire at 373 and Ξ 160, appetite at *Th*. 537) dull the νόος (cf. von Fritz, CP 38, 1943, 87-8 = Gadamer, 264-5), without giving rise to a conscious change of judgement.

323: ἐξαπατήσῃ. For ἐξ- 'thoroughly' see above, on 48 ἐξαπάτησε.

324: αἰδῶ. Not 'le sentiment de l'honneur' (Péron, 276) but "le respect des droits et des possessions d'autrui" (*id.*, 277): see above, 192 αἰδώς.

324: δέ. Has consecutive force: see above, on 18 δέ.

324: κατοπάζῃ. 'Chases away': cf. ὀπάζω 'press hard', 'chase' (LSJ III) and κατα- 'completely' (above, on 234 καταβεβρίθασι). We. capitalizes αἰδῶ and ἀναιδείη, but cf. Hom. Θ 103 χαλεπὸν δέ σε γῆρας ὀπάζει, and the use of ὀπηδέω with abstract nouns (above, on 142).

325: ῥεῖα. See above, on 5 ῥέα.

325: δέ. We. suggests that "the apodotic particle perhaps has a certain adversative value here", but apodotic δέ is a weak form of δή and emphasizes the obvious character of the connection between protasis and apodosis: see above, on 23 δέ τε.

325: μαυροῦσι. See above, on 284 ἀμαυροτέρη. For the disappearance of the α cf. Troxler, 124.

325: δέ. Has explanatory (motivating) force: see above, on 13 δέ.

325: οἶκον. See above, on 244 οἶκοι.

326: ὄλβος. See above, on 172 ὄλβιοι.

326: ὀπηδεῖ. See above, on 142 ὀπηδεῖ.

327: ἶσον. Adverbial (LSJ IV 1). It is commonly assumed that the wrong-doings are equated, either to each other or to the preceding ones (Maz., We.), but Hes. emphasizes the equality of the divine retribution (333-4): accordingly we should mentally supply μαυροῦται (similarly Proclus). Divine punishment is not the only idea connecting this section with the preceding lines: the mention of unlawful appropriation is associated with the ill treatment of suppliants and strangers because these are in continual danger of being robbed of their properties.

327: ἱκέτην ... ξεῖνον. Often coupled, e.g. Hom. θ 546, ι 270, Thgn. 143-4. They are under the special protection of Zeus Hikesios and Zeus Xenios. See further Bolkestein, 87, 91-3, Nilsson, 419-21, J. Gould, JHS 93 (1973), 90-4.

327: κακόν. For the substantival use of the neuter singular see above, on 71 ἴκελον.

327: ἔρξει. For the short-vowel subjunctive see above, on 283 ψεύσεται. We. thinks that the use of the aorist shows that "Hesiod is thinking in terms of a single act, not a habit" (as the presents at 328 and 330). But such passages as Hom. I 508 ὅς μέν τ' αἰδέσεται κούρας Διός seem to confirm the view that the aorist expresses the action as such, apart from any idea of duration: see above, on 280 ἀγορεῦσαι.

328: κασιγνήτοιο. We. writes: "as in 183-6, Hesiod passes from the guest to the brother". But in the present context ξεῖνος is a stranger rather than a guest [601], and the mention of outsiders naturally leads to that of its opposite, one's own family. We have already seen that the movement of Hes.'s thought often has an antithetic character (e.g. at 320) [602].

328: ἀνά. In his note on *Th.* 508 εἰσανέβαινεν We. suggests that "the -ανα-element in the compound refers not to getting up onto the bed but to the bedroom being upstairs". But cf. Hom. I 133 τῆς εὐνῆς ἐπιβήμεναι (similarly κ 334, 340, 342, 347, 480). It appears from α 437 ἕζετο δ' ἐν λέκτρῳ that beds were not particularly high, but ἀνα- does not necessarily imply a great difference of level.

328: βαίνοι. Editors read βαίνῃ, but the MSS. have βαίνει and βαίνοι, which points to an original βαίνοι rather than to βαίνῃ. For the use of the optative (indicating a mere possibility) between subjunctives (indicating a possibility the realization of which may be expected) cf. Hom. ζ 286-9 ῥέζοι ... μίσγηται, Thgn. 689-90 εἴη ... ᾖ, K.G. II, 429.

---

[601] Gould (above, on 327 ἱκέτην ... ξεῖνον), 93, seems to me to go too far in suggesting that "the analogy with the kin is a natural one since once the due ceremonies of ξενία or ἱκετεία are over the ξένοι and ἱκέται have become kin — 'spiritual kin' rather than kin by blood or marriage, but nevertheless members of the group".

[602] This seems to me a better explanation than the one given in *Aufbau*, 142, viz. that adultery is a violation of the right of hospitality.

329. Bracketed by Pal., Waltz, Rz., Wil., So., but the difficulty of the construction and the unusual word παρακαίριος point to genuineness.

329: κρυπταδίης. Cf. Hom. Ζ 161 κρυπταδίη φιλότητι μισγήμεναι.

329: εὐνῆς. Dative of purpose: cf. E. *El.* 720 κρυφίαις γὰρ εὐναῖς πείσας ἄλοχον φίλαν Ἀτρέως, Hom. Η 285 χάρμη προκαλέσσατο πάντας, Schw. II, 139-40, Chantr. II, 68, A. Hoekstra, Mnem. IV 15 (1962), 15 ff. Col. follows Tzetzes and Moschopoulos in reading εὐνῆς, taken to have final force, but this use of the genitive does not seem to occur before the 5th century: cf. my note on Men. *Epitr.* 348, Mnem. IV 27 (1974), 32. In his edition of 1977 (above, n. 545) he rightly reads εὐνῆς. The meaning 'sexual intercourse' (cf. Hom. ε 126 μίγη φιλότητι καὶ εὐνῇ) may be explained as *concretum pro abstracto*: see above, on 267 ὀφθαλμός. The plural (similarly Hom. θ 249) refers to repeated action: see above, on 16 βουλῆσιν and 146 ὕβριες.

329: ἀλόχου. Depends on the verbal idea implied in εὐνή: cf. Hom. ψ 346 εὐνῆς ἧς ἀλόχου ταρπήμεναι, Pind. *I.* 1, 34 τοῦδ' ἀνδρὸς ἐν τιμαῖσιν, K.G. I, 335-6. Chantraine, REG 59-60 (1946-7), 223, and *Dict. étym.*, 634, wrongly thinks that ἄλοχος always means 'legitimate wife': at Hom. Φ 499 Leto is called one of the ἄλοχοι of Zeus, and the original meaning 'partner of one's bed' is still apparent at Ι 336, where Achilles calls Briseis his ἄλοχος (Leaf wrongly takes this to refer to Clytemnestra). When Patroclus said that Briseis had to become the legal wife of Achilles, he added κουριδίη (Τ 298). Cf. also W. P. Clark, CP 35 (1940), 188-90.

329: παρακαίρια. Synonymous with παράκαιρα, properly 'beside the right measure' (cf. Hom. Δ 391 παραίσια, Schw., II, 498), hence 'improper'. For καιρός 'due measure' cf. A. *Prom.* 507 μή νυν βροτοὺς μὲν ὠφέλει καιροῦ πέρα, LSJ I, and J. R. Wilson, Glotta 58 (1980), 177 ff., espec. 180, where he compares Thgn. 199-200 εἰ δ' ἀδίκως παρὰ καιρὸν ἀνὴρ φιλοκερδέϊ θυμῷ / κτήσεται[603]. Cf. also Pind. *P.* 10, 4 τί κομπέω παρὰ καιρόν; We. observes that "unchastity is an unusual item in early Greek lists of sins", but this does not imply that adultery was easily tolerated: cf. L. Schmidt, *Die Ethik der alten Griechen*, II (Berlin 1882), 176 ff., 191 ff., Dover, 209-10[604].

330: ἀφραδίης. In a moral sense: see above, on 134 ἀφραδίης.

330: ἀλιταίνεται. Rz., Wil., Maz., Col., So. read ἀλιταίνητ', We. ἀλιτή-νεται, but the MSS. reading ἀλιταίνεται may be kept as a short-vowel

---

[603] Carrière wrongly translates 'sans attendre son heure'. Van Groningen *ad loc.* is equally wrong in suggesting that "l'idée de 'juste moment' obtient aisément la nuance de 'situation normale dans laquelle tout se fait selon les règles et sans précipitation'": "the temporal 'right time' which predominates in later Greek is clearly not original, and in 5th cent. is only one application among many" (Barrett on E. *Hipp.* 386, who refers to the spatial force of καίριος in Homer). Cf. also C. M. J. Sicking, Mnem. IV 16 (1963), 232-4.

[604] Cf. also N. Geurts, *Het huwelijk bij de Griekse en Romeinse moralisten* (Amsterdam 1928), Ch. IV. Si. concludes from our passage that "adultery is a deadly sin only when a brother's wife is involved", but Hes. obviously mentions this as an extreme case.

subjunctive: cf. Hom. A 67 (αἴ κεν) βούλεται, Μ 42 (ὅτ' ἄν) στρέφεται⁶⁰⁵.
For the meaning of the verb see above, on 241 ἀλιτραίνῃ.

330: ὀρφανά. 'Without parents' (e.g. Hom. υ 68), but also 'fatherless' (cf.
Bolkestein, 276 and n. 4). Hes. probably thinks of the children of a deceased
brother. The dark colours in which at Hom. Χ 488 ff. the fate of a fatherless
child is painted suggest that some kind of guardianship was necessary,
although it is unlikely to have already developed into a social institution in
Hes.'s time (cf. Bolkestein, *loc. cit.*)⁶⁰⁶. The obvious candidate for such a
function was the next in kin, and he might easily be tempted to abuse his
power, e.g. by appropriating the heritage: Aristotle (*Ath.* 56, 6) tells us that
actions for ill-usage of orphans lie against their guardians. Wil. observes that
Hes.'s moral point of view in considering ill treatment of orphans is unparalleled: "als allgemeine sittliche Pflicht der Menschen wird die Rücksicht
auf die Waisen nicht empfunden". This is confirmed by Bolkestein (275), who
adds, however, that the Greeks had the institution of guardianship. It may be
concluded that the emphasis put by Hes. on the moral aspect points to the
fact that guardianship had not yet been legalized.

331: γονῆα. For respect due to parents in their old age see above, on 185
ἀτιμήσουσι. For γονεύς see above, on 235 γονεῦσι.

331: γέροντα. For the substantive used as an attribute see above, on 191
ὕβριν.

331: κακῷ. Explained by Krafft (129-30) as a kind of enallage: "κακῷ wird
erst indirekt durch das Verhalten des Sohnes erklärt". But in spite of the
special situation the epithet has general force: see above, on 113 δειλόν.

331: οὐδῷ. Not the beginning or the end of old age (Ameis-Hentze on ο
246, J. Th. Kakridis, Gymn. 78, 1971, 512-3) but old age itself imagined as the
threshold between life and death (LSJ 3, Adam on Pl. *Rep.* 328 e 6, whose
assumption of two doors, however, is unnecessary). In that case γήραος is an
appositional (explanatory) genitive: cf. K.G. I, 264-5, Schw. II, 121-2.

332: νεικείῃ. See above, on 186 μέμψονται.

332: χαλεποῖσι. See above, on 186 χαλεποῖς.

332: καθαπτόμενος. Cf. Hom. σ 415 ἀντιβίοις ἐπέεσσι καθαπτόμενος.

333: δέ. Apodotic: see above, on 23 δέ τε.

333: τῷ. For the dative cf. K.G. I, 439-40, Schw. II, 167-8.

333: Ζεύς. See above, on 187 θεῶν ὄπιν.

333: ἀγαίεται. 'Is indignant'. Cf. *Lex.*, 29, *Less. pol.*, 14-5.

333: ἐς ... τελευτήν. 'In the end': cf. LSJ I 5, and see above, on 294 ἐς

---

⁶⁰⁵ Cf. Chantr. I, 458, who does not take, however, a clear stand. Schw. I, 791 n.6, too
confidently maintains: "Homerische kurzvokalische Konjunktive zu thematischen Präsentien
haben keine Gewähr". G. Arrighetti, SIFC 37 (1965), 163, follows Peppmüller in taking
ἀλιταίνεται as an indicative, but that would be very odd between 328 βαίνοι and 332 νεικείῃ.

⁶⁰⁶ See further den Boer, *Private Morality* (above, n. 527), 37 ff., espec. 38-9.

τέλος. For the idea that divine punishment may come late, but certainly comes cf. Hom. Δ 160-2, Sol. 1 D. = 13 W., 25-32, etc.

333: δέ. Has consecutive force: see above, on 18 δέ.

334: ἀντί. 'In return for': see above, on 57 ἀντί.

334: ἐπέθηκεν. Cf. Hom. β 192 σοὶ δέ, γέρον, θωὴν ἐπιθήσομεν, LSJ V.

334: ἀμοιβήν. 'Requital' (LSJ I 1).

335: ἀλλά. See above, on 298 ἀλλά. This line, not the next one (as is done by So.), should be indented.

335: ἔεργε. For the force of the present see above, on 299 ἐργάζευ.

335: ἀεσίφρονα. See above, on 315 ἀεσίφρονα.

336. The transition from social to religious duties is called "rather forced" ("ziemlich gewaltsam") by Wil., but Hes. does not draw a sharp distinction between morality and religion: we have just seen that the transgression of social rules is punished by Zeus. The transition may even be called a natural one because the duty of honouring one's parents and that of honouring the gods are often mentioned together (e.g. Pind. *P.* 6, 23-7, E. fr. 853, 2, Isocr. 1, 16). The fact that a passage about the *neglect* of social duties is followed by a passage about the *observance* of religious duties is not illogical either. They are bound together by the idea of divine retribution (334 ἀμοιβήν), and this is an ambivalent notion: punishment and reward are complementary aspects of one and the same power, and they are emphasized by Hes. alternately, as his thought takes an apotreptic or a protreptic turn. In the present case the imperative ἔεργε (335) marks the turn from an apotreptic to a protreptic point of view.

337. Suspected by Pal., P. Stengel, Hermes 27 (1892), 447 n. 4, B. Gentili, QUCC 2 (1966), 40 n. 12, because they think that ἁγνῶς refers to non-animal sacrifice, but this is a specifically Orphic conception (cf. Pl. *Leg.* 782 c).

337: ἁγνῶς καὶ καθαρῶς. The translation 'pure in soul and in body' (Tzetzes, Pal., Si.; similarly Latt. 'innocently and cleanly') is wrong: cf. *H. Ap.* 120-1 λόον ὕδατι καλῷ / ἁγνῶς καὶ καθαρῶς, E. *Or.* 1604 (Menelaus) ἁγνὸς γάρ εἰμι χεῖρας, (Orestes) ἀλλ᾽ οὐ τὰς φρένας, Pl. *Crat.* 405 b 3-4 καθαρὸν ... καὶ κατὰ τὸ σῶμα καὶ κατὰ τὴν ψυχήν. The meaning of καθαρός is 'free from defilement' (cf. Nilsson, 90), and ἁγνός means 'object of religious awe' (cf. Hom. Z 266-7 χερσὶ δ᾽ ἀνίπτοισιν Διὶ λείβειν αἴθοπα οἶνον / ἅζομαι), 'sacrosanct'[607]. For the formulaic character of the combination cf. We.

337: ἐπί. *Scil.* on the altars: We. compares Hom. φ 267 ἐπὶ μηρία θέντες Ἀπόλλωνι. Cf. also γ 178-9 Ποσειδάωνι δὲ ταύρων / πόλλ᾽ ἐπὶ μῆρ᾽ ἔθεμεν

---

[607] See further A. J. Festugière, *La sainteté* (Paris 1942), Ch. I, L. Moulinier, *Le pur et l'impur dans la pensée des Grecs* (Paris 1952), 270 ff. (whose semantic considerations are unconvincing), the literature mentioned by E. des Places, *La religion grecque* (Paris 1969), 364, B. Gentili, QUCC 2 (1966), 37 ff., *Less. pol.*, 78-81, Burkert, *Griech. Religion* (above, n. 117), 405-6.

and 273 πολλὰ δὲ μηρί᾽ ἔκηε θεῶν ἱεροῖς ἐπὶ βωμοῖς. For the tmesis see above, on 59 ἐκ δ᾽ ἐγέλασσε.

337: δέ. Has explanatory (specifying) force: see above, on 9 δέ.

337: ἀγλαά. 'Splendid': cf. Hom. Τ 385 ἀγλαὰ γυῖα, and H. J. Mette, *Lex.*, 75-7 (who wrongly translates 'fettglänzend'; similarly Maz., who refers to Th. 557 ὀστέα λευκά). See further *Less. pol.*, 72-8.

338: ἄλλοτε. Not "on the days when you do not kill an animal" (We.), but cf. Maz.: "indépendamment des sacrifices que tu leur offriras dans les circonstances importantes de ta vie, fais aux dieux tous les matins et tous les soirs des libations et des offrandes (cf. 724 sqq.)".

338: δή. Modern editors print δέ (D), but δή is often connected with temporal adverbs (τότε δή, πολλάκι δή, νῦν δή): cf. Denn., 206-7.

338: θύεσσι. 'Incense', made of citronwood or of a kind of juniper. Cf. Hom. Ι 499-500 καὶ μὲν τοὺς (the gods) θυέεσσι καὶ εὐχωλῆς ἀγανῇσι / λοιβῇ τε κνίσῃ τε παρατρωπῶσ᾽ ἄνθρωποι.

339: ἠμὲν ... καί. Cf. Denn., 287.

339: εὐνάζῃ. Maz. writes: "C'est la première fois, je crois, qu'il est question dans la littérature grecque d'une prière du matin et du soir". But cf. Hom. γ 333-4 ὄφρα Ποσειδάωνι καὶ ἄλλοις ἀθανάτοισιν / σπείσαντες κοίτοιο μεδώμεθα.

339: ἄν. We. writes: "probably = ἀνά, though cf. 543". It should be added (1) that ὅτ᾽ ἄν occurs at 427 and 467, and (2) that ἔρχομαι means 'to return' at Hom. Ν 744, α 408, Hdt. Ι 121, Pl. *Prot.* 310 c 5 (not in LSJ).

339: φάος. Cf. 724 ἐξ ἠοῦς Διὶ λειβέμεν, Pl. *Symp.* 220 d, *Leg.* 887 e.

339: ἱερόν. Day and Night are divine powers: *Th.* 123-4, 748, Hom. Θ 66, Λ 194.

340: ἵλαον. For the long α cf. Richardson on *H. Dem.* 204.

340: κραδίην καὶ θυμόν. Cf. *Th.* 611-2 ἔχων ἀλίαστον ἀνίην / θυμῷ καὶ κραδίῃ, Hom. Ι 631 τοῦ δ᾽ ἐρητύεται κραδίη καὶ θυμός, Κ 220 etc. ἔμ᾽ ὀτρύνει κραδίη καὶ θυμός, Β 171 etc. ἄχος κραδίην καὶ θυμὸν ἵκανεν. The κραδίη is the center of emotions, the θυμός (see above, on 13 θυμόν) transforms them into actions.

341: ὄφρα. Depends on 340, just as 393 on 392[608].

341: ἄλλων. Especially relatives: cf. Walcot, *Peasants*, 9.

341: κλῆρον. See above, on 37 κλῆρον.

341: τόν. For the article used in contrasts see above, on 193 ὁ κακός.

342. Wil. writes: "Ohne jede Verbindung folgen Verhaltungsmassregeln gegenüber der Gesellschaft, in welcher der einzelne steht". But there is an

---

[608] We. also compares Hom. Ο 31-2, but there the two final sentences are coordinate, just as at Γ 163-6.

associative connection: a sacrifice usually implies a meal: cf. e.g. Xen. *Mem.*
II 3, 11 ὁπότε θύοι, καλεῖν σε ἐπὶ δεῖπνον[609].

342: τόν. See above, on 266 τῷ.

342: φιλέοντα. Maz.'s translation 'qui t'aime' is misleading, for the basic
meaning of φιλέω is 'to maintain a relationship' (see above, on 184 φίλος),
and Hes. is thinking in terms of business rather than of social feelings (as is
suggested by Nicolai, 80 and n. 168, who draws the wrong conclusion that
v. 342 "spielt nur Statistenrolle"). For the ellipse of 'only' see above, on 43 ἐπ᾽
ἤματι.

342: καλεῖν. 'Invite' (LSJ I 2).

342: τόν. For the article used in contrasts see above, on 193 ὁ κακός.

342: ἐᾶσαι. 'Leave alone': cf. Hom. Υ 311 ἤ κέν μιν ἐρύσσεαι ἤ κεν
ἐάσεις, ξ 444 θεὸς τὸ μὲν δώσει, τὸ δ᾽ ἐάσει. We. writes: "The change to the
aorist seems to be for metrical convenience". It should be added that the
present denotes a state (a rule or a habit), the aorist a mere fact: see above,
on 9 ἴθυνε. For the juxtaposition of present and aorist cf. Bakker, *Imperative*
(above, n. 37), 34-5.

343: ἐγγύθι. For the importance attached to good neighbourship see
above, on 23 γείτονα γείτων. Cf. also We. on 346.

344: εἰ ... καί. Equivalent to καὶ εἰ: see above, on 321 καί. The meaning is
'not only in normal circumstances but also in case of an emergency'.

344: τοι. A *dativus incommodi*: cf. K.G. I, 417-20, Schw. II, 150-1.

344: ἐγκώμιον. Ev., Maz., We. adopt the MSS. reading ἐγχώριον, but
this is a *lectio facilior*, ἐγκώμιον commonly meaning 'eulogy'. We. argues that
ἐγκώμιον is unsuitable because "it is a private emergency, not a public one".
But Renehan (352) rightly points out (1) that the usual meaning of ἐγχώριος
is 'in the country', 'local', not 'on one's estate', (2) that "a farmer's private
problems (such as a runaway animal) are not confined to his farm proper",
and (3) that "the real contrast implied here is rather between affairs in one's
native community (whether on one's estate or not) and affairs at a distance
from home".

344: ἄλλο. Euphemistic for κακόν: see above, on 262 ἄλλη.

345: ἄζωστοι. We. remarks that "going ungirt or unshod is a mark of
urgent haste", and refers to ἀπέδιλος. But Maz. rightly points out that the
word does not refer to quickness of response but to the distance to be

---

[609] Cf. Waltz (I), 72-3, P. Friedländer, in Heitsch, 235 n. 22. Maz.'s explanation (adopted by
Kühn, 264), "la richesse dépend à la fois des dieux et des hommes (303): le poète avait déjà
montré ce que les dieux (308-9) et les hommes (311-8) pensent du travail, seule source de la
richesse; il a exposé ensuite à quelles conditions les dieux rendent ce travail fructueux (320-41): il
va dire maintenant comment il faut se conduire avec les hommes pour accroître et conserver les
fruits de ce travail", seems to me less natural: such considerations as 347 (see below on τιμῆς) are
not especially concerned with wealth. Maz. (II, 82) makes too rigid a division between "le thème
de la justice" (202-85) and "le thème du travail" (285-828).

covered: "les voisins peuvent accourir aussitôt, ὡς ἔχουσιν: les parents [this is
not correct: see below, on πηοί], s'ils habitent loin, sont obligés de s'équiper
pour se mettre en route". Cf. Hdt. VIII 120 ἐλύσατο τὴν ζώνην 'made a halt',
S. *O.R.* 846 οἰόζωνος 'travelling alone'.

345: ἔκιον. Gnomic aorist: see above, on 240 ἀπηύρα.

345: πηοί. At Hom. θ 581-3 specified as γαμβρὸς ἢ πενθερός and distinguished from blood-relations. The latter are not mentioned because they
usually stayed living in the same house or the same village.

346: πῆμα κακὸς ... ἀγαθὸς μέγ' ὄνειαρ. For the chiasmus see above, on
10 μυθησαίμην.

346: ὅσσον τε. Cf. Ruijgh, 547 ff., 893-4, who observes that the phrase here
"exprime une mesure abstraite, tandis que dans les exemples homériques, il
s'agit toujours d'une mesure proprement dite (distance, etc.)".

347: ἔμμορέ τοι τιμῆς. Cf. Hom. A 278, ε 335, λ 338 ἔμμορε τιμῆς. The
meaning of τιμή is not 'something valuable' (Maz., Ev., Latt., We., Krafft,
128, Col.), which is unparalleled[610]. Wil. rightly explains: "der γείτων wird
den Ton für die φήμη (760) angeben": cf. also 701 μὴ γείτοσι χάρματα
γήμῃς, and Walcot, *Peasants*, 45-6. It is a grave error to think that "die τιμή
[in the sense of honourable reputation] fehlt eigentlich auf der Ebene des
Bauern" (Krafft, 127): see above, on 313 κῦδος.

347: τοι. See above, on 287 τοι.

347: ἐσθλοῦ. Not in a moral sense, but 'profitable': see above, on 123
ἐσθλοί.

348: οὐδέ. Wil. prints οὐ δέ because οὐδέ would mean 'not even' (Ev.),
which is excluded by the context. But for οὐδέ = καὶ οὐ see above, on 228
οὐδέ.

348: ἀπόλοιτο. Not 'would die' (Ev., Maz.) but 'would get lost', by
wandering off or by being stolen (We.).

348: μή. The negation refers to κακός, but μή is chosen under the influence
of the optative: cf. K.G. II, 194, Schw. II, 595.

348: κακός. Not in a moral sense, but 'inefficient', 'unhelpful'[611]: see
above, on 214 κακή, 271 κακόν.

349: μετρεῖσθαι. 'Have things (e.g. corn or oil) measured out to oneself'
(LSJ II 3). For the causative use of the middle see above, on 35 διακρινώμεθα. For the absolute use of the verb see above, on 1 κλείουσαι.

349: ἀποδοῦναι. For the aorist see above, on 342 ἐᾶσαι.

350: αὐτῷ τῷ. Probably equivalent to τῷ αὐτῷ: cf. the Homeric use of

---

[610] The explanation given by Quaglia (199 n. 22), "aver un buon vicino è un onore e un
privilegio concesso dalla sorte", presuppones an impossible ellipse.
[611] I do not believe that Hes. is thinking of the evil eye, as is assumed by K. J. McKay,
Erysichthon: A Callimachean Comedy (Leiden 1962), 124 and n. 2.

αὐτός 'the same' (Μ 225, θ 107, φ 366). We. explains: "'with the measure itself' as distinct from the bonus", but the bonus is no measure.

350: καί. 'Or': cf. Denn., 292. It depends on the context whether the meaning is 'or alternatively', 'or at least', or 'or rather' (here). See also my notes on Pl. *Phd.* 67 d 8, Mnem. IV 11 (1958), 202, *Meno* 94 b 9, Mnem. IV 17 (1964), 274, A. *Prom.* 210, *Miscellanea* ... *Kamerbeek*, 456, Hes. *Op.* 401 and 533, Mnem. IV 33 (1980), 382 and 388.

350: λώιον. 'More liberally' (similarly Hom. ρ 417), properly 'more profitably' (*scil.* to the other party). For the Greek habit of doing good one's 'friends' cf. Bolkestein, 143 ff. For the tendency to overtrump one another in generosity cf. Xen. *Mem.* II 6, 35, where it is called an acknowledged virtue by Socrates, and Ps. Phocyl. 80 νικᾶν εὖ ἔρδοντας ἐπὶ πλεόνεσσι καθήκει (see further P. W. van der Horst *ad loc.*). It is inspired by the desire of asserting oneself (cf. Bolkestein, 152 ff.)[612], but also by the expectation of goodwill (cf. Bolkestein, 158-9).

351: χρηίζων. For the absolute use of the verb see above, on 1 κλείουσαι.

351: ἐς ὕστερον. For ἐς cf. LSJ ὕστερος IV 3. Similarly εἰσαῦθις.

351: ἄρκιον. Not 'sufficient' (Moschopoulos, LSJ, D. Motzkus - E. M. Voigt, *Lex.*, 1310) but 'to be relied on', 'sure': the point is to secure the neighbour's help, not the amount of his help. At 501, 577, Hom. σ 358 we might translate 'sufficient', but at Κ 304 'sufficient' would imply a tautology after δώρῳ ἐπὶ μεγάλῳ (as is pointed out by Maz.). At 370 the context (N.B. 371) requires 'sure', not 'sufficient'[613]. At Β 393 and Ο 502 ἄρκιον(ἐστί) means 'it is certain'[614], which points to an original meaning 'sure', 'sufficient' (LSJ II) being a later development (cf. Chantr., *Dict. étym.*, 110)[615]. Proclus and Tzetzes (followed e.g. by Ev.) took the object of εὕρῃς to be masculine, but 'something sure', i.e. 'help on which you can rely', seems more probable. For the neuter adjective used as a substantive see above, on 71 ἴκελον.

352: μή. The asyndeton has adversative force (cf. K.G. II, 342, and my note on Men. *Epitr.* 123, Mnem. IV 27, 1974, 23): ingratiating oneself with a

---

[612] Cf. also Walcot, *Rural Communities* (above, on 23 ζηλοῖ), 19-20: "The very fact that you are able to do someone a favour implies that you are superior and he is inferior; to safeguard his own prestige, the recipient of your generosity must attempt, in whatever way is open to him, to redress the balance, providing you with something in return that you want and so re-asserting his personal independence".

[613] Motzkus-Voigt paraphrase "es soll ihm genügen, wenn der Lohn (nur unter vier Augen) vereinbart wird", but (1) "es soll ihm genügen, wenn ..." can hardly mean 'something to be content with', and (2) the next line suggests that in the case of a φίλος, too, a witness should be present.

[614] The interpretations given by Motzkus-Voigt, 'der wird keinen Schutz haben, so dass er ... entgehen könnte' (Β 393) and 'es ist jetzt (für uns) lebensrettend wichtig' (Ο 502), are quite artificial.

[615] Although ἄρκιος is related to ἀρκέω, I do not believe that βίος ἄρκιος means 'des ressources qui écartent (la faim et le froid pour le paysan)', as is argued by J. Jouanna in *Mélanges E. Delebecque* (Aix-en-Provence 1983), 206-7.

neighbour is advisable but should not tempt one to take advantage of his favour.

352: κακά. An internal accusative equivalent to an adverb: cf. K.G. I, 310, Schw. II, 77.

352: κερδαίνειν. For the use of the present see above, on 299 ἐργάζευ and 342 ἐᾶσαι.

352: κακὰ κέρδεα. The asyndeton has explanatory (motivating) force: see above, on 267 πάντα.

352: κέρδεα. 'Desires of gain': see above, on 323 κέρδος[616].

352: ἄτησιν. Not 'madness' (Latt.) but 'ruin': see above, on 216 ἄτησιν. 'Losses' (We.) is too weak.

353-5. Rejected by Plutarch (cf. We.), but his moral reasons do not carry any weight. Wil. is inclined to reject 353-4, but his argument, "einen so schauderhaften Versausgang wie 354 gibt es nirgend", is entirely subjective, and his conclusion, "355 kann auf 352 gut folgen", is wrong (see below).

353: τὸν φιλέοντα. See above, on 342 τὸν φιλέοντα.

353: φιλεῖν. For the use of the present see above, on 342 ἐᾶσαι. We. and Renehan (352-3) give some illustrations of the principle of doing good to one's friends and harm to one's enemies[617], but do not explain the connection of this sentence with the preceding lines. That passage deals with the question of calling in a neighbour's aid, and this naturally leads to the complementary question of *rendering* aid to others[618].

353: καί. Has explanatory (specifying) force: see above, on 91 καί.

353: τῷ προσιόντι. *Scil.* τῶν φιλέοντων. The meaning is 'one who approaches you', i.e. who applies to you for help. This usage reappears in Hellenistic Greek, e.g. in *Pap. Strassb.* 57.6. Troxler (10 n. 12) defends Haupt's emendation προσεόντι, but the parallelism need not be complete, and We. rightly observes that "if it were -εόντι -εῖναι, we would expect παρ- or συν-, not προσ-; after προσιόντι it was natural to repeat προσ-, but metre imposed a change of verb" (it should be added, however, that the change of verb was imposed by sense rather than by metre: see next note).

353: προσεῖναι. We. rightly rejects ancient (Ap. Soph.) and modern

---

[616] At Hom. ψ 217 κακὰ κέρδεα βουλεύουσιν the word means 'gain', but this does not imply that Hes. could not have borrowed the phrase from Homer, as is suggested by Krafft, 130 (whose further remark, "Bei Homer wurde höchstens erst die Gewinn*sucht* verurteilt ..., dem Gewinn an sich konnte aber noch keine Schlechtigkeit anhaften", is equally inapposite).

[617] Renehan calls Hom ζ 184-5 "the oldest extant example of such a notion", but that passage does not refer to *doing* good or harm in a strict sense. See further Schmidt, *Ethik* (above, on 329 παρακαίρια), II, 366-7, C. W. Müller, *Gleiches zu Gleichem* (Wiesbaden 1965), 155 ff., Zucker, *Semantica* (above, n. 454), 156 ff., Fraisse, *Philia* (above, on 183 ἑταῖρος), Index s.v. bienfaisance, Dover, 180-4, 276-8.

[618] In *Aufbau,* 143, I wrongly connected 353 with the preceding section. The complementary character of the connection is also misunderstood by Quaglia (200-1), who thinks that "da un consiglio particolare ... si passa al consiglio generale ... di voler bene a chi ci vuol bene".

(Edwards, 114-5, who compares 208 εἰς) attempts to explain this as equivalent to προσιέναι[619], but his translation 'give your company to him that seeks it' is too weak: the context requires 'render assistance to', and this is not achieved either by Wil.'s suggestion to supply φίλον from the first part of the line: 'Wer als Freund kommt, mit dem verkehre als Freund'[620]. A pregnant meaning of προσεῖναι 'be at his disposal' may be supported by Ar. *Av.* 1315 Τύχη μόνον προσείη 'pourvu que la Tyche nous aide' (Willems), 'que la fortune seulement nous favorise' (van Daele).

354: καί. A further specification. Accordingly, a comma or a semi-colon, not a full stop (Ev., Si., Col., So.), should be put at the end of 353.

354: ὅς κεν δῷ. 'Only to one who gives', i.e. who has given or who will return a gift. For the aorist see above, on 342 ἐᾶσαι, for the ellipse of 'only', above, on 352 τὸν φιλέοντα.

354: μή ... δῷ. For the repetition in negative form see above, on 228-9.

355. Not "inhaltlich mit 354 identisch" (Wil.): the line motivates (for the asyndeton see above, on 352 κακὰ κέρδεα) 354 δόμεν: one should give only to a man who gives, but that man will remain a giver only if one returns his gifts.

355: δώτῃ ... ἀδώτῃ. We. observes that "neither form occurs elsewhere", that "'giver' is normally δώτωρ, δοτήρ, or δωτήρ; -δώτης/-δότης belongs in compounds", and that "ἀ- is not normally used to negative a noun or verb". He then gives some speculations about the origin of the words (cf. also *Less. pol.*, 171), and concludes that "it seems necessary to regard δώτης as abstracted from some other compound(s), the sequence being -δώτης > δώτης > ἀδώτης". But A. Hoekstra, AC 48 (1979), 102-3 n. 18, observes that δώτης is not a literary coinage, for it also occurs as a proper name (Archil. 57 W., 7). It may be added that the words are adjectives (used as substantives: see above, on 71 ἴκελον) meaning 'inclined to give' (Proclus δωρητικόν, Tzetzes δωρητικὴν γνώμην ἔχοντι) and 'averse from giving'. For the antithesis see above, on 3 φατοί.

356: δώς. Equivalent to δόσις: cf. Schw. I, 722, Troxler, 158, Chantr., *Dict. étym.*, 280[621]. The word refers both to δώτῃ and to ἔδωκεν, and this ambivalence enables Hes. to return to his original theme, the best way to obtain something from one's neighbour: the motivation 357-8 shows that now the giver is the neighbour.

356: ἀγαθή. 'Profitable' (see above, on 24 ἀγαθή), *scil.* to the person who wants to obtain something from his neighbour.

---

[619] One might think of reading προσῖναι: cf. ἴναι in an oracle quoted by Strabo IX 2, 22, and the metrical lengthening of the ι at Hom. Υ 365 ἴμεναι and χ 470 ἐπιέμεναι.

[620] Wil. refers to a 4th cent. epigram (*GVI* 1688) φίλο]ν τε φίλοισι προσεῖναι, but the supplement is far from certain.

[621] For Δώς as a name of Demeter cf. M. G. Bonanno, MH 37 (1980), 79-81.

356: ἅρπαξ. Elsewhere equivalent to ἁρπάζων (for the meaning of which see above, on 38 ἁρπάζων), here = ἁρπαγή (committed by the person who wants to obtain something from his neighbour). For the antithetical transition see above, on 320 δέ and 352 μή [622]. If we accept the use of *concretum pro abstracto* (see above, on 267 ὀφθαλμός), the word need not be capitalized, as is done by We. and Renehan, 354.

356: κακή. *Scil.* for the ἁρπάζων, as appears from the analogy of δὼς ἀγαθή.

356: θανάτοιο. *Scil.* of the ἁρπάζων. Wil. writes: "Dass der Raub schliesslich zum Tode des Räubers führt, ist etwas stark aufgetragen; 326 ging H. nicht so weit". But Hes. mentions an extreme case (just as at 182, 220, 240), viz. the case in which the injured person can no longer keep his temper (see below, on 362 τό) [623]. We. suggests that the bleakness of heart mentioned at 360 "feels deathly or brings the desire for death", and his quotation of S. *O.C.* 529 ὤμοι, θάνατος μὲν τάδ᾽ ἀκούειν seems to imply that he supposes the injured person to die from despair. But I have already observed that Hes. is concerned with the best way of obtaining something from one's neighbour, not with the other's well-being [624]. We. further gives some quotations from the Old Testament, but the contrast 'life-death' mentioned there is foreign to Hes.'s mind.

357: ἐθέλων ὅ γε. Neitzel (47) and We. rightly follow Friedländer (in Heitsch, 235 n. 23) in taking these words, not ὅ γε καὶ μέγα (Si., So.), together. For the emphatic function of the pronoun see above, on 246 ὅ γε. The nearest parallel for this position in the sentence seems to me Hom. Ω 206-7 εἰ γάρ σ᾽ αἱρήσει καὶ ἐσόψεται ὀφθαλμοῖσιν, / ὠμηστὴς καὶ ἄπιστος ἀνὴρ ὅ γε, οὔ σ᾽ ἐλεήσει. The difference is that in the Homeric passage the specification has motivating force, whereas ἐθέλων ὅ γε means 'provided that he does so of his own free will'. Hermann's emendation ὅτε (adopted by Maz.) is unnecessary.

357: μέγα. The adjective is used as a substantive: see above, on 71 ἴκελον.

358: δώρῳ. Equivalent to δόσει: for the use of *concretum pro abstracto* see above, on 267 ὀφθαλμός.

358: καί. Has explanatory (specifying) force: see above, on 91 καί.

---

[622] The antithetical position of δὼς and ἅρπαξ does not force us to assume that they refer to one and the same person, as is argued by Quaglia, 202 n. 27.

[623] Quaglia (*loc. cit.*) wrongly compares 325-6 and 352: the ruin of one's welfare is different from death. Neitzel (50 ff.) argues that the destruction of a whole community (as described at 246-7) is meant, but the fate of the community is not at stake in the present context. W. Nicolai, Gnom. 51 (1979), 720, points out that if Hes. had the quarrel of Agamemnon and Achilles in mind (as is assumed by Neitzel), we should rather think of the fact that Agamemnon is nearly killed by Achilles (A 190-1).

[624] As I wrongly assumed in *Aufbau*, 145 and n. 2. Maz. rightly concludes: "Tous ces conseils se ramènent donc a une générosité calculée et à une honnêteté prudente qui donnent ou acceptent dans la mesure de l'intérêt personnel".

358: τέρπεται. Because he feels himself superior as a benefactor (see above, n. 612). This is profitable (356 ἀγαθή) to the receiver of the gift because he has nothing to fear and may even expect more gifts (cf. 351 καὶ ἐς ὕστερον).

358: ὃν κατὰ θυμόν. 'With all his heart': see above, on 58 κατὰ θυμόν. For the neglect of the digamma see above, on 131 ᾧ.

359: ὅς. Equivalent to εἴ τις: cf. K.G. II, 441-2, LSJ B IV 3.

359: αὐτός. 'In a high-handed manner': Neitzel (50) compares Hom. A 137 εἰ δέ κε μὴ δώωσιν, ἐγὼ δέ κεν αὐτὸς ἕλωμαι and the similar use of αὐτός at A 161, 324, 356, 507, B 240, T 89. He also refers to A 149 ἀναιδείην ἐπιειμένε κερδαλεόφρον and concludes (54) that Hes. had the behaviour of Agamemnon in mind. This is only partly true, for 360 σμικρόν and 362 θαμά obviously refer to a different situation, and it is tempting to assume that this is the method used by Perses before he went to law to have his many ἁρπαγαί legalized [625].

359: ἀναιδείηφι. We. compares Hom. φ 315 βίηφί τε ἦφι πιθήσας and thinks that there "-φι has more of its original instrumental sense". But attempts to explain the use of -φι from an instrumental sense are not very convincing: e.g. Schw. II, 172, calls ζ 6 βίηφι φέρτεροι (a dative of limitation) an "Instrumental der Beziehung" (which is a monster), and Chantr. I, 236, wrongly takes ἶφι μάχεσθαι (which has modal force) to be instrumental. See further above, on 216 ἑτέρηφι.

360: καί τε. 'Even': cf. Ruijgh, 901-2, who observes that "καίπερ est encore très rare dans l'épopée ancienne: normalement, καί et περ y sont séparés l'un de l'autre. C'est pourquoi Hésiode a recouru à καί τε". Similarly *H. Herm.* 92 and 133 (Ruijgh, 914).

360: σμικρόν. 'A poor little amount', as the injuror may call it: see above, on 30 ὀλίγη.

360: ἐόν. The participle is used as a substantive: see above, on 5 βριάοντα.

360: ἐπάχνωσεν. Properly 'is turned to hoar-frost': Onians (46-7) points out that grief, bitter feelings, and fear were conceived by the early Greeks as freezing: cf. Hom. P 111-2 of a lion balked of his prey ἦτορ/παχνοῦται, and Ψ 598-9, where conversely Menelaus' θυμός, after having received satisfaction, ἰάνθη, ὡς εἴ τε περὶ σταχύεσσιν ἐέρση / ληΐου ἀλδήσκοντος, ὅτε φρίσσουσιν ἄρουραι. See also Zink, *Warm u. Kalt* (above, n. 412), 21-2.

360: φίλον ἦτορ. Si. suggests that "taking destroys the taker's peace of mind" (similarly Maz., Quaglia, 204 n. 29, Neitzel, 47-8, who takes τό γε as an accusative of reference). But (1) a man who is characterized as 'shameless' is unlikely to suffer from stings of conscience [626], and (2) even if such a man

---

[625] Van Groningen (286) maintains that 342-80 are not connected with Hes.'s own situation, but see also below, on 371 κασιγνήτῳ and 376 μουνογενής.

[626] And certainly would not be open to such subtle considerations as put forward by Quaglia (207), who thinks that "neppure la piccola entità del danno arrecato può dar minor dolore

could feel remorse, this could hardly be called his 'death' (356). Consequently, φίλον ἦτορ must refer to his victim (Proclus). Wil. thinks that the phrase is "leer, eigentlich falsch aus der epischen Rede herübergenommen, da es hier keinen possessiven Sinn hat". We. refers to Hom. Φ 201, but there ἦτορ means 'life', which does not suit the present context. The whole passage is concerned with the person from whom one tries to obtain something, so that he is the logical subject of the sentence: in other words, φίλον ἦτορ is used *ad sententiam*.

362: τάχα. See above, on 312 τάχα.

362: τό. 'Even a small amount may easily become a large amount': this primarily refers to the things taken away, but indirectly to the corresponding amount of irritation of the injured person: his anger will grow imperceptibly but steadily, till it will burst into destructive aggression (356 θανάτοιο). This interpretation shows that 361-2 form an essential part of the argument beginning at 357, and that Pal., Ev., Si. are wrong in putting the lines after 363.

363. An antithetical transition mediated by the term καταθεῖο: one may lay up in store (see above, on 31 κατακεῖται) other people's possessions, but this is a bad way of storing: the right way is to lay up the products of one's own labour.

363: ἐόντι. 'Something present' (the participle being used as a substantive, just as at 360), i.e. something belonging to your own store. We. compares Thgn. 515 τῶν δ' ὄντων τἄριστα παρέξομεν. Cf. also 367 παρεόντος and the Homeric phrase χαριζομένη παρεόντων (η 176 etc.).

363: αἴθοπα. Maz. and Si. print αἴθονα, but αἴθοπα is rightly defended by We., who compares the equivalence of the Homeric phrases αἴθοπι χαλκῷ and αἴθωνι σιδήρῳ. Cf. also Kamerbeek on S. *Aj.* 222 and K. J. McKay, Mnem. IV 12 (1959), 198-203 (who defends αἴθονα)[627]. For the idea cf. 'ardent desire' and German 'Heisshunger'.

364: τό. For the article used in contrasts see above, on 193 ὁ κακός.

364: κατακείμενον. 'Lying stored up': see above on 31 κατακεῖται.

365: βέλτερον. For the comparative used in contrasts see above, on 272 ἀδικώτερος. Similarly 314 ἄμεινον.

365: εἶναι. The subject is 'a product', implied in κατακείμενον. See above, on 291 ἵκηται.

365: βλαβερόν. Pal. explains: "It is not the having stores at home, but the having to get them from without, that vexes a man" (similarly Maz.). But τὸ θύρηφιν does not denote foreign import but one's own out-of-door property: cf. Hom. χ 220 κτήμαθ' ὁπόσσα τοι ἔστι, τά τ' ἔνδοθι καὶ τὰ θύρηφιν, and

---

all'ingiusto, perché di fronte al bene o al male morale non hanno valore il 'poco' el il 'molto' economicamente intesi, ma vale unicamente l'animo con cui si agisce".

[627] Cf. also *Erysichthon* (above, n. 611), 19-22, 105-6.

Troxler, 71. Si. thinks that the sentence refers to "the necessity of keeping one's goods in the house and not be lending them abroad and be constantly worrying about when you will get them back or repaid". But this idea does not suit the context. Ev. translates: 'whatever is abroad may mean loss' (similarly Wil. and We.). But there is no parallel for βλαβερός used in the sense of 'exposed to damage'. It should be borne in mind that in the earliest literature βλάπτω means 'to hinder' (properly 'thrust aside: see above, on 193 βλάψει) rather than 'to damage'. Accordingly, βλαβερόν means 'annoying', 'inconvenient', and the correct interpretation seems to be given in the schol. vet. εἰ καὶ γὰρ ἐν ἀγρῷ ἔχει τις οἶνον ἢ σῖτον, οὐκ εὐχερές ἐστιν εἰσιέναι καὶ φέρειν.

365: θύρηφιν. For the meaning of -φι see above, on 216 ἑτέρηφι.

366: ἐσθλόν. 'Profitable': see above, on 286 ἐσθλά. The asyndeton has explanatory (motivating) force: see above, on 267 πάντα.

366: παρεόντος. See above, on 363 ἐόντι.

366: ἑλέσθαι. For the aorist see above, on 342 ἐᾶσαι.

366: θυμῷ. Such translations as 'it grieves your heart' (Ev.) are too vague: θυμός is the power which urges a man to action: see above, on 27 θυμῷ. Maz. seems to me wrong in connecting θυμῷ χρηίζειν 'désirer tout bas'.

368. Connected with the preceding lines not "by the mention of enjoying what one has" (We.) but by the mention of having need of something absent: this may be something not yet present, but also something no longer present. Thus the advice of laying up stores leads to the advice of making the right use of one's stores.

368: ἀρχομένου. For the passive use cf. Sol. 1 D. = 13 W., 66 χρήματος ἀρχομένου, where Gomperz unnecessarily proposed ἀρχόμενος: for ἄρχω and ἄρχομαι with accusative cf. LSJ I 4, K.G. I, 349.

368: πίθου. For jars used to store various kinds of products see above, n. 282. We. rightly rejects the ancient interpretation that a jar of wine is meant and that the middle part contains the best quality: "Hesiod's primary concern is with thrift, not with getting the best out of the wine".

368: λήγοντος. Logically refers to the contents: similarly 815 ἄρξασθαί τε πίθου.

368: κορέσασθαι. For the aorist see above, on 342 ἐᾶσαι.

370-2. Bracketed by Wil., Col., So., Quaglia, 209 n. 36, We. It is true that the MSS. evidence is not very strong, but I do not think that much weight should be attached to the fact that the lines are missing in two papyri (as is done by We.). Proclus evidently took them to be genuine [628], and they form a

---

[628] We. argues that "the fact that the lines appear as a quotation and not as a lemma is exceptional, and suggests that ... Proclus did not find the lines in the text he was using", but the fact that the quotation is preceded by εἶπε γάρ suggests that Proclus did find it in his text.

natural sequel to 368-9 [629]: just as one should see to it that at the end of the
year or of a season sufficient supplies are left to live on, so one should see to it
that at the end of a period when a payment has to be made one will be able to
pay it in full, so that an employee may be sure of his wage.

370: φίλῳ. P. Friedländer (in Heitsch, 235 n. 24) writes: "Warum in 370
durch ἀνδρὶ φίλῳ der Geltungsbereich eingeschränkt wird, weiss ich nicht".
The obvious answer is that a fixed relationship (see above, on 184 φίλος)
makes higher demands upon one's punctuality than casual work.

370: εἰρημένος. Not 'stated by a friend' (Si.) but 'covenanted' (cf. Hom. Φ
445 μισθῷ ἔπι ῥητῷ), 'promised to'.

370: ἄρκιος. Not 'sufficient' (Wil.) but 'sure': see above, on 351 ἄρκιον.
The line was understood in this sense by Aristotle (*EN* 1164 a 27).

371. Connection with the preceding line: one should secure a similar
sureness for oneself, so that after concluding a contract there can be no doubt
about what is due to both parties.

371: κασιγνήτῳ. It may be assumed that Hes. and Perses had divided the
paternal estate (37) without witnesses.

371: γελάσας. By suggesting that the ceremony is only for fun, and so
mitigating your distrust (372 ἀπιστίαι).

372: πίστις. The MSS. have πίστεις, but in early epic this should be
πίστιες. Rz. reads πίστιες ἄρ τοι, but ἄρ τοι is unparalleled (Denn., 555,
gives only examples of τοι ἄρα). We. refers to Hom. Μ 258 etc. ἐπάλξεις, but
this is an accusative, whereas the nominative is ἐπάλξιες (Μ 424 and 430). We
may perhaps accept πίστῑς as an Aeolism (cf. Schw. I, 573): for Aeolisms in
Hes. cf. We., *Th.*, 82-4. For the plural 'acts of good faith' see above, on 16
βουλῇσιν.

372: γάρ τοι. We. withdraws δὴ ἄρ', proposed in Philol. 108 (1964), 162,
and prints a *crux*. I withdraw δ' ἄρ τοι, suggested in *Aufbau*, 147 n. 1.
Bentley's γάρ τοι is a satisfactory emendation: ΤΟΙ may have disappeared
between P and ΟΜ by haplography, and the remaining ΓΑΡ may have been
expanded to ΔΑΡΑ in order to restore the metre. For γάρ τοι cf. 302, Denn.,
549.

372: ἀπιστίαι. Examples of misplaced distrust can be found at Hom. ξ 391-
2 and ψ 71-2. For the antithesis see above, on 3 φατοί.

372: ὤλεσαν. The aorist seems to have experiential ('have often ...') rather
than gnomic force: see above, on 240 ἀπηύρα.

373. Connection with the preceding line: when property is concerned,
distrust your brother, but also your wife.

---

[629] We. thinks that after 352 would be a more appropriate place, but that passage is
concerned with loans and gifts, not with wages. we. further remarks that if we join 369 and 373
the connection would lie "in the theme of looking after one's stores". This is true, but there is a
closer connection between 372 πίστις ... ὤλεσαν and 373 μηδὲ ... ἐξαπατάτω.

373: γυνή. Quaglia (210 n. 37) thinks that "si allude genericamente alla donna astuta, che, usando tutte le sue arti, potrebbe abbindolare un uomo e attentare in qualsiasi modo al suo patrimonio", but 374 διφῶσα implies wastefulness (see below), not appropriation. Wil. writes: "Das kokette Frauenzimmer will Frau oder zunächst wohl παλλακή werden", but (1) in Homer (δ 12) concubines are slaves, and a slave's wastefulness would hardly escape the farmer's wife, and (2) if she intended to become the farmer's wife she would not ferret into his barn immediately. The context (see also below, on 376) strongly suggests that she is the farmer's wife herself.

373: σε νόον. For the σχῆμα καθ' ὅλον καὶ μέρος see above, on 28 σε. For νόος 'insight into the real situation' see above, on 323 νόον.

373: πυγόστολος. Not 'wiggling her buttocks' (Si.), for στέλλω does not mean 'to move to an fro'. The scholia suggest 'with dressed up buttocks' (similarly Maz., We.), called by Wil. 'sprachwidrig', but this rather applies to his own interpretation, 'with buttocks resembling the stem of a bird's tail (στόλος)'[630]. The ancient explanation may be supported by referring to στέλλω 'to furnish with a garment' (Hdt. III 14, 2, S. *Tr.* 612), and We. draws attention to "early archaic representations of women whose skirts are gathered in elegant folds at the rear and in some cases embroidered there rather than at the front". But this seems to be a Near-Eastern element in feminine dress, which is unlikely to have been common in Boeotia. The most conspicuous feature in archaic representations of women is a tight-fitting covering of the buttocks, which clearly marks their contours[631]. Prominent buttocks formed part of the Greek conception of physical beauty: see my note on Semon. 7, 76 ἄπυγος, Mnem. IV 21 (1968), 148. On the other hand, (1) -στολος can hardly have the pregnant meaning of 'tightly clothing', and (2) in similar compounds (e.g. κυανόστολος, λευκόστολος, λινόστολος, νεβριδόστολος, ποικιλόστολος) the first element refers to the garment, not to the part of the body clothed. We may perhaps translate 'dressed in buttocks', a neologism intended to denote an extremely tight dress. Bitter humour does not seem inappropriate in Hes.'s view of women, and enigmatic phrases are not foreign to his language: cf. Edwards, 111-3.

373: ἐξαπατάτω. For ἐξ- see above, on 48 ἐξαπάτησε. We. thinks that "Hesiod is talking about a woman ... whom you catch poking into your granary and who by wiggling her hips and telling charming lies, or actually seducing you, is able to get away with it". But the word order suggests that

---

[630] Similarly O. Vox, Glotta 58 (1980), 172-7, who thinks of a ἴυγξ. Troxler (160) compares 628 στολίσας νηὸς πτερά and Hom. A 433 ἱστία στείλαντο, but this means 'to furl' and hardly suits the comparison with a peacock, as is suggested by Troxler.

[631] Col. speaks of "vesti assai strette", but wrongly thinks that this is the meaning of the scholia.

the woman by her coquetry and wily talk diverts her husband's attention from her squandering use of the supplies (see below, on 374 διφῶσα)[632].

374: αἱμύλα κωτίλλουσα. A reminiscence of Pandora's αἱμύλιοι λόγοι (78): see above, on 91 πόνοιο.

374: αἱμύλα. See above, on 78 αἱμυλίους.

374: κωτίλλουσα. "*Prattle, chatter*, usu. with collat. notion of *coaxing, wheedling*" (LSJ).

374: διφῶσα καλιήν. Renehan (353) rightly observes that this does not mean 'poking into your granary' (We.), but his own translation 'seek after that which one does not possess' is too general: Hom. Π 747 τήθεα διφῶν, Ar. *Nub.* 192 ἐρεβοδιφῶσιν, Opp. *Hal.* 2, 435 βυθῶν διφήτορες, Herod. 7, 78 ἐξεδίφησας suggest that the meaning is 'search after something deeply hidden'. Accordingly, the woman is collecting the last remnants of the supplies, while leaving her husband under the impression that they are still amply sufficient. We. writes: "Woman stole food because they were kept half-starved by their husbands, who resented their habit of eating", referring to 704 and *Th.* 594 ff., and to some passages from Semonides 7 and Aristophanes. The latter obviously do not prove anything. It is true that at *Th.* 598-9 Hes. emphasizes women's gluttony, but this serves as a drastic expression of their craving for luxury (593 κόροιο). Similarly 704 δειπνολόχης does not refer to mere gluttony but means 'toujours à l'affût d'un repas', "c'est-à-dire de dérober en cachette ce que le mari veut économiser" (Maz.)[633].

374: καλιήν. Renehan (353) argues that this "is an instance of the container for the contained", but cf. Thphr. *Char.* 10, 6 διφᾶν τὰ καλύμματα, where the verb means 'to search'[634].

375: δέ. Has explanatory (motivating) force: see above, on 13 δέ.

375: φηλήτῃσιν. 'Thieves'. Wil., LSJ, We. read φιλήτῃσιν. Although this form is found in inscriptions and papyri and was defended by Trypho and Herodian, the connection with φῆλος 'deceitful' and φηλόω 'deceive' (cf. Groeneboom on A. *Ag.* 492) points to an original form with η (cf. Troxler, 158)[635].

We. explains the plural as 'a member of a class who are cheats', but it is more natural to observe that the singular γυναικί has generalizing force, and

---

[632] The translation 'zu etwas verleiten' proposed by J. Anastassiou, *Lex.*, 1003, is not correct: the author himself observes (1006.33): "Bei ἀπατάω wird die Person über Verhältnisse der Aussenwelt getäuscht und nicht zum Handeln veranlasst".

[633] It is equally wrong to conclude: "Offenbar taten in der Schicht zu der Hesiod gehörte die Hausfrauen und Haustöchter keine grobe Arbeit; sie waren gepflegte Luxusgeschöpfe (*WuT* 519-23)" (Fränkel, 129 n. 9): (1) 519 ff. refer to a *young* girl, and (2) Hes. acknowledges the existence of good wives (702-3), which in his utilitarian view must mean wives able and willing to help in running the farm.

[634] I take καλύμματα to mean 'slabs for closing coffers' (LSJ 9): cf. the preceding κιβωτούς.

[635] Chantr., *Dict. étym.*, 1194 and 1204, denies the connection, but admits that the etymology of both words is unknown.

that a collective singular is often followed by a plural: see above, on 133 ζώεσκον.

376. The connection with the preceding line is twofold: (1) 'wife' suggests 'son', and (2) 'a wife may ruin your stores' suggests the question what is the best way to keep your stores and manage the farm in the future: for the antithetical transition see above, on 356 ἅρπαξ.

376: μουνογενής. Not 'the only member of its kin' (LSJ) but 'only-begotten': cf. A. *Ag.* 898 μουνογενὲς τέκνον πατρί, Pl. *Criti.* 113 d 2 μονογενῆ θυγατέρα ἐγεννησάσθην. Although the advice has a general purport, Hes. may be thinking of the fact that his personal difficulties would not have arisen if he had been an only child himself (Walcot, *Peasants*, 48)[636].

376: οἶκον. See above, on 23 οἶκον.

377: φερβέμεν. For the transition from 'nourish' to 'maintain' cf. the similar use of τρέφω (LSJ III 2).

377: ἀέξεται. Originally used of living beings (see above, on 6 ἀέξει) and natural products, but in Homer also of abstract notions (e.g. Z 214 κράτος), probably imagined as living powers: wealth, too, is such a power (*Th.* 969). See further *Less. pol.*, 251-5.

377: μεγάροισιν. The house as a collection of rooms (LSJ). See further M. O. Knox, JHS 90 (1970), 117-20.

378: θάνοις. Rz., Wil., So. read θάνοι, but We. rightly points out that this is a *lectio facilior* serving to facilitate the understanding of ἕτερον παῖδα as a grandson. We. explains the wish 'May you die old' as follows: "It is good to die old with a new child in the house, secure in the knowledge that all is well for the next generation". But ἐγκαταλείπων can hardly refer to a grandfather, and ἕτερον παῖδα does not refer to a grandchild (see next note). I take the optative as a potential (for the omission of ἄν cf. Chantr. II, 216-7, Schw. II, 325)[637]: you will have a chance of attaining to a great age if you have a son who will look after you as a γηροκόμος (γηροβοσκός, γηροτρόφος): cf. *Th.* 604-5 ὀλοὸν δ' ἐπὶ γῆρας ἵκηται / χήτει γηροκόμοιο. Accordingly, the sentence expresses another advantage of having but one son: he will inherit the whole estate and so will be substantial enough to support not only his own family but also his parents.

378: ἕτερον παῖδα. Not a grandchild (We.), for ἐγκαταλείπων refers to the father, not to the grandfather. Si. explains the sentence as follows: "Should you have more than one son (similarly Ev., Latt., Renehan, 353), may you live long enough to amass sufficient wealth for them all". But the mere word γηραιός is too general to imply this supplement: other supplements have been

---

[636] For the history of the ideal of having only one heir cf. We. and G. E. M. de Ste. Croix, *The Class Struggle in the Ancient World* (London 1981), 278 and n. 6.

[637] Col. objects that θάνοις must express a wish because 376 εἴη expresses a wish, but this is no cogent argument.

suggested, such as "because by then they [the two sons] will be mature and well-established, and so less likely to quarrel" (N. J. Richardson, JHS 99, 1979, 170), and "in order to be able to oversee the fair division of the estate when the two children come of age" (Renehan), but they are equally speculative. Moschopoulos seems to me right in explaining ἕτερον as ἄλλον ἀντὶ σοῦ: cf. Pl. *Symp.* 208 ab πᾶν τὸ θνητὸν σῴζεται ... τῷ τὸ ἀπιὸν καὶ παλαιούμενον ἕτερον νέον ἐγκαταλείπειν οἷον αὐτὸ ἦν. The proper meaning is 'another, namely your son': cf. Ar. *Ran.* 515, Thuc. IV 67, 2, VII 70, 2, Xen. *An.* I 4, 2, Arist. *Pol.* 1315 a 7. For a similar use of ἄλλος see above, on 143 ἄλλο. We. objects that "where we have πάις followed by ἕτερος πάις, they cannot be the same person", but this holds good only for those readers who are not familiar with the usage of ἕτερος.

379-80. Have been added to meet the objection that parents lodging with their son still form a heavy pressure upon his budget: in favourable circumstances (Ζεύς) even old parents may lend a hand in the farm and so help to increase the substance. Solmsen, HSCP 26 (1982), 20, adopting a suggestion advanced by Fränkel (465 n. 20), thinks that the lines form a correction of Hes.'s austere view added by some rhapsodes "to please the audience", but they perfectly suit Hes.'s argument.

379: ῥεῖα. See above, on 5 ῥέα.

379: δέ. Has explanatory (motivating) force: see above, on 13 δέ. The motivation refers to the unexpressed idea that an increase of the family does not necessarily imply a decrease of the profit.

379: πλεόνεσσι. The son's family plus his parents[638]. I no longer believe that a second son is meant who might help to increase the property (*Aufbau*, 147-8): in that case the addition 'easily' would too much weaken Hes.'s advice of having but one son.

379: ὄλβον. 'Abundance': see above, on 172 ὄλβιοι.

380: πλείων. The asyndeton has explanatory (specifying) force: see above, on 11 οὐκ. For the complementary relation between divine gift and human effort cf. e.g. 299-300, 309. See further my remarks in Mnem. IV 36 (1983), 38-40.

380: πλεόνων. The farmer and his parents[639].

380: μελέτη. 'Attentive work' (similarly 412) rather than 'attention to the work' (We.).

380: δέ. The balance expressed by μὲν ... δέ has a complementary rather than a strictly adversative character: cf. Denn., 370[640].

---

[638] Van Groningen's suggestion (286 n. 4) to read κὲν (= καὶ ἐν) πλεόνεσσι is unnecessary.

[639] The genitive is wrongly taken as objective by Wil. ("die stärkere Sorge für mehrere Söhne") and van Groningen (*loc. cit.*: "à sa μελέτη de propriétaire s'est ajoutée celle de poète").

[640] This was ignored by Peppmüller, who proposed μείων for μείζων (cf. Si.).

380: ἐπιθήκη. 'Increase' (Ev.) is better than 'surplus' (We.; similarly Maz. 'profit').

381: δέ. Has consecutive (concluding) force: see above, on 314 δέ [641].

381: ᾗσιν. Rightly defended by We. and printed by So. in his second edition: see above, on 2 σφέτερον.

382: ὧδε. Primarily retrospective (see above, on 35 ὧδ' ἔρδειν), but also prospective: see below, on ἐπί.

382: καί. 'And particularly': cf. Hom. δ 95 πολλὰ πάθον καὶ ἀπώλεσα οἶκον. See further my note on Th. 33, Mnem. IV 25 (1972), 240, A. H. M. Kessels on Ps. Hipp. Medic. 23, 17, Mnem. IV 31 (1978), 131.

382: ἐπί. Primarily 'upon': work should be so steady that one work is as it were piled up on another (cf. 644 ἐπὶ κέρδεϊ κέρδος, LSJ B I 1 d). But there is a secondary meaning, 'after' (in the right order) (LSJ B II 2), which points forward to the next section.

382: ἔργῳ. For the neglect of the digamma cf. Chantr. I, 136-7 (who wrongly thinks of emendation), A. Hoekstra, Mnem. IV 10 (1957), 208-9.

382: ἐργάζεσθαι. The spondaic beginning and end of the line probably have expressive force: see We., and cf. the beginning of 623. See also above, on 291-2.

---

[641] P. Friedländer (in Heitsch, 231) takes σοὶ δέ to be contrasted with other people, implied in the preceding lines, but this is rather artificial.

INDEX OF SUBJECTS

Numbers refer to the lines of the Greek text discussed in the commentary.

INDEX OF GREEK WORDS

Numbers refer to the lines of the Greek text discussed in the commentary.